BADASS: THE BIRTH OF A LEGEND

BAD

THE BIRTH OF A LEGEND

ASS

BEN THOMPSON

Spine-Crushing Tales of
the Most Merciless Gods, Monsters,
Heroes, Villains, and Mythical
Creatures Ever Envisioned

HARPER

NEW YORK · LONDON · TORONTO · SYDNEY

HARPER

HarperCollins books may be purchased for educational, business, or sales promotional use. For information please write: Special Markets Department, HarperCollins Publishers, 10 East 53rd Street, New York, NY 10022.

FIRST EDITION

Designed by Lorie Pagnozzi and Cassandra Pappas

Library of Congress Cataloging-in-Publication Data

ISBN 978-0-06-200135-1

11 12 13 14 15   OV/RRD   10 9 8 7 6 5 4 3 2 1

I am become death, the destroyer of worlds,
engaged to destroy all beings in the world.

Of these heroic soldiers presently situated in the
opposing army, even without you none will be spared.
Now get up. Prepare to fight and win glory.

—LORD KRISHNA, *BHAGAVAD GITA*, CHAPTER 11, VERSES 33-34A

CONTENTS

The path of the righteous man is beset
on all sides by the iniquities of the
selfish and the tyranny of evil men. Blessed
is he, who in the name of charity and
goodwill, shepherds the weak through the
valley of darkness, for he is truly
his brother's keeper and the finder of
lost children. And I will strike down
upon thee with great vengeance and furious
anger those who would attempt to poison
and destroy my brothers. And you will know
my name is the LORD when I lay
my vengeance upon thee.

—EZEKIEL 25:17,
AS RECITED BY SAMUEL L. JACKSON IN
PULP FICTION

SECTION I: GODS, GODDESSES, AND OTHER KICKASS CELESTIAL BEINGS   11

1. ANUBIS   13

*Jackal-headed Egyptian lord of mummification, the
Underworld, ankhs, and everything awesome about Egyptian
mythology*

2. ZEUS   23

*The pimp-tastic ruler of Mount Olympus and head of the
Greek pantheon*

3. RAMA   29

*Indian warrior-god who battled a powerful demon with an
army of bears and monkeys to rescue his goddess wife*

4. KALI   37

*The Hindu death goddess who enjoys eating the flesh of the
dead and bathing in their blood*

A NOTE ON RELIGION

I find your lack of faith disturbing.

—DARTH VADER

DEALING WITH RELIGION CAN BE A PRETTY SENSITIVE SUBJECT, ESPECIALLY CONSIDERING THAT I'M LISTING POPULAR RELIGIOUS FIGURES ALONGSIDE OBVIOUSLY FICTIONAL CHARACTERS LIKE SKELETOR AND GODZILLA. Before we go too much further, allow me a brief moment here to explain what I mean when I say "mythological" or "legendary" in regards to prominent religious characters. It's not really within the scope of a work on fire-breathing monsters and thinly veiled penis jokes to make any kind of grand sweeping arguments claiming that a guy like Samson didn't actually exist and that God didn't grant him the power to tear down buildings with his fists, or that Kali isn't truly the all-powerful goddess in control of the cosmic cycle of death, life, and rebirth. By listing these characters in this book, I'm just saying that I took the figures' respective religious texts completely at face value, without making any attempt to verify their historical or metaphysical accuracy. So please don't go putting a hex on me or anything just because I mentioned your god in the same sentence as Optimus Prime.

BADASS: THE BIRTH OF A LEGEND

THE HERO MYTH: MAKING OTHER MYTHS LOOK LIKE BITCHES SINCE THE DAWN OF HUMANITY

FEW THINGS ARE MORE BADASS THAN HERO MYTHS. Whether it's an old-school epic poem about shanking Cyclopes in the eye with a sharpened tree trunk or a blockbuster film where some daring sea captain jumps his PT boat on a ramp and miraculously shoots a torpedo through the cockpit of a helicopter, people love hearing stories about balls-out ass-kickers slaughtering all who oppose them in order to save humanity from some kind of diabolical evil. Even back in the days before TV (when things in the world were really boring), ancient peoples used to sit around all day thinking about crazy crap to pump people up out of their minds, and to this day their stories of ball-crushing conquest are still awesome enough to make even the tamest readers want to snatch up a sword and go hunting for dragon meat. Sure, there are plenty of obnoxious, borderline-pointless ancient myths out there about how the sky is blue because some talking monkey borrowed moldy cheese from a crow and forgot how to cook a casserole, but there's also a huge amount of ultra-hardcore hero myths describing some psychotic lunatic tearing the universe a new rectum in search of ultimate glory.

But in a world where "legendary" and "epic" are routinely thrown around to describe anything from drunken keg stands to sickeningly cute pictures of baby kittens wearing jester caps, it's important to take a second to define what we mean when we're talking about the most bad-ass aspects of the fictional and mythological universe. Who are these heroes, and why do they kick so much sack?

There was a famous twentieth-century mythologist named Joseph Campbell, who dropped a metric crapton of brilliant, borderline-unintelligible knowledge on the world, the most interesting aspect being his theory that you could essentially take the greatest mythological hero tales of all time, chop-shop them down to their component parts, regurgitate it all into a JavaScript random generator, and be able to basically reproduce the plot of every fictional story ever. It was like the academic world's precursor to the TV Tropes website. Campbell summed up the entire history of epic adventure with one sentence:

"A hero ventures forth from the world of common day into a region of supernatural wonder: fabulous forces are there encountered and a decisive victory is won: the hero comes back from this mysterious adventure with the power to bestow boons on his fellow man."

That single sentence condenses the plots of everything from ancient myths to video game plots in forty-five succinct words, but let's look at the hero myth in a little more detail. What makes a mythological or fictional hero a badass? If you were going to embark on a legendary journey of heroic epicness, what would your quest look like?

MYSTERIOUS ORIGINS

The first step toward being an awesome mythological hero is to have some kind of terribly mysterious background that makes everybody think you're way more intellectually deep and psychologically tortured than you might actually be. Whether you're bitten by a radioactive spider, sent back in time from the future to save humanity, or found clinging to a piece of driftwood in the middle of the ocean without any recollection of your past, you're just not going to be taken seriously without some kind of awesome origin that makes everyone sit back and be like, "damn that guy is pretty mysterious." Maybe you never talk about your personal life unless it becomes relevant to the plot when some motorcycle-riding ninja assassins from your past show up trying to aerate your face with shotgun shells. Maybe there's a sweet ancient prophesy carved on a pyramid wall that foretells your future as savior of humanity. Maybe the only thing you know about your family is that your father was a powerful thunder god and he left you an amulet written in a language nobody speaks. Whatever. The fact remains that an evil mythological king couldn't abandon a baby in the woods without the kid getting raised by wolves or trained by Shaolin monks, and the next thing you know the disowned child is a fully grown badass and he's showing up at the castle gates with a pair of flaming nunchucks demanding vengeance. You need to be that guy.

ENTER THE PLOT HOOK

Regardless of how mysterious or awesome your origin story may be, the fact remains that at the beginning of your hero quest your life totally sucks a dong. Your people are oppressed by a tyrannical king, your rightful throne has been usurped, your family is imprisoned, and ultimate evil threatens to break free from an ancient slumber and instantaneously destroy all life in the universe. Meanwhile you're rotting in prison, cursed by an evil necromancer, hunted by a giant carnivorous alien monster, and suffering from a massive case of hemorrhoids; the girl of your dreams is either dead, in love with some loser, or locked away in a tower defended by a fire-breathing monster, and the one item that can save the world is buried in a haunted crypt on the other side of the continent, conveniently surrounded by zombie dinosaurs with katanas for teeth and machine guns strapped to their heads. Between you and victory lies an endless sea of monsters, super-villains, and forbidding terrain, and your arch-nemesis is having a hell of a great time constantly showing up at the most inopportune moments possible, and generally just pissing you off whenever he gets the chance.

No matter how boring or hopeless life seems, however, every hero has a chance to succeed, usually because they end up getting super-natural help to rise up, snap off the chains holding them down, and start building a towering pile of enemy corpses. In most mythologies, this role was typically filled by a pantheon of badass gods who de-manded bloody vengeance and pumped up their favorite mortals with the power to tear their enemies' limbs off appendage by appendage, but the quest-giver role could be filled by pretty much anybody these days. It could be a Yoda or an Obi-Wan to help you harness your inner Jedi powers; a wise, death-defying white wizard; a fairy godmother with a magic wand; a talking dog; your father's ghost leading you to an ancient, monster-slaying sword; or even just a police commissioner throwing a case file down on the hero's desk—whatever the case may be, the truth of the matter is that nearly every hero needs a quest-giver to send them beyond the limits of their mortal life and into a realm of awesomeness and manslaughter.

QUESTIN' AIN'T EASY

No matter how over-the-top and balls-out your supernatural mentor may be, vengeance-seeking gods don't just walk around handing out magic items to any moron with a beef against society, and Final Bosses typically aren't particularly keen on kicking back and opening the gates of the Citadel of Doom so some anonymous sword-toting jackass can waltz right in there and introduce their faces to the pointy end of a sharpened stick. Questing is serious work for a hero, and throughout the adventure there are going to be plenty of trials and hardships out there doing everything in their power to ass-hump you into submission. You could get swallowed into the belly of a whale, framed for murder, thrown down into the Underworld, marooned on a desert isle, or stranded in a creepy forest somewhere. Haunted volcanoes need to be summited, ancient ruins need to be raided, swords need to be pulled from stones, and princesses never seem to be in the castles you expect them to be in. Meanwhile, the Forces of Evil never get sick of opposing you—at every turn, you've got to pass through wave after wave of the king's men, alien warriors, cyborg killbots, walking dead, the Illuminati, Centaurs, Internet forum trolls, and (as is the case with nearly every video game ever) giant spiders. Lots and lots of giant spiders.

If you're going to be successful, you've got to prove that you're more badass than anything else in the world.

THE ULTIMATE SHOWDOWN

It's a proven fact that nothing is more awesome than two crazy-powerful psychopaths whaling on each other with the fate of the universe hanging in the balance, and if you're going to make it as an epic hero, you're going to need to be ready to battle your arch-nemesis to the death in a dramatic fashion. For some spiritual heroes—guys like Jesus and Buddha—the showdown comes with death itself, but for the rest of us, we're looking at fisticuffs inside the control room of a planet-eating robot or a swordfight on top of a black tower just moments before some bizarre dark ritual calls forth an evil power from another dimension.

The most important thing to remember in the Ultimate Showdown is to be as over-the-top awesome as possible. If there was ever a time to bust out the BFG 9000 or make a dramatic entrance at the controls of a mechanized Power Loader, this is it. Hold nothing back, utilize all the knowledge you gained during your epic quest, and finally destroy the villain who has threatened life as you know it.

SUPER HAPPY FUN TIME

So now you've saved the world, closed the Hellmouth, avenged the destruction of your temple, and impaled the princess-eating dragon on the point of the Seattle Space Needle. Unless you died in the process of the Ultimate Showdown (this is not recommended), you're free to return home to a victory parade or simply ride off into the sunset, content with the knowledge that your actions have ultimately changed the world for the better. You have overcome your personal issues and the bullcrap associated with your once-meaningless station in life, ventured into the unknown, vanquished your fears, and done something awesome. Now all that's left is to marry the princess, assume the throne, receive the medal, and figure out how your newfound ability to shoot bullets out of your eyes might possibly be beneficial to mankind.

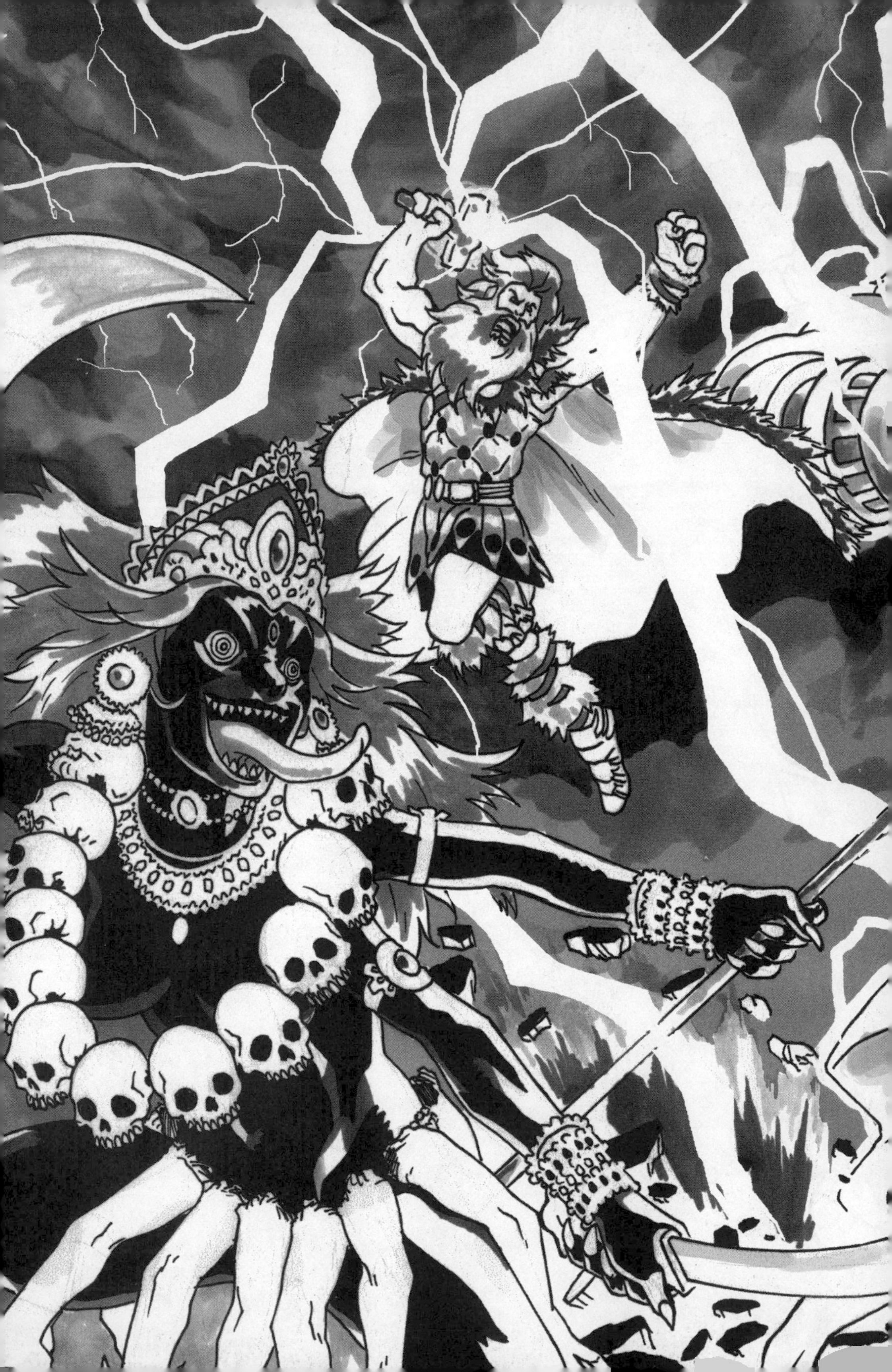

SECTION I

Gods, Goddesses, and Other Kickass Celestial Beings

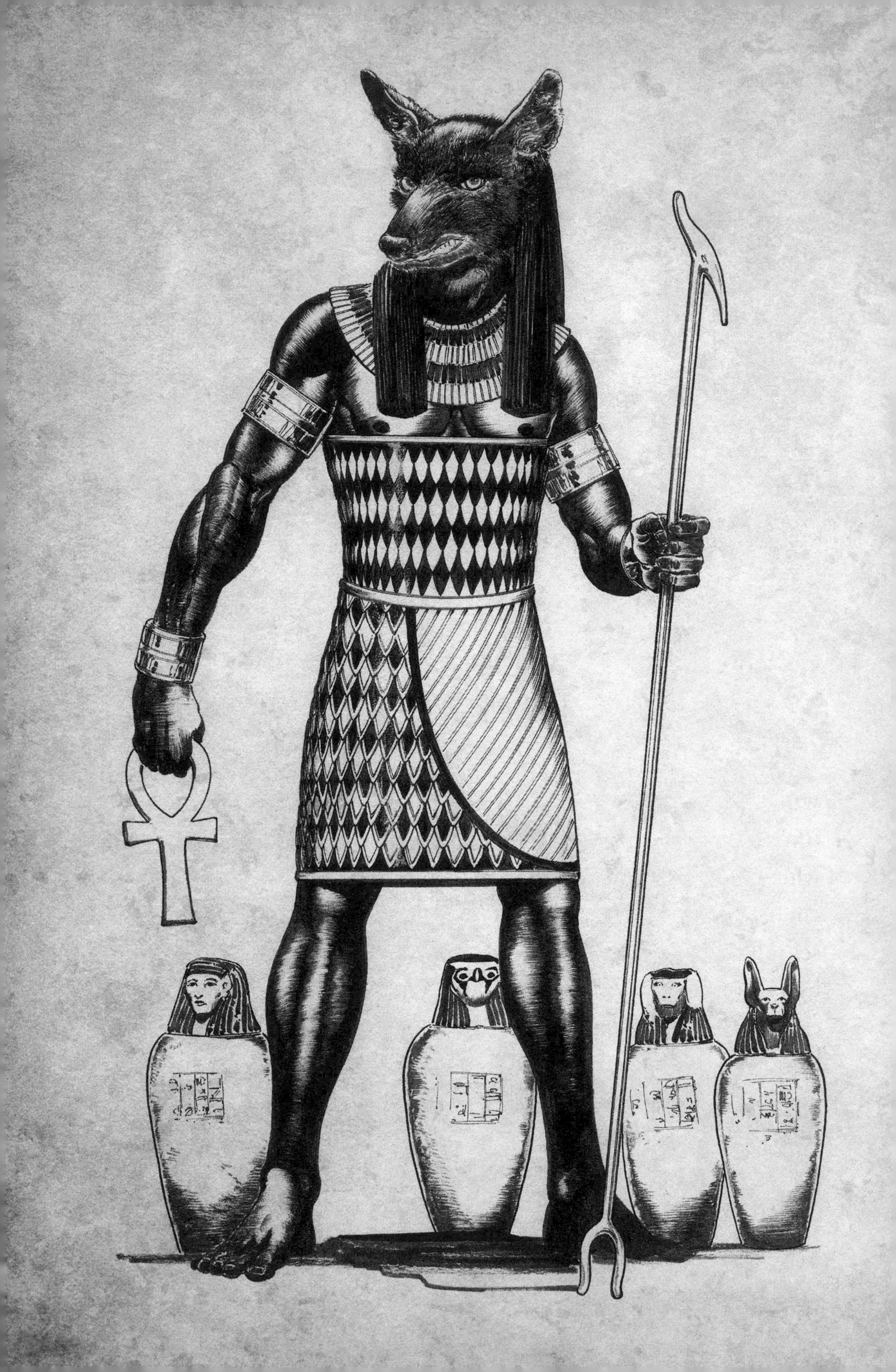

1

ANUBIS

Thee I know, and I know also the two-and-forty gods assembled
in the Hall of Justice;
They observe all the deeds of the wicked;
They devour those who seek to do evil;
They drink the blood of those who are condemned before thee.

—*THE EGYPTIAN BOOK OF THE DEAD*

WHEN PEOPLE THINK ABOUT EGYPTIAN MYTHOLOGY, THEY THINK ONE THING—TOTALLY SWEET. That's because the gods and goddesses who served as the divine rulers of the Nile were all about ridiculously cool stuff like indecipherable hieroglyphics, towering pyramids, schnozz-less Sphinxes, and gold-plated subterranean tombs protected by ancient flesh-rotting curses, and anybody who isn't down with that can feel free to catch a crippling case of mummy crotch-rot and spend eternity agonizing over their jock itch. As an added triple-shot of one hundred–proof badassitude, almost all of these bitchin' all-powerful smite-masters were represented by human bodies with insane animal heads grafted on top, making them so King Kong mega-weird-looking that it's like riding a surfboard of insanity down the Uncanny Valley. Of this massive menagerie of awesomeness, perhaps the most widely recognized anthropomorphic asskicker was the terrifying jackal-headed Egyptian deity Anubis, the god of mummification, embalming, necropolises, ankhs, and pretty much everything else that kicks ass about Ancient Egypt.

The legends surrounding this chilling god's origins are obscure at best. He was definitely the son of the goddess Nephthys, either by Osiris or Bast or Ra, but he was later adopted by the goddess Isis, who was the wife of Osiris. (Nephthys, by the way, was the wife of Set, and she, Set, Osiris, and Isis were all siblings. Still with me? If not, don't worry about it . . . it's not really all that important in the grand scheme of things, unless of course you find rampant god incest important). Regardless of where he came from initially, Anubis plays an important role in the defining event in the history of Egyptian mythology—a gloriously violent episode involving an insane death-feud between the gods Set and Osiris. Set, another sweet animal-head god who is represented by a creature so bizarre that we still don't know what the hell it's supposed to be (guesses range from an anteater to a retarded giraffe), started off on the wrong partially developed foot when he started causing trouble while just a fetus. Apparently, this guy got sick of gestating in the womb like a chump, so in the middle of the third trimester he gave his mother a C-section from the inside, tearing his way to freedom like the creature from *Alien* and then immediately going out and controlling the forces of Chaos in rebellion against order and law and decency and full-term pregnancy. Set's brother, the boringly human-faced Osiris (who was like some kind of a douchey agriculture god or some other idiocy), got all upset about it and tried to stifle Set's mojo by furiously wagging his finger at his wayward brother, but Set wasn't about to take that bullshizzle. Set killed his bro, either by burying him alive or morphing into a hippo (or crocodile) and eating him, or turning into a bull and trampling him, or turning into a malaria-infested mosquito and biting him on the foot. You'd think this would be kind of an important distinction to make, but apparently the Ancient Egyptian record-keepers didn't really feel the need to specify whether their agriculture god was murdered by asphyxiation, teeth, hooves, or vociferous microbial parasites.

Set became the pharaoh or something, but he was still really pissed off at his old dead brother for some obscure reason. In his insatiable rage, Set dug Osiris up, hacked the dude's corpse into fourteen pieces, and scattered the giblets all across the land of Egypt. This made Set feel much better. Anubis, who was at this point in the mythological cycle serving as the Keeper of the Dead, traveled around with Osiris's widow, Isis, and together they found all the dismembered body parts—except for his wang, which was eaten by fish (don't worry, Isis made him a replacement out of solid gold). Anubis then put the body back together again using his spooky Underworld magic and some mad-crazy *Tetris* skills before ritualistically eviscerating the corpse with a broken shard of glass, pulling out all of his entrails, placing them into pretty canopic urns, and turning Osiris into the first mummy, which is awesome. As a mummy, Osiris went on into the Underworld and took over. Set got ripped that Anubis had the audacity to reassemble the dismembered god and give him eternal life, so he decided to desecrate Osiris's dickless, twice-dead ass once again. This time, Anubis decided he'd had enough of this beating-a-dead-Horus bullcrap. The Keeper of the Dead appointed himself the guardian of Osiris's tomb and protected the god even through undeath, vowing not to allow harm to come to the new ruler of the Underworld. The jackal-faced ass-ruiner Anubis was pretty damn good at it, too—one time Set transmogrified himself into a leopard and tried to sneak into Osiris's mausoleum, but Anubis snatched Set with his bare hands, beat his ass, tied him up, skinned him, branded the skinless hunk of leopard meat with Anubis's personal gang sign, and then wore the skin around as a coat for a while just to prove to everyone that he was the main asskicker of the Nile.

When Set's cultists came around to recover the eviscerated macabre skin of their most favoritest deity, Anubis beheaded all of them with a scythe, then did a celebratory dance not too dissimilar from the sorts of funkalicious displays you see linebackers put on after sacking the quarterback. From that point on, Anubis's official symbol was a headless, bloody animal skin tied to a pole. If you don't think this is badass, you have no soul.

Once Set got the message and stopped being such a colossal asshat to Osiris, Anubis was able to return to his day job, where he was basically the Grim Reaper of Ancient Egypt. Not only is this black-headed jackal-man equally (if not more) terrifying than the Reaper in terms of his appearance, he also serves as the messenger of impending doom, and as the being who transports dead asses from the land of the living to the dark realm of the Underworld. It pretty much works like this—after you die, Anubis comes and cuts open your dead body to prepare you for the embalming process. Then he embalms you, wraps you in a few hundred rolls of linen to make you into a bitchin' Boris Karloffian mummy, and drags your departed soul down to the Underworld to be judged. Once you're down there, he shoves you into the Hall of Justice (the capital of the Underworld), brings you before Osiris, rips out your unbeating heart, and puts it on a scale to be weighed against the Feather of Truth. Then he quizzes you on some crap you should know, like he's a canine, shirtless, utterly-jacked Alex Trebek. If you pass the test, Anubis gives you a high-five and a kickass sandwich and then sends you along to Osiris, who makes the final judgment call on whether your eternal soul is righteous or heinous. If you fail to answer his questions correctly, or have a heavy black heart that exceeds the maximum weight requirement, Anubis pimp-slaps the fail out of you with the back of his hand, tears out your throat with his fangs, and then throws your soul down to the Eater of the Dead—a half-hippo, half-crocodile monster who munches on your balls for all eternity.

Known as "The Claimer of Souls," "He Who Counts the Hearts," "The Jackal Who Swallows Millions," and "The Master of Secrets," Anubis has a collection of diabolical, ominous-sounding nicknames that rivals the badass cred of even the most hardcore Scandinavian death metal bands' discographies. As the "Keeper of the Keys to the Underworld," he's also the patron god of necropolises—the macabre Egyptian cities of the dead—as well as of pyramids, mausoleums, and pretty much any other place where dead bodies like to congregate. He was also the only god who was allowed to be represented on nonroyal tombs, which is kind of egalitarian of him, and his penchant for smiting, destroying, and enforcing curses and hexes made him popular with necromancer cults even into the days of Classical Greece and Rome. As the inventor of mummification, Anubis was highly respected by morticians and undertakers as well—it was always a priest of Anubis who performed mummification and embalming rites at Egyptian funerals—and during the embalming process he wore a jackal mask while carrying out his duties. I imagine this looked completely unnatural/awesome. An image of the god Anubis was always included in all Egyptian funeral art and processions, usually depicted as lying on the coffin lid, simultaneously protecting and metaphorically teabagging the dead body. It's worth noting that the Egyptian Book of the Dead describes a mysterious item known as "the iron instrument of Anubis" as being an object that's inserted into the mouth of the deceased during the burial process, which sounds dirty. When he's not sort-of desecrating corpses, Anubis is generally depicted chilling out, escorting dead people around, and carrying around more ankhs than Ozzy Osbourne at a Black Mass. He also is said to have possessed the Staff of Anubis, a magical item so terribly mysterious that we don't even know what it actually did. Given what we know about the Alpha Dog, it's safe to say that it was probably totally rad.

There's another appropriately whacked-out Ancient Egyptian myth involving an unrelated man named Anubis. According to the story, this Anubis's wife tried to have sex with his brother Bata, but Bata refused her, so the wife got mad and told Anubis that Bata had tried to rape her. Anubis went off to kick Bata's ass into a protoplasmic miasma of fiction, but right before he could reach him Bata summoned a river of crocodiles to come between the two. Then Bata took a knife and cut off his own balls in a bizarrely misguided attempt to prove somehow that he didn't try to rape Anubis's wife. Anubis figured this was pretty cool for some reason, so instead of killing his bro he went home and fed his wife to his dogs, because apparently when you're a super-pissed-off Ancient Egyptian, you can't get yourself all worked up like that without violently destroying someone. I have no idea what the moral here is supposed to be, so don't ask.

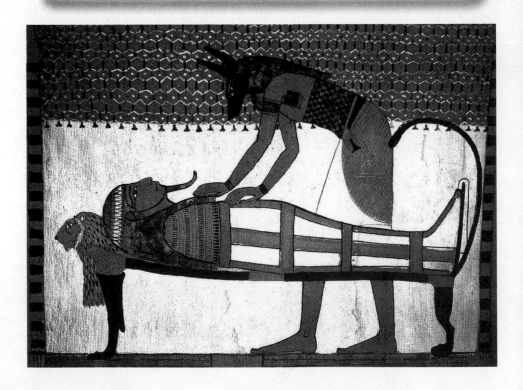

Because Osiris's penis was eaten by a fish, they were considered unclean, taboo animals. Throughout the Old and New Kingdom dynasties Egyptian priests were forbidden to consume the meat of these dick-fish.

———

During the mummification process, the brain was removed by inserting a hook through the nostril and swishing it around until the brain became a soft, jelly-like substance, which was then dripped out the nose. For all of you vocab nerds out there, the appropriate term for debraining someone is *excerebration*.

———

Even after getting the smack-down from Anubis, Set continued on being a total jackass to everyone he met. The God of Chaos eventually got into a fistfight with Osiris's son, the falcon-headed god Horus, and in the ensuing battle Horus avenged his murdered father by tearing Set's left nut off with a clenched fist and then spiking it into the turf like he'd just caught the game-winning touchdown pass in the Super Bowl. Set blinded Horus with a straight-up Ric Flair two-finger eye-gouge that popped out one of Horus's eyeballs (the plucked-out Eye of Horus is that stylized Egyptian eye you see in hieroglyphics), but it was still pretty clear that he'd gotten the worst of this particular encounter.

———

➤ ANIMAL-HEADED GODS ⬅

SOBEK

In terms of the sheer ridiculousness/awesomeness of his appearance, it's really hard to top Sobek, the crocodile-headed Egyptian god of man-devouring river fiends. The son of Neith and Set, Sobek was the Lord of the Nile, and the king of all crocodiles and crocodile-related carnivorous reptiles. This dude was like the reptilian version of Blade the Daywalker—he had all the advantages of his crocodile friends (giant teeth, jaws capable of chomping a buffalo in half, etc.), but with none of the drawbacks (short stumpy legs, cold-bloodedness, appalling lack of prehensile thumbs). Known as "The Raging One" because of his over-the-top tendency to completely flip the hell out and demonstrate his skills as the most perfect killing machine this side of a shark-armed bear with laser guns for testicles, Sobek is made even that much more badass by the fact that he was worshipped in an Egyptian city called Crocodileopolis.

Baal Moloch

We don't know a whole lot about the infamous Lord Moloch of the Biblical-age Canaanites (hell, many archaeologists aren't even totally sure that he was an actual deity in the first place), but the most popularly held belief about this horrible, gruesome, death-loving sun god was that he was a bull-headed man who enjoyed drums, loud music, and the death cries of burning children. Basically, he was Lemmy. According to some versions of his legend, the ancient Ammonites would get around a large idol of the beefy-armed, Minotaur-esque god, start a huge bonfire, and then throw a bunch of male children into the inferno as human sacrifices to Moloch. The dying yells of burning kids were a real buzzkill to the partygoers, though, so the cultists used to sing and dance and beat drums really loudly to drown out the racket. Moloch liked this for some reason. Yahweh and his posse were significantly less cool with it, so it should come as no surprise that the Bible says you're not really supposed to go around incinerating your kids just because some bull-faced dickhead thinks it would be really freaking hilarious.

Sekhmet

Once upon a time the people of Egypt decided they were going to stop worshipping the sun god Ra and start doing whatever the hell they wanted. Ra, being the all-powerful ruler of the cosmos, responded by sending the physical manifestation of his vengeance to brutally wreak havoc on them until they either changed their minds or exploded into giant clouds of bloody misery. The lioness-headed goddess Sekhmet conveyed the will of Ra by slaughtering so many people that the sands of Egypt were stained red, and before you knew it she was wading around through a thigh-deep river of flowing blood, firmly clenching her weapons and desperately looking for anything that looked even a little bit alive. The only way Ra managed to get this psychotic lioness-woman to stop massacring every sentient creature on Earth was by getting her drunk on seven thousand barrels of beer. After she woke up and got over her massive hangover, Sekhmet, the "Lady of Terror," invented infectious disease, taught herself to breathe fire, and presided over the execution of murderers, rapists, and other violent criminals. She's not all about the violence anymore, though—just as she can inflict virulent incurable pestilences on her enemies, she is also a goddess of healing and medicine, and can cure those people who wisely call on her for help.

GANESHA

The son of the Indian gods Shiva and Parvati, Ganesha was originally born looking like a regular human dude. One unfortunate day, however, Shiva (who was known for his temper tantrums and general disdain for anything other than dancing or incinerating the universe with fireballs) decided the kid was pissing him off, so he decapitated Ganesha with a jump-spinning knife-handed judo chop to the larynx. Shiva kind of felt badly about violently kung fu–ing the head off of his own son, so he grabbed the first head he could find (which just so happened to be that of a magical elephant) and grafted it onto Ganesha's cranium-less torso. Nowadays Ganesha is one of the most popular deities in Hinduism, where he's revered for his wisdom, kindness, and understanding. He is known as the remover of obstacles, and brings wealth, power, and success to people who deserve it. Ganesha fights against unfair cultural stereotypes about pachyderms by riding around the heavens on a giant mouse, and he's also sometimes credited as the original author of the classical Indian war epic, the *Mahabharata*.

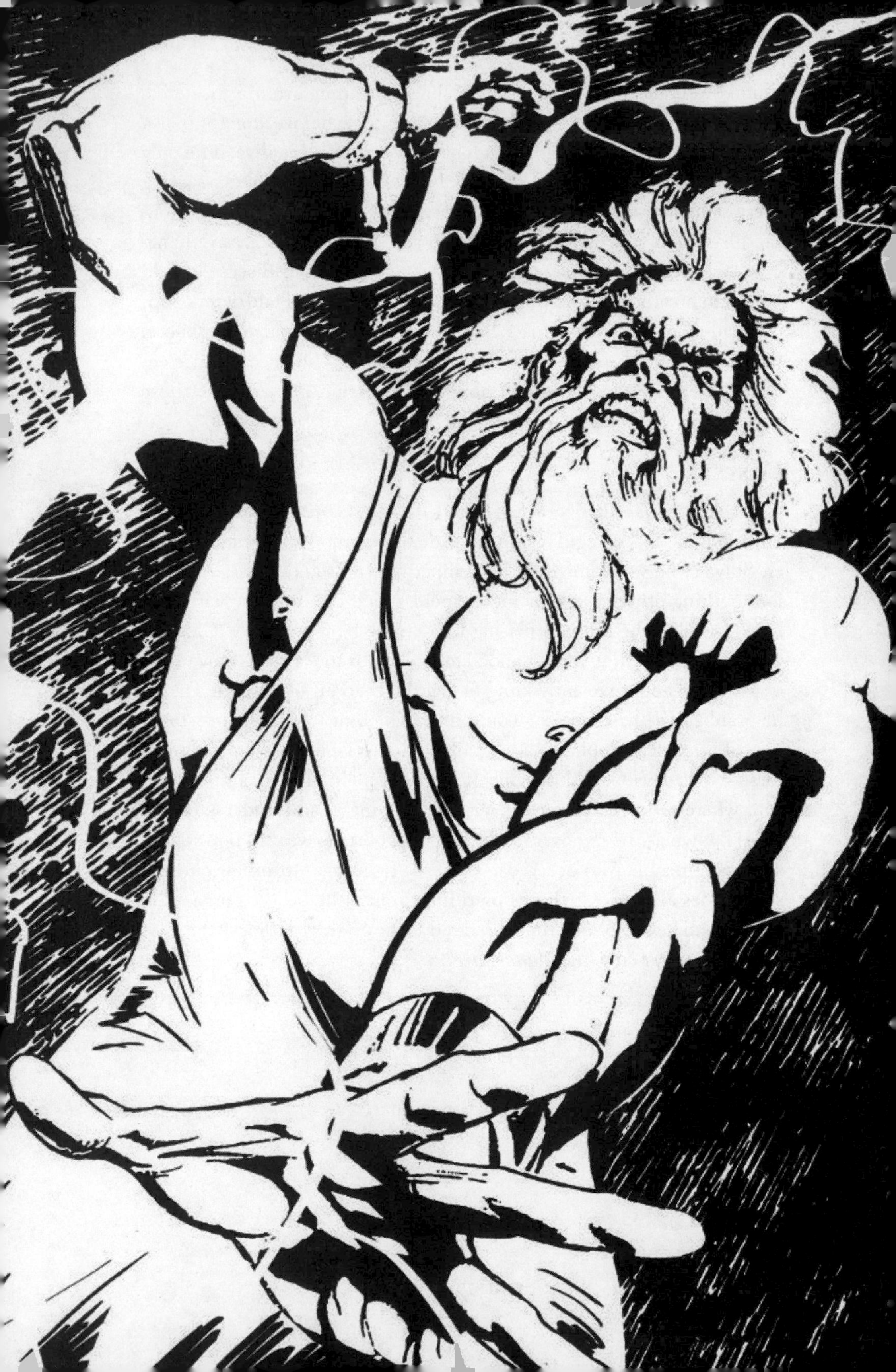

2

ZEUS

"Zeus! As in, father of Apollo? Mount Olympus? Don't f#@! with me or
I'll shove a lightning bolt up your ass? Zeus! You got a problem with that?"
"No, I don't have a problem with that."

—SAMUEL L. JACKSON AND BRUCE WILLIS IN
DIE HARD WITH A VENGEANCE

FROM ODYSSEUS TO AENEAS, GREEK AND ROMAN MYTHOLOGY IS FILLED WITH HEROIC STORIES AND EPIC TALES OF ASSKICKING WARRIORS, GODS, AND MONSTERS DOING ALL SORTS OF LEGEND- ARY, RIDICULOUS STUFF. Every myth is filled with feats of unrivaled strength and determination, and the entire pantheon just oozes things that are badass like a festering wound of awesomeness. However, among the towering acts of peerless greatness that dominate the entire mythological system, there is one figure that transcends these heroes and stands on a plane of righteous badassitude all by himself—the al- mighty Zeus, the powerful, petty, pimp-tastic ruler of Mount Olympus.

Zeus's dad was a dude named Cronus. Cronus was the king of the Titans, and generally just an all-around bastard, but things really got out of hand in his household when one day he heard some random prophecy claiming that one of his own children would overthrow him and take over as the head honcho of all existence. So Cronus (being, as I said, a bastard) arrived at the rational and logical conclusion that the best course of action to prevent his own violent overthrow was to eat his children as soon as they were born.

Well Mrs. Cronus eventually got sick of popping out babies just to have them horked down by some crazy baby-eating dumbass, so when she gave birth to baby Zeus she wrapped a rock in some baby clothes and fed that to Cronus instead. Apparently, King Cronus was so hungry he didn't even give a crap, because he wolfed that shiz down and didn't seem to notice the subtle textural and flavoral difference between a newborn infant and a large inanimate granite boulder. Zeus's mom then snuck her son off to the island of Crete, where he was raised to adulthood by a celestial goat in a cave full of mythical bees. It was . . . weird.

Cave life among the crazy goat-bees was apparently somewhat fruitful, however, because Zeus grew up with one thought on his mind—vengeance. Zeus trained himself rigorously, day after day, and when the time was right he ran out and punched his dad so hard in the balls that Cronus barfed up all of the kids he'd eaten. The kids all got together and revolted against the Titans, and under the able command of Zeus the Olympians kicked the Titans' asses off the face of Greece forever. Cronus and his defeated buddies were banished to a place called Tartarus, a horrible vortex of suck that was pretty much like the Ancient Greek equivalent of Satan's bunghole. Seriously, if Hell was the original Death Star, Tartarus was like that awful, sewage-filled trash-compactor room with the evil swimming penis eyeball thing and the walls that closed in and smashed Wookies into bloody pulps for no reason at all.

Even though the Titans lost the war, some of their homies still had their backs, and there were a couple of big revolts against Zeus. For the most part, he kicked faces and took names, but the Big Z got quite a test when the horrific monster known as Typhon showed up looking to avenge the fallen King Cronus. Typhon was the most insane of all the legendary Greek beasts—this towering hydra/dragon/lizard-man thing was like Ursula the Sea-Witch on steroids mixed with the Great Wall of China—and one day this thing showed up and started eating cities and throwing giant boulders around in an effort to eradicate all life on the material plane. Needless to say, everybody was pretty worried about that whole situation. Well, Zeus didn't give a crap about this 'roid-raging beast from some ungodly, narcotics-induced *Final Fantasy* summon spell. He nut-shotted Typhon with a couple dozen lightning bolts and then bodyslammed a mountain on top of him before shipping his ass off to Tartarus to enjoy an eternity of ball-sucking agony with his good buddy Cronus. Typhon would later father the Sphinx, the Hydra, the Chimera, the Nemean Lion, and a bunch of other bizarre abominations that would go on to in turn get owned by Zeus's children.

After all the threats to his rule were effectively face-smashed into the seventh circle of the next thing worse than Hell, Zeus took over as the head boss of everything ever. He sent his bro Poseidon to rule the ocean and his other brother Hades to oversee the Underworld, while the Z-man climbed up to the top of Mount Olympus and spent his days enjoying scenic views and having topless nymphs hand-feed him ambrosia and grapes and methamphetamines. He just hung out up there ordering around gods and mortals and smashing people's asses with lightning bolts whenever they pissed him off. As Mel Brooks says, it's good to be the king.

In addition to being the patron saint of lawgivers, kings, hospitality, and oracles, Zeus was also tasked with upholding the morality of the people as well. This is pretty ironic, because Zeus was a total manwhore who had more adulterous affairs than a Lifetime Original Movie marathon. You honestly can't pick up a book on mythology without reading some story of how the King of the Gods was out there impregnating princesses or seducing comely young maidens with his insanely good looks, or generally just getting it on with a veritable army of chicks and dudes and anything else that moved. During his wild escapades across Greece, this guy fathered hardcore gods like Ares, Apollo, Dionysus, Hermes, and Hephaestos, and produced heroes and villains like Perseus, Hercules, Orion, and King Minos. Hell, even Alexander the Great claimed to be descended from this guy, and Zeus was such a divine pimpenstein that nobody really even questioned it. This guy was so virile that one time he was just sitting around thinking about something awesome and all of a sudden the ridiculously badass warrior-goddess Athena spontaneously busted right out of his head wearing her full battle armor.

As the head of the Greek pantheon, Zeus was also the most widely worshipped of the gods, and was the focal point of many crazy religious cults. Of course, it was a good idea to worship this guy, because he was a totally petty bastard who wasn't above making your life miserable for no reason at all. Sure, he gave great rewards to good people—if you were virtuous and cool you could find yourself getting morphed into some sweet animals or receiving Time Extends on your lifespan or something—but if you were a dickhead you could expect some pretty harsh vengeance to be laid down upon your ass with the realness. Like one time a dude named Salmoneus wanted to show everyone his badass Zeus impression, so he went out and started riding around in a bronze chariot yelling "BOOM!" really loud, pretending that he could shoot lightning or something, so Zeus fragged that dumbass straight to Hades with a bolt of electricity so huge it would have made Tesla jizz. Another time a dude named Prometheus gave the secret of fire to humans, so Zeus chained him up to a rock and had rabid, pissed-off eagles disembowel him every day from that point until forever. Yet another time, a rather ambitious fellow named Ixion tried to seduce Zeus's wife, Hera, so Zeus responded by strapping the guy to a wheel of fire and having him raked over a bed of hot coals, condemning that poor bastard to an eternity of agonizing, skin-melting pain. The King of the Gods obviously transcended that whole "eye for an eye" thing.

The Temple of Zeus at Olympia was one of the Seven Wonders of the Ancient World. This place housed a towering forty-foot statue of the King of the Gods made of gold, silver, and marble, but the entire structure eventually fell apart when it imploded from the insane gravitational pull generated by Zeus's general bitchin'-ness.

3

RAMA

Wounded, faint, and still unyielding, blind with wrath the rivals fought . . .
Long and dubious battle lasted, shook the ocean, hill and dale,
Winds were hushed in voiceless terror and the livid sun was pale,
Still the battle lasted, until Rama in his ire
Wielded Brahma's deathful weapon flaming with celestial fire.

—*THE RAMAYANA*

LORD RAMA WAS THE SEVENTH PHYSICAL INCARNATION OF THE
INDIAN GOD VISHNU AND THE CENTRAL FIGURE OF THE BELOVED
POEM *RAMAYANA*, ONE OF THE TWO MAJOR EPIC TALES IN HINDU
LITERATURE. To this day, the illustrious Rama stands as a representation of the ideal man, the perfect model for benevolent kingship,
and the complete embodiment of honesty, loyalty, bravery, and duty.
He also had blue skin, once led an army of anthropomorphic bears
and monkeys in a full-scale war against cannibalistic, elephant-riding
shape-changers, debated religious philosophy with a talking vulture
prince, incinerated trolls with a fiery spear forged by the gods, and
rescued a beautiful princess from the clutches of the brutal King of all
Demons.

The firstborn son of the king of India, Rama was trained at an early age in the badass arts of archery and hand-to-hand combat by the Brahman sage Vasistha. One of the seven great sages of the Vedic religion, Vasistha was kind of like the Indian version of Merlin, only instead of directing young kings toward haunted, sword-filled lakes, this guy took the Indian prince out into the woods to hunt demons and save religious enclaves from the clutches of evil heathen devils by detonating their torsos Rambo-style with some bitchin' explosive-tipped arrows. Vasistha was also the owner of the sacred Mother of All Cows, Kamadhenu, who is said to have granted wishes to those she deemed worthy. That last part isn't really relevant to the story, but I find it impossible to leave out when discussing Vasistha.

One day, Rama was wandering around a nearby kingdom when he heard that the local princess, a mega-super-babe named Sita (who herself was an incarnation of Lakshmi, the Goddess of Prosperity), was holding a contest where she had agreed to marry the first man strong enough to string the massive Bow of Shiva. Now, according to Hindu tradition, Shiva the Destroyer is the dude who's tasked with obliterating the universe at the end of time, making him basically like all Four Horsemen rolled up into one multiarmed ass-smasher, so you can be pretty sure that his personal weapon was the sort of thing that would only be appropriate for someone capable of eradicating the entirety of existence. Getting a bowline on this bastard was like trying to string up a goddamned siege engine. Since Sita was so insanely hot, about five thousand jock meatheads all lined up and gave themselves hernias trying to operate this behemoth, and after watching all these fools look like a bunch of monkeys trying to hump a football she soon began to worry that there was nobody in the kingdom man enough to be her husband.

That's when Rama rolled into the town square. The blue-skinned prince silently walked up to the gigantor bow, cracked his knuckles, strung the weapon in one fluid motion, and then pulled the bowstring back so far he cracked the friggin' thing in half. Rama had such a blast trashing the ancient holy artifact that he would later go on to snap the Bow of Vishnu as well, but that time it was less about meeting chicks and more about just being awesome.

Of course Sita swooned, and the two had an incredibly lavish wedding ceremony where everyone partied harder than Andrew W.K. wearing a sarong and wading through a kiddie pool full of PBR. Most of the guests woke up a week later in a total daze completely covered in henna tattoos, but it was totally worth it.

A few years later, Rama's dad decided to retire, but while Rama was the rightful heir to the throne, the queen (Rama's stepmom) decided she wanted her son to take the crown instead. She called in a favor the king owed her, and had the king declare her son as his successor. As if that wasn't bad enough, she then had the king exile Rama to the wilderness for fourteen years, which also sucked a satchel of dicks. Everybody kind of knew this was a huge steaming pile of fresh horsecrap, but they also understood that it was their duty in life to honor their promises and live by the code of dharma. The king fulfilled his promise, and Rama packed his bags and headed out for a decade-long camping trip to nowhere.

Rama, Sita, and Rama's younger brother Lakshmana wandered around the woods for a while until they found this really kickass grove full of fresh fruit, quiet streams, and other sorts of stuff that made it basically paradise on Earth. They chilled out Walden Pond–style for a while, getting their Ralph Waldo Emersons on, but things went downhill quickly when the Demon Lord Ravana snuck into the grove when Rama and Lakshmana were out fighting demons and kidnapped Sita by throwing her into the back of his flying chariot and taking off like a gangsta.

Rama returned home to find his wife gone, his house trashed, and an assassination party waiting to ambush him. Needless to say, he wasn't happy. He and his brother were then immediately attacked by a bunch of demons riding a huge elephant, but those chumps were no match for

Rama's now boundless, uncontrollable kill-rage. Even though he was going up against a hulking possessed elephant holding a sword in its trunk and swinging it around, the Indian prince ice pick–lobotomized his enemies and unceremoniously left giant piles of mangled corpses in his wake. Ravana would not get away with this.

Without any clues or leads, Rama and Lakshmana roamed the Indian countryside looking for any trace of Sita or Ravana. They had a bunch of adventures on their quest, but it wasn't until they entered the Land of the Monkeys that things really started to take a turn for the awesomer. It was there that Rama met the former King of the Monkeys, a down-on-his-luck regent who had been languishing in exile ever since his stupid brother usurped his throne and started hooking up with his wife. Rama volunteered to assist the King of the Monkeys, challenged the usurper to a duel, and then blew the dude's head off by shooting an arrow into his neck with roughly the same force of impact as a thermonuclear warhead. Overjoyed at reclaiming his throne, the King of the Monkeys ordered the Monkey General Hanuman to assist Rama in his quest. Hanuman, who was the son of the Wind God, immediately put together an army of monkeys and started flying around trying to figure out where the balls Sita was being held prisoner.

Hanuman tracked Sita to Ravana's super-secret evil fortress on the remote island of Lanka. The flying monkey commander crossed the ocean, snuck into Ravana's lair, and found Sita in a gloomy valley surrounded by hundreds of heavily armed Rakshasa pig demons who looked like they meant business. Hanuman learned that Ravana was bound by some spell or other that prevented him from raping the captive princess, but that he'd given her a pretty straightforward ultimatum—if she didn't let him get to third base within the next three months, he would chop off all of her limbs, set her on fire, and throw her in a hole somewhere to rot.

Well, Rama would have rather dipped his balls in a deep-fat fryer than seen his wife run through the *Kama Sutra* by some repugnant dickwad from the douchiest recesses of the moral spectrum, and he immediately got his game face on and got ready to prove to the Demon Lord that he didn't fake the funk on a nasty dunk. Hanuman put together the Army of Monkeys, and then went to the King of the Himalayas to enlist the help of an army of bears (!), and together this insane group of weapon-toting war-animals marched toward glory. The Monkey Army built an impractically giant bridge from the Indian coast to Ravana's island, and Rama personally ran out and led the charge against Ravana's massive army of elephant-riding Rakshasa demons.

The battle that ensued was one of the most over-the-top engagements you could imagine. Rama and his monkey/bear army were on one side, charging forward with gnashing teeth and claws and God knows what else, while opposite them were pig demons, cannibals, corrupted evil men, sword-swinging elephants, and a sorcerer who was able to make giant, thirty-foot-long pythons fall out of the sky. Rama blitzed ahead, multi-shotting a half-dozen arrows with a single pull of the bowstring and stabbing with his spear the faces off of anything left standing. In the near-limitless and utterly ridiculous devastation that followed, Rama's brother was seriously wounded by a poison-tipped spear and almost died (Rama would avenge Lakshmana by shanking his assailant in the eye), the God of the Eagles swooped down and devoured the Master of Serpents, and Rama single-handedly defeated a twenty-foot-tall green-skinned monkey-smashing ogre that made Tolkien's cave trolls look like arthritic nursing home grandmas swinging their canes around.

Finally, after weeks of searching, hours of fighting, and a kill count that rivaled that of an early John Woo movie, Rama and Ravana met up for a final neck-smashing epic showdown of death. The hero nocked an arrow, clenched his teeth, and prepared to exact blood-drenched vengeance on the vile creature responsible for imprisoning and attempting to pork his beloved wife.

Unfortunately, it turned out that the King of the Demons was actually a bonkers-ass ten-foot-tall dude with ten heads and twenty arms, and each arm was whirling around a different pointy object of extreme bodily mutilation. Forget dual-wielding—this guy was decuple-wielding everything from tridents and daggers to rusty chains and giant boulders he broke off from mountaintops.

The catastrophically psychotic battle that followed was like ten tons of Mentos being dumped into a nuclear reactor filled with diet cola. Ravana was running around slinging spiked balls and handmade ninja stars; Rama was diving out of the way, pegging his nemesis in the eye with a few dozen arrows and impaling him in the kidneys with a magical spear. Both warriors were suffering the sorts of heinous, soul-sucking wounds that would have left most people lying facedown in an explosive crater of their own internal organs, but their intense, undying hatred for one another made this one of the most gruesome and brutal deathmatches ever contested. Eventually, after a battle so hardcore it made the Earth itself cringe, Rama rushed up and chopped off a couple of Ravana's heads, only to feel somewhat discouraged when Ravana

un-decapitated himself hydra-style, sprouting brand-new heads within seconds of the old craniums being lopped off.

Half dead from the battle, Rama was starting to run out of ideas. So, as a last-ditch effort to save his wife and murder the holy living cheeseballs out of the physical embodiment of evil in the universe, Rama whipped out the Spear of Brahma (a perpetually flaming, epic-level spear he'd looted from the body of one of Ravana's henchmen), faked like he was going to stab at a face Musashi-style, and then jammed the pointy part of the weapon straight into Ravana's cold, black heart.

That did the trick. Ravana keeled over like a top-heavy SUV, falling faces-first into the dirt. After witnessing Rama go all Voltron Blazing Sword on the King of the Demons, the Rakshasa army lost their will to live, and were promptly disemboweled by the Monkey-Bear Army of Ultimate Insanity. Rama was reunited with his lost love, and he, Sita, and Lakshmana returned home as heroes. Rama's half-brother (the one who had taken over as king) immediately abdicated the throne on their arrival. Rama and Sita ruled India for a thousand years, leading their people to an unprecedented era of peace and prosperity, and are still worshipped today in many parts of India and Southeast Asia.

A few hundred years after the original poem, some fun-hating killjoys tacked on a sequel where Rama abandons his pregnant wife in the woods because some jackass commoner makes a douchey remark about how she got it on with Ravana while in captivity. This addition pissed a lot of people off (think of it like the classical Indian equivalent of the *Star Wars* prequel trilogy), and as a result many people prefer to ignore it. The Tamil people wrote a much better sequel, the *Catakantaravanan,* in which Ravana's brothers come for vengeance and Sita takes them down herself.

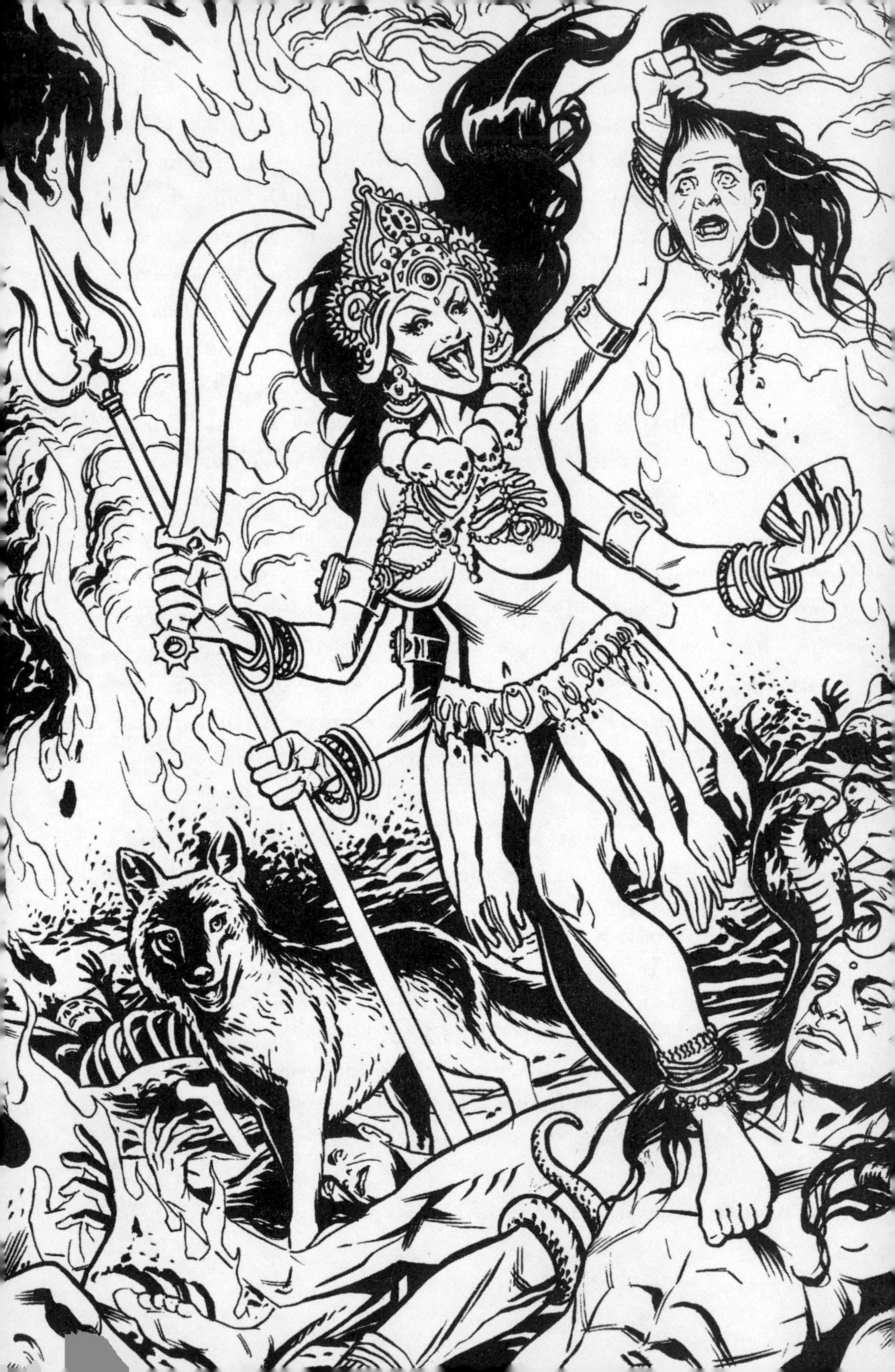

4

KALI

IT TAKES A SPECIAL KIND OF GODDESS TO BE WORSHIPPED IN THE MIDDLE OF A SMOKE-FILLED CREMATION FIELD, SURROUNDED BY WAFTING ASHES, FLICKERING FLAMES, AND OMINOUS CHANTS TO MALICIOUS GHOSTLY SPIRITS. A goddess whose devotees delight in relaying exceedingly gruesome stories about ritualistic sacrifice, cruel murderous vengeance, and eating the flesh from burning corpses like something out of a Tony Roma's franchise operated by Hannibal Lecter.

If that sounds like a fun way to spend a Saturday night, then the Dark Mother Smashana-Kali is the deity for you!

For starters, the Indian death goddess Kali is probably one of the most pants-soilingly terrifying things you'll ever see. The vicious, bloodthirsty aspect of the Great Goddess Parvati, this ass-wrecking mistress of fatality and destruction is about as cuddly as a Cthulhu teddy bear made out of razor blades and broken glass and coated in the venom of an Australian box jellyfish. With pitch-black skin (or, in some cases, such a deep midnight blue as to appear black), wild, untamed hair, and fiery eyes, she's usually depicted as being surrounded by snakes, ravens, and decapitated corpses blasting fountains of blood out of every orifice like something out of an over-the-top ultraviolent Japanese cartoon. She's generally shown as being completely naked except for a long, epic necklace made from fifty strung-together human heads, each one branded with a different letter of the Sanskrit alphabet. When she's feeling particularly saucy, she enjoys laying out the heads and spelling different words and phrases—my guess is that the majority of these are presumably violent threats, soon-to-be-fulfilled curses, or withering profanity about the quality of your maternal lineage, but I don't actually read Sanskrit so it's hard to say. She also wears a belt of severed forearms around her waist and bracelets made from serpents, and is generally shown either straight up standing on the prostrate body of her husband, Shiva (the Hindu Lord of Destruction), or tearing out his intestines with her teeth. When she's not consuming the entrails of the gods, getting drunk on human blood, performing her Dance of Annihilation, sticking out her Gene Simmons–esque tongue, or shouting horrific insults at people who may or may not deserve it, she shoots blood out of her mouth like a fire hose. Throw in the fact that she has four arms with which to make the goat-horn hand sign, and she's pretty much the most totally metal being ever.

Born from the Ocean of Blood at the beginning of the universe, Kali represents the limitless void, and the physical embodiment of the cosmic, planet-destroying power of Shiva—a god so tough that the word "shiv" appears in his name (though I suppose "smash" appears in

"Smashana-Kali" as well). She is the inevitable demise and destruction of all things. Assisted by her dark attendants, who range from jackals and ravens to goblins and dark female spirits, she resides in the cremation fields, battlegrounds, and spooky temples of India, where she burns away, devours, and/or axe-murders life and everything associated with it so that all that remains is her.

In addition to having a fine appreciation for a few thousand assloads of blood, Kali is also the Goddess of Tantra and the patron deity of sex, drugs, and rock 'n' roll. And ritual animal sacrifice. And maybe war, depending on who you ask. Those who join her wild Tantric sects fear nothing, indulge in their every desire, and believe that death is simply an inescapable eventuality of life. As you can imagine, the Drinker of Blood tends to attract some pretty odd ducks to her cult. While the Priests of Cybele definitely bear mentioning (these dudes castrate themselves with ceremonial daggers as a way of honoring her), the most infamous of her devotees were the notorious Thuggee. A mysterious, secretive cult of murderers and bandits, the Thuggee used to worship Kali and then go out to ritualistically kill people, rob them of all their worldly possessions, and dump their dead asses into wells. According to the beliefs of this antisocial brotherhood of bandit jackasses and highwaymen, Kali was doing battle with an evil demon one day, but when she cut him in half all of his blood droplets sprouted into full-size duplicates of the monster. Since the requisite gore-fest that generally follows Kali around like the paparazzi resulted in a huge throng of duplicated demons in a very short period of time, Kali flipped out and created a couple humans out of her sweat to help her fight the monsters off. She gave these weird sweat-dudes some special yellow handkerchiefs, instructing them to strangle the demons to death without spilling a single milliliter of their blood. Then she gave them a sacred pickaxe with which to bury the corpses, which was helpful. The Thuggee reportedly killed 2 million people over the course of a couple centuries, and created one of the most kill-crazy organized-crime syndicates in history.

It should be mentioned that the Thuggee are rather loosely portrayed in *Indiana Jones and the Temple of Doom*, where the badass shaman/priest/crazy person Mola Ram covered himself with red war-paint and tore a dude's heart out through his chest cavity with a stone-cold open-hand punch to the sternum (awesome). The eponymous fire-spewing Temple of Doom was actually supposed to be a temple of Kali-Ma, and you've really got to respect any god or goddess who has their place of worship—fictional or otherwise—referred to as anything even remotely associated with being "of doom."

By the early twentieth century, the Thuggee were all but wiped out by a mix of British colonial authorities, gnarly mine-cart accidents, and gnashing crocodile teeth, but you can probably guess that it's going to take a little more than the complete destruction of her favorite cultists to satiate Kali's undying desire to go head-first down a waterslide fueled by fresh, flowing crimson rivers of blood. As recently as 2002, Indian police estimated that at least one Kali-related ritual human killing was taking place in the country every month, which is kind of insane and also super-scary. Sure, this is a vast improvement over past centuries, when the altars of Kali's temples were adorned with piles of severed animal heads, and human males were being ceremonially dismembered in her name at the rate of roughly one per day, but I'm not necessarily sure we can refer to this as "progress" as much as just "marginally less terrifying."

Admittedly, much of the info we have on these aforementioned "kill a kid a day and then eat a baby harp seal just to prove how incredibly evil I am" kinds of sacrificial rites come from marginally reliable European colonial missionaries who weren't exactly taking the time to understand the intricacies of the indigenous religion, and I should point out that many of Kali's followers get a little upset by this harsh portrayal of her as a gore-spewing juggernaut capable of decapitating four to six people at a time (depending on how many sword-bearing arms that particular iteration of her is sporting). They argue that she's not bad; she's just drawn that way. Rather than a stone-cold black widow who enjoys completely covering herself in the warm, flowing blood of her freshly dismembered enemies, she can also manifest herself as a mother, a protector, and a preserver, and in some cases, the ultimate and supreme being in charge of the universe. She not only saves the world from evil by going into a famous kill-frenzy and imploding demons' heads with her bare hands, but just as the Blood Drinker aspect of her nature snuffs the life out of people who probably deserve it, the Sex Goddess and Dark Mother aspects can also grant wealth, power, long life, nine-hour orgasms, and success on those who need it. She offers retribution to those who seek vengeance, leads her worshippers to victory on the battlefield, bestows children on those who desire to procreate, and offers an end to misery to those who follow her teachings. I personally have a tough time seeing "warm and fuzzy helper-goddess" in a statue of a sword-swinging woman crotch-stomping a half-dead guy and shooting blood out of her eyes while headless torsos run around in the background, but hey, I guess anything's possible.

Many religions and pantheons share the idea of an all-encompassing "Triple Goddess"—a trinity of female deities (or three aspects of the same goddess) that represent different facets of the classical notion of womanhood. The Maiden aspect is generally a young virgin who signifies spring, rebirth, and prosperity; the Mother embodies sex, fertility, childbirth, protection, and nurturing; and the Crone is sort of like the crazy old cat lady who runs around casting death spells on furniture she doesn't like and chasing neighborhood kids off her porch with a Weedwhacker.

DURGA

Another badass (yet somewhat less sociopathic) aspect of Parvati/Kali is the warrior-goddess Durga. Durga, whose name means "inaccessible" or "unapproachable" in Hindi, is a multiarmed, Devil-smiting doom-bringer who rides around on a giant lion looking for punk-ass demons that need a half-dozen razor-sharp tridents rammed into their disgusting, dripping mandibles. She is said to have been created by the fire spewed from Shiva and Vishnu's mouths while they were fighting a ridiculous mutant buffalo-monster. Durga's primary cosmic responsibility is to violently combat evil—particularly when that evil takes the form of giant-ass, previously unkillable fiends that can only be defeated by having their necks twisted into knots by superpowerful kill-mongers. When this four-armed, sword-swinging demon-huntress isn't relentlessly hacking armies of thirty-foot-long brain-eating toothy creatures into bucketloads of shark chum, she keeps in shape by doing yoga, which she invented.

FREYJA

Norse mythology is so hardcore that even the goddess of love, beauty, and fertility—Freyja—is also the goddess of war, battle, sorcery, and death. This multitasking divine being is not only a spicy-hot sex symbol who serves as a serious object of lust for mortals, gods, and giants alike, but she's also an armor-bearing warrior goddess who rides through battle-torn lands and claims the souls of one-half of the slain warriors for herself. She and Odin split the battle-dead between Odin's fortress Valhalla and her golden hall Sessrúmnir, which is located in the Warriors' Fields of Asgard. She wears a jeweled necklace that shines brighter than the sun, travels through the heavens on a chariot pulled by horse-size cats, owns a gold-bristled boar named Battle-Pig, and can turn into a falcon at will. On the rare occasion that she cries, she shoots red gold out of her eyes instead of tears, which is sweet.

ENYO

Her name might bring up thoughts of the sort of narcolepsy-inducing soothing ambient music preferred by massage therapists and yoga enthusiasts the world over, but the Greek goddess Enyo wasn't the sort of kickass hellion who took long relaxing bubble baths with exotic moisturizing lotions when she could have been laying waste to battlefields and flagellating warriors' faces off with the bloody scourge she carried with her at all times. According to Homer, the goddess of frenzied combat delighted only in the sounds of battle, and everywhere she went she was followed by the ruthless din of war. Enyo's primary role in the pantheon of asskicking was that of Ares' close associate and wheelman, driving the God of War's chariot from battlefield to battlefield while he pitched gold-plated javelins into people's eyes and insulted their mothers while grabbing his crotch. She specialized in the besieging and destruction of cities, and was said to have been present any time an invading army was plundering or pillaging a vanquished town.

HEL

Another ruthless Norse goddess, Hel is the monstrous daughter of Loki and the powerful, fierce, exceedingly cruel ruler of the Nine Underworlds. Half of her body is pitch-black, and the other half is bone-white, which is pretty cool, and she's in charge of cheerful stuff like hunger, famine, sickness, and epic, earth-smashing natural disasters. From her inescapable realm far beyond the mythical Corpse-Gate, this dark goddess rules over souls that die of illness and old age and don't have the good sense to be brutally eviscerated in battle with a great warrior's sword lodged in their brain. The worst spot in her nine realms is reserved for oath-breakers and murderers—these bastard-coated bastards are thrown into a hall made entirely out of serpent spines, where they constantly wade through a waist-deep river of blood while giant evil snake heads spit venom in their eyes. It's not a whole lot of fun. Hel and her minions lie in wait for the battle at the end of the world—Ragnarok—when the bowels of the Underworld will empty and she and her creatures will return to Earth to fight against the gods who have imprisoned them.

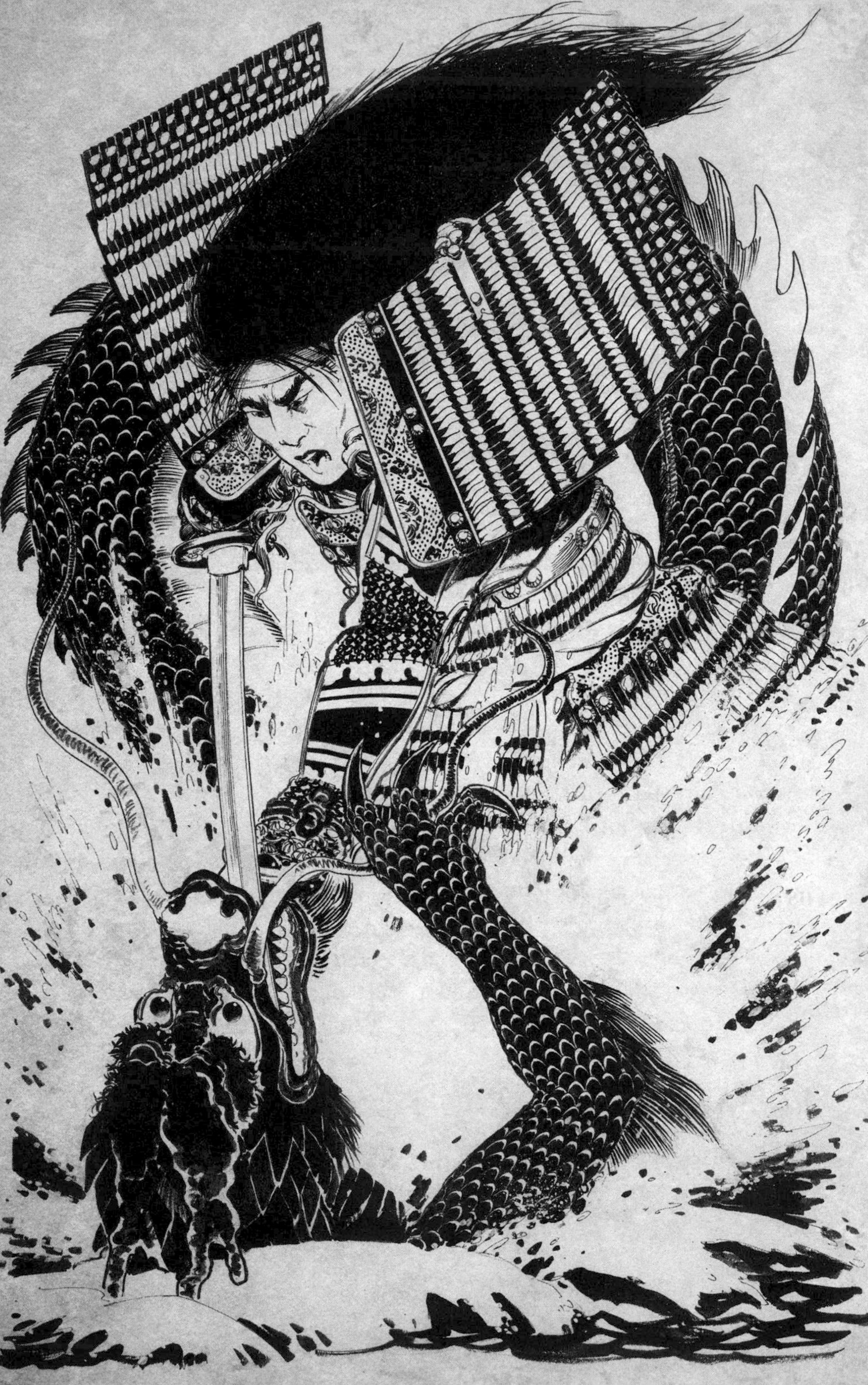

5

BRAVE-SWIFT-
IMPETUOUS-MALE

Brave-Swift-Impetuous-Male, drawing his Ten Grasp Sword,
severed its heads and belly,
cutting it into eight small pieces, each of which became a
Thunder-Kami and flew up into the sky,
and the river flowed on—a river of blood.

—*THE KOJIKI*

HIS BRAVE-SWIFT-IMPETUOUS-MALE AUGUSTNESS IS A DUDE WHO LAYS IT ALL OUT FOR YOU RIGHT IN HIS NAME. Sure, here in the West some authors try to sound professional by transliterating his incredibly hyphenated name to Susano, Susanoo, Susuanowo, Susano-O, or some arbitrary combination of the letters *s, u, n,* and *o,* but this doesn't change the fact that the Shinto god of thunder, storms, the Underworld, and being an asshole was so manly and hardcore that he is now remembered by those who worship him simply as a non sequitur mash-up of words describing precisely how manly and hardcore he is.

Brave-Swift-Impetuous-Male was created at the beginning of the universe, though his creation wasn't exactly a super-glamorous affair—he came into being when he was accidentally shot out of the nose of the Great God of the Shinto faith in one of the most epic sneezes ever recorded. Exploding forth from the third-grossest orifice of the human body really isn't something you want to go around bragging about, because let's face it—there's really not a lot of good stuff that comes out of noses these days.

Despite being a boy named Sue, Susanoo eventually managed to overcome the unfortunate circumstances surrounding his creation and go on to be one of the toughest heroes and most unabashed jerks in mythology. Not long after being born out of a giant nostril (the likes of which might only have existed on the set of *Double Dare*), Brave-Swift-Impetuous-Male was sent to Earth, placed in charge of the sea, and made the all-powerful master of the ocean and all of its domains. Unfortunately for cosmic order of the universe, Susanoo (perhaps understandably) decided that he didn't want to be some Aquaman jackass merfolk who floated around all day talking to porpoises and singing songs like a dumbass, and refused the position. So, despite technically being the Japanese edition of Poseidon, there's no record of Susanoo ever actually presiding over his vast aquatic domain. Instead of ruling the seas with a magical trident and a handful of crabs, Susanoo rage-quit his job, decided Earth blows goats (which, in his defense, it sometimes does), and stormed back up to Heaven to chill out like the immortal badass that he was. His tempestuous departure was so savage and hate-filled that as he stormed away the mountains fell apart, the forests turned to rotted brown piles of sludge, and humans started spontaneously combusting into vapor trails of blood for no reason at all. I think we've all been there at some point during our professional careers, but this guy took the whole "take this job and shove it" mentality and cranked it to the next level.

Brave-Swift-Impetuous-Male went back to Heaven and immediately got his sibling rivalry on with his sister, the much-revered and incredibly powerful sun goddess Amaterasu. Amaterasu was nice enough, I guess, and is a primary goddess of the Shinto faith, but Susanoo was such an insane-in-the-membrane jackass to her that it's hard not to be amused by his over-the-top antics. For starters, he once took a dump in Amaterasu's sacred worship hall right before her yearly harvest festival. This isn't even hyperbolic exaggeration—the dude seriously pulled off the roof of the structure, upper-decked the congregation, and then ran out laughing his head off. That's kind of awesome. Another time, Amaterasu was sewing a garment of some sort, and Susanoo flayed a horse backward (apparently, there is a right and a wrong way to flay a horse, though I'm not familiar enough with the art to be able to make an effective commentary one way or the other), ran over, and chucked the skinless equine right in his sister's face when she was in the middle of her seamstressing. He also screwed around with her rice crops, causing floods and natural disasters that ruined his sister's harvest. At least, that's how I'm choosing to interpret the literature when it claims that Susanoo "erected rods in her rice fields" and "filled up her irrigation channels." For the sake of avoiding any further discussion of celestial incest, I'm just going to stick with the literal translation and quickly move along.

Amaterasu eventually had enough of her brother's hilarious-yet-cruel dorm room–grade pranks and locked herself in a cave. The eight hundred other Shinto gods got a little concerned that the sun suddenly stopped shining, and frantically tried to convince her to come back out of the cave. Amaterasu only emerged after the other gods brought her a full-length mirror, had one of the goddesses perform a sexy striptease, and passed a decree mandating that all of Susanoo's hair be cut off, that his fingernails and toenails be ripped out, and that he be banished from Heaven forever. That did the trick. The sun returned to the land, and Susanoo was shorn, shredded, and once again shipped off to the hellhole that is Earth. Susanoo, apparently being kind of a stand-up guy beneath all those layers of jackassery, eventually texted his sister, apologized, and then proved his devotion by crunching some jewels into dust with his teeth, blowing them into the wind, and having the spit-dust sprout into male children. That last part doesn't make a whole lot of sense, but she bought it anyway. He then scattered his shaved hair to the wind, where the strands of his ultra-manly beard became sacred trees that are now used for building shrines, warships, coffins, catapults, and other awesome wooden things.

Like all good Kurosawan samurai asskicking heroes, His Brave-Swift-Impetuous-Male Augustness was now doomed to wander the Earth with nothing but his sword, his guts, and his brave-swift-impetuousness. Having now seen that it doesn't really pay to be such a preposterous ass clown all the time, Susanoo decided that the best practical application of his particular skill set was to travel the land slicing people in half longways with the magical Ten-Grasp Sword, fighting demons, and murdering Giant Enemy Crabs by striking them in the weak point for massive damage. This guy took on every mercenary job he could find, no matter how intense, and constantly proved to everyone that he had the hugest ballsack in all of mythological Japan. Nowadays there's a lot of traditional Japanese art depicting Susanoo wrestling sea monsters and other magical beasts, and I think we can all agree that it kicks ass any time religious iconography depicts a god wrestling a Kraken.

One day, Brave-Swift-Impetuous-Male heard a story that some giant eight-headed dragon was tormenting a nearby kingdom with its hugeness and hydra-headed villainy. This beast, who was so huge that trees were growing out of its hide, had apparently decided that the only way it would refrain from devouring the entire population of the kingdom was if the king fed him one delicious princess every year, forever. The king, wanting to do what was in the best interests of his people, appeased the monster in this way for seven years, but he only had eight daughters and was understandably concerned when he realized he was rapidly running out of edible princesses.

Luckily, Susanoo was there to help. With violence. The out-of-work Japanese thunder/ocean god didn't like the idea of some jackass mountain-sized monster thinking it was better than him, and the prospect of saving princesses is the sort of thing that has always appealed to asskickers of all cultures, no matter how brave, swift, or impetuous they may or may not be. So Susanoo showed up, told the king that he was there to save the day, and promptly morphed the princess into a comb, which he then stuck into his now regrown hair like a 1970s Afro pick.

While most people probably wouldn't have any idea what the hell to do with an eight-headed, red-eyed dragon that breathes fire (did I mention that he breathed fire? I think he also shot lightning bolts out of his dick like Lo Pan, but I can't seem to find any legitimate sources to verify that last part), Susanoo had a totally awesome plan. First, he cut down a bunch of trees and used the wood to build eight giant towers outside the creature's lair. Then he filled up eight kiddie pool–size tubs with rice wine, and placed one on top of each tower. The Eight-Headed Serpent of Koshii crawled over to investigate the crazy lumberjackery that was going on, saw all the sake, chugged it, got wasted, and passed out like a lightweight. As soon as the creature was down and out like a freshman during pledge week, Susanoo drunk-shamed the behemoth by going around cutting off all of the heads with mighty blows from his monster-cleaving sword. Before he was even half-finished, the entire land was completely flooded with the blood of the monster, but Susanoo somehow managed to swim through it to complete the job. Inside the corpse of the beast he found another magical sword, the Heavenly Sword of Assembled Clouds, which he added to his rapidly increasing collection of magic katanas. Another Japanese imperial prince would later use this sword to escape from a magical brushfire by cutting apart all the grass in his general vicinity, and the Heavenly Sword of Assembled Clouds became known as the Grass-Cleaving Sword, or, alternatively, the Herb-Quelling Sword. It seems to me that if your friggin' samurai sword doesn't cleave grass, you've got a problem that goes well beyond dealing with building-size monsters that can devour you in one bite, but whatever. The people of Japan seemed to dig this magical power, because the Herb-slayer Sword ended up becoming a holy artifact of Japan and the symbol for the physical manifestation of the power of the emperor, and stayed that way until some dude lost it in the ocean in the twelfth century.

His Brave-Swift-Impetuous-Male Augustness turned the princess back to human form, married her, built a sweet palace, and took over as king after the eventual death of his new father-in-law. Susanoo's descendants would go on to be progenitors of the imperial family of Japan (to this day, the emperor still traces his lineage back to the thunder

god), and after his mission of slaying dragons, throwing horses ass-first at goddesses, and spawning the elite rulers of Japan was over, Susanoo descended into the Underworld, wrested control from the punk who used to be in charge, and took over as the God of Death. Nowadays, the Eight-Headed Serpent of Koshii is on the currency of Japan, and Susanoo's legacy lives on in a bunch of really weird, super-violent, and borderline-accurate anime movies depicting his adventures. I'm sure this is how he would have wanted to be remembered.

I don't know if it's antiquated translations, unconventional naming practices, or just general awesomeness, but Japanese myth has some seriously sweet names for their gods. In the early tales of their celestial history, you run into folks with names like Foot-Stroking-Elder, Wondrous-Deity-of-Eighty-Evils, Deity-Princess-of-Great-Food, The-Brave-Rustic-Illuminator, and Truly-Conquer-I-Conquer-Conquering-Swift-Heavenly-Great-Great-Ears.

Some of the most evil creatures in Japanese mythology are the vicious Oni—giant, horned, red-skinned hairy ogres who carry spiked clubs, kidnap young women, consume human flesh, and drink the blood of mortals. The legendary warrior, archer, and swordsman Minamoto Raiko is famous for dedicating his life to scouring the land of these lecherous bastards and everything they stand for. During his adventures whomping ogre-sacks around the time of the Emperor Murakami, Raiko reportedly destroyed an Oni tribe that lived on Mount Oeyama and pretended to be an enclave of Buddhist monks, defeated a giant wine-connoisseuring cannibal known as Chief Drunk Boy, and rid the country of a video game–style giant spider that could shoot webs out of its abdomen and disguise itself as a beautiful woman whenever it felt threatened.

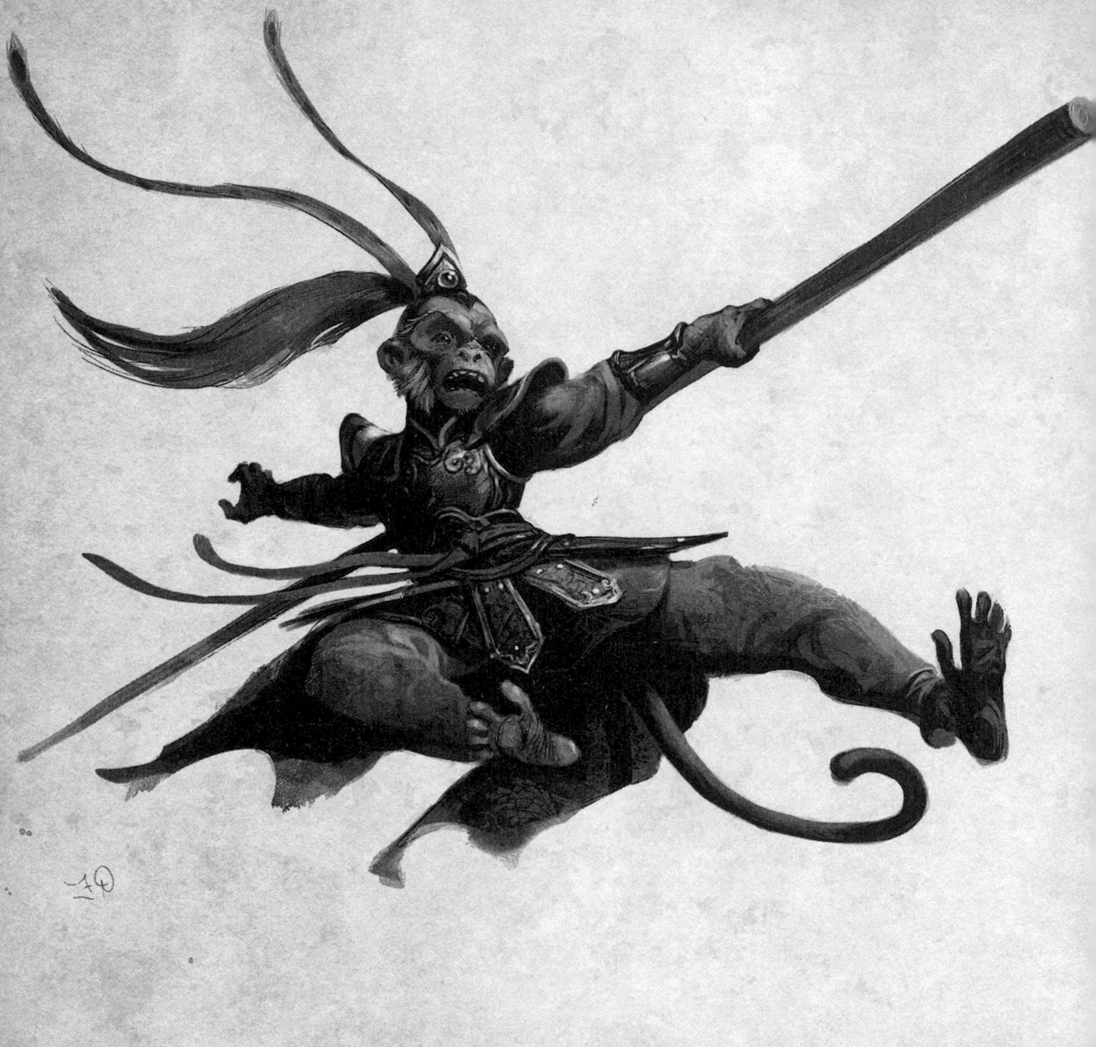

6

THE MONKEY KING

Don't believe your eyes. You say I am small, but I can make myself as
tall as I please. You claim I am unarmed, but with these hands
I could tear the moon out of the sky. Hold still, and we will see
how you like the taste of Monkey's fists.

SUN WUKONG, BETTER KNOWN IN THE WEST AS THE MONKEY KING,
IS A BELOVED TRICKSTER-GOD WHO STARS IN THE CLASSICAL CHI-
NESE EPIC *JOURNEY TO THE WEST*—AN EXISTENTIAL TALE ABOUT
SPIRITUAL ENLIGHTENMENT, HEROISM, AND THE JOURNEY OF A
SMALL GROUP OF MONKS IN SEARCH OF THE HOLY TEACHINGS OF
THE LIVING BUDDHA. He was also an ill-tempered bipedal talking
monkey who was smarter than Dr. Zaius, more diabolical than Go-
rilla Grodd, so incredibly hardcore that Jet Li played him in a movie,
and his story is so crap-your-pants insane that I could tell it straight-up
without any of my beloved hyperbole and you would still think it was
one of the most over-the-top things you've ever heard.

Born in the Mountains of Flowers and Fruit when a magic stone
laid an egg that was transformed by the wind into a stone monkey, this

celestial chimp spent his early years in existence shooting light beams out of his eyes and befriending the monkeys, tigers, leopards, apes, elephants, wolves, and bears of the land. While regular monkeys wanted to do normal monkey-related things, like eat bananas and fling poop at stuff, the Stone Monkey discovered a magical paradise by jumping through a waterfall and landing in Heaven on Earth. The beasts and ferocious animals of the land were so impressed that they made him their king and started bowing down to him all the time, and he took the imperial title "Handsome Monkey King."

Monkey ruled over the beasts for a few centuries, but that got boring so he went on a ten-year voyage west, climbed a mountain on the Western Continent, and became a student of one of the great patriarchs of Taoism. For the next several months Monkey trained with the Tao master, learned the secrets of immortality, and was taught seventy-two different magical kung-fu styles, like how to fly, turn invisible, summon monsoons, breathe water, belch smoke bombs out of his mouth, and spontaneously shape-shift into a humongous, evil-looking megademon with three heads and six arms and possibly four asses.

Monkey was unceremoniously expelled from the temple by the patriarch for turning himself into a pine tree without proper authorization, so he somersaulted onto a cloud and flew home, only to discover that his people had been displaced and oppressed by a giant, sword-swinging monster known as the Demon King of Havoc. Monkey, who is basically the ultimate god of not taking crap from anything or anyone regardless of rank and/or stature, ran out to the Dark Lord's lair and challenged the monstrous creature to a duel by insulting him vociferously and without mercy. The Demon King was roughly about the size of Godzilla wearing a suit of plate-mail armor and carrying a two-handed razor-sharp sword, but Monkey overcame the substantial size difference by spontaneously cloning himself into a hundred smaller monkeys, all of which flew through the air and kicked the behemoth warrior in the head in a fifty-hit freak-monkey face-kick combo. While the demonic monster was distracted by all the flying baboons pummeling the crap out of his facial, the Handsome Monkey King tore the massive sword right out of the bastard's hand, jumped up ridiculously high into the air, and split the foul creature's skull with a simian death-blow that was like an axe cleaving through a water balloon. The monkey clone army shrieked like overexcitable chimps, grabbed sticks, overwhelmed all of the demonic imps in the Demon King's army with brute force, and set the imp homeland on fire until everything was dead.

Monkey returned to tell his loyal subjects about how he once again bailed their asses out, and then ensured that similar levels of demonic enslavement would never happen again by breaking into a powerful nearby city, plundering the armory of all its weapons, and training his army of monkeys and tigers in hand-to-hand combat. Realizing that no mortal weapon was badass enough for him, however, Monkey then went to the bottom of the ocean, met the Dragon King of the Eastern Sea, and demanded the dragon fork over a death implement worthy of Monkey's unwaveringly intense badassitude. The Dragon King gave Monkey a suit of gold armor, a Phoenix plume helmet, and a gigantic iron cudgel that had once been used by a mighty hero to pound out the ocean floor. This was sufficient, but the Monkey King was such an arrogant jackass about the whole thing that the Dragon King went complaining to the Jade Emperor of Heaven, who sent the planet Venus to arrest Monkey and bring him to Heaven.

Monkey voluntarily traveled to Heaven (he figured it was time he saw what the big deal was anyways), and the Jade Emperor was amused enough by Monkey's assholish behavior to give him a chance at redemption. Monkey was appointed to be the stable-boy of the gods, but our self-aggrandizing antihero deemed the post too insignificant for someone of his stature, so he violently flipped over a fully loaded super–buffet table, fled back to Earth, and declared his new title to be "Great Sage,

Equal of Heaven." Of course, this blatantly awesome display of *cojones* pissed off the gods, who sent a powerful celestial warlord named General Mighty-Mighty to beat Monkey into submission. Mighty-Mighty went down to the Mountains of Flowers and Fruit looking to make a little bit of charred monkey brain paté, but to his surprise, his entire army was single-handedly battered into paste by the cudgel-swinging chimp and his righteous rod of cranial destruction. Realizing they couldn't beat the Monkey in the arts of war, the gods called him back to Heaven and decided to keep an eye on him by making him the guardian of the Peaches of Immortality, which was a significantly more prestigious task than the whole stable boy thing. They even let him keep his title—Great Sage, Equal of Heaven—because it's not like they could really do anything about it anyway. Unfortunately for the gods, they had yet to realize the time-honored axiom that you can never trust a monkey—no sooner did the gods turn their backs than Monkey ate all the Immortality Peaches, broke into the home of Lao-Tsu (the real-life historical founder of Taoism), drank all of his wine, and fled Heaven once again, incredulously laughing about how all the gods could be so amazingly idiotic.

That was it. The full might of Heaven's army converged on Monkey's palace in the Mountains of Flowers and Fruit, but once again the Great Sage didn't give a crap. Monkey personally defeated the planets and the stars in battle, smashed the main army of Heaven, and it was only after a super-intense, planet-spanning battle that Monkey was subdued by the nephew of the Jade Emperor. Monkey was dragged back to Heaven to be executed, but he had eaten so many of the Peaches of Immortality that he had actually become invincible, and not even the weapons of the gods could harm him. Monkey took advantage of the situation, broke free, and did battle with thirty-six Thunder Gods, but then the Buddha showed up, turned his hand into the Mountain of Five Elements, and slam-dunked the Himalayas on top of the Monkey King. Monkey was imprisoned beneath this hellacious mystical mountain, pinned down in such a way that he could only move his head, and every couple days some heavenly messenger would show up and throw a pot of molten-hot copper into Monkey's face. It sucked.

For five hundred years, the Handsome Monkey King was trapped beneath the Mountain of Five Elements. Finally, one day a wise monk named Hsuan-Tsang came by on a holy quest—he had been tasked with journeying 108,000 miles over land from China to India and recovering the sacred scriptures from the Buddha himself. The old wise man was definitely in need of a bodyguard capable of cranking demons' heads off with his prehensile thumbs and murdering river gods by cracking them in the balls with a baseball bat made out of angry piranhas. While crossing the Himalayas, Hsuan-Tsang came across Monkey in his unfortunate state and freed him from his ridiculously uncomfortable incarceration. Monkey, having been taught a little humility over the course of five hundred miserable years underneath the soul-crushing weight of the most devious monolithic monstrosity geology has to offer, agreed to do some penance, become a Buddhist priest, and serve as Hsuan-Tsang's disciple along their journey. Hsuan-Tsang, understandably a little hesitant to journey around with a talking Monkey god that once tried to face-kick the Buddha himself, ensured his own personal safety by tricking Monkey into putting on a stylish magical hat. The hat was rigged so that any time the Monkey acted like a jackass, all Hsuan-Tsang had to do was recite a quick spell and the Monkey suffered such an excruciatingly painful migraine headache that his eyes would bug out of his head like a cartoon character's.

Even though he was a little upset about being cock-blocked every time he tried to murder his new master, Monkey made the best of what he had to work with. His first act of freedom was to warm up his muscles by killing a tiger with his bare hands and turning its coat into a robe; and, not long after, by slaughtering six punk brigands who tried to rob Hsuan-Tsang.

For the next fourteen years, the two heroes journeyed across the land, passing through unexplored caverns, treacherous cliffs, impenetrable mountains, and impassable rivers, never deterred from their sacred quest. They took on a few disciples—a pig-headed demon named Pigsey, who fought with a nine-pronged muckrake given to him as a gift by the Jade Emperor; a red-haired river demon who wore a necklace of nine skulls; and a water-dragon prince that turned himself into a white horse for the monk to ride—and got help from wise bodhisattvas and an army of ghostly spirits, but in the end it was Monkey who usually ended up saving the day through his wise and judicious use of extreme physical violence. When he wasn't boasting about how awesome he was, taunting his enemies, citing bizarre nonsensical proverbs, or calling his friends idiots, fools, or whimpering simps, Monkey stole a water-breathing horse from a giant Bull Demon, seduced the Goddess of Fire Mountain (and then called her a "hussy" as he was running away), and achieved spiritual oneness with the world somehow. Together, the funky monks overcame eighty-one ordeals, recovered the sacred scriptures, met the living Buddha, and ultimately saved the souls of the populace by giving them spiritual enlightenment and general awesomeness. Monkey was promoted to the rank of Living Buddha, becoming known by the honorific title "Buddha Victorious in Strife," because every time there was a battle to fight, he ended up seated on top of a pile of beat-to-hell corpses. Nowadays he is easily considered the greatest and most popular folk hero in Chinese mythology.

I'm told that Monkey is the inspiration for the main character of some obscure niche Japanese cartoon called *Dragonballz* (or something along those lines), but, quite frankly, this means nothing to me.

———

The Green Dragon Crescent-Moon Blade was a magical weapon forged from the body of a green dragon and wielded by the great hero Guan-Yu in the Chinese historical epic *The Romance of the Three Kingdoms*. Guan-Yu was a man so badass that he is actually worshipped as a god of war in some sects of Taoism, and his fearsome six-foot halberd allegedly weighed in at somewhere between fifty and a hundred pounds. In the hands of this stalwart, excellently bearded warrior, the impressive weapon was responsible for the deaths of some of the most formidable generals and champions of medieval China. It was known as the "Frost Blade," because snow used to stick to the warm blood whenever he fought outside in the winter.

———

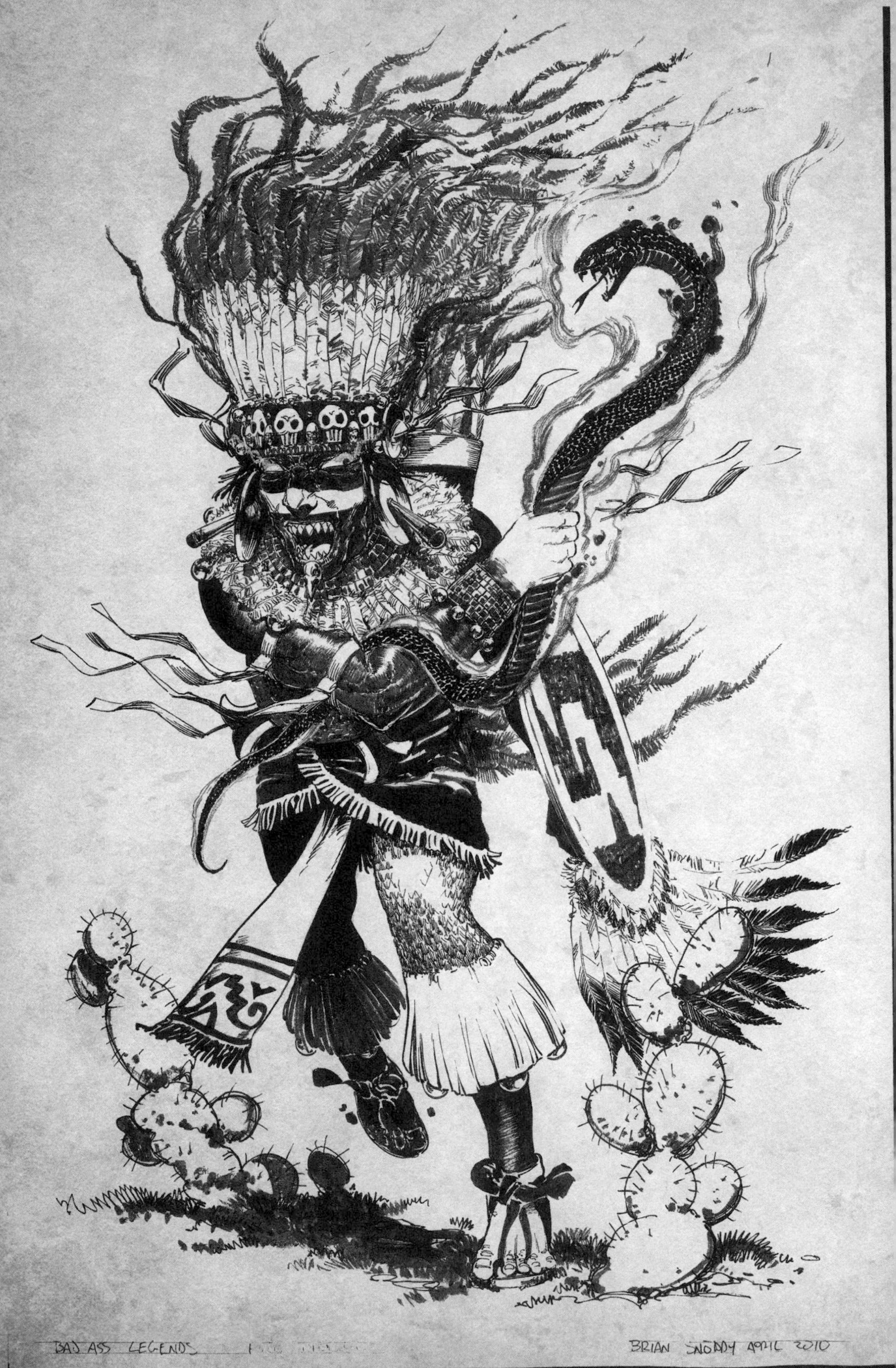
BAD ASS LEGENDS
BRIAN SNODDY APRIL 2010

7

HUITZILOPOCHTLI

Then he pierced Coyolxauhqui, and then quickly struck off her head. It stopped there at the edge of Coatepec. And her body came falling below; it fell breaking to pieces. In various places her arms, her legs, her body each fell.

—*THE FLORENTINE CODEX*

A PRISONER OF WAR WAS LED SLOWLY UP THE BLOODY STONE STEPS OF THE MASSIVE PYRAMID, THE BRUTAL AFTERNOON SUN BEATING DOWN ON HIS NECK. He reached the top—the highest place he had ever seen in his life—just as the Aztec priest rolled a bloody corpse from the stone slab in the center of the platform. The prisoner was grabbed, thrown down onto the bloody altar, and the priest efficiently cut out his heart with all the subtlety of a grizzled space marine performing triple bypass surgery with a chainsaw bayonet. The heart was torn out, held up toward the sun, and then, somewhat unceremoniously, cast down at the foot of the red-and-white, skull-encrusted shrine that stood atop the pyramid. Just another vicious sacrifice to the Aztec sun-god Huitzilopochtli. But it would not be enough. If the Aztecs wished to continue their way of life and preserve civilization as they knew it, much more blood would need to be shed on this day. The priest rolled the heartless body from the slab and looked toward the staircase, where guards slowly led an equally hopeless victim toward him.

Huitzilopochtli's birth story, like the origins of many other heroic and godly fellows, seems like it was conjured up after some dudes ate way too many magic mushrooms. It started with a nice young goddess named Coatlicue, who went by the nickname "She of the Serpent Skirt" because of her propensity to wear giant, pissed-off snakes as part of her favorite outfits. One day, Coatlicue's snake-pants failed in their secondary function as a fanged, venomous chastity belt, and she somehow became impregnated by a large ball of feathers. When Coatlicue told her one daughter and four hundred sons about the happy occasion, they were all like, "What the hell is that all about?" because even in mythology the whole "knocked up by a ball of feathers" thing is kind of a tough sell. The four hundred and one children of Coatlicue got really pissed off, and plotted to avenge their upstanding reputation in the godly community by honorably murdering their pregnant mother with pickaxes. Coatlicue climbed to the top of Serpent Mountain (she really, *really* liked snakes, apparently), but her evil kids caught up with her and got ready to massacre her with a delightful assortment of shiny metallic objects.

Just as the kids were closing in and preparing to deliver a few hundred gargantuan death blows, a horrifically insane, fully grown war god busted out of Coatlicue's abdomen wearing armor, carrying a vicious-looking variety of fiery weapons, and notably missing all the skin on his body. This musculo-skeletal insta-madman took his sword and immediately sliced the head off the leader of the Four Hundred, decapitating the goddess known as She Whose Face Is Painted with Bells (whatever that means) with a mighty blow from his pimp-slapping arm. As her headless corpse began to reel backward, he took the weapon in his off-hand—a flaming spear that just so happened to be made from the fiery body of a constantly burning snake—and cut out her heart with it. The rest of the Four Hundred attempted to avenge their only sister by swarming around and kicking the crap out of the blood-lusting skeletal berserker with the flaming snake spear, but Huitzilopochtli obliterated those mother-killing smeg-heads with an unstoppable series of fire snakes to the eyes and disgusting skinless-knee strikes to the balls. Only a handful of the Four Hundred escaped with their lives, and Huitz celebrated his brutal victory by jamming his slain sister's head on the top of Serpent Mountain to serve as a warning to others. Suck on that, trolls. Haters always gotta hate.

Huitzilopochtli went on to grow some skin and become the Aztec god of the sun, war, fire, soldiers, kings, wealth, success, and vicious systematic ritual sacrifice. Known by the seemingly innocuous nickname "The Hummingbird of the South," this guy was generally depicted as a man with a blue shield, blue body paint, and feathers on his head and legs, and idols in his honor typically feature awesome crap like snakes, human hearts, skulls, and tortillas. Sure, this is a pretty bizarre assortment of items, but when you're dealing with a god who feeds on blood and commands an army of priests that are capable of cutting out a man's heart in the time it takes most world-class surgeons to scrub up, you don't ask a whole lot of questions.

The only deity in the Aztec pantheon that wasn't co-opted into their culture by a conquered civilization, Huitzilopochtli was revered and honored as the founder and leader of the Mexica people. He gave them fire, provided them with food and nourishment, and when the first Mexica explorers were wandering through the wilderness looking for a good spot to build their capital city, Huitzilopochtli spoke to them through a human skull they carried around with them Monkey Island–style. The talking Murray the Head skull-god showed them that present-day Mexico City was the place to rock for awesome fi-

estas, good crops, and bloody human sacrifices, and under Huitzilopochtli's guidance, the Aztecs founded Tenochtitlan—the City of the
Gods. Constructed on a five-mile-wide island in the middle of a huge
lake, Tenochtitlan's skyline was dominated by a giant pyramid built in
Huitzilopochtli's honor. The Templo Mayor, as it was known, was the
main epicenter of the Aztec faith and, according to some archaeologists,
is perhaps the single bloodiest site in human history.

The Aztecs believed that Huitzilopochtli's epic battle with his siblings was recreated every day, and that the sun crossing the sky and
chasing off the Moon and the stars was their heroic deity once again

owning the faces of his mortal enemies. Despite his innate asskicking abilities, however, Huitz's followers were fairly confident that in order to repeatedly slaughter the Four Hundred and One every single morning for the rest of eternity, their favorite darkness-slaughtering god needed nourishment—only instead of Powerade and high-fiber granola bars, this guy required human blood and hearts to fuel up for his endless war against the darkness. The Aztecs firmly believed that if horror-movie amounts of gore were not spilled atop the Templo Mayor, their Dracula-like hero-god would lose his strength, the sun would not rise, and the world would end. While we may never know the real statistics, it's believed that hundreds of thousands of men were brutally sacrificed to Huitzilopochtli to power his infernal sunrise machine.

This may sound pretty bizarre to regular science-loving freaks like you and I, but the Aztecs took this whole "end of the world" thing pretty seriously. They were already one of the most warlike and bad-ass civilizations to ever exist, and their quest for still-beating hearts really puts them over the top as being some completely balls-out face-wreckers. These guys would go to war with anybody and everybody they could find, and instead of winning glory by slaughtering their enemies, Aztec warriors would dress themselves in the skins of flayed jaguars and go to war solely for the purpose of capturing opposing warriors alive and dragging them screaming back to Tenochtitlan to be brutally executed in front of the entire city. These fighters saw themselves as holy warriors struggling to exert their dominance over their enemies, appease their bloodthirsty god, and preserve life on Earth as we know it. That's kind of an epic charge there. If they perished in their search for warm hearts, fallen Aztecs could look forward to Mexican Valhalla, which is kind of like Norse Valhalla only with margaritas and mariachi music. Rocking in the afterlife, they'd chill in Huitzilopochtli's home, eat blood, drink the juice of flowers, and enjoy the company of hot Mexican babes. Sounds like a good deal to me.

But Huitzilopochtli wasn't all about having people's vital organs pulled out through their chest cavities. When he wasn't battling the night or presiding over a few gajillion sacrifices, he also liked singing, dancing maidens, tortillas, and high-fives, and many super-fun festivals were held in his honor. The most interesting of these was the Festival of God-Eating, where local women would make a giant statue of H-Poc out of tortillas, cut it up, and feed it to the kids of the city. According to a group of horrified sixteenth-century Spanish missionaries, the tortilla dough was kneaded with honey and the blood of sacrificed human children, but those missionaries may have just been overreacting to all the slaughter they'd witnessed at the Templo Mayor and started hallucinating that there was blood involved in every aspect of Mexica life. Maybe there was. Who knows.

Another thing Huitz dug like crazy was gladiatorial sacrifice in his honor. Basically, if one of the enemy soldiers had shown particular valor in combat, he would be dragged to an arena, chained to the Stone of Combat (a large, carved circular stone lined with a bunch of sluices for quickly draining blood away from the battlezone), handed a blunt spear, and sent up against a gauntlet of badass Aztec warriors. If he could beat seven of them in a row, he was released, but otherwise he was disarmed and sacrificed by an Aztec priest the instant he received a mortal wound from one of his assailants. Sure, this wasn't an ideal situation, but Huitzilopochtli was such a hardcore warmonger that he at least offered his most valiant enemies the opportunity to die a true warrior's death.

Bran the Blessed was a gigantic Welsh hero who traveled to Ireland to avenge his sister against her evil husband. In the war that followed, the Welshmen defeated an army of cauldron-born zombie Irishmen, but Bran's head was sliced off in the fighting. The head continued to talk, and had "pleasant conversations" with his men as they carried it all the way back from Ireland to London. The head was buried at the site of what is now the Tower of London, and it is said that as long as Bran's face was shoved down under there, England would never be invaded by a foreign enemy.

Zardoz is a crazy seventies-tastic movie about a flying stone head god that barfs out guns and yells a bunch of stuff about how penises are evil and automatic weapons are awesome. It stars Sean Connery wearing a diaper and orange plastic suspenders, which is a significantly less attractive look than when Milla Jovovich wore a similar getup for *The Fifth Element*.

Huitzilopochtli was so nut-crushingly hardcore that they put the temple of the rain god Tlaloc alongside Huitz's temple atop the Templo Mayor. The reasoning there was that if Tlaloc got fresh and decided to start punking out on the Aztecs with some bullcrap droughts or floods, Huitzilopochtli would be right there to crack him in the holiest of holies with a fire-spewing snake and thump his ass back into submission. He was like the god of making other gods his bitch.

→ BEASTS AND MONSTERS OF NATIVE AMERICAN MYTH ←

NALUSA FALAYA

According to Choctaw legend, the Nalusa Falaya were a race of man-size, swamp-dwelling monsters with small eyes, large noses, and huge pointed ears. At night, these evil goblinoid Vulcan-Elves would take off their skin and fly around, and were so terrifying in appearance that hunters who saw them passed out from fright. While the hunter was unconscious, the Nalusa Falaya would run up and stick a small thorn into one of their feet. The hunter would then return to his tribe, but the thorn acted like the damned rage virus, driving the dude completely psychotic and making him start mindlessly attacking people for no reason at all.

SIATS

The Ute Indians used to freak the holy living hell out of their children by warning them that if they wandered into the woods alone they would be captured and eaten by the Siats—a horrible race of cannibalistic clowns who lived in the wilderness. These evil clowns not only devoured children while juggling bowling pins made out of fireballs, but they were almost completely indestructible; the only way to kill them was by shooting them with an obsidian arrow. I can honestly think of nothing more mind-humpingly freaky than a killer evil clown that can only be slain by a weapon I would have absolutely no way of obtaining.

RAW GUMS

Raw Gums was a horrible evil child from Arapaho legend who, while still an infant, snuck out of his crib every night and ate all the neighboring chieftains in the region. When Raw Gums's parents found out that their kid was a chief-eating murder machine, they covered him with animal fat and tried to feed him to some dogs. It didn't work out too well—Raw Gums summoned forth the skeletons of his slain enemies, which danced around, chased off the dogs, and scared the people of Raw Gums's tribe right out of their pants. Leaving his now-deserted hometown, Raw Gums wandered around, eventually meeting a shaman named White-Owl Woman. White-Owl Woman gave Raw Gums a couple logic tests, which he passed, and then, when he got sick of doing a bunch of stupid trials, he just crushed her skull with a stone tomahawk and knocked out her brains.

HÎNQÛMEMEN

Also known by the badass and much more pronounceable moniker "The Engulfer," this was a legendary killer lake hidden deep in the forests of Canada. The Inuit believed that if you ever took water from Lake Engulfer, the lake itself would flip out, hunt you down no matter how far away you got from it, grab you, drag you below the water, and drown you. There aren't a whole lot of things more humiliating than getting your ass kicked by an evil body of water.

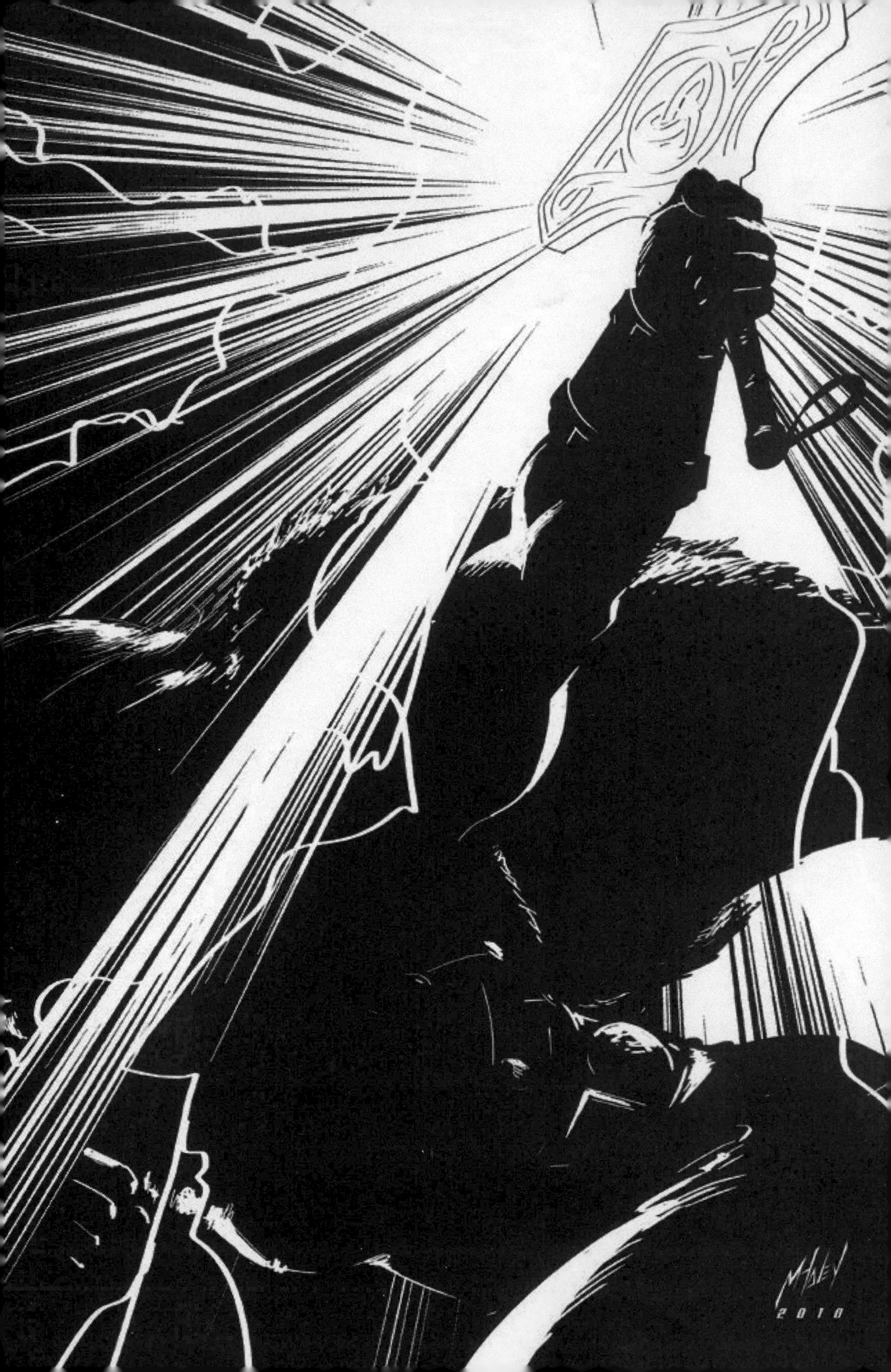
2010

8

THOR

THOR WAS THE HEAD-SMASHING NORSE GOD OF LIGHTNING, THUN-DER, STORMS, BEING AWESOME, AND KILLING GIANTS BY HITTING THEM IN THE FACE WITH A MEATNORMOUS MAGICAL HAMMER. The son of the god Odin and the goddess Fjörgyn, Thor was the defender of the heavenly land of Asgard, the toughest warrior among the gods, an original Avenger, best friends with Captain America and Iron Man, and the guy who everybody called on whenever they needed some pompous douche's ass kicked out through his forehead.

The life of Thor reads like a loosely associated amalgamation of badass battles and duels thrown together into one epic narrative of carnage and destruction. This bloody succession of continual ass-beatings usually takes place at the expense of the hapless race of the Frost Giants, a group of impossibly large hardcore humanoids who Thor intensely detested for a variety of borderline-justifiable reasons.

For instance, one time a giant architect threw an unnecessarily violent temper tantrum when the gods stiffed him on the tab after building a set of impenetrable fortifications for Valhalla, so Thor paid the guy back by caving his skull in with a hammer. Another time, some giant snuck into Thor's house, drank all of his ale, and boasted that he was going to go off and have a rape-tastic threesome with Thor's wife and the fertility goddess Freyja, and it took the take-no-bullcrap Norse hero roughly five seconds to haul ass back home, crash his glorious, flowing locks through the walls of Valhalla like a blond wrecking-ball, and challenge that soon-to-be-excerebrated d-bag to a one-on-one death-match. The dude showed up to the dueling field clad in armor made from stone and accompanied by a twelve-foot-tall clay golem, but nothing was going to deter Thor's implacable fury and insatiable desire for giant homicide. The Defender of Asgard was so ferocious and pissed about the whole "I'm going to rape your wife" comment that the golem took one look at this guy and started urinating uncontrollably on itself, whizzing so hard that liquid piss melted the clay and dissolved the creature down into a fetid pool of failure and defeat and golem urine. That's right, folks—Thor was so crap-your-pants scary that he could make inanimate constructs spontaneously spawn an excretory system solely for the purposes of wetting themselves. In the ensuing battle between god and giant, Thor got a broken-off hunk of a whetstone lodged in his head but didn't even blink—he just hucked his hammer right through the giant's eye, blowing his brains out like a close-range headshot with a sawn-off twelve gauge.

In addition to being utterly terrifying, super-strong, and rocking a glorious 1980s hair metal mane that was, according to the stories, "more beautiful than gold," Thor was also the owner of the legendary weapon Mjolnir. Mojlnir was a fully rad warhammer that never missed its mark when thrown and always seemed to bring about the vicious blunt-force trauma death of anyone Thor deemed worthy of a painful demise. This kickass hunk of enchanted runestone was so intensely hardcore that if you even so much as touched the thing without wearing a special pair of iron gloves, the magical energy exuded by the weapon would freak out and melt your hand.

While Mjolnir is easily one of the sweetest blunt weapons from mythology, Thor didn't need its super-crushing powers to go out and pummel you into a bloody smear on the asphalt. One time Loki was captured by the giant Geirröd and his three evil daughters, and in exchange for freedom, the patron god of being a total douchebag agreed to trick Thor into venturing into Giant Land without his signature weapon. Thor showed up, looking to save Loki from imminent peril, and was immediately ambushed. First, one of the giant ogress daughters angered Thor by taking a piss in a river while he was trying to walk through it, so he killed her by flinging a rock through her head. Then two more giantesses tried to crush him by smashing him repeatedly against the ceiling of their stone cottage, but he got both hands on the ceiling, pushed down, and snapped both their backs with one mighty shove. Then Geirröd himself showed up and started taunting the already-berserk Norse god, so Thor grabbed a piece of molten hot iron out of the fireplace and threw it so hard that it went through a solid stone pillar and Geirröd's torso, and blew a hole in the wall behind him. I like to think that after all this happened, Thor grabbed a flagon of mead, chugged it in one gulp, and smashed the empty container down on the ground before making a pithy James Bond–style one-liner and walking off like nothing happened.

Thor lived in a gigantic 540-room Valhalla-style fortress called Bilskirnir, which was appropriately situated in the middle of the Plains of Strength. His favorite hobbies included drinking mead by the barrel, wading through rivers, riding around on a chariot pulled by horse-size goats, and making expeditions into uncharted lands for the sole purpose of wasting as many giant asses as he could fling his hammer at (which turns out to be a lot). This guy was so good at getting crunked up on fermented honey and using his mallet to hammer people into the ground like meaty tent pegs that, according to Norse myth, thunder was actually the sound of Thor bashing a guy's head into pulp, and the tides were believed to have been created when Thor sucked down half of the ocean as part of a drinking contest after a giant magically transformed it into mead.

Another good drinking story has Thor getting invited to feast at the palace of some random member of the Frost Giant nobility. If you were a giant, you'd think Thor would be the last guy you'd want to have hanging around your dinner table, but apparently this particular household didn't possess the common sense necessary to come to this conclusion themselves, and they thought it might be fun to die painful deaths at the hands of the Norse God of Smiting. Interestingly, things were actually going fine until everyone in attendance soon became kind of horrified when, during the course of one all-you-can-eat super-buffet smorgasbord feast, Thor ate an entire ox, eight salmon, and chugged three full barrels of mead. When the giants (who, by the way, were largely portrayed in Norse sagas as ogre-like barbarians) gave Thor a hard time about consuming half of their food in the span of a few dozen ultra-manly gulps, the bane of giant-kin decided that for dessert he would just kill everyone in the dining hall with a hammer, because screw them for talking smack about his etiquette skillz. So he did.

Thor was also a master of fishing, which seems like it would be kind of counterintuitive for a guy who shoots lightning out of his hammer. Nevertheless, the presumably superconductive god once went with his buddy on a weekend fishing trip aimed at catching the horrifically evil Midgard Serpent—a giant-ass sea monster so enormous that its body measured the entire circumference of the Earth. Thor rowed out to the edge of the world in a crappy little wooden boat, threw his line in, snagged the beast, and lifted it up out of the water, but just as he was getting ready to bust the creature's skull (hammer-fishing is way more hardcore than spear-fishing, by the way), Thor's buddy freaked out and cut the fishing line, sending the ghastly monstrosity back below the waves. Thor was so pissed off that he punched the dude in the mouth, kicked him overboard, and rowed home by himself.

The Maestro of Hammer-Humping Giants in the Mouth also plays a central role in one of the crucial events of Norse mythology—the incredibly bizarre death of the god Baldur. The short version of the myth is that Baldur, Thor's half-brother and the god of being inoffensive, cool, and beloved by everyone, was murdered one day when the prankster god Loki tricked a blind dude into throwing a sprig of mistletoe at him. Why Baldur was so allergic to mistletoe that a relatively unsharpened branch flung vaguely in his direction caused him to spontaneously combust into a cloud of death is somewhat incomprehensible, but, needless to say, everybody was pretty pissed off about the whole situation. Thor led the funeral service, blessed his half-brother's funeral pyre, and swore vengeance on Loki. Then, out of the blue, some random jackass dwarf started being disrespectful and talking really loudly during the funeral service, so Thor booted the jerk into the flaming pyre with a swift kick to the balls. I find this hilarious.

Thor's next mission was to track down Loki and make sure that he was brought to some incredibly painful, Viking-style justice. He tracked the Trickster god down, cornered him in a river, and when Loki morphed into a salmon and tried to swim away, Thor grabbed the fish by its tail and hauled it down to the Underworld. Loki's firstborn son was then disemboweled, and the dripping entrails were used to strap Loki down to a huge-ass rock. The gods then positioned a giant, disgusting snake overtop of Loki so that it dripped super-venomous poison right into his eyes like a Chinese water torture device from some sadistic corner of Hell. From that point on, the Norsemen believed that earthquakes were caused by Loki screaming out in agony and attempting to break free. If strapping your ex-friend down with his dead kid's intestines sounds a little excessive to you, that's because Thor never half-assed anything in his life—especially revenge.

Don't feel too badly for Loki, though—he'll get his crack at vengeance eventually (and Thor will get a rematch battle with the Midgard Serpent), but I'll deal with both of those tales a little later, when I talk about Surt.

Thor's stepson Ull was the Norse god of hunting, archery, dueling, cage fighting, skiing, snow forts, and ice hockey. When this extreme-sports aficionado wasn't impressing the ladies by gliding across frozen lakes on skates made from animal bones or doing bitchin' backside 180 tailgrabs while riding his shield around like a snowboard, he enjoyed shooting people in the face with arrows and imbuing his followers with the power to go berserk and tear their enemies limb from limb in bloody trials of single combat.

One time, Loki tried to impress a girl by tying one end of a rope around a goat's beard and the other around his own ballsack, and then playing tug-of-war with the goat. I'm not even kidding.

✦ *FINAL FANTASY* SUMMON SPELLS ✦

The *Final Fantasy* video game series sold over 85 million copies between 1987 and 2009—a number that's larger than the populations of Norway, Sweden, Iceland, Finland, Denmark, Greece, Macedonia, Israel, Ireland, Saudi Arabia, Mongolia, and the State of Louisiana combined—so if the name "Odin" conjures up thoughts of Chocobos and Espers rather than runestones and medieval Icelandic poetry, you're not alone. Many of the summon spells you know and love have a basis in mythological history, however, so here are the stories behind some of our favorite materia-based, board-shaking damage spells.

ODIN

The leader of the Norse pantheon and the god of death, magic, and wisdom, Odin is known as the All-Father, Thruster, Spear Shaker, and the Fulfiller of Desire. When he's not trying to decide on which of those porn-star names he'd prefer to be called, Odin rides around Heaven on a super-fast eight-legged horse named Sleipnir, casts magical spells, inscribes runestones, and throws his never-missing spear, Gungnir, at anyone who deserves it. One day, Odin traded in one of his eyes in exchange for limitless knowledge and the ability to see the future. While this may have helped him win a lot of sports bets in Vegas, he also foresaw his own violent death by being mashed between the champing jaws of a gigantic, fiendish dire wolf named Fenrir. It turns out that previewing your horrific demise and the destruction of the universe is a lot more depressing than you might think, and, as a result, Odin is generally detached, aloof, and constantly deep in thought.

BAHAMUT

In *Final Fantasy*, Bahamut is an awesome, fire-breathing flying dragon who nukes your enemies from orbit like a high-tech military satellite, but his mythological counterpart is noticeably less about incinerating civilization and a lot more about aimlessly floating around and being tremendously large. In Islamic mythology, Bahamut the World Fish is a huge-ass cosmic space tuna so incomprehensibly gigantor that the entirety of Earth is supported on a small portion of his back. The only person to ever see this beast in its full form was Muslim Jesus, and his mind was blown probably just as hard as some people's minds were blown when they just read that the Islamic faith has stories about Jesus Christ.

SHIVA

One of the three manifestations of the prime deity of Hinduism, Shiva the Destroyer is the celestial being responsible for obliterating the universe. Repeatedly. He's often symbolized by a giant erect penis, though for some reason the *Final Fantasy* series opted not to represent him in that way. Every once in a while, when he gets bored, Shiva dances around, shoots fireballs out of his third eye (I'm under the impression that this isn't a euphemism, and he actually has a third eye in the middle of his forehead, though I suppose it's anyone's guess), destroys the planet in flames, and wipes off a clean slate for the god Brahma to come in and re-create it. If it helps to think of this Earth-destruction/rebuilding process as kind of like wiping your hard drive when it gets old and crappy and starts locking up on you all the time, then Shiva is like the mythological equivalent of typing "Format C:" into a DOS prompt.

IFRIT

One of the five types of djinn in Islamic myth, ifrits aren't the wish-granting variety of genies as much as the kind that pulls your backbone out through your rectum and then breaks your girlfriend in half by swinging your disembodied spine around like a whip. These malicious, brutal spirits breathe fire and smoke, sprout giant horns on their heads, and enjoy torturing and tormenting humans whenever they get the opportunity. Ifrits typically have cloven hooves for feet, so eating them is definitely not kosher, and they live primarily in deserts, where they're occasionally known to grab wayward children and pull them down beneath the burning sands.

PHOENIX

The Phoenix was a large, reddish-purple Egyptian bird said to be able to live for about five hundred years, though most ancient people were significantly more interested in the last hours of this fiery creature's lifespan than what it did with the rest of its time. Near the end of its days, this bizarrely pyromaniacal bird would go around and build a special nest of spices and twigs and gasoline and then set itself on fire, incinerating itself in a kind of awesome blaze of glory. Then, just when you're like, "Holy crap did that bird just torch itself to death?" all of a sudden from the ashes of the smoldering nest a brand-new baby Phoenix would shoot out through the flames like Lando Calrissian escaping the destruction of the second Death Star. This cycle would supposedly repeat indefinitely, though the fact that there aren't Phoenixes running around the world anymore might indicate that somewhere down the line evolution must have corrected the glitched-out perpetual-Phoenix machine.

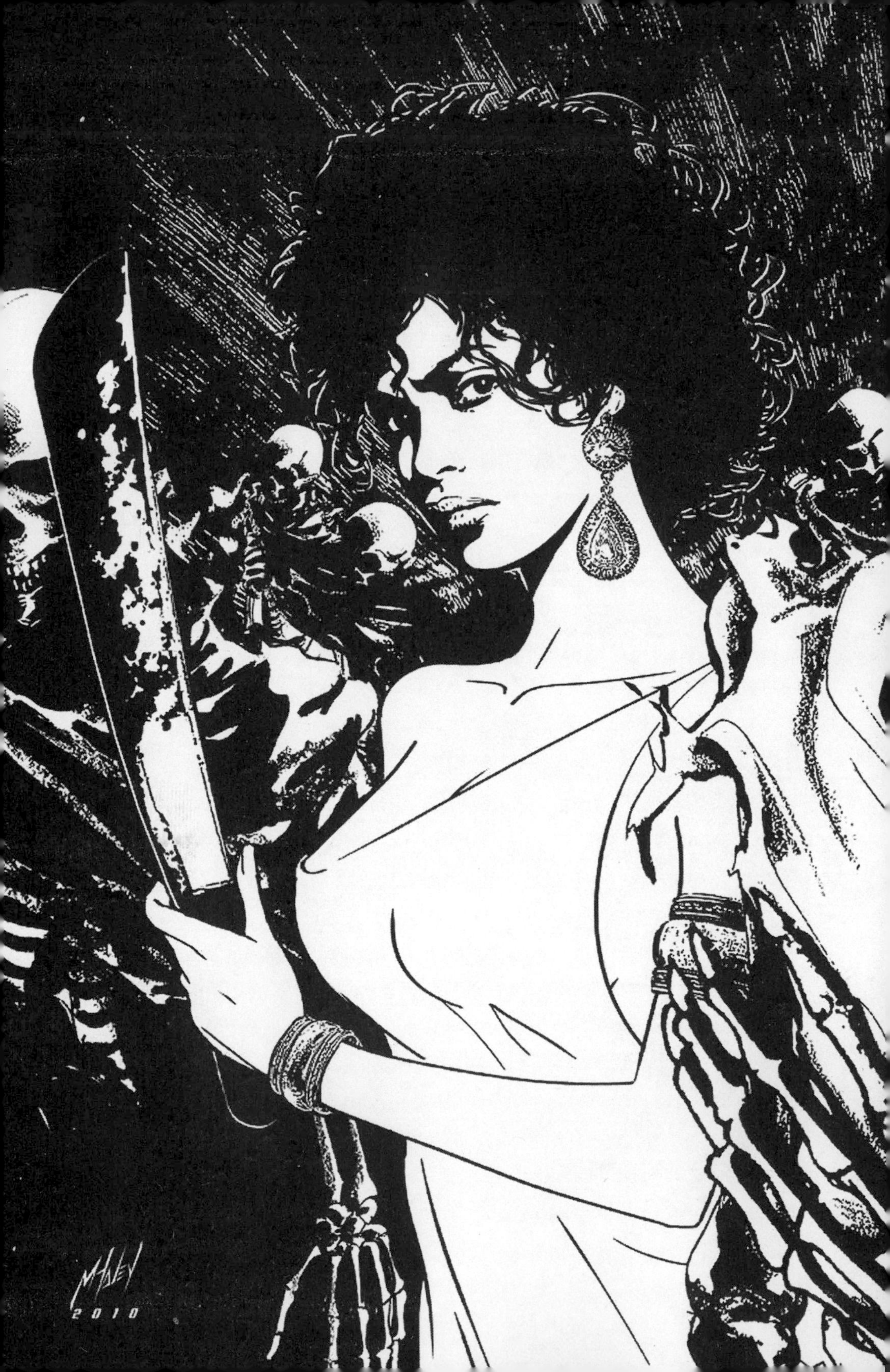

9

OYA

Wind of Death
Tears the calabash, tears the bush.
Shango's wife
With her thumb tears out the intestines of the liar.
Great Oya, yes.

—TRADITIONAL YORUBA SONG

WHAT DO YOU GET WHEN YOU CROSS STORM FROM THE *X-MEN* WITH A VOODOO DOLL, A BOTTLE OF RED WINE, A BEARD, AND A MA-CHETE? Meet Oya, the African goddess of warfare, destruction, death, storms, hurricanes, rebirth, and inexplicable Chuck Norris–style spontaneous beard growth. This chaotic, death-slinging cyclone of suckbag-annihilation is the most kickass spirit in the ancient religion of the Yoruba people, and is so head-splittingly tough that she's been incorporated as a main deity in two of the most intensely hardcore and universally misunderstood faiths in the world today—Vodoun and Santeria.

Oya's story starts with a dude named Shango. Shango was a fairly powerful West African king way back in antiquity, but for whatever reason he never really made the jump from "mediocre regional warlord" to "all-powerful iron-fisted emperor with a summer home made out of gold bars and the skulls of his vanquished rivals." One day, Shango was just chilling out near the Niger River when all of a sudden a random water buffalo morphed into a super-hot babe and started talking to him, telling him that he needed to buck up because you never know when you're going to get over that hump and become a tyrannical master of all the land which you survey. The two got married, and the buffalo-babe revealed herself as the goddess Oya—the mistress of lightning and all-powerful queen of earth-rending storms. With her help, Shango went on not only to crush the lands of West Africa beneath his heel, but eventually to ascend into godhood himself, becoming the deity of dance, thunder, and epic, flaming two-hour-long drum solos.

Together, these two ass-beaters were utterly unstoppable. Shango was a hyper-giga-tough ruler, sure, but Oya didn't get a bunch of dope nicknames like "The One Who Puts on the Pants to Go to War" and "The Wife Who Is Fiercer Than the Husband" just by sitting around looking pretty and not cleaving people from head-to-groin by flinging a bladed boomerang through them like they were made out of cardboard. She got it by going Leeroy Jenkins into battle and making sure that anyone that got in her path ended up dry-humping a machete with their face. In times of combat, she blasts lightning from her hair and fingertips and spits fireballs at unsuspecting jerks, which is cool, but perhaps the most badass part of Oya's combat ability is the fact that any time she gets ready to rush into battle she immediately grows a super-huge, majestic beard. This beard-and-armor look is a little bit of a departure from Storm and the X-Men charging into action in an uncomfortable-looking assortment of skintight lycra/spandex body gloves, but it's damn near impossible not to give appropriate cred to anyone—man or woman—who responds to life-or-death situations by busting out a vicious beard and unsheathing a blood-stained machete.

Even though Shango's Empire hasn't appeared on too many maps in recent years, Oya continues to rage and kick ass in the metaphysical realm just as hard as she did in the good old days when the two of them forged an empire out of blood and steel and beardage. As a prime orisha of the Yoruban faith, Oya is in charge of quite a few incredibly awesome yet unrelated items. The vast, largely incongruous array of tangible and intangible concepts she represents includes rum, red wine, tobacco, goats, cemeteries, grotesque masks, businesses, bullwhips, water buffalos, the Niger and Amazon Rivers, witchcraft, revenge, pregnant women, fertility, the colors purple and dark red, copper, magic, locusts, eggplants, and the number nine. Representing an array of things that reads like a *Sesame Street* sponsor list is cool, sure, but first and foremost, Oya is a hardcore, chaotic storm goddess who rains destruction down from the sky at her whim. This intense, tempestuous spirit can call down floods, whirlwinds, and hurricanes whenever the hell she damn well pleases, moving her body like a cyclone and completely devastating entire lands in her intense, rampaging dance of demolition. She's just that hardcore. My Yoruban pronunciation is a little rusty, but I also envision her name being pronounced "oh yeah," much in the way the Macho Man Randy Savage says it right before heartily snapping into a Slim Jim, or like Lou Ferrigno would utter the first part of the phrase "Oh yeah, now I'm definitely going to sew your ass to your face."

While nobody is going to deny the fact that being fragged in the balls with a thunderbolt isn't exactly a great way to spend an afternoon, Oya isn't simply a wanton, heartless killing machine. Sure, there's some of that, but she's also in charge of life-giving rains and rivers, and is totally cool about protecting those who are in need of a guardian. Oya particularly champions women, standing up for them against oppression and general douchery. The storm goddess is not only believed to bestow powers onto those who wish to take matters into their own hands (in Santeria, many dark cults that focus on destructive and revenge magic are devoted to channeling her dark wrath), but she also won't hesitate to drop a lightning bolt on evildoers' asses whenever she doesn't feel like decapitating them so hard that their heads fly off into the stratosphere and dent the moon. In terms of the musical catalogue of German 1980s hair metal band the Scorpions, she's like "Winds of Change" and "Rock You Like a Hurricane" together in one epic power ballad. A fierce lover, devoted mother, and stalwart defender of those in need, she generally seeks to accomplish the defense of her people by violently disposing of their oppressors, either by straight-up kicking them in the balls with a funnel cloud until their testicles pop out of their noses or by driving them berserk and forcing them to unwittingly destroy everything that they love. She reserves her most brutal eviscerations for liars and thieves, personally pinning them down with a figure-four leg lock and tearing out their intestines with her thumbs.

While I suppose you can't understate her position as the Goddess of Eggplants (and therefore mortal enemy of perennial digital toolshed *Kid Icarus*), Oya's other prime aspect is that of a death goddess. It is Oya's sacred job to take the last breath of a dying person, conduct their soul to the Underworld, protect them in the afterlife, and even occasionally call them back into her service. Yes, that's right—Oya is capable of summoning undead warriors to do battle in her name. Generally, she just uses the spectral armies to scare the crap out of poor Shango when her husband doesn't want to see things her way or take out the garbage, which is pretty hilarious if you ask me.

In the Santeria religion, where Oya is also syncretized with Saint Theresa and Our Lady of Candelaria, a priest of Oya performs funeral rites, and in both Santeria and Vodoun, cemeteries, necropolises, and graveyards are considered sacred ground to the tempestuous goddess. The practitioners of Vodoun even take her position as a death goddess one step further, as she's the spirit that you invoke during the creation of so-called voodoo dolls. Sure, the real-life iteration of those little guys isn't the same thing as those semi-adorable stuffed pincushions you see in movies and TV, but it's still safe to say that being on the wrong end of the physical embodiment of Oya's wrath is generally the sort of thing you'd like to try to avoid if you don't enjoy being kicked in the head by a tornado or having the breath of life sucked out of your lungs by a little bit of divine anti-CPR.

It's hard to talk about temperamental goddesses of obscenely dangerous natural disasters without mentioning the Hawaiian fire goddess Pele. This volatile spirit is said to reside in the magma-filled volcanic crater at Kilauea—the most active volcano in the world and a spot where lava bombs have been known to shoot nearly fifteen hundred feet into the air—so you know she means business. Pele only really likes to take time out from spewing fireballs to do things like have sex with hula dancers and piss off her sister Namaka, the water goddess. The ancient Hawaiians honored Pele and sought to appease her unbridled rage by throwing things like flowers, silks, booze, and virgins into the burning magma of her volcanic craters. This only worked some of the time.

You probably know Baron Samedi best as a flamboyantly dressed Bond villain, but he's actually the Vodoun sprit in charge of debauchery, obscenity, sex, death, and resurrection. Generally depicted as a man with a skull-like face, a black tuxedo, a black top hat, and super-cool dark sunglasses, the Baron is kind of like a hard-partying, hard-drinking version of Grim Fandango that sports a totally sweet pimp cane, a tobacco pipe, a bottle of rum, and a huge boner. Samedi talks trash Skeletor-style in a high-pitched nasal voice, possesses partygoers and makes them get funky on the dance floor, and is also the Vodoun spirit who is called upon in the creation of the Haitian *zombi*—real-life predecessors of the George A. Romero–style zombies we know today. Appropriate offerings to Baron Samedi involve leaving inordinately huge quantities of booze on his altar, and festivals in his honor generally circulate around drinking, dancing, partying, and having Caligula-grade orgies. They just don't make deities like that anymore.

10

SAINT MICHAEL THE ARCHANGEL

And there was a great battle in Heaven, Michael and his angels fought
with the dragon, and the dragon fought and his angels: and they
prevailed not, neither was their place found any more in Heaven. And
that great dragon was cast out, that old serpent, who is called the Devil
and Satan, who seduceth the whole world; and he was cast unto the
Earth, and his angels were thrown down with him.

—REVELATION 12:7–9

IMAGINE THE BIGGEST, MEANEST, MOST DIABOLICAL, PUPPY-KICKING,
SPINE-CRUSHING, INSANE-O-TRON DEMON YOU CAN POSSIBLY THINK
OF. Then multiply that by some factor of infinity and throw it in the
back of a cement mixer with a thick slurry of nitroglycerine-infused
TNT and the complete works of H. P. Lovecraft and you get SATAN—
the big dog of Hell, the Prince of Eternal Darkness, and an entity so
all-consumingly evil that the mere mention of his name is enough to
make people start spontaneously shooting blood out of their eyes and
writhing around on the ground like spastic morons. Given the ridicu-

lous, super-hateful nature of this ultimate enemy of everything that is good, just, and holy in the universe, it would stand to reason that you couldn't possibly write a book about the great face-melting badasses of the spiritual realm without giving due propers to the sadistic being that single-handedly took on the power of Heaven and gave God Himself the finger, right?

Wrong.

Nowadays, the term "angel" has become more or less synonymous with "pussy." It conjures up images of disproportionately huge-breasted ninety-pound lingerie-clad Victoria's Secret models having sweaty pillow-fights in the clouds, or innocent-looking fat kids playing the harp and blowing kisses at butterflies and rainbows. It's a term used for wussbag cherubs that shoot love arrows at teenage couples having picnics in the park on summer afternoons, or the sort of thing a grand-mother coos out when looking at a photo of a human child no matter how cute or hideous it may actually be. With all this lame-ass angelic bullcrap going around, people unfortunately tend to forget that the most hardcore of all the Harley-riding, heavy metal–listening, battle-axe wielding, cocaine-snorting bastards from Hell got his snot epically annihilated by the biggest badass Heaven has to offer—the Archangel Michael: the Chief Justice of Wrecking Evildoers' Faces and leaving behind a trail of severed tendrils, ichor-stained carcasses, and broken-in-half demon giblets.

Just to refresh your memory, the story goes like this: Once upon a time, the powerful Archangel Lucifer decided that he didn't see what the big deal was about God, so he led a massive revolution against the throne of Heaven just to be a raging dickhead. The Prince of Darkness turned one-third of the angels to his cause, gave the old man the single-finger salute with a taloned claw, and started running amok with the unholy destruction of everything that even vaguely resembled decency, justice, sanity, or cleanliness/godliness. His angels all morphed into blood-drinking spiny demons that gave everyone thermonuclear wedgies, shook down the fat kids for their lunch money, and tried to get all of their friends to cut Sunday school class and start huffing glue out of specially constructed glue-coated unholy scuba tanks. Lucifer started telling everyone to call him Satan, the once-chill denizens of Heaven started kidney-punching people without any warning, G. G. Allin started recording music, and there was so much chaos and anarchy that nobody had any damn clue what the hell was going on anymore.

While the lesser angels were all trying to decide whether or not it would be awesome to join up with the Morning Star and start ball-knocking cherubs in their potentially nonexistent nutsacks with a couple spike-laden spinning roundhouse kicks, one hardcore heavenly ass-whomper knew what he had to do. The Archangel Michael, commander of the forces of light, chief prince of Heaven, and general all-around hardass, took off his sunglasses, cracked his knuckles, strapped on his armor, and got ready to show the traitorous angels that when you step to the G-Man, you end up getting a holy-as-hell flaming longsword mercilessly punched straight into your brain.

In the battle that ensued, Satan attempted to take down Michael with an imposingly horned head-butt and a mouthful of fire-breath, but the Patron Saint of Badasses punched the King of Hell in the solar plexus, face-planted him to the turf, and then curb-stomped the Prince of Darkness into the ground with a sandaled foot, grinding that douche's nose into the earth like the flagrantly incompetent ass-hat that he was. Check it out sometime—nearly every sculpture and painting depicting the battle between Lucifer and Michael features the stone-cold, humorless archangel standing over the fallen demon, with his sword raised over his head, a tough-as-hell expression on his face, and one of his feet planted firmly on the neck of his much-hated and appropriately humiliated enemy. I love this, because Michael is also universally represented as having huge-ass feathered angel wings, and probably doesn't really ever need to actually set foot on the ground for any reason, yet he still realizes that when you're wrecking the archenemy of God in mortal hand-to-hand combat with the fate of all existence hanging in the balance, you really need to take a moment to make sure your pitiful defeated opponent knows that he's a punk bitch. It's like the equivalent of teabagging a noscope sniper kill, or going over to your buddy's house the day before his big final exam and using a Sharpie to draw a huge penis on his face while he's passed out. It may be better to rule in Hell than to serve in Heaven, but getting your head stomped by a disgruntled archangel pretty much always sucks balls, regardless of where it's happening.

In addition to preserving the natural order of the universe by dry-gulching Satan with an elbow-strike to the larynx, mutilating an army comprised of one-third of all the angels in Heaven, and power-bombing all of these traitors spine-first onto a fire hydrant so hard that they blew a hole through the earth and landed face-first in the ever-burning brimstone fires of eternal Hell, Saint Michael is a defender of justice, a slayer of dragons, and an all-around stifler of douchebags in all three Abrahamic traditions. A typical day for Mike would go a little something like this story, which we get from the awesomely mysterious Dead Sea Scrolls: One fine afternoon, the Demon Belial, the Angel of Darkness and the Patron of Idolatry, flipped out David Koresh–style, proclaimed himself the Messiah, and told everyone to worship him instead of God. Belial raised an army dubbed the Sons of Darkness, and moved to conquer the world by popping people's heads off with his boner. Michael heard about this, broke out his über-holy battle gear, formed the Sons of Light, and put on his best Ash impression, blowing the heads off of the Army of Darkness with a combination of chainsaw arms and close-range shotgun blasts to the face. By the time the smoke cleared on the corpse-strewn war zone, Michael and the heavenly equivalent of the Justice League of America had completely wrecked the faces of

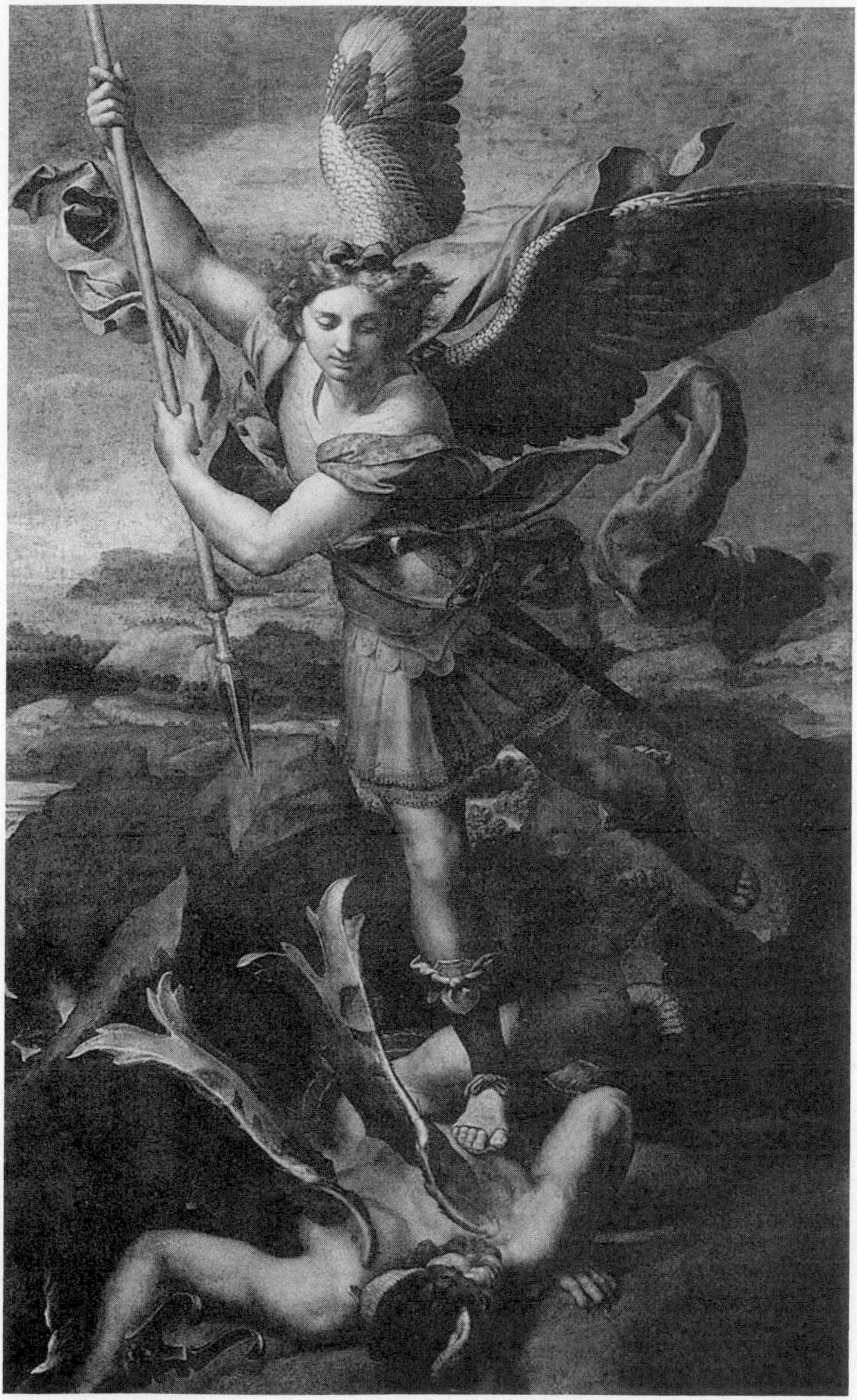

the "Sons of Pussies" (Mike's term for them, not mine) and left behind a prostrate assortment of whimpering heretics and decapitated demon corpses so impressive it makes the Devil-murdering main characters from the *Diablo* series look like those granola-eating pacifist ministers who got ordained on the Internet from some unaccredited Central American seminary.

Another time, the fallen Seraphim Samael, the former Angel of Death and the Demon of Lust and Wrath, decided he was going to start trouble with Moses and the Israelites while they were chilling out in the desert with the Ark of the Covenant, so Saint Mike flexed his authority as the Protector of Israel, challenged Samael to a brutal, steel-cage death-match, pummeled him into an unrecognizable mash-up of feathers and meat pulp, and added the former Angel of Death to the list of bitch-slapped devils who have kissed his Converse. During his epic career laying down some Old Testament–style justice as the bare-knuckled fist of God, Michael also single-handedly routed a marauding Assyrian army under King Sennacherib by busting into Sennacherib's camp in the middle of the night and slaughtering 185,000 battle-hardened soldiers in the span of a few hours. That's a hell of a lot of warriors, even for an archangel. We can only assume that pissing off this guy was kind of like programming a nuclear ballistic missile submarine to simultaneously fire all of its warheads directly into your rectum.

In addition to being a master of sandaled face-kicks and stepping on demonic necks so hard that his enemies' eyes bugged out of their heads, the Shepherd of the Righteous stands as the pinnacle of pretty much everything badassery-related. He's the patron saint of chivalry, knightly orders, soldiers (particularly paratroopers, combat medics, and fighter pilots), police officers, face-punching, the Nile River, the City of Kiev, and anyone who enjoys taking things right into the danger zone whenever humanly possible. He's a defender of justice and order, a healer of the sick, and an all-around kickass dude who is respected as the ultimate warrior by Jews, Muslims, and Christians alike. Universal acclaim like that is kind of hard to come by, but when you stomp as many disfigured monster balls as Michael does, it's hard to argue with it.

You can say what you want about JC and his whole "turn the other cheek" mentality as it applies to neck-crushing badassitude, but the second coming of Jesus in Chapter 19 of the Book of Revelation treads a fine line between being intense, hardcore, and totally insane. In Saint John's account of the Apocalypse, the King of Kings busts out of Heaven on a white horse, wearing robes drenched in blood and shooting a huge, double-edged sword out of his mouth. He smites the Armies of Darkness with the mouth-blade, chokeslams the Devil and his evil minions into a burning lake of fiery brimstone, and then rides off into the sunset, leaving behind nothing but a bloody field of bird-eaten corpses. That's kind of awesome.

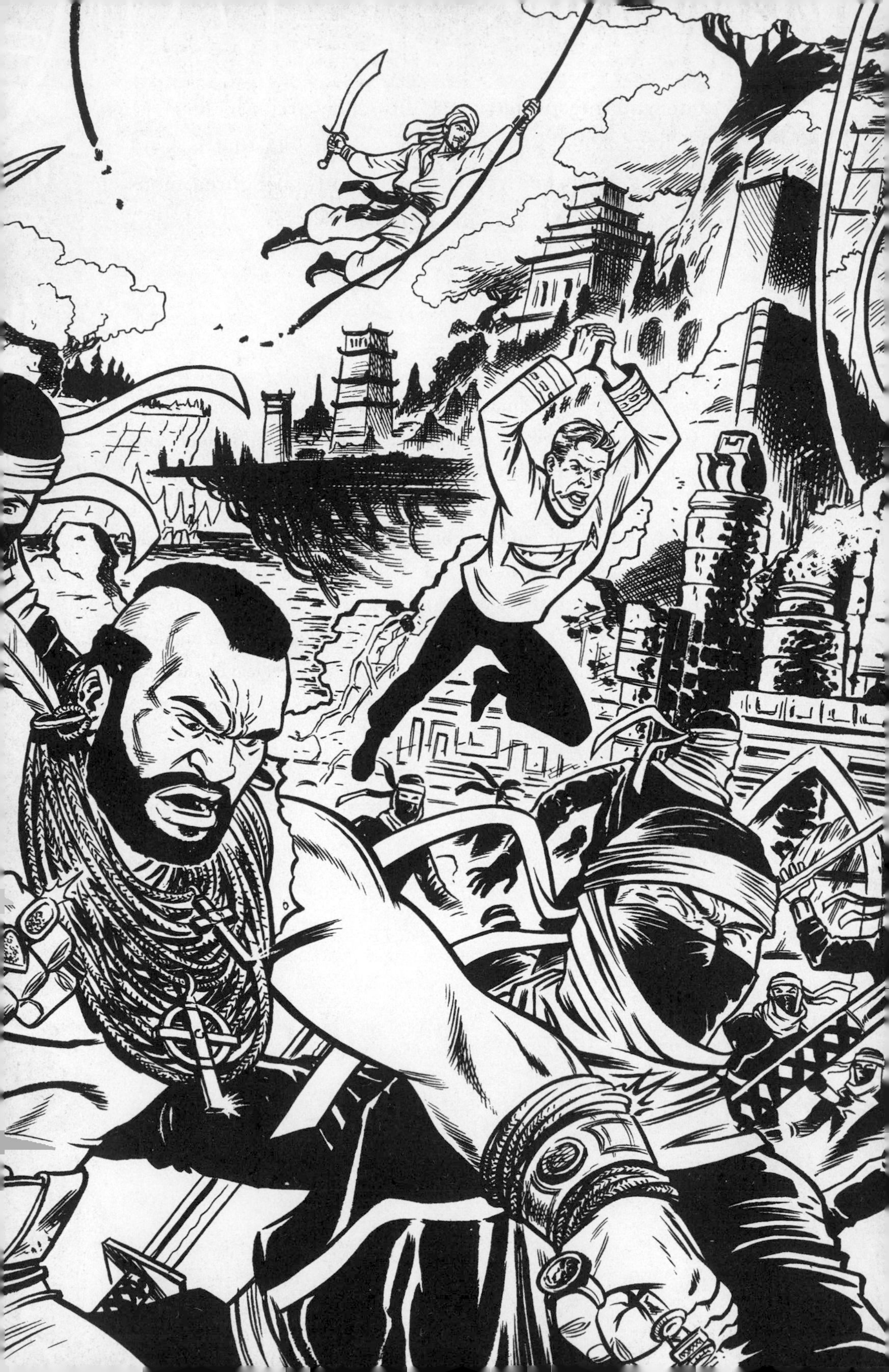

SECTION II

Heroes, Heroines, and Over-the-Top Do-Gooders

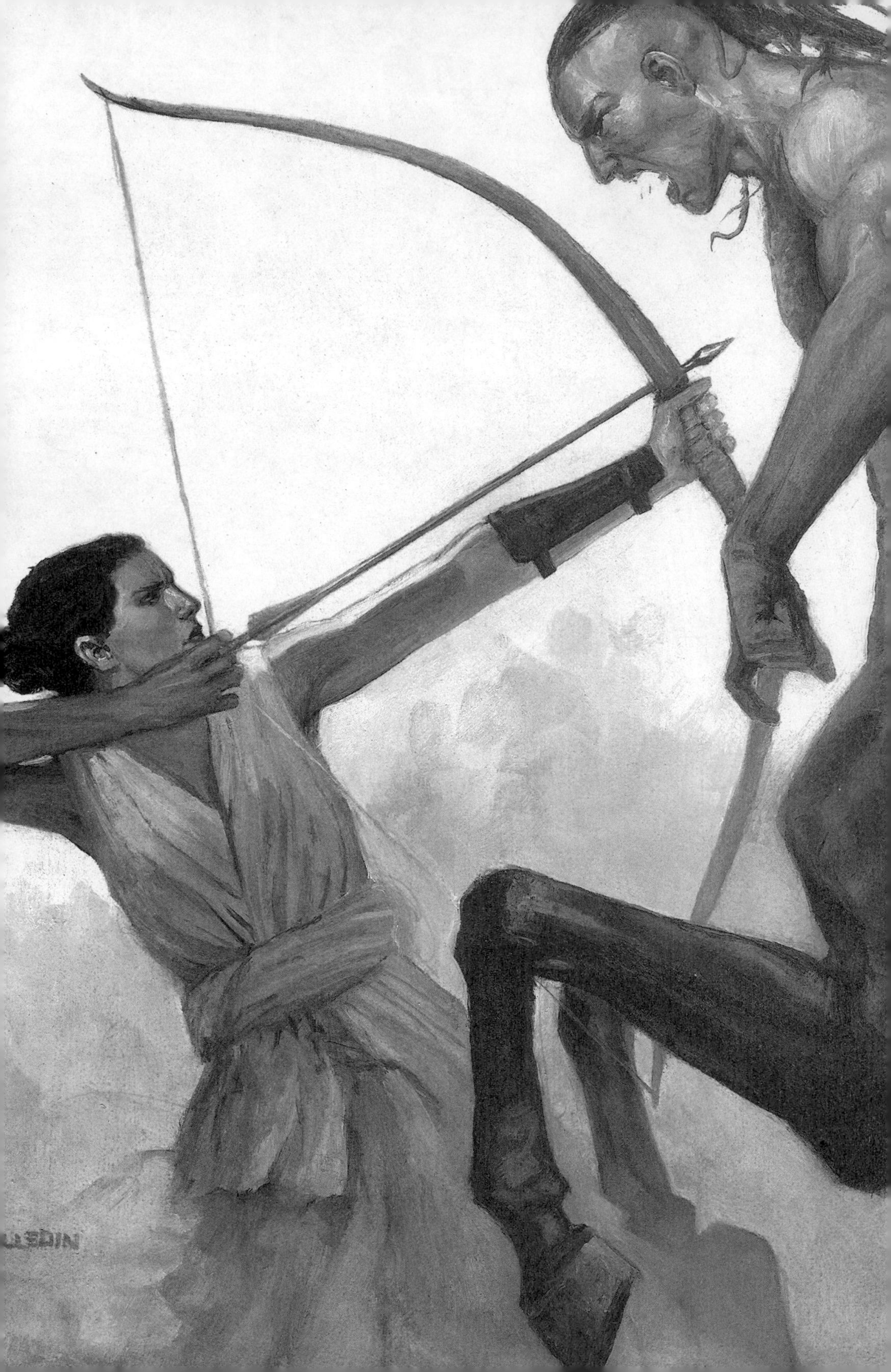

11

ATALANTA

No man's wife am I unless he wins the race.
For speed the prize is wife and wedlock;
for the slow the price is death: Upon that rule the race is run.

CLASSICAL MYTHOLOGY ISN'T EXACTLY WELL-KNOWN FOR ITS OVERWHELMINGLY POSITIVE PORTRAYAL OF STRONG, INDEPENDENT WOMEN WHO HEAD-BUTT VELOCIRAPTORS BACK INTO THE LATE CRETACEOUS PERIOD, DRAGON-PUNCH POWERFUL HEROES THROUGH THE FORTIFIED WALLS OF ANCIENT STONE TEMPLES, OR DO PRETTY MUCH ANYTHING OTHER THAN PLOT HATEFULLY EVIL DEEDS, PRODUCE HOPEFULLY MALE CHILDREN, CHEAT ON THEIR HUSBANDS, AND/OR RUN AWAY FROM A VAST ARRAY OF CREATURES AND GODS THAT ARE TRYING TO SEXUALLY ASSAULT THEM. Atalanta is one of just a few notable exceptions to this rule—not only does this hardcore, head-smashing huntress perform enough towering deeds of heroic awesomeness to list her among the greatest heroes to ever grace the pages of mythology, but she also travels to mysterious uncharted lands, battles unkillable monsters, participates in some of the most legendary quests ever recorded, and utterly emasculates every man who attempts to challenge her in any test of physical ability.

While Atalanta would grow up to become one of the most groin-stabbing badasses in the Golden Age of Greek Heroes, things didn't start out so hot for our would-be heroine. You see, her jerk-ass dad really wanted a son for his firstborn child, so when Atalanta's mom had the audacity to defy her husband's wishes and maliciously produce a female baby instead, this flaming douche-canoe totally stepped up and did the honorable thing, which in this case meant taking the day-old infant out into the woods and leaving her there to die a miserable, lonely death from exposure and starvation.

Luckily for Atalanta, she was rescued when a massive, ill-tempered, face-rending momma bear came out of nowhere and took the abandoned child in as her own. Now if mythology has taught us anything, it's that being raised by wild animals whips more balls than a dominatrix, and growing up surrounded by man-eating grizzlies and eating a bunch of strawberries and freshly dismembered meats was probably way more awesome than anything Atalanta would have ended up doing with her boring dad anyway. She grew strong and was able to run woodland creatures down on foot, slap a clinch-hold on them, and Murph those suckers with nothing more than bared teeth and an unbreakable kung-fu grip. After life among the bears grew a little too tame for Atalanta, she moved out of her hibernation cave and joined up with a clan of grizzled old woodland hunters. These venison-munching lumberjack commandos taught Atalanta how to utilize weapons and tools to further increase her capability to stab, pierce, puncture, and generally just completely massacre anything with a pulse until it was a smashed-apart cloud of meat-vapor. From that point on, the mighty huntress was rarely ever seen without a javelin, a well-crafted bow, and a suit of armor stained with the gore of some sort of freakishly horrific monster she just finished snapping in half with an atomic backbreaker or three.

Speaking of freakishly horrific monsters, Atalanta first busted onto the mythological asskicking scene during a particularly death-o-rific episode known as the Calydonian Boar Hunt. Basically, the story goes that one day some bumblenuts king forgot to mention Artemis when he was honoring the gods, so the Goddess of the Hunt responded by summoning a wild boar the size of a city bus to tear ass through the kingdom, eviscerate people with its tusks, trample their crops, and smash the place into one endless strip-mine of ball-sucking. King Bumblenuts sent out his best hunters to battle this hellacious fiend, but the Calydonian Boar head-butted them all into bloody giblets in a horrific, gleaming-tusked typhoon of pointiness. The king had no choice but to fire up the Bat-Signal and plead for all of Greece's best hunters to come kill this damn thing, and before long his palace was chock-full o' dudes looking to carve this hate-filled abomination into a few thousand strips of sweet, delicious demon-bacon.

You can probably imagine how things went down when Atalanta showed up looking to join the fight. Even though she was decked out in all of her most badass-looking war gear, most of the chauve-tastic dudes in attendance were all like, "What the hay, bro? What the hell is this chick doing crashing our sausage party?" Before they could respond to their own rhetorical questions, however, the completely INSANE wild boar came flying out of nowhere and disemboweled two heroes with one sweep of its massive, supersharp tusks. Everybody started scrambling around like morons trying to battle the monster, but this thing just turned around and bit one dude in a hamstring, dropping him like a sack of cannonballs. A couple guys got their crap together and flung their javelins at the boar, but not only did they miss wildly (how the hell you miss a bus-sized boar with a javelin I have no idea) but they actually ended up hitting their own buddies with the spears, killing or wounding them and honestly just making the whole assortment of brave heroes look like part of a Three Stooges skit.

Atalanta watched these dudes flailing around like spastic losers, said something pithy, and calmly drew an arrow back on her bow. Right as the boar was charging full-speed over to skewer a couple helpless dudes who had been knocked to the ground, Atalanta loosed a perfectly aimed arrow that struck the creature behind the ear, mortally wounding it. In its death throes, the creature continued to rage blindly at everything around it, castrating one guy with a cringe-inducing nut-shot, and disemboweling its seventh victim with another fierce tusk-thrust. Mercifully, some guy ran up and stabbed it, putting both the creature and the Greeks out of their collective misery. For dealing the mortal wound that brought the beast down, Atalanta was awarded the pelt of the skinned boar, which sounds totally gross but was a kind of a big honor at the time.

That's just how Atalanta operated. She didn't give a crap what people thought about her—she just went out there, kicked ass, and didn't let people screw with her. Like this one time she was just hanging out in the woods minding her own business when all of a sudden these two jerkburger Centaurs (monstrous creatures with the upper body of a man fused onto the body of a horse) came up and decided to gang-rape her because they didn't have anything better to do. While most mythological women would have either called out to the gods for help (and hopefully been turned into a tree) or futilely tried to outrun a couple of super-buff dudes with horses for torsos, Atalanta's default fight-or-flight response was firmly entrenched in the realm of "bloody, murderous vengeance." With these two equine dirtbags bearing down on her at top speed, Atalanta squinted her eyes, took note of the wind conditions, and decided it was these bastards who were going to get the horse-cocking. She calmly nocked a couple arrows, drew the bowstring, and sent the bronze-tipped projectiles point-first through the brains of these two unsuspecting dillholes at point-blank range.

The next stop on Atalanta's adventures was the land of Thessaly, where she heard that a guy named Jason was trying to recruit the toughest warriors in the land to help him recover the fabled Golden Fleece from the far-off land of Colchis. We're not entirely sure what role our heroine played in the events surrounding one of the most famous quests in mythological history—Apollodorus mentions her involvement fighting off the Colchian army and being wounded in combat while escaping with the Fleece, which would indicate that she had been out there with the Argonauts, sailing, rowing, fighting off monsters, singing sea shanties, getting turned on by the Sirens, and beating up indigenous warriors alongside the greatest heroes of Greece throughout the entire epic, but then again, Apollonius doesn't even list her among the crew members, so we don't really know what to believe. Personally, I tend to think that Apollonius is a moron, but I suppose you're free to say whatever you'd like about the guy.

What we do know definitively is that after the crew of the *Argo* returned home, Atalanta was present at the funeral games that were held for the recently slain King Pelias of Iolcus. Since the footraces would have been too easy a victory for her, Atalanta entered the wrestling competition instead. She defeated all comers, reached the final round of the tournament, and then defeated a powerful Greek warrior (and fellow Argonaut) named Peleus in a spirited, violent bout of Greco-Roman wrestling. I should mention that Peleus is the father of a guy named Achilles—a dude you may know as the single greatest, strongest, and most head-crushingly invincible war hero in the entirety of Greek mythology—so taking down Peleus in an MMA-esque battle of hand-to-hand combat wasn't exactly like arm-wrestling a Jack Russell terrier or some other trivial bullcrap.

Between the Calydonian Boar Hunt, the Argonautical Asskickery, and judo-flipping Achilles' dad in a no-holds-barred Muai Thai kick-boxing match, Atalanta had earned some serious badass cred. So, of course, all of a sudden her bunghole dad decided he wasn't so ashamed of her after all. He invited her back home, un-disowned her, and then—in the same breath—told her he was going to marry her off to some rich jerk in exchange for craploads of cash.

Needless to say, Atalanta wasn't really super-pumped-up about this. A loner for most of her life, this warrior-huntress wasn't particularly interested in getting hitched to some no-nuts loser. Yet, by the same token, she also didn't want to piss off her jackwagon dad now that she'd finally been able to reunite with him for the first time in twenty-some years. So she compromised. She said that any guys that wanted to marry her would have to face her in a straight-up hundred-yard dash. If she was defeated, she'd submit to marriage, but if she won, she reserved the right to execute the dude on the spot by ramming a sharpened stake into his heart. Atalanta's dad, seeing an opportunity to get a total ba-dass to marry his daughter, agreed.

What pops didn't bank on was the fact that Atalanta was the fastest mortal on the planet. Once she got her Usain Bolt on, nobody could keep up with her, and in the span of a few short months, she'd amassed a body count so impressive that Ares himself flew down from Mount Olympus to give her a flying chest bump.

Well, Aphrodite—the goddess of love, fertility, sex, lust, and all-around slutty behavior—kind of took it personally when she came across a woman who didn't want to get laid, and Atalanta's virginity was kind of pissing her off. So the Love Goddess went out and found a tall, dark, and handsome bachelor named Melanion and decided to fix him up with the lightning-quick huntress. Melanion was a decent guy who had a mad crazy crush on Atalanta, but he wasn't exactly Carl Lewis getting ready to break the sound barrier on foot and then long-jump through a ring of fire over seventeen exploding buses, so, like any good personal trainer, Aphrodite hooked him up with some performance-enhancing goodness to help give him an unfair competitive advantage. Instead of shooting him full of HGH, however, she found something significantly weirder—she brought him three magical apples crafted from solid gold, which were said to be so beautiful that anyone who saw them would covet them instantly, and when Melanion raced Atalanta, he was to throw these apples in front of his running-away bride. Theoretically, she would stop to pick these priceless gifts up, giving Melanion a second or two to get ahead. Of course, if it didn't work, this poor chump could look forward to having a spike rammed through his heart, but apparently this was a risk he was willing to take.

When the day of the big race came, Melanion used the apples, and he actually ended up winning when she stopped to pick them up. I would argue that Atalanta let the dude win because she liked him, and possibly because he was less about trying to exert his physical dominance over her and more about hooking her up with a bunch of sweet presents, but I suppose that's just speculation on my part. It just seems to make more sense to me, since it's obvious that she probably could have run circles around him if she'd actually wanted to.

Whatever the case surrounding the circumstances of their betrothal may be, it seems that Atalanta and Melanion ended up being pretty happy together. They had a son, who went on to be one of the Seven Champions Against Thebes, which was pretty cool (though one source claims that this child was fathered by Ares and not Melanion . . . this was back in the days before Maury would hook you up with paternity tests, so we'll never know for sure whether or not she actually got some from the God of War). Eventually, after quite a few years of married life, the two lovebirds snuck off to get it on in a sacred grove somewhere, and the gods got mad that their field was defiled by naked manass, so they transformed the couple into a pair of lions, thus allowing them to run around nude and get it on outside whenever they wanted. This really doesn't seem to me like that bad of a punishment, because being a lion would be kind of awesome.

It shouldn't come as a surprise that Atalanta dedicated herself to Artemis, the Goddess of the Hunt. For those of you who aren't down with her, Artemis was the sister of Apollo, the protector of the forests, and the only god other than Ares with a Greek cult that made explicit provisions for ritual human sacrifices. Being in tight with this super-vengeful goddess had its perks—not only did Artemis grant bonuses to attack rolls and critical hit damage, but she was also known to spontaneously shoot water out of rocks when Atalanta was really tired and thirsty from massacring wolves or bison or whatever the hell else she was hunting at the time.

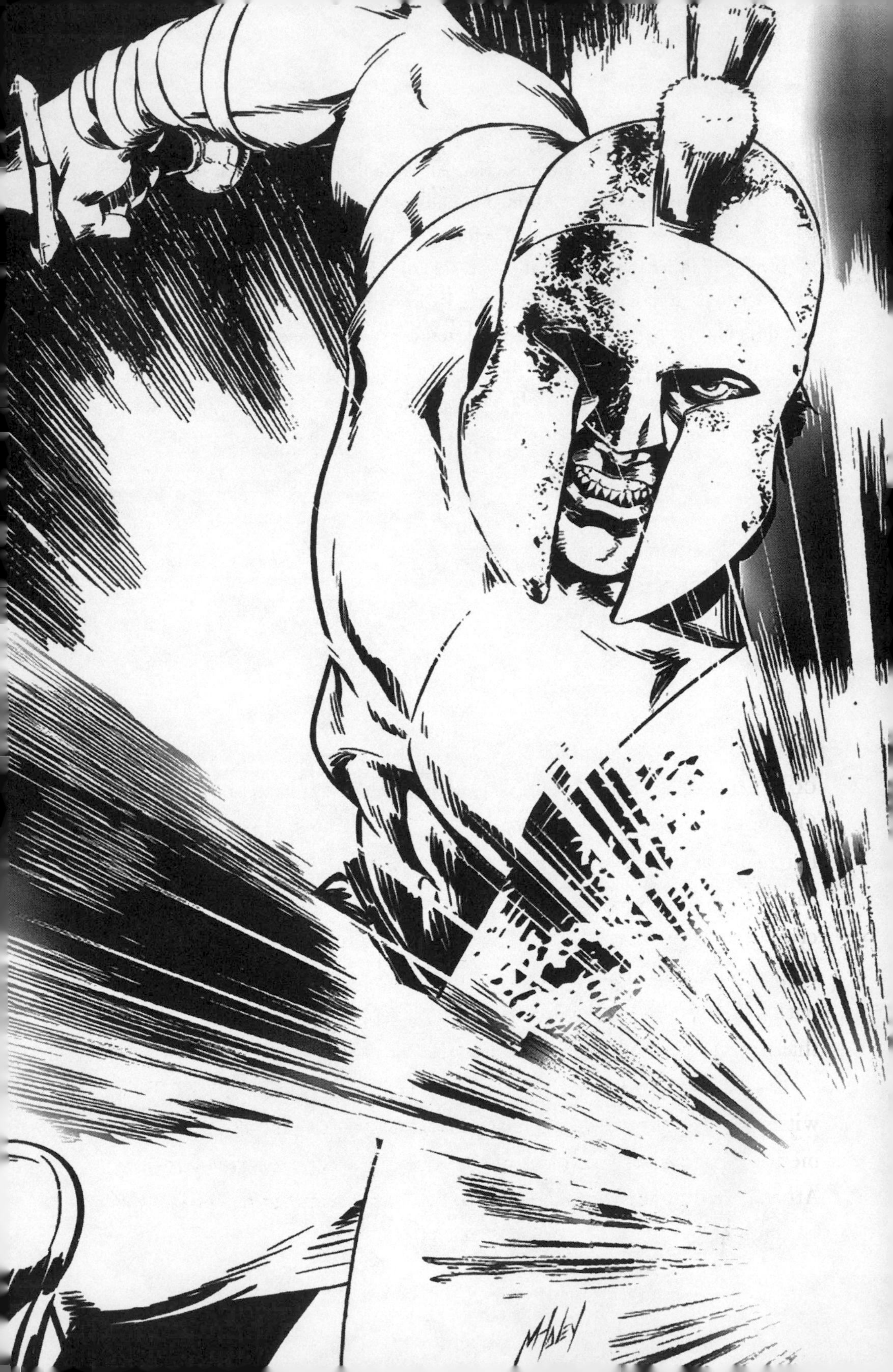

12

DIOMEDES

*He fights with fury and fills men's souls with panic. I hold him mightiest
of them all; we did not fear even their great champion Achilles, son of
an immortal though he may be, as we do this man: his rage is beyond all
bounds, and there is none can vie with him in prowess.*

—THE ILIAD

DIOMEDES MIGHT POSSIBLY BE THE MOST UNFLINCHINGLY HARD-
CORE HERO OF THE TROJAN WAR. Sure, Achilles, Ajax, Hector, and
Odysseus get most of the ink when you're talking about sack-tearing
hardasses from the epic ten-year Ionian bloodbath, but the significantly less talked-about king of Argos performed towering acts of bone-
crunching awesomeness on par with the greatest deeds of any of those
mighty warriors. Plus he fought against three gods and went into battle
with a shield that also doubled as a flamethrower, and this is a point
that I can't possibly emphasize enough.

Even before the glory days assaulting the golden walls of Troy
with a giant spear drenched in the blood of torn-to-hell Trojans, Diomedes kicked ass. A favorite of the mega-hardcore warrior-goddess
Athena (and the only mortal man to have ever seen her in her full di-

vine form), Diomedes was blessed with wisdom, strength, and cunning well beyond his years—a skill set he usually employed in the business of twisting the helmets of his enemies into scrap metal and bone dust with a sharpened blade. The first chumps to feel this wrath were the citizens of Thebes. Diomedes' father had fought alongside Atalanta's son as a member of the Seven Against Thebes—a legendary group of seven warriors who led an army against the heavily defended city of Thebes. The Seven were defeated out of hand, their leader was slain, and those who didn't run for it like bitches were left to die in a field somewhere. Diomedes' father returned home reeking of failure and defeat and cabbage, and Diomedes swore to avenge this affront to his family's honor. As a teenager, he joined the Epigoni, a military force comprised of the seven sons of the Seven Against Thebes. The Epigoni relentlessly attacked the city once again, destroyed the defending forces, sold the surviving populace into slavery, and tore down the walls of the city with their teeth.

Incidentally, Diomedes' involvement in this campaign meant that the young king of Argos had more military experience than many of the other commanders at Troy. Though Diomedes was the youngest king to lead his black ships across the Aegean, he was also among the wisest, the strongest, and the most accomplished. It also bears mentioning that when he departed the shores of Greece, he brought eighty ships with him, making the Argos force the second largest invasion fleet behind only that of Agamemnon, the overall commander of all Greek forces in Troy. So he was a pretty big deal.

Once the war was in full swing, Diomedes only continued to assert his thoroughly bronzed balls and subtle knack for cleaving people apart at the neck. For starters, this guy was huge, jacked, permanently pissed, and so intimidating in combat that Homer refers to him as "Master of the War Cry." This rampaging man-monster charged into battle wearing a near-impenetrable armor hand-forged by the blacksmith god Hephaestus, which was impervious to arrows and emblazoned with images of some badass pointy-tusked wild boars. If it's not enough that he carried a wide variety of weaponry and wore sword-proof body armor, he also had a shield and a helmet that were enchanted by Athena to blast out fireballs at will like some kind of godly Homeric flamethrower.

Igniting enemy warriors with a searing-hot jet of flaming liquid is great, but Diomedes generally preferred to opt for the more direct route and kill his enemies the old-fashioned way. According to Homer, this head-crushing behemoth was second only to Achilles in terms of fighting ability and blood-raging fury, a fact that seems to be supported by the ridiculous body count he piles up throughout the *Iliad*. In the brutal ten-year showdown, Diomedes killed a couple princes of Troy, some Amazons, a few hundred soldiers, several cavalrymen, and really whatever the hell else he felt was pissing him off at the time. The *Iliad* lists nearly thirty names of warriors personally eviscerated by Diomedes, along with several other excerpts mentioning him "freaking the hell out and murdering a ridiculous number of people," so we can assume that this guy was eminently competent when it came to the task of single-handedly wading into the middle of an enemy formation and laying waste to anything in his wheelhouse. Plus, he was significantly less of a whiny punk bitch than Achilles, which is refreshing and greatly appreciated.

But the wanton slaughter of faceless jobbers is just the beginning of Diomedes' awesomeness, and it doesn't fully express the fact that this was one of the most high-octane mortals to ever heft a spear in Greek mythology. At one point during the war, Diomedes actually came face-to-face with another epic hero—the mighty Trojan Prince Aeneas, a hero described by Homer as being both "godlike" and "lord of men" and the Rome-founding hero of Virgil's *Aeneid.* The powerful Diomedes took one look at this warlike member of the Trojan royal family, cracked him in the face with a huge-ass rock, and then ran in to slice the dude's head in half and face him in the brain. The goddess Aphrodite, seeing Aeneas in trouble, swooped down from Olympus, snatched the badly wounded Trojan hero up into her arms, and ordered Diomedes to halt.

Diomedes told her to get sacked. With Athena guiding his blade, Diomedes charged forward, striking Aphrodite in the arm and causing her to cry out in pain. Aphrodite dropped Aeneas and fled back to Olympus clutching her wound, while Diomedes yelled taunts at her for her cowardice and interference.

If beating up fertility goddesses isn't hardcore enough for you, this was only just the beginning of Diomedes' tremendous ability to flex his nuts independently of one another like Arnold Schwarzenegger making his pec muscles dance in the *Conan* movies. No sooner did Aphrodite beat a hasty retreat than the hero-god Apollo swooped down to save Aeneas from a visceral, quick death in combat. Apollo, the heavily worshipped Greek god of archery, light, music, order, and a bunch of other things, snatched the wounded Trojan in his arms and rushed in to carry Aeneas away, but even that didn't stay Diomedes' hand from battle. The king of Argos attacked Apollo three times, only to be repelled by blinding flashes of light each time. This guy just didn't give a crap—he would take on anyone, anyplace, anytime, regardless of their potential status as being immortal, or, you know, whether or not they were *his gods.*

Never was this more intensely awesome than when Diomedes, the mortal son of some moderately important guy, went straight-up against Ares, the Greek God of War, in mortal combat. That's right, this guy was so utterly fearless that he fought the deity responsible for warlike bloodshed, and the being whose sole job is to decide who won victory in battle. Diomedes didn't care. As soon as he saw Ares' chariot smiting Greeks alongside the Trojans, the king of Argos rushed over to face him. Amazingly, this wasn't even a hopeless battle—as Diomedes was charging in to do battle with Ares himself, Athena warped down into Diomedes' chariot, guided his arm, and the Greek hero threw an epic spear that *wounded the God of War*, sending Ares running back to Olympus crying and howling like a bitch. The only analogy I can really make here is that this is like playing a game of *D&D*, deciding to have your character attack the Dungeon Master, and winning.

It's hard to top something like stepping to the God of War in a duel, but it does bear mentioning that Diomedes also bests many of the Trojan War's greatest heroes in tests of strength and skill. He defeats Hector in single combat by cracking him in the skull with a javelin, and the commander of the Trojan Army only escapes with his life when he gets a little assistance from the gods. Diomedes beats up the superstrong hero Ajax in a full-contact sparring match, which is actually stopped by the Greek generals when they see Diomedes' fury and fear for Ajax's life. He outruns Odysseus in a footrace, and wins a badass *Ben-Hur*-style chariot race against many of the other Greek heroes.

Diomedes also played an understated role as a Greek special-forces black ops commando during the war. He and Odysseus went on a couple of espionage missions that had far-reaching implications for the allied victory against Troy, including one time when they broke into the city and stole the Palladium (the most holy and revered artifact the Trojans had, as well as a badass element of the periodic table), and another time when they assassinated the king of Thrace in his palace and stole his horses. The most famous of these covert operations, however, was the story of the infamous Trojan Horse. Diomedes was one of the Greek commanders inside the belly of the wooden horse that was led into the city, and he was one of the assholes that set fire to Troy in the

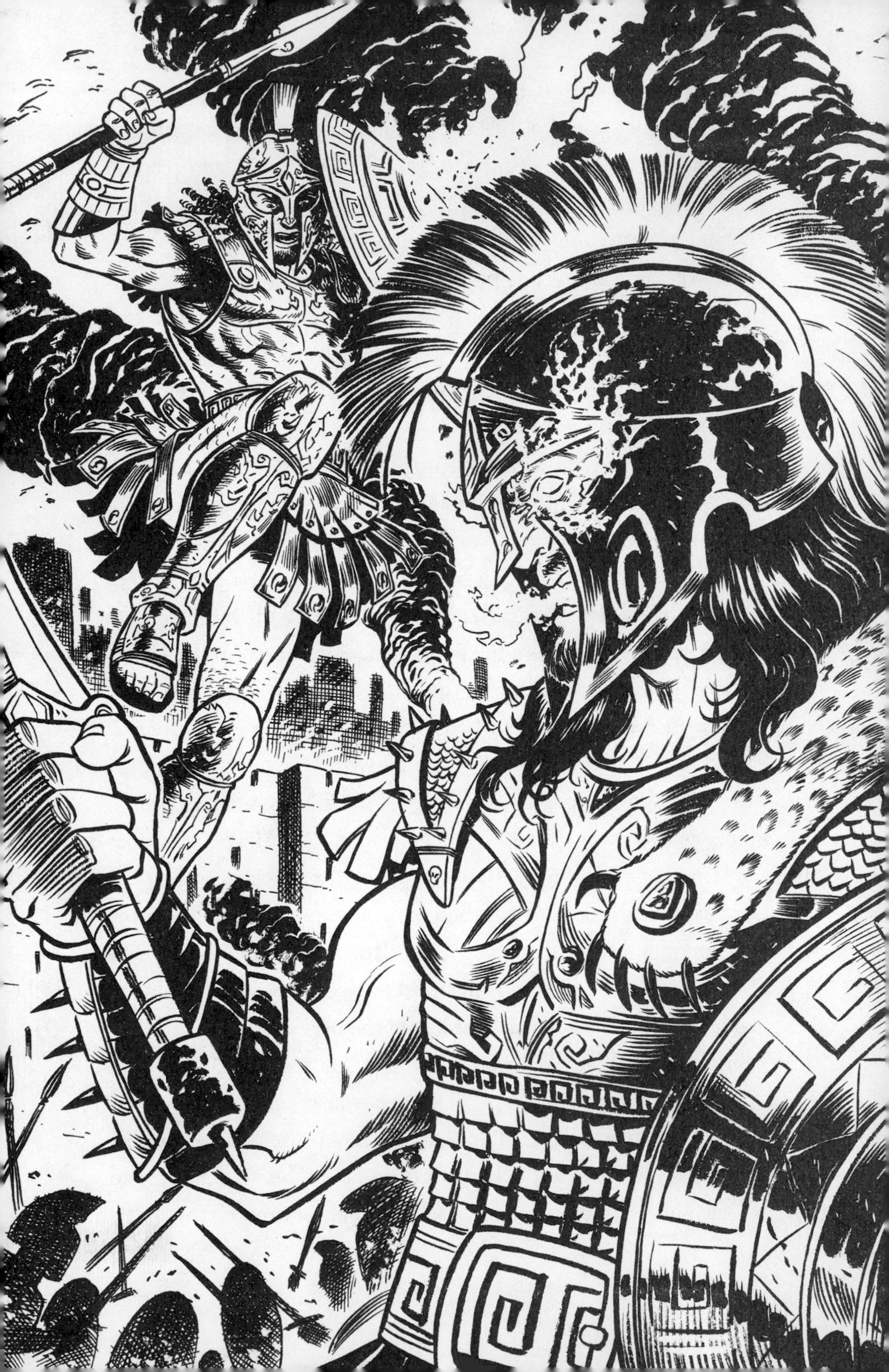

middle of the night, destroyed the city, and ended the war in a giant cataclysm of bloody explosions.

After the war, Diomedes returned home to find that his wife was no longer interested in having him around (the myths attribute this change of heart to the work of Aphrodite, who was still understandably a little upset about the whole being-shanked-in-the-arm thing), so he just ditched home and traveled around the Mediterranean having all sorts of wild adventures along the way. He ventured across North Africa, Italy, and Greece, built some cities, killed a few people, and then promptly just faded out of history without anyone having any idea where he went off to. No sources exist explaining what the hell happened to Diomedes ... some classicists speculate that he died of old age as the ruler of a distant land, while other folks are convinced that Athena granted him immortality and brought him up to live out eternity on Olympus. Dante, of course, claims that Diomedes and Odysseus are encased in a sheet of flame down in the Eighth Circle of Hell, but that's Dante for you.

> *Seducer, a worthless coward like you can inflict but a light wound; when I wound a man though I but graze his skin it is another matter, for my weapon will lay him low. His wife will tear her cheeks for grief and his children will be fatherless: there will he rot, reddening the earth with his blood, and vultures, not women, will gather round him.*
>
> —DIOMEDES, TO PARIS

If you're down with sheer brute strength and demolishing your enemies' faces with nothing more than a giant, ham-sized fist, then the Indian hero Bhima is a guy you should familiarize yourself with. This ferocious giant was the master of kicking the asses of demons, evildoers, and various supernatural beings, and he plays a prominent role in the epic battles of the *Mahabharata*. Described as the "greatest warrior of them all," this guy went into battle dual-wielding a pair of diamond-hard maces, swinging them around with skull-crushing brutality, and basically spends several chapters playing whack-a-mole with entire regiments of pathetic enemy warriors. One time, this tack-eating madman tore a demon in half by grabbing his legs and ripping him apart down the middle. Another time, a group of pork bandits tried to sexually assault one of his friends, so Bhima flipped out, chased down her would-be rapists' chariot (on foot, no less), pulled them out of the car by their hair, and kicked them in the ribs until their lungs collapsed and they died painfully.

→ THE CHAMPIONS OF ATHENA ←

The Greek goddess of wisdom, art, and justice, Athena was a straight-up war deity so hardcore that some ancient writers claimed that in terms of battlefield tactics and strategy, she was superior even to the totally meatheaded war god Ares. She was always down with adventure and heroic deeds, and always ready to help out Greece's toughest heroes. Here are a couple notable examples of guys who benefited from the supernatural aid of the patron goddess of badasses:

HERCULES

One of the most vicious, brutal, and throat-crushingly hardcore mammals to ever nut-punch a lion unconscious by swinging a couple King

Cobras around like a pair of serpentine nunchucks, Hercules was the ultimate pinnacle of neck-snapping brutality among the Greek heroes. The son of Zeus and a mortal woman, Hercules fistfought the gods, once impregnated fifty women in a single night, and defeated a legendary, half-immortal wrestler by giving him some amateur chiropracty with a badass bear-hug that warped the dude's spine and crushed both his lungs into useless, fleshy, deoxidized sacs of misery. Hercules caught a little bit of flak among the Greeks when he became "seized by madness" and killed a bunch of kids, so the Oracle of Delphi sent him out to accomplish twelve impossible labors as penance for his crimes. The details of all twelve labors ranged from adventures as epic as battling the Hydra to something as mundane as the time when he went into Hades and punched out Cerberus, the three-headed hellhound guardian of the Underworld (yawn). You'd think Hercules would have been on his best behavior after doing all those labors, but not long after he got back from his court-appointed community service, he had one of his trademark psychotic episodes, once again turning into a giant raging dickhead and hurling some poor dude from a tower to his death for no reason at all. After a long career destroying cities, sailing with the Argonauts, and massacring the families of his enemies in vindictive blood feuds, Herc was eventually killed when his wife gave him a coat lined with the blood of a Centaur rapist, which burned the hero's skin off as soon as he put it on. Because he was so awesome, the gods raised Hercules from the dead and brought him up to Olympus so he could eat ambrosia all day and hook up with Hera's daughters whenever he wanted.

PERSEUS

Perseus was reportedly created when Zeus came on a hot princess as a shower of gold and impregnated her with a great hero, but this kind of seems like crap to me because everybody knows you can't get pregnant from golden showers. Either way, Perseus' grandfather (who had heard a prophesy that his grandson would murder him) wasn't happy with the pregnancy, so he locked Perseus and his mom in a box and threw it in the ocean. They were found by King Polydictes of Mycenae, who immediately decided he was going to try to get busy with Perseus' mom. Polydickcheese needed to get Perseus up off his bozak in order to make his move though, so he sent the now-teenage boy out on a suicide mission to defeat the evil, snake-haired Medusa. At this point, Athena swooped in, gave Perseus a bitchin' mirrored shield, a pimped-out adamantium sickle, a pair of "Air Hermes"–brand winged sandals, and a couple handfuls of curly fries, and Perseus got psyched up, snuck in, and sliced off the Medusa's head while she was sleeping. Pegasus, a huge-ass winged horse, flew out of the Medusa's chest cavity, so Perseus hopped on, rode around, and saved a hot naked babe named Andromeda from the chomping jaws of a maiden-eating sea monster. The two got married, and at their wedding Perseus got the added bonus of killing his wife's douche ex-boyfriend by whipping out the Medusa head. The dude turned to stone, Perseus made an insanely witty penis joke about how that guy no longer had to worry about erectile dysfunction, then he and his wife went back home, killed Polydictes, and took over as king and queen of Mycenae. Athena kept the Medusa head and bolted it onto her shield.

ODYSSEUS

As the wily hero who came up with the idea of the Trojan Horse and ordered the midnight assassination of the royal family of Troy, Odysseus was also the poor chump who bore the brunt of the gods' anger for his allegedly less-than-badass way of dispatching his hated enemies. He was doomed to ten years of wanderings at sea before he would finally return home, and ended up going on a balls-out series of adventures across the Mediterranean. During his journey, Odysseus killed the Cyclops, seduced a sorceress, avoided sea monsters and Sirens, and watched as his inept crewmen got eaten off one by one by horrific sailor-devouring monstrosities. After finally atoning for his sins by traveling to the Underworld and pouring one out with his dead homies, Odysseus returned home only to find that his wife was being hit on by like a hundred chump-ass suitors who were disrespecting Odysseus' home and drinking all of his High Life. Odysseus freaked out and killed all the suitors with arrows and spears, and the great hero was finally able to lead a nice quiet life with his beloved wife.

KRATOS

Originally the name of the Olympian God of Strength, nowadays the name Kratos is primarily used to refer to the ultra-hardcore, deity-smiting badass from the unbelievably epic *God of War* video game series. In the mythology of the game, Kratos was a Spartan commander who sold his soul in exchange for battlefield victory, and ended up serving as Ares' personal asskicker for quite some time, beating people to bloody pulp by decapitating them with a set of razor-sharp blades that Ares grafted to his forearms with huge chains. Aided by Athena's wisdom, Kratos atoned for the accidental murder of his wife and daughter by serving the gods, but eventually freaked out and killed them all (except Aphrodite, who he slept with), as well as all the Titans, most of the heroes, and everything else in existence.

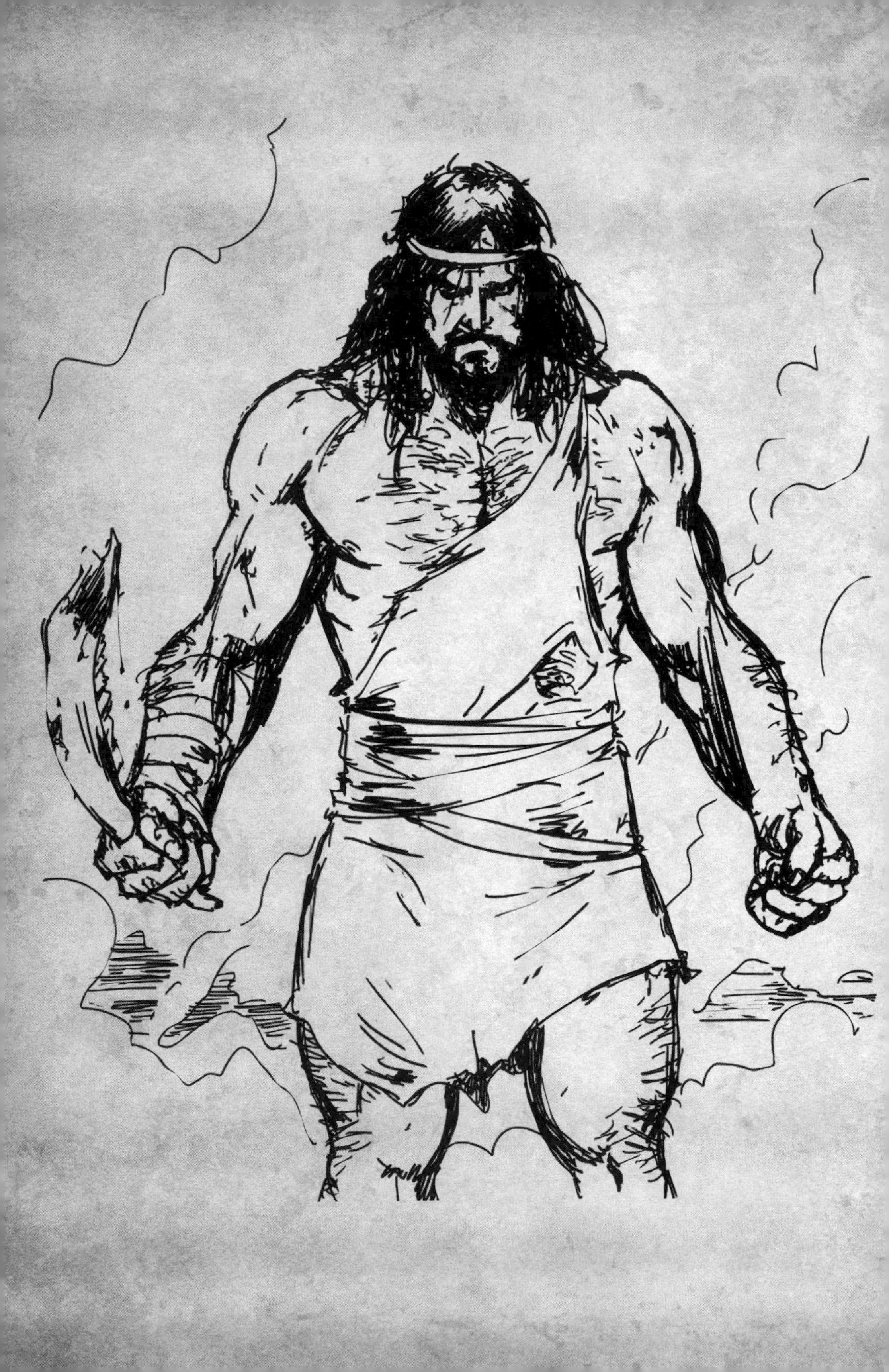

13

SAMSON

*Then the Spirit of the LORD came mightily upon him; and the ropes
that were on his arms became like flax that is burned with fire, and his
bonds broke loose from his hands. He found a fresh jawbone of an ass,
reached out his hand and took it, and killed a thousand men with it.*

—JUDGES 15:14–15

ONCE UPON A TIME, THERE WAS AN ISRAELITE GUY AND HIS WIFE
WHO GOT BUSY LIKE ALL THE TIME BUT COULDN'T CONCEIVE A
CHILD. One day the wife was walking home from buying a loaf of bread
at the supermarket and cursing her inability to procreate when all of a
sudden she met an Angel of God chilling in an alley somewhere. The
angel came up to her and was like, "Hey you know how you can't get
pregnant? Well, God says that you're going to get knocked up and have
a kid who will be a total badass as long as you never cut his hair for any
reason. Also you should keep kosher and lay off the booze while you've
got one in the oven because you don't want this kid to have any kind of
screwy birth defects or anything." Within weeks, the couple became
pregnant just as the angel had predicted, and nine months later they
proudly introduced the world to a guy who was going to spend the ma-

jority of his life bench-pressing motorcycles, pulling fifty-thousand-ton express trains with his teeth, and tearing a hole in the fabric of the universe by dead-lifting cattle—the ultimate Biblical asskicker, Samson.

Samson spent his early days whipping people to death with their own intestines. One day, after he reached manhood, he was walking through town when he saw a fine-as-hell Philistine babe who decided to go out with him. A couple days later, he was headed out to his date with this chick when all of a sudden a huge-ass PISSED-OFF LION jumped out of the brush and started tearing ass toward Samson, baring its razor-sharp teeth, but Samson was not impressed. He just snatched the creature out of the air mid-leap and pulled it apart with his bare hands like it was a piece of paper made out of beef. Then he ate it raw and washed it down with some honey from a nearby beehive.

After destroying the King of the Jungle with nothing more than a bad attitude and the ol' meat hooks, Samson went off on his date. They got some Starbucks and hung out, and decided they were going to get married because they were totally into each other and they both really enjoyed the mellow grooves on the new Jack Johnson album (Samson listened almost exclusively to chill stoner acoustic soft-rock, because anything more intense immediately sent him hurtling into berserker rampage mode).

Things were going well until Samson got a little overexcited during the rehearsal dinner and all of a sudden challenged thirty of his Philistine wedding guests to a test of wits. He told them that if they couldn't solve a riddle he just came up with, they each had to give him one of their finest robes. However, if they were able to solve the riddle, then he would give one fine robe to each of the thirty Philistines. The guests got all psyched up about the idea of getting some free swag, so they agreed. Samson presented them with the riddle: *Out of the eater, something to eat, out of the strong, something sweet.* The Philistines, of course, had no idea what the balls this lunatic was talking about, and couldn't figure out whether they even needed to formulate their response as a question or a statement.

The guests eventually got pissed at this bullcrap riddle and told Samson's fiancée that they were going to set her and her father on fire if she didn't tell them the damn answer. She immediately went home and convinced Sam to give her the correct answer (Samson could not be defeated by any man, yet he seemed to get worked over by women with a pretty noticeable regularity), which she then took back to the Philistines. The next day, the guests were able to answer Samson's impossible brainteaser by giving him the inscrutably correct answer: *What is stronger than a lion? What is sweeter than honey?* Just like that, Sammy had to come up with thirty fine robes, because apparently this was the response he was looking for. Luckily, Samson, being the resourceful man that he was, knew just how to show the Philistines his displeasure at their having cheated on the test: he got SUPER-omega pissed, traveled to the Philistine village of Ashkelon, killed thirty dudes with his bare hands, stripped them of their robes, and presented his asshole wedding guests with the pilfered materials. That'll show 'em.

After a long day of slaughtering Philistines for no good reason, Samson got drunk and went to his fiancée's house for a booty call. He knocked on the door to her home and her father answered. When Samson was all like, "Hey I'm going to go upstairs and get some busy," his soon-to-be father-in-law was like, "Dude, I thought you hated her for giving away the answer to the riddle, so I married her off to your best man instead! If you want though, you can marry her younger, hotter, significantly more-limber sister . . ."

Samson was stunned. This was the final straw that finally made him blow a gasket and become a man who dedicated his life to ripping people limb from limb and hurling their appendage-less torsos into the Sun. The massive, muscle-bound hero looked his would-be father-in-law in the eyes and said, "From this day I shall be blameless in what I do against the Philistines: For I will do you evils." And he did.

Samson then proceeded to get pissed in the sort of totally balls-out way that people got pissed in the Old Testament. He rounded up an army of foxes with razor blades for teeth, slapped horned Viking helmets on them, tied a bunch of torches to their tails, and then set them loose to run amok in the Philistines' farmlands and vineyards. By the time the psycho fox-pillagers were done running around incinerating everything, the entirety of the Philistine croplands had been reduced to smoldering ashes. The Philistines were understandably pretty angry at Samson for destroying all of their food and wine, so they were like, "Okay jackass, if you like fire so much let's see how you enjoy this!" They captured Samson's ex-fiancée and her father and made good on their previous threat to incinerate them to death with fireballs.

This would prove to be a mistake. Samson didn't even really like his two-timing ex-girlfriend that much anymore, but badasses in the Old Testament don't just back down when you go around setting their former loved ones on fire. They seek brutal, delicious, munchy-crunchy chocolatey vengeance, and they do it in the most over-the-top way they can think of.

Samson got the biggest sword he could find, headed into town, and started cleaving through Philistines like a left-handed MMA fighter viciously mangling his way through a thin sheet of rice paper with a pair of non-lefty scissors. The Bible is a little hazy on the details, simply saying he "cut them to pieces in a great slaughter," but that's descriptive enough that you get the idea.

After he beat the insubordination out of every Philistine he could get his hands on, Samson went to the land of Judah and took up residence in a nice quiet cave on the Rock of Etam. After being involved with so much death and destruction in such a short period of time, he just decided to find a place to get away from it all, return to nature, and relax with his John Mayer albums. Unfortunately, the Philistines were not in any mood to let him get away. They put together a huge army and marched on Judah.

Since the people of Judah weren't in any position to go to war with the Philistines, they made a deal—the Judahites (or whatever you want to call them) agreed to hand over Samson if the Philistines would spare them from all the looting, destruction, and agony that always seemed to travel around with massive armies. The Philistines agreed, and the high council of Judah headed to the Rock of Etam to get Samson. When they showed up and pleaded with Samson to turn himself over to the authorities, the Hebrew Sledgehammer was just like, "Whatever. Go ahead and tie me up, but don't kill me. Just take me to the Philistines alive so that I can see the looks on their faces when I tell them all to cram it up their cram-holes." So they bound him with two strong ropes and marched him down the mountain toward the justice that, in all honesty, he probably deserved.

When the Philistines saw their mortal enemy tightly bound up with strong rope and seemingly helpless, they all started screaming insults and headed toward him with their weapons drawn.

But Samson wasn't about to be executed like some kind of chump.

He flexed his giant manly Yahweh-powered pecs and the ropes holding him exploded off in a thousand different directions. The Philistine army immediately froze in panic and collectively muttered "oh fffffuuuuuuuuuuuhhhhhh . . ." under their breaths. Samson then grabbed the closest thing he could find, which in this case happened to be the jawbone of an ass, and started beating the holy living crap out of EVERYONE EVER. He was charging around with this broken-off hunk of donkey bone, smashing skulls with his fists, clubbing people's heads into craters, and rampaging around like King Kong on a bad acid trip.

When the dust finally settled, this goy-crushing madman had slaughtered one thousand Philistine soldiers with a freaking bone club. I think this beatdown is where the phrase "kicking ass" originally comes from.

Once he was done single-handedly destroying an entire regiment of Philistine infantry with little more than a blunt piece of equine anatomy, a tireless weapon arm, and a frightening amount of determination, Samson sat down on a rock and realized he was half-dead from dehydration. Fighting an army all by yourself is hard work, even for a dude like Samson. So he looked up to the heavens and cried, "Hey God I killed a thousand Philistines but now I'm thirsty as a bastard!"— so God came down and gave him some sangria. Samson got refueled by fruit-juice power and went home, where he went on to serve as the Judge of Israel for twenty years.

The Biblical judges weren't kings, but they weren't really litigators either. They were kind of like judges in the *Judge Dredd* sense more than anything else; they couldn't raise armies or increase taxes, but they did double as political and military leaders, arbiters of disputes, and general asskickers who annihilated any potential threats to the people of Israel. This was a position that was right up Samson's alley, and he was actually one of only twelve people to lead his civilization in the period between Joshua and King David. We don't know much about what happened during his tenure, which probably indicates that Israel's neighbors had the good sense not to mess with the people of Abraham as long as they were being led by a dude who once killed hundreds of people with a donkey.

Many years later, Samson fell in love with this chick named Delilah, but, as we've seen, this guy didn't really do a great job of hooking up with women that didn't lead him head-first into steaming piles of dead Philistines. The Philistines, who were understandably still irked at Samson for a variety of reasons, came to Delilah one day and offered her a buttload of gold if she could discover whether or not Samson had any weaknesses. Delilah kept pestering him until eventually he told her about the source of his unmatched power: his *Dreadlocks of Hill Giant Strength +4*. Samson told her that he had never shaved in his entire life, and that the key to his power, like that of any good rock star, was his hair. Delilah immediately sold her boyfriend out and relayed this to the Philistines, and then one night when Samson was sleeping, Delilah shaved his head like a bad dorm roommate. The Philistines then busted into his home, bound him up with bronze shackles, gouged his eyes out, and strapped him to a millstone to serve a life sentence of hard labor.

Not long after Samson was locked up, the Philistine leaders decided to throw a huge banquet to celebrate their victory over this guy who had been their public enemy number one for over twenty years, and who had massacred a noteworthy percentage of their population. The entire nobility, along with about three thousand other Philistine officers, courtiers, and important people all got together at the temple of the god Dagon to get wasted and offer up burning animal sacrifices to signify their excitement, because apparently that's what people did back in these days. Once the party really got hopping and everyone started to get a little tipsy, the senior administration decided to bring Samson in so that everyone could yell mean things, throw tomatoes, and point and laugh. So the guards fetched the fallen Israelite hero from prison so he could serve as the entertainment to the heathen jackass Philistines.

Samson couldn't see (having your eyes cut out sucks like that), but he somehow convinced his captors to place his hands on two huge pillars that served at the primary supports for the temple. The guards obliged him and then went back to whatever they were doing, and Samson exploited their temporary lack of judgment by placing one hand on each pillar and calling out for God to give him the strength to exact vengeance on his mortal enemies. God was totally down with brutal vengeance and crushinating destruction back then, so he suddenly restored Samson's superstrength. Samson pushed against the columns with all of his seemingly endless might, toppling both pillars, bringing the entire temple crashing down on top of the Philistines, and massacring the entire flower of the Philistine nobility with one feat of strength reminiscent of those *World's Strongest Man* competitions you see on ESPN 8 at like two in the morning. Everyone was flattened to death, including Samson, but you can be pretty damn sure that the last thought on his mind was about how great it was to go out in a blaze of glory and take everyone else down with him.

King Solomon built the First Temple in Jerusalem, strengthened the land of Israel into a dominant, wealthy, successful world power, and is at the center of a bunch of really kickass legends. Like how he was married to seven hundred women ranging from pharaoh's daughters to Hittite princess, had a veritable army of three hundred concubines on the side, and could allegedly sleep with seventy different women a night, every night, forever. Super-wise and powerful, Solomon once tried to end a custody battle by chopping a baby in half with a sword, and ruled from a gold-plated ivory throne flanked by ivory lions. He is the progenitor of the Rastafari religion through an alleged relationship with the Queen of Sheba, and according to Islamic tradition, he could speak with animals, had power over all creatures, flew around on the wind, and ruled over an army of genies that carried out his every whim.

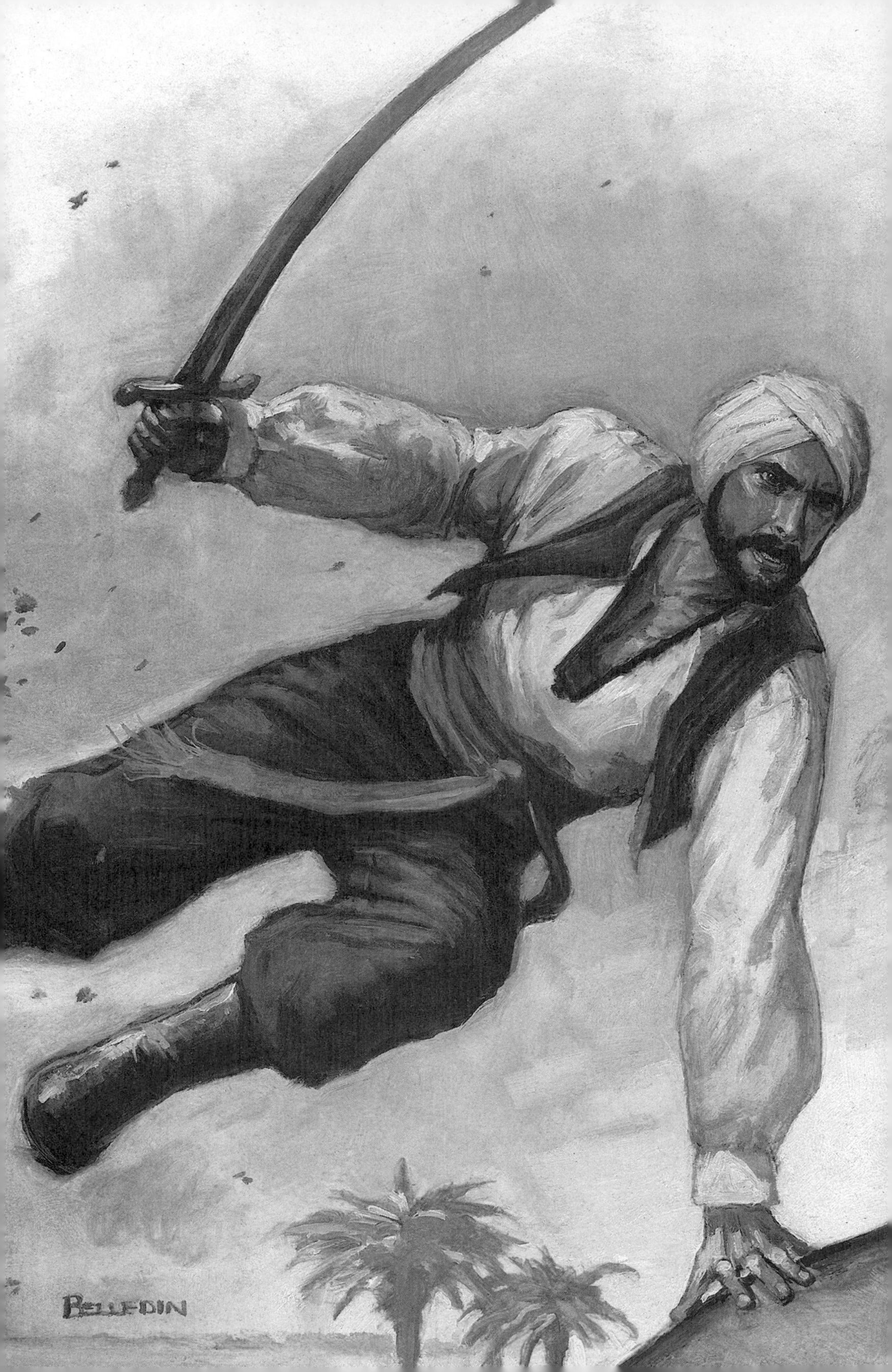
BELLEDIN

14

SINBAD

Presently, my brother, you shall hear the tale of my fortunes and all the hardships that I suffered before I rose to my present state and became the lord of this mansion where we are now assembled. For only after long toil, fearful ordeals, and dire peril did I achieve this fame. Seven voyages I made in all, each a story of such marvel as confounds the reason and fills the soul with wonder. All that befell me has been pre-ordained; and that which the moving hand of Fate has written no mortal power can revoke

SINBAD IS ONE OF THE MOST INTENSE HEROES TO EVER HOIST A MAINSAIL AND GO CAREEN HIS SHIP FULL-SPEED INTO A HEAD-ON COLLISION WITH SOME JAGGED ROCKS JUST BECAUSE HE FELT LIKE MAYBE THOSE ROCKS WERE CONCEALING SOME ADVENTURE BEHIND THEM. In his seven incredible voyages covering every corner of the globe and every possible variety of giant, revolting, man-eating monsters, Sinbad accumulated a vast horde of wealth, pummeled the snot out of a few thousand disgusting monstrous beasts, hooked up with princesses from a half-dozen long-lost civilizations, and clawed his way through more dangerous exotic locations than Bear Grylls, Les Stroud, and the entire cast of *Gilligan's Island* all crushed together into one face-punching clusterbone of survival skillz with a *z*.

One might look at the fact that every single one of Sinbad's seven cross-ocean voyages resulted in our hero being shipwrecked on some remote desert island and think that this guy was probably one of the worst seafarers to ever clumsily attempt to buckle a swash, but you can rest assured that Sinbad the Sailor isn't just a delightfully sarcastic epithet or anything like that. Sure, there were a couple of occasions where this salty, knot-tying sea dog accidentally smashed the mast in half or busted a hole in the hull simply by accidentally whipping out his gigantic titanium balls while he was standing on the deck, but most of the time the complete destruction of the ship and the brutally grisly murder of the entire crew was brought about by some random, completely unforeseen event that no mariner worthy of his sea legs would have possibly been able to prepare for. Once the ship was boarded and captured when a super-agile race of mini-Bigfoot-style hairy midget ape-men climbed onto the deck, beat up the crew, and took command of the helm. How the hell are you supposed to account for something like that when you're planning your expedition? Another ship was smashed when it put ashore on an island that turned out to be the back of a gigantic, several-mile-long whale. As soon as the crew started up a fire, the whale got burned and pissed, crushed the ship, drowned the entire crew, and Sinbad found himself all alone clinging to a wooden trough in the middle of the ocean, fighting off shark attacks by swinging a two-by-four around like a baseball bat. Again, not the guy's fault, even though he probably should have noticed a lake-size blowhole. If nothing else, you've actually got to give this balls-out sailor bonus points for being completely unafraid to climb right back into the crow's nest time and time again and not letting something like almost being smashed into jetsam on six consecutive expeditions deter him from still going out, somehow finding a willing crew, and seeking out new adventures, excitement, and wealth. If the definition of insanity is doing the same thing over and over and expecting different results, then it's safe to say that this guy was insanely awesome.

Sinbad's pops (we don't know his name, exactly, but I really hope it was Sindad) was a super-wealthy and influential merchant in Baghdad, the City of Peace. This is great and all, but Sinbad really didn't want to fall into a boring life haggling over the black-market price of genie lamps, flying carpets, and magical Yeti parts, so when his dad kicked it and left Sinbad a veritable sackload of gold, jewels, and expensive exotic goods, our hero promptly liquidated his assets. And, of course, by "liquidated his assets" I mean that he sold everything for booze money. Sinbad went on an epic bender of Lindsay Lohanic proportions, blowing his father's entire life savings on women, alcohol, parties, and huge piles of delicious cured meats in the span of just a few months. He finally awoke one morning to find that he only had about three thousand dirhams left to his name, and so, bored of a life of extravagance and ready to do something useful with the last shred of wealth he had left, Sinbad bought a boat, stocked it with merchant wares to sell at faraway ports, and set sail for awesomeness.

What followed was a series of epic adventures of hardass survival at sea against all odds and all definition of reality. While this guy's ability to successfully stay onboard any floating vessel larger than an inflatable inner tube is perhaps questionable at best, there's no doubt that Sinbad routinely kicked the scrotums of all manner of mythological and legendary beasts whenever they stood directly between the wreckage of his recently trashed ship and the location of some hidden civilization rife with hot babes and wealth itching to fall into the waiting arms of our hero. During his exploits, Sinbad took on a race of aquatic horses that ran up out of the ocean and devoured regular, wussier land horses, did battle with a trio of ship-devouring sea monsters, and escaped from the land of a jacked-up race of bat-winged Satan-worshipping demon-men.

Of all the near-death experiences this dude put himself through (and there were many), one of the most famous of his expeditions involves his adventure in the land of the Rocs. Ridiculously giant eagles known to carry off elephants and rhinos in their talons and munch humans down like popcorn shrimp, the Rocs were a vicious, bloodthirsty species of carnivorous birds that just so happened to inhabit a gemstone-rich area known as the Diamond Mountains. While shipwrecked in this wealthy-yet-insanely-deadly locale, Sinbad decided he was going to get out there and start grabbing as many diamonds as he could stuff down his pants, just in case he somehow miraculously survived and found himself in a city that put a premium on guys who could pull giant-ass diamonds out of their lederhosen. The daring, treasure-hunting hero tied himself to a Roc's leg, sailed through the air strapped to the creature's undercarriage, climbed down from the bird's nest to a particularly diamond-studded valley floor below, and survived a harrowing night inside the lair of an oversize man-eating serpent before somehow emerging with so much ice that you could have mistaken him for a glacier.

Another time, Sinbad and his crew were captured by a humongoid man-eating giant with a penchant for impaling men, roasting them over a spit, and chowing down on them along with a nice glass of red wine (you would think that human would be more of a white-wine dish, but you would be mistaken). This revolting culinary behemoth was as tall as a palm tree, with red eyes, boar-like tusks, and claws the size of a lion's, but Sinbad didn't give a crap. This able seaman wasn't going to sit around and let that thing stuff a sharpened stick up his poop deck, so one night, as the creature was getting ready to cook dinner, Sinbad grabbed the hot stake out of the fire, rammed it through the creature's eyes Odysseus-style, and then led his crew back to the coast, where they tried to escape on a homemade raft. Now Sinbad's track record of not getting shipwrecked was bad enough when he *wasn't* being pursued by man-eating giants while trying to row around on a lashed-together series of logs, so you can probably imagine how successful his daring seaborne escape went. Sinbad's men barely shoved off before the monster's pissed-off girlfriend showed up, flung a boulder through the raft, and obliterated it like it was made out of friggin' popsicle sticks. The party members who weren't pulverized by the rock drifted over to a nearby island where they were immediately eaten by a huge-ass fiendish anaconda from Hell. Sinbad was, of course, the only man clever and daring enough to escape the crush-hungry coils of the tremendous serpent, presumably by drawing from his years of experience fighting the ridiculously oversized monsters that seemed to jump out and try to bite his balls off every time he stopped to take a whiz in the woods.

On another occasion, Sinbad and his crew were captured by an uncomfortably weird tribe of wild, naked men. This was awkward at first, but things got even weirder when the cannibals busted out a bunch of giant-ass grilled foods like they were a race of nudist Burger Kings. Sinbad tried to warn his fellow seamen that you really shouldn't eat food given to you by a sweaty, naked villager, but the jerks ate all the burgers anyway, got super-fat, and were promptly devoured by the cannibals. Sinbad made himself as un-delicious as possible by starving himself Gandhi-style, and then his scrawny ass bolted for it in the middle of the night. He spent eight days in the mountainous wilderness before arriving at a land where his tale of survival made him an instant hit with the ladies. Sinbad married a baroness, one of many he would bag in his career on the high seas, but when she died, he tragically learned that these people's custom was to throw the husbands into the tomb with their deceased wives. Sinbad was dumped into the Cavern of the Dead, somehow survived being buried alive for two weeks, clawed his way out of the tomb, and continued listing aimlessly toward home again.

In yet another bizarre encounter, Sinbad was attacked by an evil old ogre who jumped on our hero's shoulders and refused to let go. Sinbad tried to throw the dude off, but the Old Man of the Sea had legs like bear traps and couldn't be moved. Our resourceful adventurer ended up feeding the dude some superstrong home-brewed pomegranate wine until he was super-trashed out of his mind, and as soon as the old guy loosened his grip, Sinbad flipped him into the turf and bashed in his skull with a rock.

After his seven incredibly insane voyages across the sea, Sinbad eventually succeeded in his goal of being impossibly rich and famous. He moved into a massive palace surrounded by servants, exotic dancing girls, eunuchs, money, wine, and spiced meats, possessed incredible treasures, and spent his days regaling friends, family, and strangers alike with self-aggrandizing tales of his bravery and general overall cool-dudery. Sinbad was also so loaded and generous that he distributed much of his extra wealth to widows, orphans, and the poor, and everyone thought this was so totally dope that they never talked smack about how inept he was as a sailor.

It's worth noting that Sinbad is also the hero of a couple of action-adventure movies featuring the work of badass visual effects master Ray Harryhausen and his stop-motion monsters of extreme awesomeness. The film-Sinbad's exploits range from swordfighting a skeleton to shacking up with the super-hot Caroline Munro, but the highlight of his adventures was probably that scene in *The 7th Voyage of Sinbad* when he saved his four-inch-tall princess girlfriend from the clutches of an evil wizard by shooting a fire-breathing dragon with a ballista and having its corpse fall on top of the sorcerer. Sure, there's really no evidence that the literary Sinbad had ever done anything quite like this, but I really wouldn't put it past him, either.

⇸ MYTHICAL PLACES ⇷

ATLANTIS

From the Ancient Egyptians to the Native Americans, several cultures have stories about advanced civilizations in the middle of the Atlantic Ocean that met untimely demises when they were powerbombed beneath the waves by angry gods, but the tale of Atlantis as we know it comes from the Greek philosopher Plato in his famous *Dialogues*. A powerful, warlike civilization that lived many centuries ago on a no-longer-existent island west of Europe—Atlantis was the center of a world-domination-hungry empire that stomped balls across the Mediterranean from Libya to Italy. After crotch-knocking all of Europe, the Empire of Atlantis attacked Greece with a force so huge it made Xerxes' infantry hordes look like an army of miniatures on a *Warhammer 40k* battlemat being rolled over by an M1 Abrams tank, but the men of Athens stood strong, holding their ground and somehow turning back the assault with sheer force of their own giant, unrelenting nutsacks. After splintering the spine of the

Atlantean army, the Athenians pressed on, liberating Egypt and the rest of the continent, but just as they were getting ready to invade Atlantis and personally cock-punch the emperor, the gods beat them to it. A single day of earthquakes, floods, and storms tore the island a new bunghole and sunk it into the sea, never to be heard from again.

Hy-Brasil

Back before Brazil was famous for wrecking everyone in international soccer competitions and pushing unbridled hedonism to the limit with their always-epic Carnival festival, it was actually the name of a mysterious phantom island off the coast of Ireland, supposedly fading in and out of etherealness and appearing only once every seven years. One of the few stories of adventures in Hy-Brasil comes from the wild, unsubstantiated ramblings of some random nutjob known only as Captain Nesbitt. According to Nesbitt's delirious blatherings, he landed on Hy-Brasil once, passed through a super-thick forest, and found a creepy castle that was stocked with wealth but guarded by three super-scary-looking old dudes. Nesbitt, the young, fit sea-captain, bravely ran screaming away from the old geezers, hopped in his ship, and sailed away while the island sunk back beneath the waves. Nesbitt later claimed that Brasil was the land where fairies lived.

The Seven Cities of Gold

In 1540, a Spanish explorer named Francisco Vásquez de Coronado heard some rumor that there were seven golden cities located somewhere in the uncharted lands of present-day New Mexico, so he mortgaged his wife's estate, bought a suit of gold-plated armor, put together an expedition of 320 soldiers, and spent the next two years stumbling aimlessly through the American Southwest without any damn clue where the hell he was going. In a shocking turn of events, the Seven Cities, which were supposedly founded by seven wealthy bishops who had fled Portugal after the Moorish invasions in the ninth century, weren't there, and Coronado had to settle for plundering six mud-constructed Pueblo villages instead. It just wasn't the same.

El Dorado

Here's a fun fact—El Dorado wasn't a place; it was a guy. According to legend, the "Gilded Man" was a South American king who covered himself in gold dust once a year, sailed out to the center of a huge lake, threw a bunch of treasure into the water, and then washed off his *Goldfinger*-style paint job by cannonballing off the royal barge into the water. The Spaniards figured that if this guy could afford to coat himself in gold once a year, he probably had a pretty dope treasure somewhere, so dozens of expeditions plowed groin-first into the Amazon rain forest looking for this crazy eccentric freak and his supposedly endless stores of gold (and cinnamon, because who controls the spice controls the universe). The Conquistadors encountered endless danger in the form of disease, mutiny from their cutthroat mercenary soldiers, and relentless attacks by vicious tribes of native warrior-women (this, incidentally, is where the Amazon River gets its name), but never found this crazy bastard or his gold.

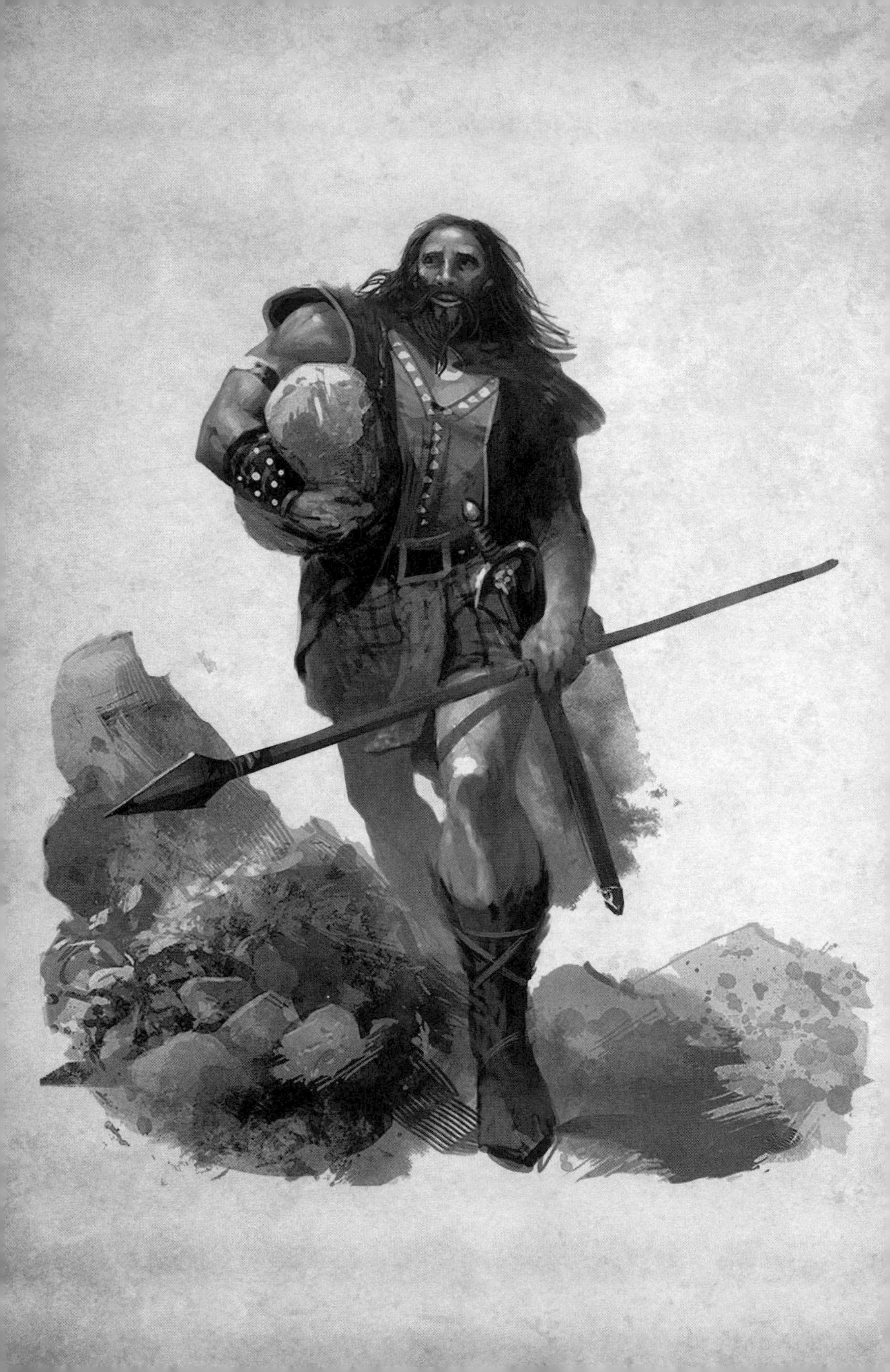

15

FINN McCOOL

His courage rose and he quickened his hands and he plied his blows, so that his bird of valor arose over the breath of the royal warrior, so that crowds of warriors were unable to stand against his prowess, so that men fell round his knee and a heap of them was piled up in their maimed-bodied and bloody-truncated necks and litter of gore wherever he would go into the battle . . . and the crushing of thighs and shin-bones and halves of heads under the edge of his sword in the battle was like the smiting of a smith in the forge, or like the uproar of withered trees cracking . . . the royal warrior never ceased from that onset until the battalion of the "pillars" was annihilated both by slaughter and flight.

—THE VIOLENT DEATH OF FINN

ANY DISCUSSION REGARDING THE GREAT BADASSES OF IRELAND'S FOLKLORE HAS TO MENTION THE MAN BELIEVED BY MANY TO BE THE BIGGEST, TOUGHEST, AND MOST EPIC HERO TO EVER GRACE THE EMERALD ISLE WITH HIS SIZE 47 BOOTS, UNBELIEVABLY FOUL TEMPER, AND ONE OF THE GREATEST-SOUNDING NAMES OF ALL TIME FINN MCCOOL.

Finn's legend starts back in the third century. Cumhaill, Finn's pops, was a ruthless warrior who served in a hardcore association of knights and soldiers known as the Fianna. One day, Cumhaill decided he wanted to marry the daughter of a powerful, high-ranking Druid, but the Druid wasn't too keen on this and he responded to Cumhaill's request by giving him the finger and whacking him in the crunch really hard with a shillelagh. Cumhaill, being the fearless, face-wrecking hard-ass that he was, wasn't going to be dissuaded by something as pathetic as a bone-shattering cudgel blow to the family jewels, so he busted into the Druid's house in the middle of the night, grabbed the girl, and carried her off into the darkness. In my research, I wasn't able to determine whether or not the blushing bride was a willing participant in this home-invasion/elopement/kidnapping, but I suppose that when you're dealing with medieval marriages this is only a minor detail.

Unfortunately for poor Cumhaill, the Druid was in tight with the High King of Ireland—a guy who went by the moniker Conn of the Hundred Battles—and the bride-stealing Irishman would soon discover that it's never a good idea to step to a guy who has a badass name describing how many different military engagements he's somehow managed to survive. Conn expelled Cumhaill from the Fianna, declared him an outlaw, and sent the fearsome, unstoppable brotherhood of knights out to capture and kill their former member. The commander of the Fianna personally tracked Cumhaill down, kicked him head-first into a ditch, and promptly introduced his skull to the pointy end of a lance a few dozen times.

Even though Cumhaill had been successfully killed the hell out of, there was still a little bit of a problem. You see, not long after the absconded Druish princess returned home, it became obvious that she had contracted a rather noticeable case of pregnancy. Her dad, being the virtuous religious leader that he was, concluded that the only possible way of resolving this unfortunate situation was to tie the poor girl to a stake and set her on fire until she died from it. Conn of the Hundred Battles disapproved of the daughter-torching idea for some strange reason and issued an order of protection, and when the baby was born he had the kid sent off to live with a couple of crazy-ass warrior women in the middle of the woods.

Young Finn McCool (who, by the way, is also known as Fionn Mac Cumhaill or Finn, son of Cumhaill—I, of course, chose the McCool spelling because it is probably one of the most awesome names ever) spent his formative years growing up in a magical forest surrounded by insane man-eating monsters and being trained in the arts of war and hunting by his face-melting Druid priestess aunt and her best friend, the legendary blademistress Liath Luachra. As you can imagine by his slightly unorthodox childhood, Finn had a bunch of weird adventures growing up. Like one time, he saw some chick crying tears of blood because her kid was slain by a badass warrior from the Fianna, so of course Finn McCool went out there, snapped the guy in half with his bare hands, and stole all of his treasure in an effort to make the poor girl feel a little bit better about herself. Another time he helped a wise and powerful sage catch the Salmon of Wisdom, a magical fish that granted the gift of supreme intelligence to the first person who ate it. (As a bizarre side note, the Salmon of Wisdom got its interesting powers by eating the Nuts of Wisdom. There's no mention of where the nuts came from, but I kind of love the fact that there's such a thing as mythological nuts of wisdom.) Finn was cooking this crazy thing but burned his finger on it, and when he instinctively put his thumb in his mouth to soothe the flesh-searing discomfort, the brain-expanding powers of brilliance instantaneously transferred from the magic salmon to him. From that point on, Finn McCool was able to divine the correct solution to any question simply by sticking his thumb in his mouth.

Not only was Finn McCool a super-mega mastermind capable of calculating the rotation of the Earth down to the nearest degree per minute simply by quickly jamming his thumb in his mouth, but he also grew into a tough-as-hell giant who stomped balls all across the Emerald Isle. When this guy grew up, he decided he wanted to restore honor to his family name and prove himself as a reckless destroyer of faces who exploded the brains of anyone foolish enough to stand within two hundred yards of his sword arm, so he went out to the capital and decided to save the town from a badass monster known as Aillen the Burner.

Aillen was kind of like a third-century Irish version of Trogdor the Dragon-Man. Once a year, this bastard-faced demon crawled his way out of the horrible depths of the underworld, wailed out a flaming solo on his harp so powerful that it put everybody to sleep, and then torched the town into cinders. Finn decided to put an end to that quick. He visited the town, kept himself awake through the harp-playing by stabbing himself in the face repeatedly with his own poisoned spear, and then ran out to confront Aillen the Burner as soon as the creature appeared. Aillen tried to breathe a huge fireball onto Finn, but the Irish giant smothered the flame by throwing his cloak over the demon's head and sucker-punching him in the chops. The pyromaniacal monster, displeased by this unforeseen turn of events, turned around and started running full-speed away from the crazy, face-smashing Celt with a bad attitude. Well, Finn wasn't going to let this medieval terrorist-monster get away with nothing more than the old "coat-over-the-head, punch-in-the-face" routine, so he took two steps toward the fleeing beast, hucked his spear at it, and impaled it from long range with enough force to puncture concrete. Then he casually walked over and kicked it in the head until it died.

After witnessing this righteous display of badassery, the High King of Ireland (Conn's grandson) immediately promoted Finn to commander-in-chief of the Fianna. Finn was pretty pumped up about bouncing the man who killed his father out of his prestigious position, and would go on to lead the Fianna to victory in tons of battles against everything from Viking marauders to armies of goblins from the Underworld.

The Fianna were pretty awesome, if you ask me. These powerful, head-cleaving knights were independent contractors under the nominal command of the king, sort of like mercenary commandos with huge beards and battle axes, and they did whatever they wanted to whoever they wanted whenever the hell they felt like it. These guys spent their summers hunting and camping out in the wilderness, and then their winters chilling with the king watching Irish dancing babes and eating giant hocks of beef and pork. They carried the fabled Weapons of the Gods, were pretty much unbeatable in combat against even the most battle-hardened asskickers, and they were all capable of pounding enough Guinness and whiskey to send most normal men into a coma. Of course, when you've got an organization like this, you can't just go around letting any idiot with a sword into your frat, and the Fianna had a pretty insane entrance examination. For starters, you would be buried in a waist-deep hole armed only with a shield, and you had to defend yourself while nine berserkers attacked you relentlessly with spears. If you were wounded in the melee, you were sent packing. If you somehow survived the pointy onslaught, you were set loose in the forest, and had to escape while the rest of the knights of the Fianna tried to hunt you down like an animal. If you were caught, stepped on a branch, or messed up your hair, you were expelled (just like their modern counterparts—metal-dudes—these guys took their hair VERY seriously). If you succeeded, you were rewarded by being sent off to battle against a bunch of gnarly otherworldly monsters like a true badass.

As commander of this Order of Ass-Beatery, Finn went on a bunch of crazy adventures all across Eire. He defended his homeland from invaders several times, had a bunch of wild parties, killed his own nephew in an argument over a babe, owned a pair of totally sweet battle dogs, and married a goddess who could turn into a deer. According to some legends, he also defeated the Celtic God of War in single combat by pummeling him senseless with a car battery, and you have to think that defeating the Irish equivalent of Ares is an accomplishment you really can't take lightly. Another story claims that he created the Giant's Causeway by throwing a bunch of rocks from Ireland to Scotland so that he could fistfight another giant over there, and in a similar geography-related incident, he also created the Isle of Man by trying to hurl a chunk of Ireland at a guy who was pissing him off. Finn just didn't give a crap.

All good things must come to an end, however, and for Finn McCool, that end came in the form of a story now known as "The Violent Death of Finn." It seems that over the years, McCool let all the praise go to his head, and kind of turned into a total jackass. The king turned several members of the Fianna against him, and at the Battle of Gabhair, Finn was jumped by a bunch of jackasses and murdered. The Fianna was then disbanded, because without Finn they were substantially less interesting. Finn's grandson went on to write a bunch of epic poems about him and to party with Saint Patrick, which is pretty sweet, and nowadays McCool's sweet name lives on in that he has a bunch of colorful Irish hooligan pubs named after him.

—————

The Horn of Bran Galed was a magical item said to be one of the greatest treasures of medieval Britain. Functioning as a cool-looking mix between a Thanksgiving cornucopia, a Viking helmet, and a *Star Trek* replicator, all you needed to do was grab this thing and speak the name of an alcoholic beverage, and all of a sudden the horn would be filled with the drink of your choice. Needless to say, Bran got invited to a lot of parties during his lifetime.

—————

Banshees are spectral Irish ghosts famous for their ability to foretell impending doom and/or scream super-loudly all of the time. Basically, a couple days before you were fated to kick the bucket, you would see the ominous, spectral apparition of a beautiful woman yelling, wailing, and prematurely mourning your dead body. If the banshee didn't really feel like shrieking her head off on that particular day, she might also appear to you in the form of a handmaiden washing severed heads or bloodstained armor in a river. Either way, if you saw them, you were screwed.

—————

Some people think that the ancient tales of Finn McCool and the Fianna were the inspiration for the epic stories of King Arthur and his Knights of the Round Table. These people are called the Irish. As is the case with most things, the English tend to disagree with them on this.

—————

✦ CUCHULAINN ✦

One Irish hero who could rival Finn McCool for sheer badassitude was the mighty death-slinging warrior Cuchulainn of the legendary Red

Branch Knights. A famous hurling champion in his youth (and I use the word "hurling" to refer to the field hockey–like sport and not the act of competitive vomiting), this brash, attractive, bone-crunchingly powerful asskicker was both lusted after by women and feared/respected by men across the land. Trained in the mysterious Fortress of Shadows by the warrior-goddess Scathach, Cuchulainn was given his ultimate test when his mentor's evil sister Aoife randomly showed up looking to destroy her sis in a vicious duel. Cuchulainn jumped into the middle of the dueling circle, took on the warrior-goddess himself, defeated her in combat, and then slept with her. He was apparently one of the few guys who could be a lover and a fighter *at the same time*.

Cuchulainn's secret weapon was a magical javelin known as the Gae Bolg. The Gae Bolg (which may or may not be pronounced "Gay Bulge") was an insane device carved from the bones of a giant sea monster, and Cuchulainn would swing this thing around and then kick it at his enemies at hard as he could. As soon as this flying shank penetrated a man's skin, thirty barbs would shoot out of it, killing the poor chump instantly and horrifically. Since the barbs made the weapon act like a hardware anchor, the only way to remove it from a person was to cut it out of their dead body with a sword. Yikes.

When this guy wasn't kicking the hell out of spears and replacing people's ribcages with a set of razor-sharp spines, he was also known for completely flipping out ninja-style and launching into something known as the "Warp Spasm"—a violent, bloodthirsty berserker rage that generally resulted in the horrible mutilation of everyone in his general vicinity. While in full-on freak-out mode, Cuchulainn's face contorted into a hideous position where one of his eyes bulged out of his head, and his ability to vaguely resemble the "pwned face" was probably equal parts intimidating, psychotic-looking, and awesome. One time, this unstoppable crush-o-matic warrior single-handedly won a battle against a rival army by separating the lobes of a few hundred dudes into their left and right hemispheres, but was so jacked up on adrenaline and bloodlust and PCP that he just kept bifurcating people's faces even after the war was over. The only way to get this psycho to chill out and stop violently murdering everything in sight was for the King of Ulster to send a detachment of a hundred hot topless babes to run out and distract him by jumping around on trampolines or something. I'm told that this worked.

Cuchulainn's most famous adventure was when his men of Ulster went to war with the armies of Queen Medb of Connacht. The queen, who was also a powerful sorceress, put the Ulstermen under a spell that would make them feel labor pains constantly, and while women are tough and can handle physical pain like eyebrow-plucking and waxing their bikini lines and birthing and God knows what else, men are total wusses when it comes to that stuff. The Ulstermen were all rolling around crying and complaining, and Queen Medb sent her forces in to invade the now-undefended land.

Because he was beardless, Cuchulainn was somehow left unaffected by Queen Medb's bizarre ability to simultaneously kick every single man in Ulster directly in the ballsack over and over again, and he alone marched out to meet the queen's forces. He positioned himself in the ford of the River Dee, and then challenged the entire Connacht army to a Rite of Combat. Queen Medb agreed that her army would not invade Ulster as long as Cuchulainn controlled the ford, and that she would send one of her greatest warriors out to duel him every single day until he was finally killed. For roughly two weeks, Cuchulainn slaughtered all the challengers he faced, including one battle against a crazy Druid and his twenty-seven kids, all of whom brought poisoned spears into the fray. No one could overcome the Irish champion—Cuchulainn single-handedly held off the entire army until his buddies could snap out of their unfortunate situation and get back to business. By this point, the men of Connacht were so demoralized that they didn't stand a chance.

Cuchulainn died when he inadvertently pissed off the goddess Morrigan by refusing to boink her. She sent a huge group of Druids out to murder his ass. The warrior fought bravely, killing several of them, but was mortally wounded by a magical heat-seeking spear that nailed him in the chest. Dying, Cuchulainn stumbled over to a large rock and strapped himself to it, so that even in death he could face his enemies standing. His death was later avenged by Conall the Victorious, which is presumably where that guy got his cool nickname.

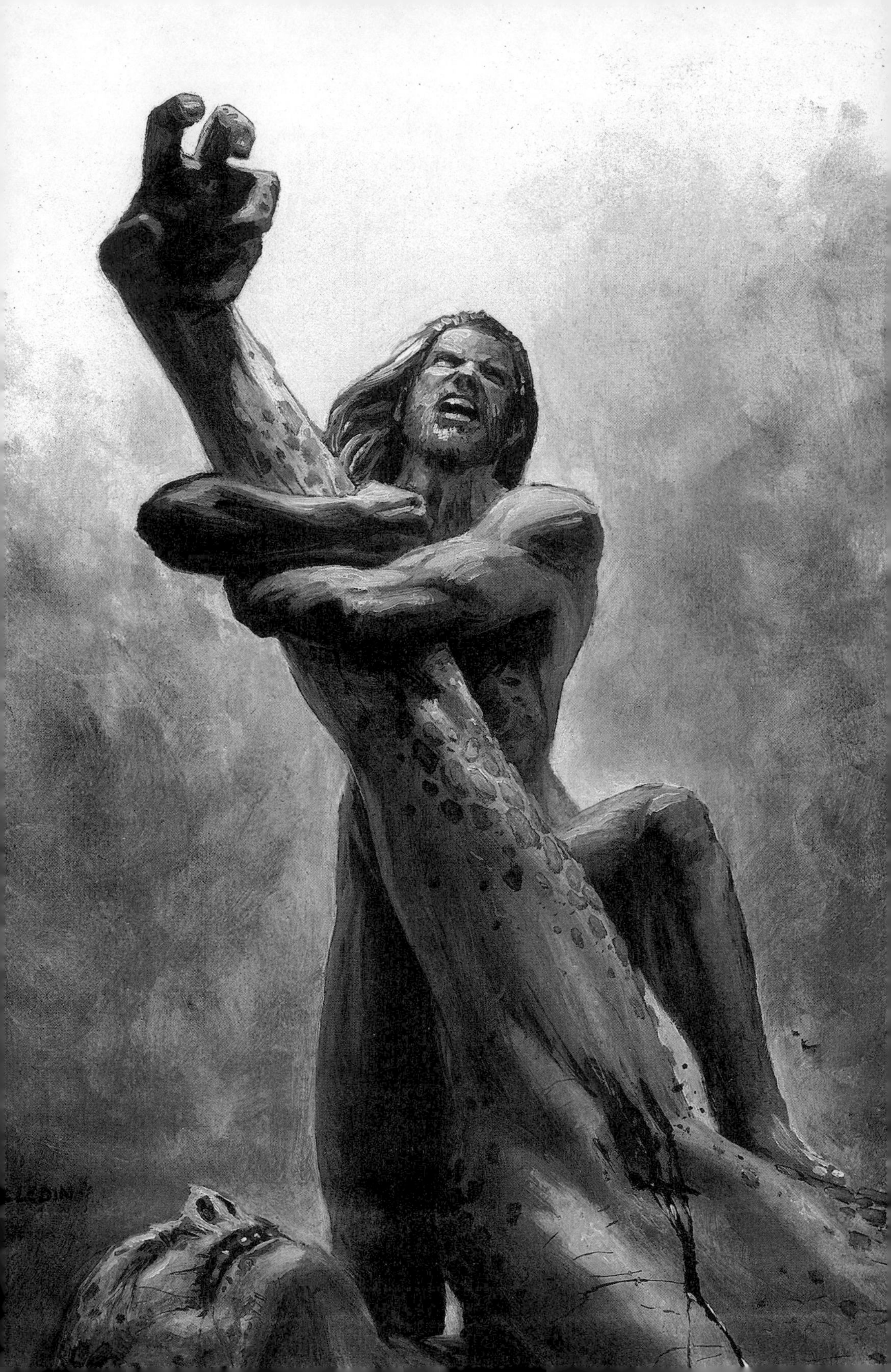

16

BEOWULF

Wise sir, do not grieve. It is always better to avenge dear ones
than to indulge in mourning.
For every one of us, living in this world means waiting for our end.
Let whoever can win glory before death.
When a warrior is gone, that will be his best and only bulwark.

FOR TWELVE LONG YEARS, THE MYSTERIOUS MAN-EATING MONSTER GRENDEL TERRORIZED THE POOR CITIZENS OF DENMARK, BUSTING INTO THEIR HOMES IN THE MIDDLE OF THE NIGHT, EATING THEIR CHIPS, AND THEN BITING THEIR FACES OFF WITH HIS GIANT, GLEAMING YELLOW FANGS. Over time, pretty much everybody got used to having their relatives devoured by a giant, disgusting, superpowerful monster, and no hero was tough enough to liberate the Danes from the oppression of this wretched beast. Well, one badass from the distant realm of Geatland took a particular interest as to what was transpiring on the shores of this mysterious land, and he decided he was going to sack up and do something about it.

The great Anglo-Saxon literary hero Beowulf did what any video-game protagonist would have done in a similar situation—he put together a raiding party of hardcore medieval warriors, strapped on his most righteous battle gear, and went out to kill himself some damned demons. This guy was no stranger to wiping the floor with the mutilated corpses of disgusting mythical beasts—he had already slain everything from sea monsters to water demons in his admittedly brief career—but he'd never tested his mettle against something this insane before. It was an awesome challenge so hardcore that he got mega-pumped-up just thinking about it, and with visions of glory and bloodshed dancing in his head, Beowulf put together a badass Led Zeppelin mix CD, jumped in his boat, and went to find out what the hell was rotten in the state of Denmark.

Beowulf and his homedogs crashed onto the shore of Denmark and immediately made their way out to tell the king what was what. When the big boss-man heard Beowulf's noble intentions, he held a righteous feast in the hero's honor, complete with kegs of booze and giant carved Thanksgiving turkeys and cranberry sauce and all that good stuff, and people ate meat right off the bone like the barbarian badasses they were. Everything was going pretty well until some jacknut had the mind-numbingly brilliant idea to call Beowulf out right in front of everyone. This dude got up and started talking mess about how he heard that Beowulf had lost a swimming race against a lesser warrior or something. The room fell silent at this accusation. All eyes turned toward the newcomer, who leaned forward in his chair, his face hard as poured concrete, his expression as grim as a funeral.

Beowulf slowly rose to his feet, pounded his fist on the table, and said, "Go hump yourself, ass-hat—when I'm in the water I'm like a cross between a coked-up dolphin and a blender permanently stuck on the 'melt faces' setting. Not only did I whip that guy's balls off in the swimming race, but I also set the world record in the hundred-meter butterfly AND had time to choke out a sea monster with my bare hands in the process. Oh yeah, then this giant Kraken tried to drown my ass by wrapping me up with its tentacles, so I sucker-punched that multi-tentacled monstrosity in the junk until it was comatose! What have you ever done, punk? You're obviously not out there killing any Grendels, that's for sure, so why don't you just sit here complaining about your aching ballsack and let a real hero go out there and show you how a ba-dass handles things?"

Then somebody in the audience yelled, "OH SNAP!" because this douche-bubble just got seriously told. The dude ran off crying into his handkerchief, and everyone else went back to their epic feast and got wasted on mead and wine and tryptophan.

Well, as luck would have it, Beowulf wouldn't have to go far to get the fight he was looking for. The monster Grendel just so happened to show up that night while everyone was asleep, and he immediately started slaughtering and devouring dozens of battle-hardened warriors like they were prepackaged containers of cooked beef. The demon then kicked in the door to Beowulf's hotel room and ate one of his soldiers, but our hero, despite having spent the entire night chugging enough ale to intoxicate most inanimate objects, popped out of bed without a hangover. Grendel reached for this fearless challenger, but Beowulf jumped up, totally ass-naked, head-butted the ogre to the floor, grabbed the monster's arm, and tore it off with his bare hands just to show the beast that it was being a bitch. The monster ran away and crawled into a hole to die, and Beowulf triumphantly hung the severed limb in the Danish king's dining hall, turning the feasting room into one of those family-dining-style chain restaurants with all the wacky crap hanging off the walls. For defeating the horrific creature in such a badass man-ner, the king gave the warrior-hero more weapons, armor, gold, cake, and jewelry than he could carry. Then they had another huge party and everybody got trashed again, because that's what people did back in the Dark Ages before the Internet.

Well, it turned out that the whole "getting devoured head-first by man-eating monsters" thing wasn't over yet for the good people of Denmark, because Grendel's mom got all cheesed off and decided to exact bloody retribution on the people who brutally and horrifically dismembered her son. This EVEN HUGER and EVEN MORE LIVID creature showed up in the middle of the night, super-wicked pissed off, killed a bunch of sleeping Danes, and ganked the disembodied arm off the wall of the king's dining room. The next morning, when everybody saw the carnage, Beowulf knew what he had to do. He put together a force of loyal warriors and rode out to the swamp to teach that mother of crap a lesson in getting clubbed with the severed appendages of her own children.

The adventurers rode out to a super scary swamp in the middle of nowhere. Knee-high fog obscured the ground, the dead vegetation was littered with dried blood, snakes, bat turds, and human remains, and everybody was so freaked out they pretty much had myocardial infarctions right there on the spot. Everybody except Beowulf, that is. He took one long look at this nasty-ass swamp, strapped on his armor, and dove into the freezing-cold stagnant black water of some disgusting, fetid lake.

Beowulf swam down to the bottom of the bog, where he busted into the foul lair of Grendel's crazy mom. She freaked out and started trying to kick him in the grundle with her taloned feet, but he drew his monster-smiting blade and lopped her head off with one fatal swing. Then, when he noticed that the now-deceased mommy dearest had dragged Grendel's armless corpse down to the bottom of the lake with her, Beowulf went over and chopped Grendel's head off as well, just to make sure he had the complete set of decapitated Grendel family trophies.

Back on the surface, everybody pretty much thought Beowulf was dead, because, holy crap, how can someone hold their breath for that long, right? Well, just as everyone was getting ready to say, "Screw it," and head back home, Beowulf emerged from the murky waters carrying twice the number of severed heads he had originally intended to retrieve. He returned to the king's palace, where he was lauded as a hero yet again. With the land of Denmark scoured of unholy flesh-eating monsters, Beowulf decided to head back home.

When the epic hero got back to Geatland, he gave most of his treasure to his king and queen, because that's what good noble heroes were supposed to do back in those days. The king kept Beowulf as his personal champion, heaped rewards on him, and sent him out at the head of his army to battle the Swedes in a couple of wars. Eventually, the old king died, and for his bravery and service to the throne, the dying king handed the crown over to his greatest champion.

King Beowulf ruled justly and honorably for fifty years, and everybody thought he had more balls than a high school gymnasium. Then one day, all of a sudden, this massive fire-breathing dragon showed up out of nowhere and started laying waste to the countryside like a mother. Beowulf, now like seventy years old and knowing that his time here on Earth was growing short, donned his war gear for the last time and rode out to the dragon's apparently not-so-secret lair. When none of his fellow warriors had the sack-o'-nuts required to take on this creature, this legendary face-smashing hero wasn't going to let something like "being seriously decrepitly old" stand in the way of performing towering acts of heroic asskickery. He charged balls-out into the dragon's lair, weapon at the ready. This thing breathed a huge fireball right in Beowulf's face, scorched off his cool, super-long white beard, and bit him in the shoulder with its poisonous fangs, but Beowulf still managed to stab this thing in the heart repeatedly until it exploded *Contra*-style. The last of his energy expended in the badass act of killing a giant, man-eating monster, Beowulf died, going out in a badass blaze of glory. His body was burned on a funeral pyre like Darth Vader, and then the great Geat hero was buried under a large hill along with a bunch of the dragon's treasure for some reason.

The Sub-Saharan African version of this monster-wrestling warlord is the legendary folk hero Heitsi-eibib. Born to an ordinary peasant woman who somehow got pregnant by eating a handful of grass, Heitsi-eibib went out to save his people from a powerful monster that enjoyed beating up mortals and throwing their broken bodies down a huge, bottomless hole. Heitsi-eibib hulked up and wrestled this creature, mano-a-beasto, but after a long battle the hero was suplexed down into the hole himself. Rather than give up and plummet to his death like a chump, Heitsi-eibib somehow managed to grab the side of the pit, climb out, defeat the abomination in hand-to-hand combat, and destroy the beast by judo-flipping it into its own hellacious chasm. Heitsi-eibib is also credited with defeating a magical, enormous flying lion that had been terrorizing the countryside. The humorless warrior ran out, wrestled with the Griffon-like creature, cut off its wings with a dagger, and when the wounded beast climbed a tree to escape Heitsi-eibib's wrath, the African hero promptly grabbed a torch and set the tree on fire.

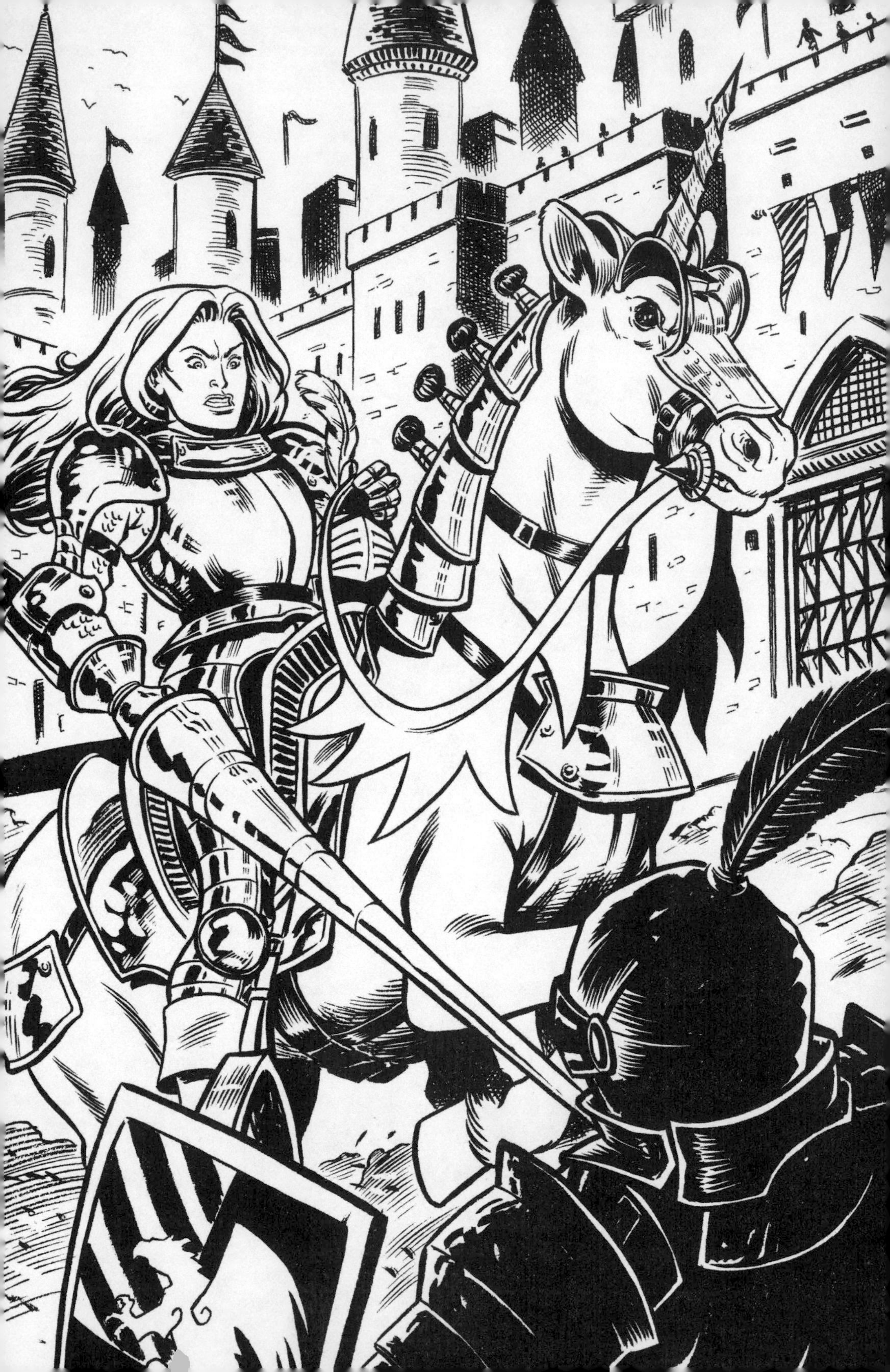

17

BRADAMANT OF CLAIRMONT

Did I not tell you that you would have done better to carry my message than to be so eager to joust with me? Now please ask your king to choose from among his army a warrior who can match me; let him not waste my energy against the rest of you, who have little experience in arms.

DAMSELS IN DISTRESS ARE OVERRATED. While I certainly won't deny the fact that most guys out there have, at some point or other in their lives, secretly wished they could ride out, slay some gruesome dragon, and rescue a hopefully large-breasted maiden from the darkest reaches of some foul, god-forsaken citadel, there's also something to be said for a kickass chick who doesn't take crap from anyone and can take care of herself in any situation, no matter how impossibly dangerous it may be. The badass warhammer of a warrior-maiden Bradamant of Clairmont, the heroine of Ariosto's immortal sixteenth-century epic *Orlando Furioso*, not only defies the damsel-in-distress archetype— she completely pile-drives it onto a tile floor and tears out its spleen with a gauntleted fist.

The *Furioso* is one of the most popular medieval epics of mainland Europe (in France and Italy, it is more widely read than even the King Arthur stories), and Bradamant is a hardcore knight on par with the most intense, face-crushing heroes of medieval Christendom. A valiant paladin in the service of the real-life Frankish king Charlemagne, this chivalrous heroine is unique in legend because she's actually the one who has to save her boyfriend from the clutches of an evil wizard. This questing battle-maiden scoured the countryside one eviscerated corpse at a time, searching for the brave knight Ruggiero—a mighty Saracen warrior she had fallen for after battling him in combat. The two had shared a brief moment of love at first sight on the battlefield, each one hearing the greatest romantic ballad of all time—Marvin Gaye's "Let's Get It On"—softly playing in their heads while limbless torsos cartwheeled through the air behind them in slow motion spraying blood around in circles like waterwheels as they flew past. After a brief profession of undying devotion for all eternity, the mighty champions immediately had to get back to the serious business of smiting the infidelity out of whichever soldiers they considered to be heretic godless heathens, and both were left wondering what might have been. After the battle, Ruggiero searched for the kickass chick he had seen viciously cleaving her way through his countrymen's heads, but before he even had a chance to wipe the blood from his sword he was ambushed, captured, and imprisoned by an evil sorcerer who dove down through the sky on a winged half-eagle, half-horse monster and wielded a shield that made people pass out and piss themselves whenever they looked at it. The sorcerer dragged the unconscious Ruggiero back to an ominous steel fortress and threw him into a god-forsaken dungeon with a bunch of other chumps he'd collected during his seemingly purposeless adventures around Spain and France and everyone spent their time together sitting around thinking about how boring the place was. The fortress was situated at the peak of a mountain high in the Pyrenees, surrounded by a moat filled with waters from the River Styx that caused the instant death of anyone who even so much as touched them, and the odds of getting this guy out were about as good as the odds of me spontaneously shooting a lightning bolt out of my balls.

Bradamant didn't give a crap—she was determined to rescue the dude in distress from the clutches of this madman, and anything that stood in her way was going to get impaled by a magical golden lance that hit so hard it was like being kicked in the sternum by a T-Rex—and a real badass, old-school T-Rex, not one of those bullcrap feathered bitches you see flapping around like morons in science journals these days. She started her adventure alongside another knight, who was seeking to rescue his girlfriend from the same evil fortress, but for some asinine reason the douche-head cut the rope while she was rappelling down a cliff face into an unexplored cave (wearing full armor, no less), sending her plummeting to the darkness below. Bradamant would later avenge herself on this jackass knight by spinning him backward off his horse in a joust, chasing him on foot through the ankle-deep waters of a foggy swamp, and stabbing him a hundred times in the back, but that's not really relevant right now. She survived her fall somehow, met the ghost of Merlin the Wizard, and rapped for a while with a mysterious yet bizarrely normally-named sorceress known as Melissa. Melissa told Bradamant that she would need a one-of-a-kind magic ring to resist the blinding powers of the sorcerer's evil shield, but unfortunately that ring was in the possession of a really hardcore knight who lived all the way off in some distant land somewhere. Bradamant, never one to be discouraged by stupid crap like geography, hunted the guy down, caught up with him in a tavern in the middle of nowhere, beat his ass into a crumpled heap with the flat part of her sword blade, and wrenched the ring off of his lifeless finger as he lay passed out on the floor. Then she journeyed back through the Pyrenees, climbed the foreboding mountain, and approached the fortress where Ruggiero was being held.

Bradamant, somewhat concerned about the instant-death-water moat, decided to just call the evil wizard out of his citadel the good, old-fashioned way: by standing out in his front yard yelling insults at him until he got so angry that honor compelled him to show himself. The pissed-off sorcerer flew out on the back of the hippogriff—a mythical animal with the body of a horse and the wings and head of an eagle—teleported around through the sky, and then swooped down from a high altitude for the kill. Bradamant quickly dodged this attack, and when he showed her the coma-inducing shield, she immediately pretended to fall down unconscious. The wizard, thinking he'd sufficiently roofied her up, ran over to tie her down and drag her back to his wicked lair, but right at the last second, she sprang to her feet and cold-cocked the dude in the jaw with a gauntleted fist, sending that jerkwad sprawling to the deck. The dude hurtled through the air, smacked head-first in the dirt, and skidded for a few feet. Bradamant ran up, kicked the shield and lance out of his hands, put her sword at his neck, and forced him to release his captives. When the guy desperately told her he'd trade her the flying eagle-horse and the magic shield if she would just leave him alone, she informed him that he had no authority to offer her things that were now obviously already hers, and that if he knew what was good for him, he'd just suck it up, take it like a man, and do everything she told him to. Then he begged her to kill him, but Bradamant, who had a badass code of honor, wasn't willing to just kill an unarmed dude, no matter how badly he deserved it. She told him to go hump that flying horse-bird thing he was riding earlier, and that if he really wanted to die, he should just sack up and do it himself. Seeing that arguing with this chick was useless, the sorcerer finally waved away the fortress with his hand, and all the knights and ladies imprisoned inside were immediately freed.

Ruggiero came running out and the two briefly reunited. I say briefly, because Ruggiero was actually kind of a total dumbass, and as soon as he saw the awesome hippogriff, he thought it was pretty much the most bitchin' thing since a rocket-powered motorcycle and jumped on its back. The second he landed in the saddle, the bizarre eagle/horse combo got spooked, took off into the air, and flew off in some random direction. Ruggiero, who had very little experience riding magical half-mammal/half-bird monstrosities, was dragged screaming along for the ride, and just like that, he was gone again.

The hippogriff took Ruggiero to some kind of crazy island where sorceresses rode around on unicorns and morphed men into trees, and for all of her searching Bradamant couldn't track him down. She eventually conscripted the sorceress Melissa into rescuing Ruggiero, sending her off with the magic ring and a letter professing her love, and got on with her life. While she was waiting for Melissa to do her thing, Bradamant killed time by commanding the defenders of Marseilles against a massive invasion of Saracen warriors, marshaling her men with all the intricacy of a hardcore professional South Korean *Starcraft* master micro-ing a Zergling horde against a Protoss base. After winning the war single-handedly, she saved a kidnapped princess from being carried off against her will by unhorsing her would-be abductor in a joust, shattering the dude's shield, and breaking his spine in the process, but that's basically the sort of thing this warrior-maiden did on a daily basis, and it barely warrants mentioning.

Ruggiero eventually returned from the island of unicorn bimbos, defeated a sea monster in a fistfight, and got back to the serious business of searching for his lost love, Bradamant. Not long into his quest, however, he was badly wounded in battle when he was ambushed by a teeming pile of rectum sandwiches, and was barely rescued by another warrior-maiden—the hyper-hardcore Saracen knight Marfisa, who nursed him back to health in a Saracen military camp along the battle-front. When word came back to Bradamant that not only was Ruggiero back in town but that he was shacking up with some random, sword-swinging blond bimbo (untrue rumors were also going around that the two were betrothed), Bradamant once again put the cute-and-cuddly girlfriend thing to the side and went on the goddamn warpath after him, ready to exact pointy revenge on this punk two-timing bastard by ramming the sharp end of her lance through his eye socket at high velocity. While raging across the countryside in a berserker blood-frenzy, she came across the kings of Norway, Sweden, and Gothenburg, who were in town for a diplomatic mission with the queen of Iceland and thought it would be funny to try and screw with the badass warrior-damsel, so Bradamant showed them a little diplomacy of her own by face-kicking them off their horses in a driving rainstorm and unceremoniously dumping their Scandinavian asses forcefully into the mud. Twice. In a row. The dudes were so disgraced that they took off their expensive gold-plated armor and tossed it into a moat, and spent the rest of their miserable existences walking around half-naked. Next she met the king of Algiers, who at that time apparently had nothing better to do than stake out a subterranean fortress on the side of the road, beat up traveling knights, and steal their armor, but that poor douchebag picked the wrong day to try and stand in the path of Bradamant of Clairmont—the rampaging paladin beat him down in such a soul-crushingly overwhelming manner that the guy threw his sword down on the battlefield and ran off to live in a cave for a year as a hermit. She slowed down just long enough to return the suits of captured armor to their rightful owners before charging lance-first into Ruggiero's military camp with nothing but ultimate destruction on her mind.

Bradamant pulled up outside the Saracen camp and loudly challenged Ruggiero to a duel, calling him out as a flaming crap-burger unworthy of death by drowning in a bucket full of urine. Three of the toughest Saracen champions heard these virulent threats and rushed out in their full armor, telling her that she would need to deal with them first. Bradamant responded by saying, "Go back, and tell your liege from me that I haven't come forward for the likes of you: I have come here to seek battle with a warrior worthy of the challenge," which is paladin-speak for "Don't waste my time, losers." Understandably insulted, the warriors charged ahead, and, one by one, she plucked them off of their weenie horses and dumped them to the ground with her lightning-bolt lance and unquenchable anger. After those guys were toast, Marfisa herself rode out to challenge Bradamant, because (as you will see) Marfisa was also incredibly tough and unwilling to back down from any challenge.

Marfisa wasn't someone you wanted to mess with. Raised by lionesses in the North African desert, this armored battle-axe had been sold into slavery in the court of an Arab king, but when the king got a little too frisky and tried to rape her, she killed him, slaughtered his entire family, seized control of his palace guard, and took the kingdom for herself. By the time she was eighteen, she had conquered seven neighboring kingdoms, and is credited by Ariosto as being undefeated in over a thousand duels—including one bloodbath where she impaled a guy with her lance and then skewered two other knights with the first dude still shish kabobbed on her weapon. She also carried a lance so heavy it took three men to lift it, and wore a suit of armor forged in the fires of Hades.

Marfisa and Bradamant rushed at each other, lances couched, and Bradamant once again unhorsed her rival with one piercing strike. Marfisa got super-angry, jumped to her feet, and charged again on foot, but Bradamant lashed out and lanced her back down to the ground. The ensuing fight quickly became so vicious that all the Christians and Moors watching it got really pissed and charged into a huge melee, and the next thing you know everyone was running around getting killed all over the place. During the fight, Bradamant defeated three hundred enemy warriors, cleaved her way through the rabble to Marfisa, and resumed her fight—the two women going at it with lances and swords, and then, after those shattered, with fists and feet.

Just as it looked like the two most ferocious, balls-out warriors on the battlefield were going to physically tear each other limb from limb, Ruggiero showed up, and it was revealed to Bradamant that Marfisa was actually Ruggiero's twin sister and that Bradamant was truly the love of his life. The three were reconciled on the spot, and got so pumped that they celebrated by riding out to the castle of a super-evil king and avenging a couple of local maidens that the dude had wronged. The evil tyrant had already earned a reputation for torturing, tormenting, or murdering any women he found on his lands, so Bradamant, Marfisa, and Ruggiero charged out, and the three of them killed all of his bravest knights and destroyed the dude's castle. Marfisa personally took the dude down in a joust by throwing down her lance and *punching him from horseback* while galloping full-speed, which is almost unspeakably awesome. The damsels then tied the bastard up and threw him to the oppressed peasantry so that they could exact their own revenge. Then they returned to France to chill with Charlemagne for a while, fight some battles, and beat the hell out of anyone who screwed with them.

After a while, Ruggiero finally realized Bradamant was completely awesome and worthy of a similarly badass guy, so he decided to straighten up and fly right, and the two got married. The ceremony was attended by thousands of cheering guests and administered by Charlemagne himself, and everybody was really pumped up about the whole thing. Well, everyone except the king of Algiers—that old bastard showed up in armor and tried to break up the wedding as revenge for Bradamant having busted in his face a year earlier, but Ruggiero ran up and stabbed the dude through the visor of his great helm a couple times and everyone lived happily ever after.

One time Marfisa was walking up to register herself on the combat lists at a tournament when she noticed that the weapons on display as prizes were actually a sword and a mace that used to belong to her (she had dropped them while chasing a vanquished enemy through the countryside a few days earlier—the weapons were slowing her down, so she'd needed to jettison some weight to catch up to the guy). Instead of entering the tournament, this battle-loving warrior just walked right up and grabbed the two weapons out of the display case without saying a word. Everyone in the general vicinity drew their weapons and jumped her, but she didn't even care—Marfisa took on the entire field of challengers, the king, his bodyguards, and an angry throng of peasants all at once, cutting her way through the crowd and escaping with her recovered gear.

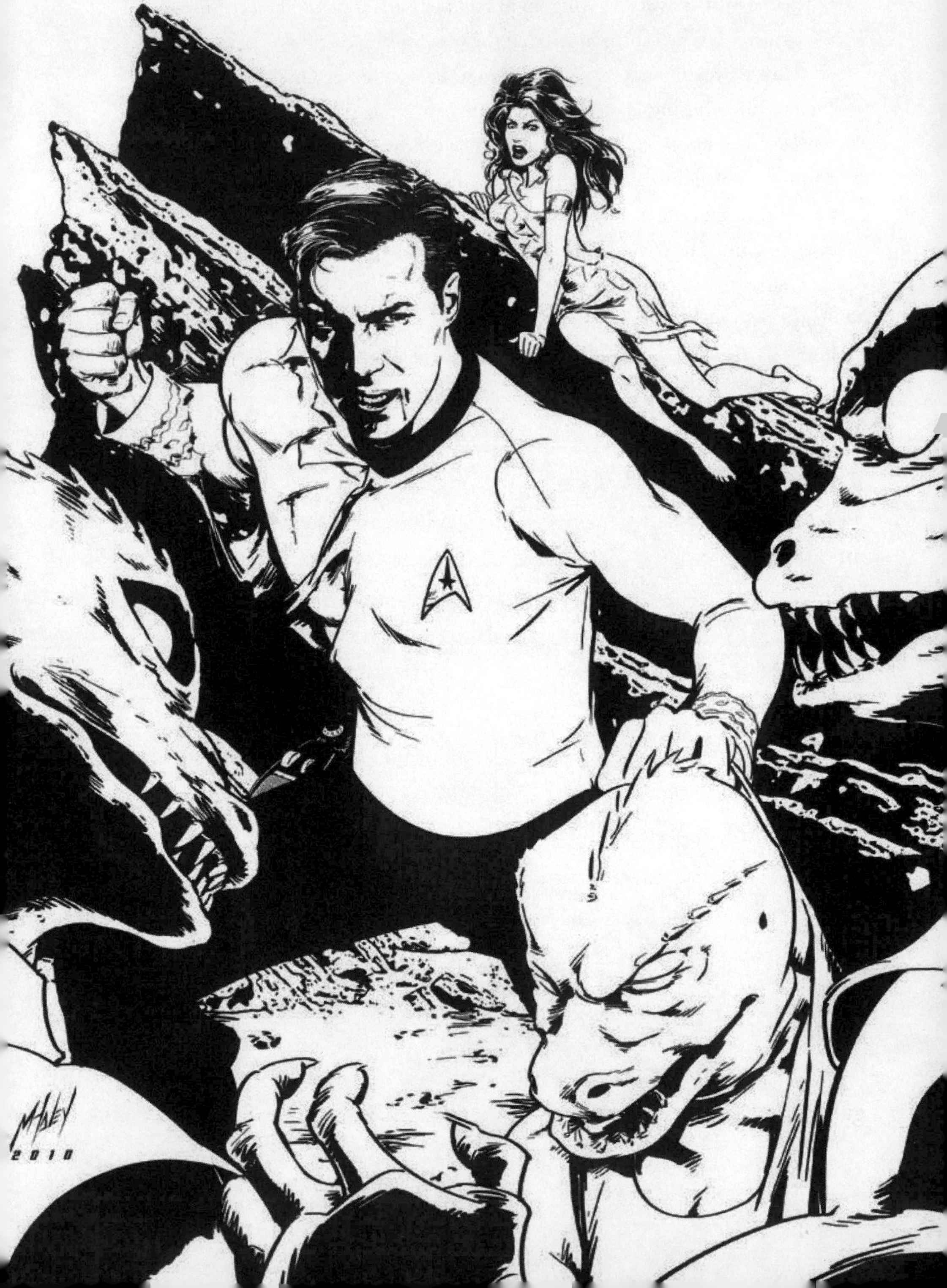

18

CAPTAIN JAMES T. KIRK

One of the advantages of being captain is being able to ask for advice without necessarily having to take it.

THROUGHOUT THE YEARS, THERE HAVE BEEN HUNDREDS OF SCI-FI CAPTAINS AIMLESSLY HURTLING THEMSELVES THROUGH THE UN-DISCOVERED COSMOS IN SEARCH OF ALIEN LIFE FORMS TO BATTLE, SEXY ALIENS TO ROMANCE, UNCHARTED PLANETS TO EXPLORE, AND NEW AND INTERESTING CIVILIZATIONS TO MAKE CONTACT WITH. These dashing heroes handle every situation with decisive action, and by constantly pushing their ships and their crews to their physical and structural limits. They achieve greatness and victory in the name of humanity, and sci-fi nerds the world over eat that stuff up like it was a big bag of sour-cream-and-onion potato chips. But while many of these daring heroes can make claims to their own badassitude, there is one immortal, incomparable man who has spent the past forty years serving as the ultimate paragon of awesomeness, and a template for what it means to be a heroic space adventurer—Captain James Tiberius Kirk, commander of the USS *Enterprise*.

We love Captain Kirk because he was a man of action—this hardcore, galaxy-traveling starship commander was a no-frills asskicker who shot first, didn't ask questions, sucker-punched the dead bodies, and then made out with the hot alien widows. He didn't give two craps about introducing himself to a newly discovered alien species by giving them a homemade spaceman knuckle-sandwich and then stomping on their genitals, hopping in the *Enterprise* and firing enough torpedoes to destroy the solar system, or reverse-engineering some crazy makeshift weapon and using it to slaughter an entire civilization that was pissing him off. He had no compunctions about self-destructing enemy vessels, violating long-standing peace treaties, and basically doing whatever he wanted to whomever he wanted at all times. He didn't bow down to a bunch of bureaucratic, unrealistic Starfleet regulations, shoved the Prime Directive up everyone's cloacas, and he didn't screw around when it came to weird xenomorph ham doctors that were just asking to have their space asses wrecked. He was such a lover that all the women under his command always wore supertight miniskirts and go-go boots, and such a fighter that he couldn't leave the ship without some red-shirted jobber getting frakulated by radioactive space-lightning or vaporized by a subatomic disintegration ray.

A big part of Kirk's badassery stems from his unrivaled prowess in martial arts, and his unbelievable willingness to settle most intergalactic diplomatic situations by directly insulting alien ambassadors to their faces and then pummeling them senseless if they get offended. He also preferred to beat his enemies down like a man, and usually took the most direct approach when dealing with jerkwads. The best example of this is probably the time he was in some mine on an uncharted planet, holding an old dude at gunpoint while the guy dug for something important. The old guy totally called Kirk out, giving him some crap about having an unfair advantage, so Kirk responded to this insult by ditching the phaser and beating the dude down with a mining trowel.

When Kirk breaks out the fisticuffs, nothing can stand before his powerful Shat-Fu. The Captain of Carnage had no compunctions about hurling himself into battle with a vicious, flying, double-leg drop-kick, flinging himself at his enemies like he was shot out of a damn cannon and ramming a pair of well-polished boots right into the fleshy parts of his enemies' disgusting alien abdomens. If that didn't immediately render his foes unconscious, Kirk could also unleash a vicious series of hammerfists (both one- and two-handed variants), as well as an ultra-badass open-hand JUDO EFFING CHOP to the neck so intense it could drop a blood-lusted Minotaur in its tracks. When Kirk drops the chop, it's all over, my friends. No creature in the universe can withstand its righteous ferocity. The brave captain had a wide range of attacks, bordering from the awesome to the ridiculous, but even though he couldn't really seem to kick above his waist, and tended to get slapped around by Spock whenever they battled, you still loved him anyway. That's primarily because this guy's first instinct in any fight-or-flight situation was to either punch or kiss—or, in the case of the time he escaped from an intergalactic penitentiary by seducing some random green-haired alien babe, by kissing and then closed-fist punching her in the mouth immediately afterward.

But it's not all just about cracking alien fighter pilots in their stupid space-faces, breaking Klingon bat'leths over his head, and photon-torpedoing Romulan vessels into the Delta Quadrant for Kirk. He understood the Holy Trinity of Space Captaining—you drop the flying hammerfist on the hideous evil alien spacemen, you blow up any vessel that doesn't have your country's logo emblazoned on its hull, and you make out with every hot alien babe you can get your hands on. And holy crap was he a space player. The women he met on his intrepid expeditions could have six heads, purple skin, four arms—it didn't matter. All chicks in the galaxy understood the universal language of Captain Kirk's space package, and all of them swooned like wounded doves every time he emerged from a fistfight with a giant taloned alien monster with half of his uniform top ripped off. He had hot alien women flinging themselves at him all across the universe, and didn't give two craps about ignoring Starfleet regulations, disobeying direct orders, and swooping down to the Bikini Beach Blanket Bingo planet for a couple days of 1960s-style surfing parties and scoring with every scantily clad bipedal alien female he thought was even remotely attractive. He was such a space pimp that it's no surprise that he was in on the first interracial kiss in American television history—and I'm not just talking about that time that he got it on with Uhura, either, because he was also responsible for the first televised human–Vulcan kiss, human–Green-Skinned Alien Chick kiss, human–Robo-Cyborg Space Dominatrix kiss, and human–Alien Psycho Murdering Shapeshifter Babe make-out session as well. He was a pioneer in the art of space-frenching.

The closest thing Kirk had to a lasting arch-nemesis was the evil tyrant Khan Noonien Singh, though even Khan had a tough time dealing with the JTK. Khan was a super-warrior from the futuristic 1990s, genetically engineered to have superhuman strength, unrivaled military intellect, and freakishly overdeveloped, rubbery pectorals, but our intrepid star captain wasn't impressed by any of that weak-sauce bullcrap. Kirk defrosted the toughest dictator in Earth's history from his cryogenic sleep, harassed him at the dinner table, beat him down with a lead pipe, then dumped him off on a remote, uninhabited planet on the fringe of the galaxy and completely forgot about him. Without even trying, Kirk accidentally pissed Khan off so hard that the dude spent the next fifteen years plotting revenge at all costs, eventually pursuing the *Enterprise* around the Antares Maelstrom and around Perdition's flames, but then Kirk denied him his space vengeance by tearing the guy's starship a new bunghole with a half-dozen well-aimed photon torpedoes and then celebrating by bringing a bunch of Klingons aboard the *Enterprise* and self-destructing it.

Basically, Kirk was awesome. This guy wasn't interested in any problem that couldn't be solved by making out with a hot babe or kicking an alien in the junk; he had one of the coolest first officers in the history of science fiction; and his job was just to fly through the galaxy in a top-of-the-line spaceship having all sorts of crazy adventures. When he was on a planet and had to fight a superstrong Gorn lizard-warrior leader in a green rubber monster costume, he friggin' built a homemade howitzer out of materials he found lying around in the desert in the middle of a duel, shot the alien in the face with his space cannon, and saved the *Enterprise* from destruction. Without even trying, he made a Vulcan princess fall in love with him so hard that Spock got pissed and tried to lop his head off with a razor-sharp *American Gladiators* jousting mallet. Kirk even came face-to-face with God once, and was just like "whatever, dude." That's how he rolled.

The Klingons are a pretty hardcore race of leather-clad space bikers, and their mythology is no less face-rending than they are. According to the ancient mystical history of the Klingon people, their race was created by the gods, but then rebelled against their makers, slaughtered all of them, and incinerated Heaven with blowtorches. Their most famous legendary hero was a dude appropriately named Kahless the Unforgettable. The founder of the Klingon Empire, its first ruler, and the greatest of all the warriors in Klingon history, Kahless was a righteous head-cleaving insane person who fought entire armies by himself, invented the bat'leth, overthrew a brutal tyrant, and passed on a badass code of honor to his people. Though Kahless's physical form departed the mortal realm long ago, he now rules Klingon Valhalla—a place called Sto-vo-kor, where all honorable warriors go after being slain in bloody combat.

Star Trek II: The Wrath of Khan is based on *Moby-Dick*, except Khan is Captain Ahab and Kirk is the whale. To bring the whole thing full-circle, in the made-for-TV version of Melville's classic, Ahab was portrayed by Patrick Stewart, who, of course, was Captain Picard on *Star Trek: The Next Generation*. The whale in that one was played by an actual whale.

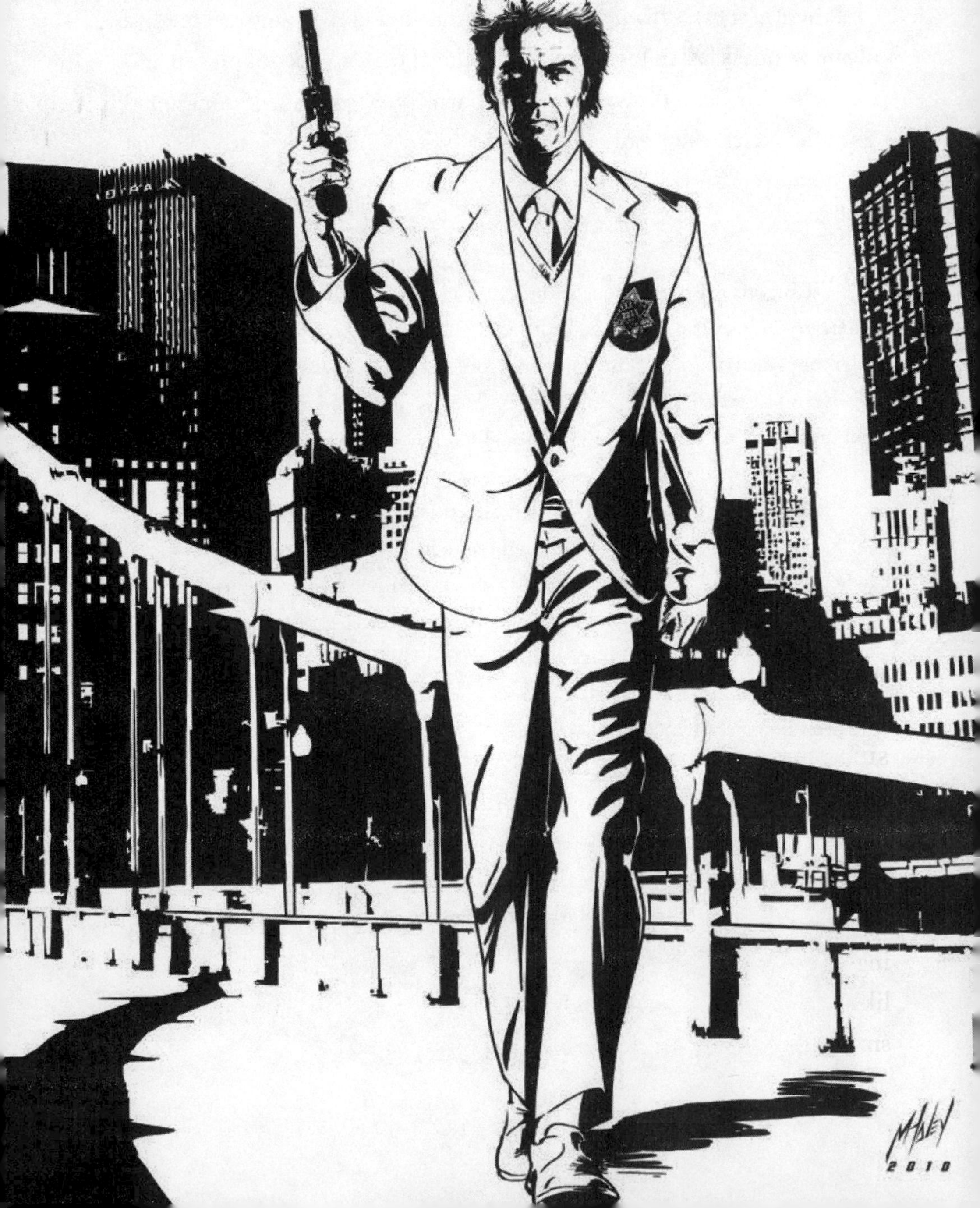
2010

19

INSPECTOR HARRY CALLAHAN

I know what you're thinking—"Did he fire six shots or only five?" Well, to tell you the truth, in all this excitement I kind of lost track myself. But being as this is a .44 Magnum, the most powerful handgun in the world, and would blow your head clean off, you've got to ask yourself one question: "Do I feel lucky?" Well, do ya, punk?

IF SOMEONE WERE TO ASK ME TO DEFINE WHAT I MEAN BY THE WORD "BADASS," I WOULD TELL THEM TO JUST GO OUT, RENT THE FILM *DIRTY HARRY*, AND PREPARE TO BE PISTOL-WHIPPED INTO SUBMISSION BY THE ULTIMATE PHYSICAL EMBODIMENT OF LIVING BADASSITUDE. The first film in the epic saga of the mind-blowingly hardcore San Francisco Police Inspector Harry Callahan is like an instructional guide to not giving a crap about anything except bashing punks in the face with a half-dozen bullets, explosively destroying everything within a two-block radius, handing out ass-whippings like parking tickets, and slowly walking away with nothing but flames, smashed cars, and smoldering carnage in your wake.

Needless to say, much of his apocalyptic awesomeness stems from the fact that Dirty Harry is played by Clint Eastwood. It's a well-documented fact that Clint is the ultimate existential man, and easily one of the most daunting human beings to ever live—between his unblinking, withering stare, his "one eye opened, one eye half-closed and twitching" look of fury, and his gravelly, commanding voice, he's one of the few people in the world who can make the word "marvelous" actually sound tough. This isn't a guy who tears your nuts off with his fist—this is a guy who can intimidate you into tearing your *own* nuts off and eating them. Seriously, I'd take an eighty-year-old Clint Eastwood straight-up in a street fight against anyone, ever, without hesitation.

By association, Harry Callahan is the sort of guy who wins battles before they've even started. This fearless hardass doesn't blink, he doesn't show fear, he doesn't back down, and he completely hates everything. Like, a lot. This guy even hates people trying to commit suicide—one time he "talked a guy down" from a ledge by insulting the would-be jumper, punching him in the face, and dragging the poor face-punched chump's unconscious body down the side of the building. His threats are so convincing and he's so openly hostile and intimidating that lesser men don't even attempt to stand in his way—they throw down their weapons without even putting up a fight, which is always an intelligent move when you're staring down the barrel of Callahan's Smith & Wesson Model 29 revolver. Everybody around him spends so much time crapping themselves, you'd think he'd set his cell phone ringtone to the brown note, and punks rarely feel lucky enough to test his patience. For instance, when Callahan took down some ultrapowerful mob boss (a high-profile arrest so routine for Callahan that the films didn't even bother to show it on-screen), he had the kindness to leave the dude with a functioning respiratory system for some reason. Unfortunately for the Mafia, the colossally stupid incarcerated criminal mastermind had the balls to thank Callahan by sending a bunch of hit men out to assassinate him. Instead of doing something rational, like requesting police protection or looking underneath his car in the morning to check for C-4 explosive charges tied into his ignition system, Callahan just got super-ripped pissed-off, jumped in his sweet car, road-raged down to San Quentin State Penitentiary, and personally threatened the guy so viciously that the mob boss actually hired thugs to follow Callahan around and protect him from any other potential dangers that might somehow arise. (Callahan pummeled both of them senseless, of course, telling them, "Don't [fornicate] with me buddy or I'll kick your ass so hard you're going to have to unbutton your collar to take a [defecation break].") Just for fun, he also threatened a different Mafia boss at the guy's granddaughter's wedding and freaked the don out so hard that the guy died of a heart attack on the spot. Harry was so gargantuanly tough that he would have kicked Al Capone in the lunchbox in front of his own gang if he had the chance, so you can imagine how he dealt with guys who weren't high-ranking leaders of all-powerful criminal organizations.

I can say without exaggeration or hesitation that Inspector Callahan is probably the most badass man ever. This guy just oozes testosterone out of every pore of his body. He doesn't have any friends, his partners all end up either in the hospital or the morgue, and his girlfriends can generally just expect to get shoved violently to the floor at the first sign of danger, because violence is the only emotion he is capable of openly displaying. He destroys everything he touches, and the only things that seem to make his day involve shooting pool, eating greasy food, drinking black coffee, throwing back Schlitz out of the can, and smoking punks in the face with large-caliber handgun ammunition. He has absolutely no respect for authority, traffic laws, reporters, his own safety, or the Bill of Rights, and seems to break five amendments every time he arrests a guy. Every other minute he's getting his ass chewed out by his superiors for excessive violence or being too awesome or some other such inane bullcrap, but he totally doesn't even care about any of that as long as he gets his man and brings him to a special blend of justice that falls roughly somewhere between due process and back-alley vigilantism. Callahan doesn't run fast, he doesn't jump high, he has a hard time driving a car without crashing it or almost killing pedestrians, but he's unyielding, relentless, and ball-chillingly ruthless once he's on the job. He always gets his man, no matter how many people he needs to destroy to do it, and you'd better not get in his way unless you enjoy being kicked in the head repeatedly with your own severed leg.

Plus, for some reason, it seems like everywhere he goes there are topless 1970s babes, even if it doesn't fit into the plot in any meaningful way at all. You still appreciate it anyway (usually).

Beyond the fact that this guy is the prototypical American badass, Inspector Callahan's service record speaks for itself. He won the police combat shooting championship every year except for one, and he ended up eventually killing the dude who beat him. For whatever reason, Callahan seems to particularly excel at the moderately uncomfortable "shoot a man's crotch" targets—so much so that one time, in a full live-fire combat situation, he shot a thug in the dick while the dude was running up a flight of stairs in a futile, impotent effort to escape our pipe-laying hero. He beat a confession out of a corrupt priest in a church confessional. He hung on to the roof of a speeding school bus full of kids being driven by a crazy pedophile psychopath, then had an epic showdown with the dude in an abandoned rock quarry. He told the chief of police to cram his badge up his ass (referring to it as a "six-pointed suppository") moments before receiving a commendation for bravery, then, while suspended from the job, he stormed Alcatraz without a warrant, shot a Communist terrorist off a lookout tower with a ship-mounted fire hose, blew a guy apart with a LAWS rocket, and saved the mayor of San Francisco from militant kidnappers. He broke up a tense hostage situation by crashing his car through the front window of a liquor store and busting a half-inch of lead into the torsos of a dozen shotgun-toting criminal scumbags. When he went up against a trio of corrupt motorcycle cops, he plowed one of them with the hood of a badass 1970s muscle car, karate-chopped another in the throat like a thousand times, and out x-tremed the third by jumping over an aircraft carrier on a motorcycle. He also impaled a serial killer with a harpoon gun that once belonged to Guns N' Roses guitarist Slash, which was pretty damn weird, though not as bizarre as the time he dropped a rapist onto the horn of a merry-go-round unicorn at an abandoned fairground.

Dirty Harry can't even eat lunch without people being carted off in body bags. On one particularly hardcore occasion, he bought a hot dog, then shot three guys, smashed a car, demolished half a city block, and stopped a bank robbery in progress before he was even done chewing. Another time he was getting a burger at the airport and the next thing you know, he was going undercover as an international pilot (despite not actually knowing how to fly an airplane), and thwarting a terrorist hijacking by shooting through a passenger-filled airplane cabin and smoking a couple Tangoes' heads apart with his Magnum. The only time we ever see him go out on a date, he gets in a glass elevator that gets shot apart with Uzis and has to blast a couple guys in the back while they spinelessly flail away from him. That doesn't stop him from hooking up with her, of course . . . she was a hot reporter babe that wanted to do a story on him, but not only does he not do the story; he ends up sleeping with her, too. Did I mention that he's the ultimate "man's man"?

In *Dirty Harry* for the Commodore 64, you replenished your health bar by eating chili dogs. It's hard not to like a character that has a mechanic that delicious built into his video game.

→ TOUGH COPS ←

ROBOCOP

A giant walking cyborg police officer with bulletproof armor and a machine pistol built into a hidden compartment in his leg, Robocop is an emotionless automaton of thug-smiting justice. Forged together from a mix of top-of-the-line military equipment, old car batteries, and the limited remains of Detroit patrolman Alex J. Murphy, Robocop always walks around like he has a stick lodged in whatever remains of his anus, and has trouble with magnets from time to time, but his body-count is so prolific that you can't possibly deny his cred. In addition to proving to the mentally unstable ED-209 that having chain guns for arms is no match for a good set of workable legs, Robocop is one of the few to avenge his own death—a task he performs by throwing the dad from *That '70s Show* through like a hundred windows and then stabbing him in the neck with a Wolverine-style fist-spike. I also once saw him shoot a ninja's head off.

CORDELL WALKER

Texas Rangers are serious business in any situation, but never is this statement truer than when that Ranger is Chuck Norris. The ultimate mega-hero in every possible way, Cordell Walker is capable of performing tremendous feats of awesome without warning, at all times. Every car he shoots immediately explodes, he communicates telepathically with animals, and teaches valuable life lessons to the kids, all while taking down the Dallas–Fort Worth metro area's toughest evildoers by roundhouse-kicking them so hard that their rib cages explode out through their spines.

In true Chuck Norris fashion, Walker's preferred method of rescuing the assistant district attorney when she's inevitably captured by the bad guys is by launching a one-man assault on a heavily defended terrorist compound, commando-rolling away from danger like a bearded panther, and obliterating all opposition with a series of brutal face-kicks, slow-motion face-kicks, and super-slow-motion face-kicks. Things explode while he is doing this.

INSPECTOR TEQUILA

John Woo's mass-murdering detective with a flair for the ridiculous, Chow Yun Fat's character in the grossly underappreciated action flick *Hard Boiled* is one of the toughest bastards to ever fly backward through the air shooting people in the kneecaps with a matched set of pistols. Don't be fooled by the eccentricity associated with being named after a distinctly non-Chinese brand of alcohol, his propensity for playing the clarinet, and his love for fizzy drinks—this guy is stone-cold. Whether he's sliding down handrails in a bullet-riddled tea shop, shooting up a terrorist-controlled hospital with a thermonuclear shotgun, or leaping through fireballs while clutching a baby he just met, Tequila can't seem to go anywhere without that place turning into a raging warzone. He's so murder-rific that he even overcomes the limitations of firearms and physics—every gun he touches is blessed with the IDKFA infinite-ammo cheat and immediately has ten to twenty times the stopping power of its real-life counterpart, allowing this Hong Kong cop to detonate motorcycles with a shotgun and cause a trail of explosions to follow him everywhere he goes.

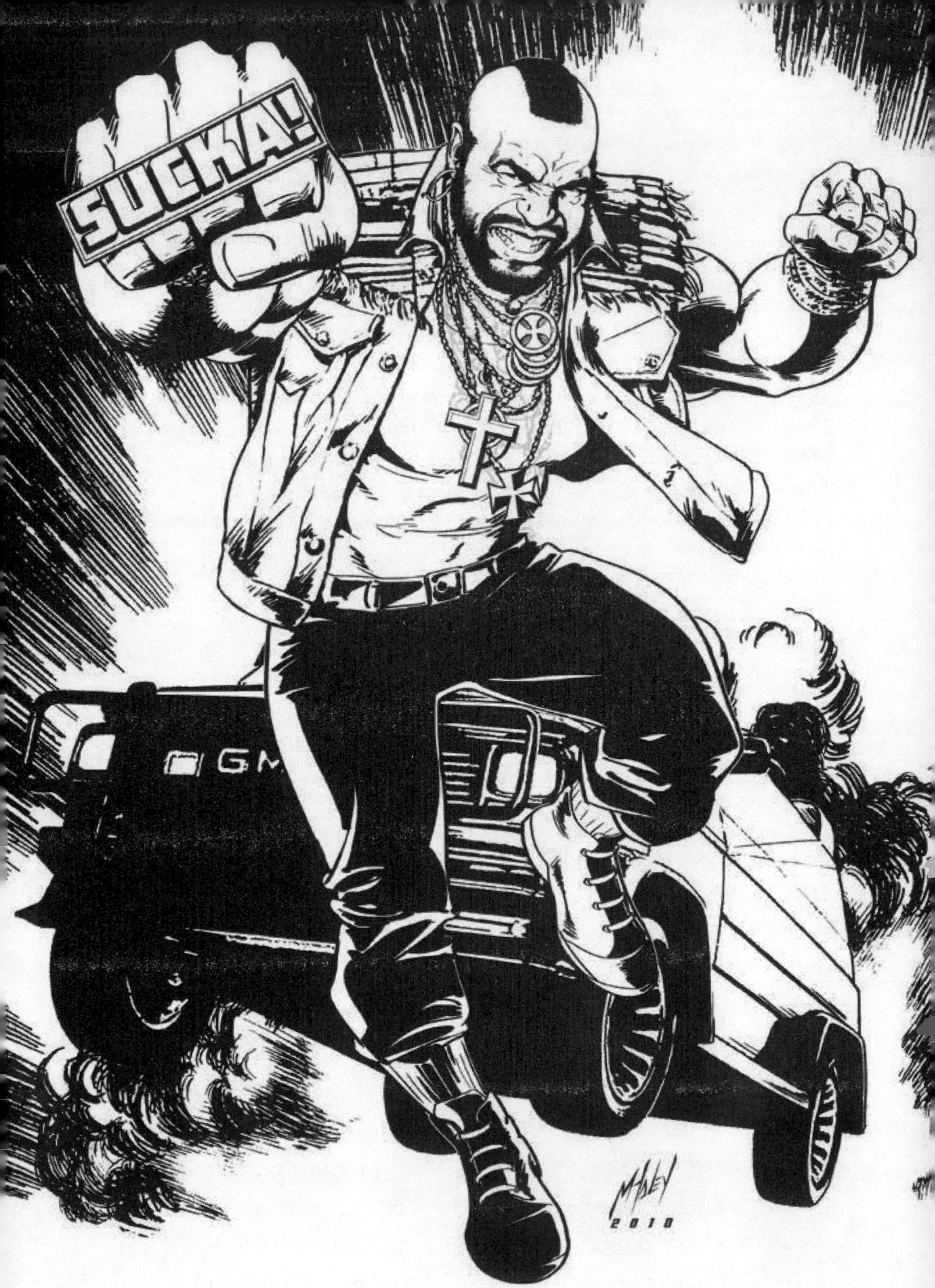
SUCKA!
2010

20

B. A. BARACUS

We don't file grievances. We file death reports.

B. A. BARACUS WAS AN EX-MILITARY MERCENARY FACE-PUNCH-FOR-HIRE WHO WAS SO HARDCORE THAT HE'S BECOME A CULTURAL ICON FOR 1980s TELEVISION BADASSES. A sergeant in the U.S. Army Special Forces during the Vietnam war, B. A. overcame the seemingly crippling obstacle of being named "Boscoe Albert Baracus" by intimidatingly responding to any inquiries involving his name that his initials stood for "Bad Attitude," then daring anybody to suggest otherwise. "Bad Ass" would perhaps also have been an appropriate ackronym, but only if Mr. T was one of those guys who for whatever reason felt bizarrely obligated to break badass out into two words. While kicking asses, curb-stomping scrotums, and saving Hulk Hogan's life alongside the Green Berets in 'Nam, B. A. was a heavy-weapons expert and a mechanical genius who could build, fix, or jerry-rig anything from a broken bicycle chain to a full-scale Mad Cat OmniMech. While it's true that Bad Attitude had a nasty habit of punching out his commanders any time they failed to successfully curtail the jibber-jabber, the sorts of beatings he laid upon the enemy were so much more cringe-worthy that nobody really seemed to mind the occasional gross misconduct or charges of assault on superior officers.

If you go back to the whole argument that everything badass in fiction has already been done before, Baracus's story actually bears some pretty striking similarities to the myth of Hercules. Baracus, like Herc, was a super-strong, bone-crushing asskicker who was unbeatable in hand-to-hand combat, and both dudes had a propensity for clutching fools by the jugular, military-pressing them over their heads, and then hurling them through the air like meat-grenades until they exploded through a second-story window. Also like Hercules, Baracus was an epic hero who ended up getting into some serious trouble for a crime he only sort-of committed.

Despite what the opening sequence of *The A-Team* may have you believe, Baracus was part of a top-secret government mission that went deep behind enemy lines to rob the Bank of Hanoi in an attempt to throw North Vietnam's economy into disarray. True, he was only acting on orders, but when his commanding officer ended up dead and all trace of the mission was destroyed, he found himself getting arrested and tossed into a maximum-security stockade in Fort Bragg, North Carolina. Baracus escaped with the help of his former team members, presumably by tearing the wall off of the prison with his bare hands and walking into the sunset still clutching the ripped-in-half cinderblocks, and then, much like Hercules, he sought to atone for his crimes by traveling the land, helping out any defenseless people in need of a guy so strong he could rip a guy's arm clean off at the elbow. Whereas Hercules performed his labors solo, with only the occasional help of some ambitious gods (which was totally cheating, by the way), Baracus traveled around with a crazy lunatic pilot, a cigar-chomping tactical mastermind, and Lieutenant Starbuck from *Battlestar Galactica*. Violence ensued, as it did pretty much any time Mr. T went anywhere or did anything.

B. A. Baracus excelled in putting his initials on dirtbags' brains, then hurling them into their fellow-dirtbag associates. Sporting a sweet Mohawk modeled after the hairstyle of the Mandika tribal warriors of Western Africa and pimped out with a pirate treasure-chest worth of gold chains and a pair of earrings made from human scalps, Baracus forged new and wondrous things upside his enemies' heads by cracking them in the skull with a fist weighted down by twenty pounds worth of diamond-studded gold rings so hefty it makes a roll of quarters in the fist look like a boxer punching a guy with a giant pink carnival teddy bear duct-taped to his knuckles. Everything he touched ended up registering a ten on the BA scale, with ten being TOTAL PAIN. Unbeatable in one-on-one tests of strength, Baracus also benefited from being seemingly immune to all manner of physical attacks. He was never shot, he survived horrific car wrecks and explosions, and any attempts to strike him with something less powerful than a nuclear explosion just resulted in Mr. T blankly staring his assailant down *just long enough* for the sucka to realize he was boned, before concussing his lights out with one rock-hard haymaker of inescapable doom.

Aside from his crippling fear of air travel, Baracus wasn't afraid of anything, and he never backed down from a fool looking for a fight. One time, this crazy ninja totally flipped out hard, whipped out two swords, and started trying to demonstrate his katana skillz, but B. A. Baracus—who was holding the dude at gunpoint at the time—calmly handed his revolver to Hannibal, cracked his knuckles, and laid the ninja out with one swift jack to the face. BA, being awesome, then looked down at the broken-faced ninja lying on the deck, and defiantly exclaimed, "Hiya THAT, sucka!" During his missions helping the poor and underprivileged peoples of the world, he showed that violence sometimes actually can solve all of life's problems. Baracus beat up Nazis, cultists, guerrillas, terrorists, hijackers, dope dealers, and anything else that stood in his way. One time, he blew a couple of dudes up with a nineteenth-century cannon just to be eccentric and diversify his pain portfolio. This guy was so hardcore with his powers of getting pissed and not giving a crap that he even flipped over a table and punched out a couple military policemen during his own court-martial, then subsequently tried to intimidate the firing squad that was sent to execute him for treason.

There were really only four things that Baracus exceled at, but they just so happened to be four of the primary prerequisites of badassi-tude—intimidation, punching, cooking chili, and driving. While he was comfortable behind the wheel of anything larger than a moped, there's no doubt that he's best known for his skills in the driver's seat of the iconic black-and-red 1983 GMC A-Team van. In the hands of B. A. Baracus, this ordinarily creepy, spoiler-clad windowless conver-sion van handled like the *General Lee* and hit like Optimus Prime in truck mode. It was right up there with the Airwolf chopper, KITT, and Marty McFly's flux-capacitor-equipped DeLorean in terms of sheer 1980s awesomeness. This thing was so hardcore that it couldn't even drive down the street to the grocery store without a couple of open-top jeeps speeding in out of nowhere, exploding, and flying a few hundred feet into the air.

An iron-fisted crusader for justice, Bad Attitude wasn't interested in any-thing that didn't involve cracking skulls or stomping on a gas pedal. Air-borne vehicles were his primary adversary, though he also hated dentists, vegetarians, brass bands, Irish proverbs, coincidences, sleeves, and his own coworkers. He didn't have time for the jibber-jabber, he didn't wear disguises, he pitied fools, and he usually made good on the excellently cre-ative threats he dished out with almost the same frequency as face punches.

Despite the fact that it's hard to envision a situation in which B. A. Baracus wasn't shattering someone's jaw with a right hook, he still tried to make an honest effort to use his powers only for good. He tried to help people out, rarely accepted payment for his services, and always made sure that the kids drank their milk, stayed off drugs, said their prayers, and were good to their mothers. B.A. is just cool like that.

I've been writing about badasses long enough to know that it's never really a good idea to disrespect super-ripped dudes named Rampage, but as far as I'm concerned, B. A. Baracus will always be synonymous with one man—Mr. T. The second-youngest of twelve kids, T spent most of his youth living a hard life on the South Side of Chicago. His single mother somehow provided for her family on a salary that could probably best be described as "laughable," and the family often had to go without food. As an adult, Mr. T played football, and even tried out for the Green Bay Packers, but after he blew his knee out during tryouts he joined the Army and served as a military policeman for a while. After serving his country, T became a nightclub bouncer, and was so hardcore that he won NBC's reality TV contest "The World's Toughest Bouncer." Deciding that soldier, football player, and bouncer were all jobs that didn't provide him enough excitement during his daily life, he turned to the carefree life of a bodyguard instead. T ended up serving as a bodyguard to Muhammad Ali, Steve McQueen, and Joe Frazier—three super-hardcore dudes who could take care of themselves in most situations, though it never hurts to have a giant ass-wrecking psycho like Mr. T watching your back. Not even lymphoma could take this guy down—in 2004, he beat cancer, probably through a daily regimen that involved standing in front of the mirror and directly threatening his own lymph nodes.

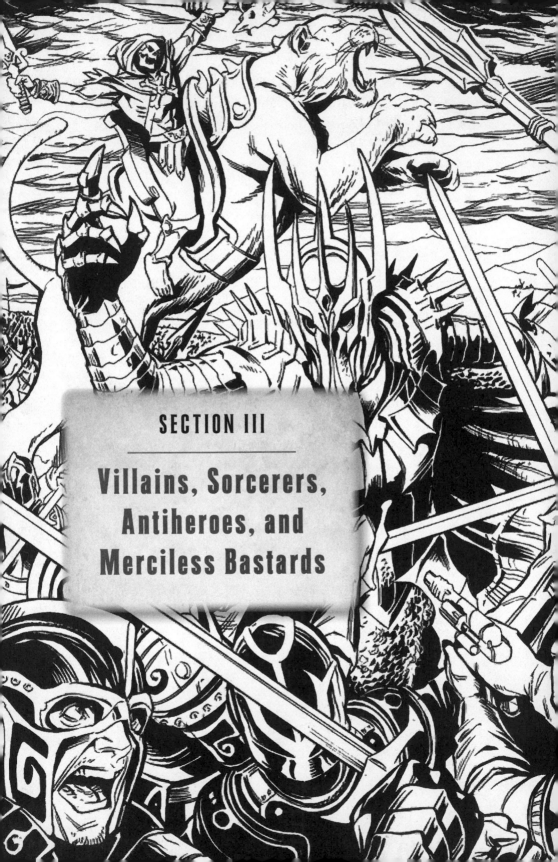

SECTION III

Villains, Sorcerers, Antiheroes, and Merciless Bastards

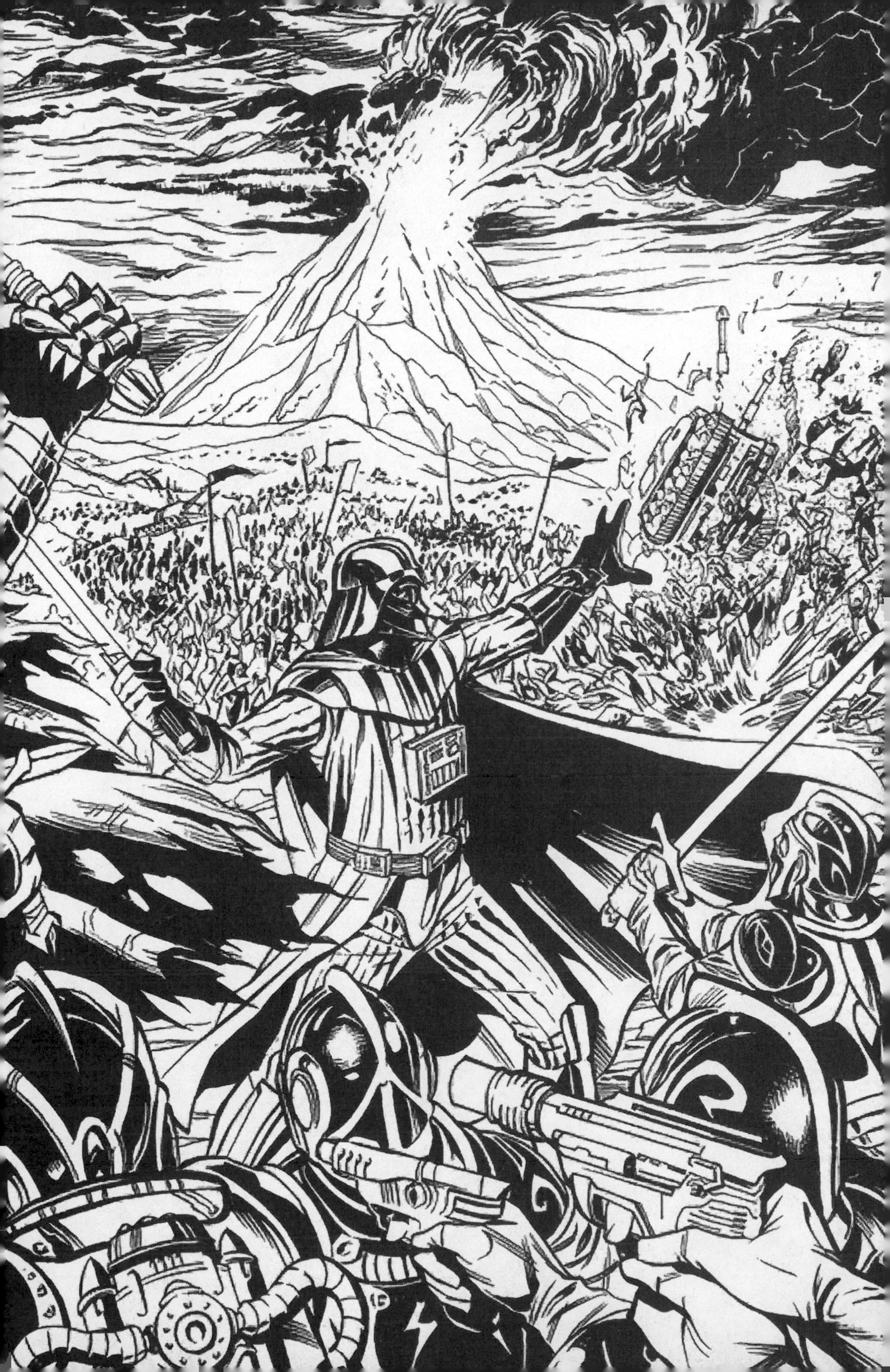

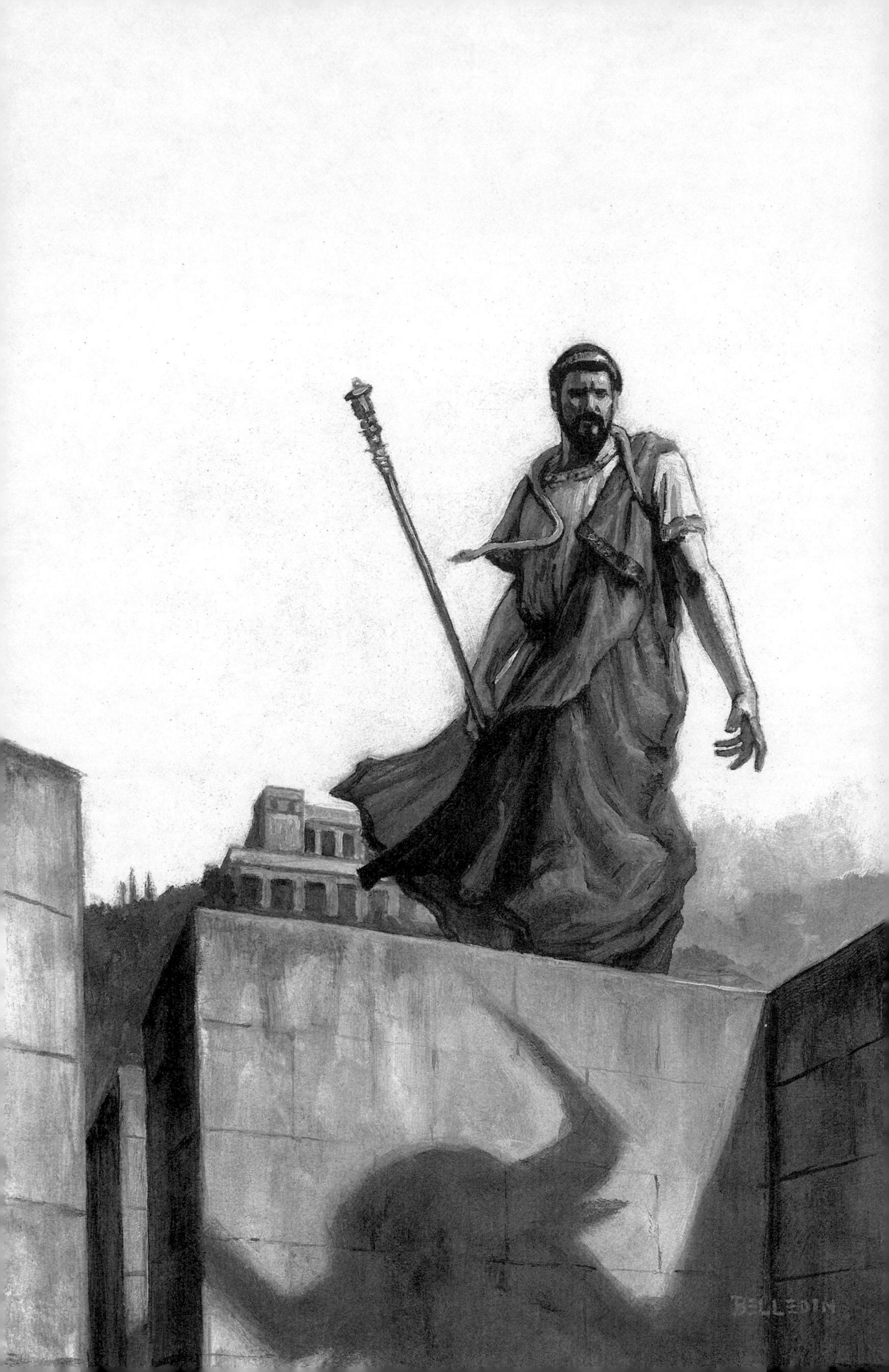
BELLEDIN

21

KING MINOS

Minos was there, scowling and terrible,
Examining the faults of new arrivals;
He judges them, and sends each to his place.

—DANTE, *THE INFERNO*

KING MINOS WAS CONCEIVED WHEN ZEUS MORPHED HIMSELF INTO
A GIANT BULL AND GOT IT ON WITH EUROPA, THE MORTAL WOMAN
WHO NOW LENDS HER NAME TO THE CONTINENT OF EUROPE. As
I mentioned previously, Zeus was more of a "love 'em and leave 'em"
sort of guy than a devoted father who sent graduation cards and took a
bunch of boring home videos, so young Minos ended up being passed
off to be raised by the king of Crete. After the death of the king, Minos
exterminated his half-brothers—presumably the rightful heirs to the
throne—in a good old-fashioned bitter succession war, pried the crown
from his father's corpse, led Crete to a period of unprecedented power
in the Mediterranean, and started a bitchin' career that would make
him the primary antagonist in some of the most popular and over-the-
top Greek myths ever recorded.

Early in his career as supreme dictator of Crete, Minos was

MC'ing a festival when he got totally pumped up and started free-styling a bunch of crazy nonsense into the mic about how Poseidon should send him a magical bull that he could sacrifice to the gods in his honor. Poseidon, who was always down for a good spontaneous animal sacrifice, responded by sending a huge majestic white bull charging horns-first out of the ocean in a one-beast albino stampede that left everyone standing around rubbing their eyes in disbelief. Minos took one look at the majestic killing machine and was like, "Holy fart balls, dude, this thing is totally sweet—there's no way I'm chopping this bad boy up!" So he sacrificed his second-best bull instead, and led this behemoth out to the royal pastures to chillax for a while. Poseidon, who is known for responding to any perceived disses with his trademark unyielding death-rages, was all like, "Okay, dude, if that's the way you wanna play it, let's go," and he turned Minos's wife into a rampaging font of bestiality. She fell madly in love with the white bull, and after some freakiness I don't really care to go into right now, she gave birth to the Minotaur—a giant, totally jacked muscle-man with a bull's head, a cool-looking nose ring, and totally sweet horns for goring the ever-loving ass out of people. After fathering the Minotaur, the white bull completely blew a gasket in the part of its brain that makes it not completely flip out, and ran around Crete in an unstoppable riot of stabbing, smashing, and maiming, and raising all kinds of hell before Hercules eventually showed up and choked some sense into the beast with his iron Kevin Sorbo fists.

Even though he wasn't super-happy that his wife banged a bull, Minos realized that not a lot of wealthy kings can say that they have totally sweet man-eating bull monsters for stepsons. He did what any good, loving father would have done in this situation, and built an awesome, brain-bustingly confusing Labyrinth for the creature to run around in and eat people at its leisure. Minos named the creature Asterion, but everybody just called it the Minotaur, because that was way easier to remember. It's also a mash-up of "Minos" and "Taurus," and is sort of like the Ancient Greek way of saying, "King Minos's Awesome Head-Smashing Bull Man."

It should go without saying that Minos didn't construct the Labyrinth by himself, because when you're a maniacal dictator you can just hire people to do that sort of stuff for you. For this particular project, the Cretan tyrant found a convicted murderer and disgraced evil genius architect named Daedalus. Daedalus was pretty much the closest thing Greek myth has to a mad scientist—"mad architect" doesn't necessarily carry the same connotation, but you get the idea. Daedalus had been in a little bit of trouble back in Athens when he became jealous of another builder and ended up flinging the dude off the top of the Acropolis, but Minos had no real moral compunctions about hiring a psychotic madman to construct a sprawling subterranean terror-drome—it probably made him better-suited to the job.

Since Minos was already commissioning the creation of gigantic ridiculous things, he also had the blacksmith god Hephaestus forge Talos—a giant, fifty-foot tall bronze golem who ran around Crete all day and lobbed hull-smashing boulders at passing ships for no good reason. As if it wasn't sweet enough that this thing was the forerunner of gunslinging mechs, this huge, steam-powered robo-bastard is also said to have killed a bunch of Sardinians by jumping into a fire, making his metallic body super-hot, and then breaking off a thermonuclear man-hug that incinerated a dozen guys on the spot.

But it wasn't all about huge palaces, giant androids, and secret underground lairs for King Minos—like with any decent evil genius, there was also the whole world-domination thing. While smashing armies and exerting his dominance over Greece, Minos went to war with King Nisus of Megara over something that may or may not have been important. The Cretans were victorious when Nisus' daughter, princess Scylla, fell madly in love with Minos and betrayed her own father for him. She destroyed her dad, subverted the city, and then threw herself at Vitamin M when he marched his armies triumphantly through the gates of Megara. Minos, however, had no respect for anyone who would kill their own parents, and when he saw this chick, he just shrugged and sailed out of town without her. Scylla swam after the boat, desperate to get a piece of that sweet sweet Minos action, but he didn't even slow down. She eventually got tired and drowned.

That's just how things went down when Minos rolled into town. This guy was a brutal autocrat, sure, but chicks dig that sometimes, and this dude more or less had half-nude women flinging themselves at him everywhere he went. He got busy with maidens, nymphs, goddesses, and anything else he could get his hands on, and he ended up having like twenty kids from a veritable harem of girlfriends and mistresses, both mortal and divine. His wife eventually got pissed and placed a curse on him that made him randomly shoot scorpions and snakes out of his junk, which sounds kind of awesome in theory but was probably a lot less so in practice. Also, from that point on, any woman who slept with him died immediately afterward, which pretty much sucked. You'd think that since this guy's wife had once cheated on him with a friggin' bull, she wouldn't have a whole lot of room to talk about marital fidelity, but there you have it.

The most famous myth involving Minos has the king sending his favorite son to Athens to compete in some hardcore Festivus-style feats of strength. Minos Jr. did well and all, but things took a turn for the worse when he was betrayed and backstabbed to death by the jerkface leader of Athens. Minos, being the humorless conqueror that he was, responded by blockading the city, crushifying the Athenian military, and then ordering the gods to call down droughts, famines, and earthquakes to ruin the asses of everything in mainland Greece. The Athenians, utterly ruined, begged the Cretan King for mercy, and Minos agreed to call off the impending apocalypse if the Athenians swore to provide seven men and seven women every year to be served up as food for the Minotaur. The Athenians agreed.

For the next decade or so, the Athenians shipped off fourteen youths a year to the Labyrinth, and the Minotaur bit their faces off and devoured them. Things were going great until some jerk hero named Theseus got his tunic in a wad about the whole Minotaur head-nomming arrangement and volunteered to go to Crete and slay the semi-cannibalistic creature. Unfortunately for Minos, his daughter fell in love with Theseus when she saw him walking in at the head of that year's King Minos' Annual New Year's Death-Buffet Parade. She slept with him, divulged the secrets of the Labyrinth, and gave her new boyfriend a magical ball of thread that would help him find his way back out of the maze alive. Theseus snuck into the Labyrinth in the middle of the night, valiantly killed the Minotaur in its sleep, escaped, stole a boat, and led the rest of the Athenian prisoners to freedom. The intrepid hero repaid Minos's daughter for her invaluable aid by abandoning her on an island somewhere in the middle of the ocean, and then on the way home he accidentally caused the violent death of his own father by forgetting to give the signal that he was returning home safely. He would later end up getting imprisoned in Hades for trying to bone the queen of the Underworld. Theseus was kind of an inept dickhead, if you ask me, yet people still seem to love him for some reason.

Needless to say, Minos was pretty upset that this punk kid had swooped in, cheap-shotted the Minotaur to death, and then marooned the princess on an uncharted island. Unable to find Theseus, the Cretan ruler instead directed his uncontrollable anger at Daedalus, who not only had built a crappy, substandard Labyrinth, but who had also had the brilliant idea of creating the magic ball of thread that the Minotaur-slaying hero had used to escape the dungeon alive. Minos grabbed the crazy artificer, locked him and his son, Icarus, in a tower, and started thinking about how badass it was going to be when he slowly tortured the two of them to death. While imprisoned in the tower, Daedalus somehow managed to MacGyver together two sets of working bird-like wings, and he and Icarus jumped out the window and started to fly around by flapping their arms up and down like lunatics. Unfortunately for Daedalus, his son was a total moron, and flew too close to the sun—his wings melted or caught on fire or something, and Icarus plummeted a few thousand feet down into the ocean, dying from the most epic belly-flop ever recorded. When King Minos heard about this, he laughed his ass off for like a week straight.

Daedalus, however, managed to escape by flying across the sea to a nearby island, but Minos's navy was hot on his trail. The Cretan king hunted the mad architect down and prepared to gut him with a butter knife, but the night before he was going to make his move, the D-Train got the drop on him and killed his would-be captor by climbing up on the roof of Minos's hotel, putting a pipe through the ceiling of the royal bathroom and dumping boiling pitch on the dude while he was in the tub. This is an awful way to go.

King Minos's body was entombed in a Temple of Aphrodite, who didn't seem to mind the snakes-out-of-the-crotch thing all that much. His spirit went down into the Underworld, where Hades was so impressed by his kickass administrative skills and blazing-fast words-per-minute typing ability that he put the deceased ruler in charge of deciding whether dead souls were escorted to the beautiful paradise of the Elysian Fields or hurled into the black pit of Tartarus. Evidently, Minos's talents were still marketable even after Satan took over for Hades, because in Dante's *Inferno*, Minos is still chilling in the Underworld, working as Hell's version of Saint Peter and determining which Circle of Hell is an appropriate level of eternal face-melting agony for your pitiful condemned soul. I guess if you've got to be stuck doing the Devil's bidding and spending eternity burning in Hell, that has to be one of the sweetest gigs out there, so good for him for sticking with it.

According to Dante's *Inferno*, the Nine Circles of Hell, in ascending order of suckitude, are reserved for the virtuous non-Christians, the lustful, the gluttons, the greedy, the wrathful, the heretics, the violent, the corrupt, and the traitors. Satan himself is trapped in the middle of the Ninth Circle, encased in a waist-deep layer of ice from which he can never escape. He has three heads—one red, one black, and one yellow—and spends eternity chowing down on the hapless soul of Judas Iscariot, as well as those of Brutus and Cassius, the two men responsible for the betrayal and assassination of Julius Caesar. In Lucifer's defense, those guys had it coming.

—————

Minos is what we in the mythology biz like to refer to as a "semi-legendary king." This is really just a fancy-pants way of saying, "Yeah, there may have been an actual King Minos of Crete who did some pretty awesome stuff, but he probably didn't feed people to a giant cannibal bull-man and shoot scorpions out of his pants, and in general there was probably a lot less bovine genitalia involved in all aspects of his story."

—————

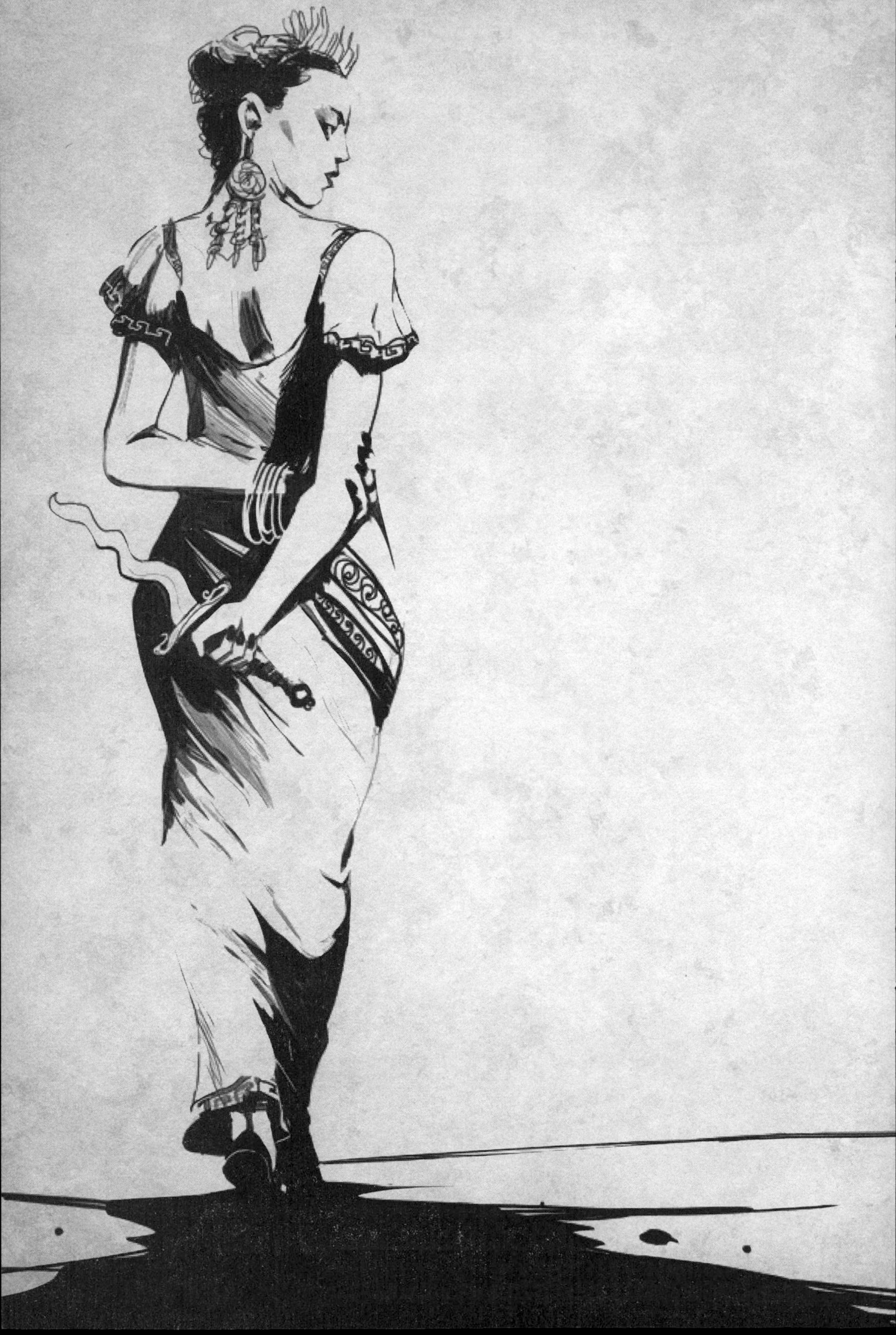

22

MEDEA

In craft and in darkness I will hunt his blood . . . sword in hand,
full-willed and sure to die,
I will yet live to slay them. For all their strength, they shall not
stab my soul and laugh thereafter!

MEDEA IS THE SORT OF HARDCORE CHICK THAT WOULD HAVE
SPENT MUCH OF HER TIME IN MYTHOLOGICAL GREECE GRACING
THE COVERS OF THE MOST BRUTAL AND HORRIFIC EDITIONS OF *US
WEEKLY* EVER PUBLISHED. Her life had all the juicy intrigue—love,
sex, betrayal, revenge, divorce, occult dealings, and bad-hair days—of
those trashy mags, and she capped it all off with a brutally overdeveloped love for murder, violence, and flammable substances so profound
that if "setting people on fire" were a Facebook status, Medea would
have Liked it.

We don't know a whole hell of a lot about what Medea's life was like
before the Argonauts drunkenly stumbled into her boring, peaceful little homeland, but we can assume that she probably spent most of her
time bitch-slapping dumbasses with fireballs and turning her father's
political rivals into shriveled, toxin-soaked corpses with an astonish-

ing array of freshly blended hemlock daiquiris. We know that she was the moderately goth princess of the island kingdom of Colchis, and a powerful devotee of Hecate, the chthonic Greek goddess of sorcery, witchcraft, necromancy, de-nutting people with a grapefruit spoon, and cheap canned Mexican beer.

Medea's life changed dramatically the day that the handsome adventurer Jason arrived in her father's court asking about the most sacred artifact in Colchis—the legendary Golden Fleece. Jason and his daring crew, a veritable All-Star team of mythological Greek heroes, had already guided their ship, the *Argo*, through an impossible number of tasks just to reach this far-off island. By this point in their quest, the Argonauts had already saved a miserable wretch from the clutches of the fearsome Harpies, fought the deadly iron-feathered Stymphalian Birds, accidentally slaughtered the peace-loving civilization of the Doliones, and bravely navigated their way through a treacherous island teeming with horny naked babes looking to shack up with them nonstop and deliver death by snoo-snoo.

Jason had accepted the quest for the Fleece because his evil uncle Pelias (an underhanded ass-casket who had usurped the throne from Jason's father) promised to relinquish the crown if Jason would first complete a mission to prove his worth. Jason, seeing an opportunity to do something awesome and make his uncle look like a jackass in the process, ran out and hired a crew. Jason was, however, completely oblivious to the fact that Pelias was playing him like Donkey Kong grandmaster Billy Mitchell working over a worn-out arcade cabinet in an empty old-school pizza parlor. Pelias knew damn well that Medea's dad was more likely to french Bigfoot than he was to hand over his kingdom's greatest relic to some tunic-wearing schmuck from the mainland, and when Jason came asking for handouts, the king set up a series of impossible tasks before this dude would even think about coughing up the goods. First, he had to yoke up these two cantankerous fire-breathing, bronze-hoofed bulls. If he somehow managed to hitch a plow to those bastards without detonating his head into a cauterized chunk of melted flesh, he then needed to sow a huge field with a bunch of dragon's teeth, each of which would spontaneously sprout into a cheesed-off, spear-swinging, armored warrior that Jason would then have to fight to the death. No problem, right?

After hearing his tale and realizing that young Jason was about twenty-four hours away from becoming an inside-out shell of what was once an endearingly moronic adventurer, Medea took pity on the poor guy's plight. She also thought he was really hot, which helped his case considerably. That night, the princess snuck out of her father's castle, made her way down to the beach, and professed her undying love for Jason. She promised to help him overcome these impossible trials with the power of evil magic if he would swear by the gods to marry her and take her away from this crappy miserable island she was stuck on. Jason, understandably seeing the "marry hot princess and get Golden Fleece" offer as a win-win situation, agreed. Medea gave her new first-date fiancé an *Epic Potion of Fire Resistance* to withstand the flaming bronze bulls and a custom-made magical rock of PCP that he could throw into the midst of the warriors and it would make them all get totally whacked out on angel dust and start beating the snot out of each other indiscriminately.

The next day, when the king saw Jason actually hitch up the plow, plant the field, and then defeat the warriors, he totally crapped a brick. With no interest in relinquishing the Fleece, and no way of honorably going back on his promise, the king figured that the best course of action at this point was just to hire a bunch of assassins to go into the Argonauts' camp in the middle of the night and stab everyone in the balls until they discovered what the insides of their scrotums looked like. Medea overheard her father's villainous plot to murder her new boyfriend and snuck out to warn Jason of his impending crotchal destruction. Under the cover of darkness, the Argonauts prepared the ship for departure, while Medea led Jason to the secret cave of the Golden Fleece. The Fleece was guarded by a gigantic killer dragon (which, like every other animal on this damned island, also breathed fire), but Medea put it to sleep with a magic spell that allowed Jason to straight-up snatch-and-grab the artifact from its narcoleptic protector.

When Medea and Jason returned to the *Argo*, they were confronted by Medea's brother, who was a little less than interested in letting these two lovebirds ditch town with the only non-lethal artifact the island of Colchis had to offer. Medea, being a woman of action, no matter how criminally insane it might be, responded to her arrest by knifing her own brother in the face and dragging his corpse aboard the *Argo*. The next day, when the king awoke and realized what was going on, he launched a huge fleet of warships to track down Jason and bring him back. Medea once again saved the Argonauts' asses in a gruesome manner—when the king's flagship was bearing down on the *Argo*, she sliced, diced, and cubed her brother into a bunch of tiny pieces and threw the disassembled corpse, bit by bit, into the ocean. The horrified king ordered his fleet to stop and recover all the pieces of his incredibly dead son so they could give him a legit burial, an order that slowed down his pursuit and gave the Argonauts time to escape. Hey, she may be a little misunderstood, but Medea doesn't get written up as a villain for nothing.

Since dismembering your family is rarely a reliable way to acquire positive karma points, Medea wisely directed the Argonauts to land on the island of the sorceress nymph Circe—Medea's aunt, a powerful magic-user, and a sly seductress best known for once turning Odysseus' men into pigs when they pissed her off (she eventually offered to turn them back to human form if Odysseus would agree to have sex with her . . . the women in this family obviously had a knack for negotiation). Circe purified the crew of their sins, and nobody commented on the irony of the situation. After that, the Argonauts passed the island of the Sirens, whose luring calls were drowned out by a flaming lute solo belted out by the mythological A-list rock star Orpheus, and landed on Crete, where they were promptly challenged to a molten-hot arm-wrestling competition by King Minos' giant iron man, Talos. Medea, being the sort of a chick who didn't take crap from fifty-foot-tall metallic golems no matter how serious they were, defeated the virtually indestructible mechanical construct by using her magic to yank a nail out of his ankle and bleed him of all his oil. Talos face-planted the Cretan beach, and before you know it, the *Argo* was beaching itself like a whale on the shores of Jason's homeland.

Jason's uncle, the evil King Pelias, was obviously a little perturbed that the suicide mission on which he sent Jason turned out to be slightly less murderous than he had hoped. Likewise, Jason wasn't too happy when he heard that Pelias had killed Jason's mom and dad, and that after all the bullcrap he'd been through, Pelias still had no interest in giving up the throne. Jason came to the cold, hard realization that the woolly hide of a golden ram didn't really have a whole lot of interesting powers that might help you overthrow a powerful king, which kind of put him into a minor existential meltdown. Well, forget the Fleece— the truth of the matter is that the most powerful weapon the Argonauts acquired on their journey was Medea herself. The homicidal sorceress got revenge on Pelias in a pretty hardcore way—not by murdering him directly (that would be too easy), but by manipulating the king's stupid daughters to slice their dad up and boil his dismembered corpse in a cauldron. Medea had convinced the daughters that this would restore their father to his youth and vigor. It didn't.

Jason and Medea were run out of town for the charge of regicide, moved to Corinth, and enjoyed ten years of married life, producing two children. Everything was going fine for the happy couple, until one fateful day when the king of Corinth decided he wanted to marry his daughter off to the renowned hero, the notably already-married

Jason. Jason, being a witless douchebag of epic proportions, decided that being a prince would be a really awesome endeavor, so he divorced Medea on the spot and agreed to marry this hoochie instead. When Medea got pissed about Jason ditching her for a newer model and renouncing the oaths he made to the gods, Jason had the balls to tell this serial murderess that he still liked her, and intended to keep her around as a concubine on the side. Then he offered her some money to shut her up.

Okay. I think I speak for most married men when I say that if I tried to pull a stunt like that on my wife, she would go on a berserker rampage that would make Medea's most ruthless escapades look like Malibu effing Barbie driving a pink Corvette through Candyland. This woman didn't bail Jason out of a dozen life-or-death situations, abandon her homeland, betray her family, and assassinate her own brother just to be one step above a prostitute, and saying that she was "a little upset" about this proposed arrangement would be like saying that self-trephining with a cordless drill is sort of a bad way to cure a hangover.

Medea's first act of vengeance was to give the princess of Corinth a seemingly innocuous engagement present—a luxurious silk robe that spontaneously burst into flames as soon as the girl put it on. When the present demonstrated its special powers, the king went running over to extinguish his bonfire of a daughter, but as soon as he touched her, he, too, turned into a human-size pillar of red-hot fire. Jason had the good sense not to touch either of them, and when he ran home to confront Medea about the conflagration massacre, she had already killed their kids and was in the process of taking off from the roof of her house in a fiery chariot pulled by dragons. That totally sounds like the sort of thing you'd see airbrushed on the side of a 1980s conversion van.

In her defense, it's possible that Medea gets a bad rap. According to some accounts of the myth, the Colchian priestess didn't actually murder her kids—she wasn't able to take them with her on the flying dragon-chariot, so she left them in the care of the priests at a local temple of Hera, where they were discovered and murdered by the Corinthians in revenge for the death of their crispified king. Others argue that she feared torture, slavery, and slow deaths were in store for the children, and she chose to give them a quick, merciful end rather than to see them suffer at the hands of their enemies. Either way, Jason should just be glad that he made it out of that relationship with his genitals intact after trying a bullcrap stunt like that.

Medea's dragon cart landed in Athens, where she eventually married Theseus' dad and became the queen of Athens. The couple had a son named Medos, who went on to conquer a ton of land in the Middle East and found an empire, which he named Media after himself. This is pretty significant, considering that when the Ancient Greeks talked about Media, they were talking about the area we know as Persia. Eventually, Medea was run out of town again, this time for trying to poison the ever-obnoxious Theseus to death, but when Theseus sent men to execute her she disappeared in a cloud of smoke ninjitsu-style. After a little more wandering and murdering, Medea finally returned home to Colchis. She arrived to find her father had been overthrown by his skanky brother, so Medea took out the usurper with some of her murder-magic, reinstated her dad, and reconciled with her family over the whole abandonment-fratricide-mutilation thing. Nowadays, Medea spends the afterlife in the Elysian Fields, the Greek version of Heaven, where she gets it on all the time with Achilles, a dude who was revered by many as the greatest war hero in mythology. Jason went on to live the short, boring, and lonely life of a tactless dumbass, and eventually kicked it when a piece of the *Argo* broke off and crushed him to death with irony.

The Arthurian version of the diabolical sorcerous femme fatale was the infamous enchantress Morgan le Fey. Based on a mythological Irish warrior-goddess known as the Morrigan, le Fey focused all of her skills as a spell-caster and a seductress into destroying King Arthur and his Knights of the Round Table. During her incessant battles with Camelot, Morgan stole Excalibur twice, beheaded a Welsh king with his own sword, kidnapped Sir Lancelot, and once created a Medea-style shawl that caused people to burst into flames whenever they put it on. Her magic could put people to sleep or turn men into rocks, and when she wasn't incinerating chivalrous nerds, she traveled in style, being followed around by four knights who held a large green canopy over her head to block the sun. The queen of Gore (so known because she was actually the queen of a province called Gore, and not because she always seemed to be followed around by dead knights with gruesome stab wounds in them) eventually reconciled with Arthur, and after the legendary king's death, she was one of the mysterious pallbearers who carried his body off to its final resting place at Avalon.

————

For the Ancient Greeks, the Oracle of Delphi was the pinnacle of sacred power and the primary conduit for asking your dumb questions to the gods. In the first month of spring, a priestess of Apollo would receive questions from everyone from commoners to kings and would channel the spirit of the sun god into her body, perform some strange rituals, and come up with an appropriately cryptic answer that was so terribly mysterious that it must have been true. In the old days, the priests used to use teenage virgins as oracles, but when one enterprising Thessalian guy seduced the priestess in exchange for a favorable prophesy (he later ended up sneaking her out and marrying her), they started choosing old women instead.

————

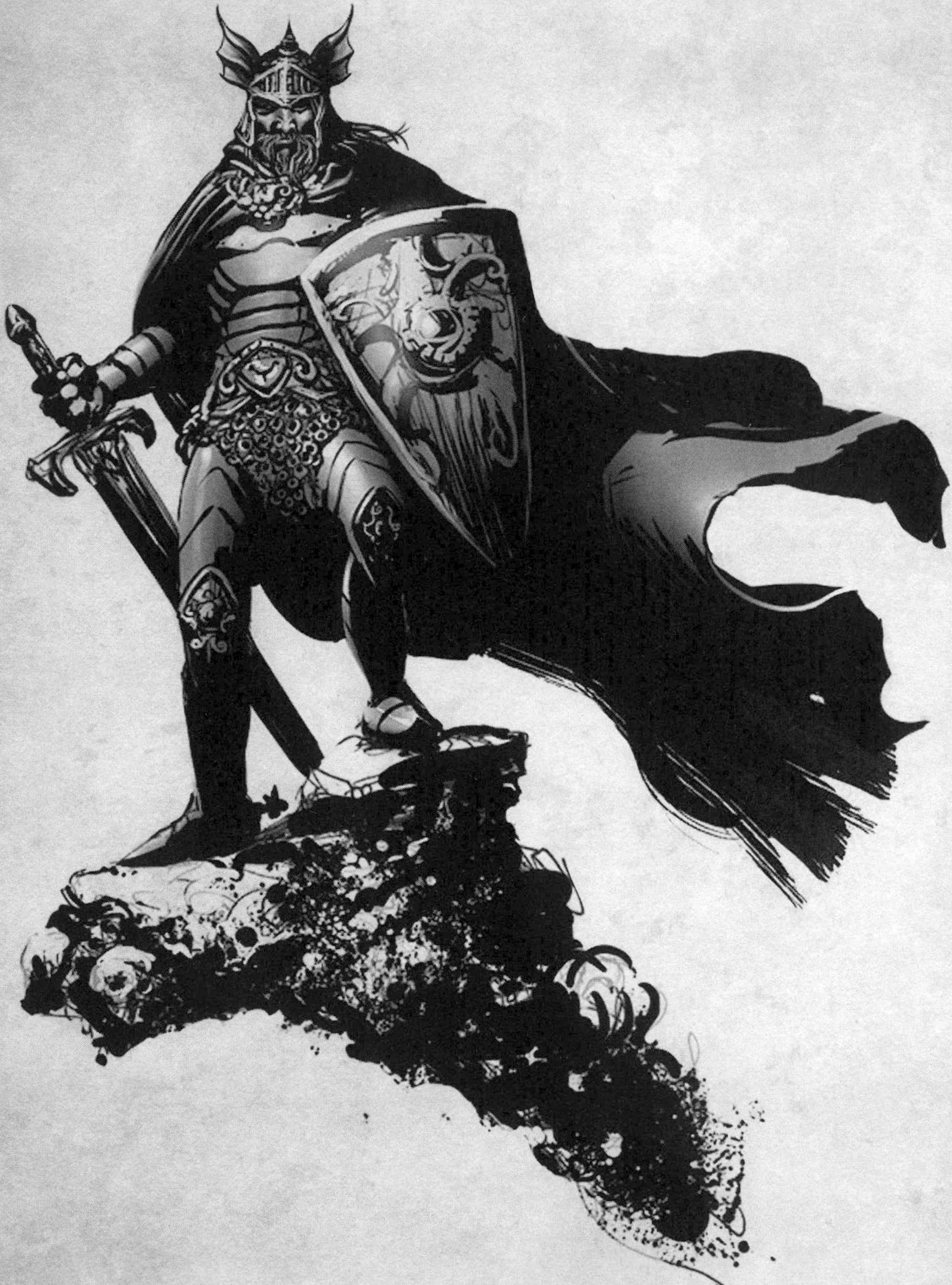

23

SIR MORDRED

And Mordred, as he was the boldest of men,
and always the quickest at making an attack,
immediately placed his troops in order, resolving either to conquer or die.

—GEOFFREY OF MONMOUTH,
HISTORY OF THE KINGS OF BRITAIN

SIR MORDRED WASN'T THE STRONGEST OF THE ROUND TABLE KNIGHTS. He wasn't the bravest, the handsomest, the best jouster, or the guy who got picked first every year at the annual Camelot kickball tournament and wild boar barbecue-a-thon. He didn't discover the secrets of the Holy Grail, slay an evil sorcerer, or win the hand of a beautiful damsel by saving her from some hellacious fiend from the deepest recesses of some H. R. Geigerian clusterhump. He was, however, the man who single-handedly brought about the destruction of Camelot, the end of the Round Table, the disgrace of the once-proud champion Sir Lancelot, and the violent death of the legendary King Arthur.

The whole sordid story begins with a woman named Queen Margawse. Early in the reign of King Arthur, Margawse was sent by her husband, King Something-or-Other, to go spy on the young ruler and report back about whatever harebrained world-domination schemes he was cooking up behind the walls of Camelot. Margawse came to Arthur's court, ostensibly as a foreign dignitary on a diplomatic mission, but before long she decided to stop spying on her husband's behalf and start seducing Arthur instead, because apparently when he was a young buck he had really great abs. Arthur was down with this, and he ended up hitting that so hard that whoever pulled him out could probably have made a case for being named the king of England themselves. After a few nights of crazy monkey-humping, Margawse discovered she was pregnant, and her husband decided that would probably be a good time to recall her from her post.

Unfortunately, adultery was going to be the least of their problems. One day, as though he were the ghost of Obi-Wan Kenobi materializing inside the Rebel base on Hoth ten minutes too late, the powerful mystic wizard Merlin busted into Arthur's throne room and dropped a groin-kickingly tragic ten-ton bombshell that made everyone simultaneously crap in their chain mail: Queen Margawse was actually Arthur's half-sister.

I can only assume that what followed this incest-tastic revelation was something akin to the infamous scene from *The Crying Game*.

Just as Arthur was getting ready to scour his eyes out with lye and take a bucket of bleach to his urethra, Merlin inflicted yet another piece of soul-suckingly unfortunate data on the horrified king—it gets worse somehow. In case you're wondering what could possibly be worse than treating your sister like a porn star and then spawning a human child from the transaction, try this one on for size: their child was going to become a mighty warrior, slay Arthur, and overthrow the kingdom he had worked so hard to build. Goddamnit, Merlin.

This aggression would not stand, man. Arthur immediately resolved to give his sis a postpartum abortion, quashing any future threat to his rule and erasing all physical evidence of his ridiculously inappropriate affair with Queen Margawse. Once again, however, the Fates resolved to judo-chop Arthur in his metaphorical nutsack—Margawse had already had the baby, and had given it up for adoption. Arthur, unable to locate his bastard son and desperate to somehow alter his destiny, decided that the preservation of his rule required significantly more drastic measures. He issued an order that all children born on May Day (Mordred's birthday) be brought to Camelot for a special "I Promise Not to Kill You" springtime celebration of happy fun time-ness. As soon as all the kids were in his castle, Arthur snatched them up, unceremoniously chucked them all onto an unmanned, provisionless plywood boat, and set it adrift in the ocean, figuring that starvation, exposure, and drowning was easily the most humane way to dispose of a boatload of helpless babies. The ship sank at sea, and every child on board died. Every child, that is, except one.

Young Mordred clawed his way out from the wreckage, clung to a piece of driftwood, and made his way back to shore, where he was taken in by local villagers who raised him to adulthood. From that point on, the boy who would one day be known as the Arch-Traitor of Camelot plotted his bloody, delicious, best-served-cold vengeance on the man who had screwed him over so epically.

Mordred trained his ass off, day and night, to become a powerful warrior. Finally, once he was ready to face his father, Mordred was brought to Camelot and identified by Merlin as the son of Queen Margawse and King Arthur. At this point the king had settled down a little and didn't have the heart to execute his own kid on the spot, and Mordred was able to ride his own knightly valor, his standing as Arthur's son, and the reputations of his heroic half-brothers (Margawse's sons Sir Gawain and Sir Gareth) to get himself a seat at the Round Table in Camelot. As a Knight of the Round Table, Mordred performed many feats of complete head-cleaving asskickery, including one time when he went to a tournament in a faraway land and, together with just two other Camelot knights, defeated sixty warriors in one day of battle by slapping them all around like ginger bitches. When he wasn't jousting, fighting, plotting, or questing, Mordred was also known for sleeping with lots of hot babes, regardless of their marital status, and then, if their husbands came by to yell at him, he would punch them in the face repeatedly until they were unconscious. It turned out he had kind of a double standard when it came to adulterous affairs, however, because when Mordred found out that his mom was hooking up with the noble Sir Lamerok, he ran up and impaled the knight by ramming a two-handed sword through one of the dude's kidneys, sneak-attack backstabbing for triple damage.

Sir Mordred spent most of his time at Camelot hanging out with the insanely powerful and infinitely more famous Sir Lancelot. Much of this time was spent lurking in Lancelot's shadow, however, because in terms of kicking ass, Lancelot was like Michael Jordan to Mordred's Scottie Pippen. The paragon of knightly virtue, Lancelot raided castles, had busty maidens falling in love with him every time he turned around, and was undefeated in combat, wasting all of Europe's most powerful knights and kings in jousting, hand-to-hand combat, and thumb-wrestling competitions. His life was so intense that he once saved a damsel in distress by chasing an evil knight across the countryside while riding in a rickshaw pulled by dwarves and nobody even thought twice about it. A lot of illuminated manuscript ink is devoted to singing the glorious praises of the mighty Sir Lancelot, from his youth being raised by the Lady of the Lake and his quest for the Holy Grail to his stunning good looks and his heroic efforts battling the enemies of Camelot by cleaving them from groin to head with mighty blows from his holy kill-sword. Lancelot also spent quite a bit of time violently and ferociously defending the honor of Arthur's wife, the mega-babe Queen

Guinevere, by engaging her enemies in all manner of physical combat and crushing anyone who didn't seem to think that she was the greatest thing since oxygen. Of course, all his efforts to prove how pure and admirable she was kind of backfired when the two fell in love and carried on a decade-long illicit affair that would bring about the ruin of Camelot. But whatever.

Honestly, Lance was kind of an a-hole, if you ask me. This dude was the Alpha Dog of the Round Table and he knew it, and he wasn't afraid to let everyone know about how much he kicked ass. He was like Camelot's version of the high school football quarterback who not only goes out with the cute head cheerleader that won't give you the time of day, but who's also banging the smoking-hot, fresh-out-of-college Spanish teacher on the side also. He defeated everyone in battle, the other knights all had to suck up to him, the peasantry thought he was cooler than a Lamborghini Diablo made out of cupcakes and boobs, and he made no real effort to conceal the fact that he was running around boning the queen whenever he wanted. I can only imagine that even though Mordred and the other knights played along because Lance could easily kick their asses, they all secretly hated his stinking guts. Plus, Lancelot was French. Did you know that?

No one ever talked smack about Lance and Gwen, though, because throwing down a charge like adultery in the Middle Ages would have been a certain death sentence for both the queen and her champion. What was worse was that unless you could have caught them in the act or proved infidelity somehow, Lancelot would have had the opportunity to dispute any circumstantial accusations by declaring a Trial of Combat—a sword-to-sword contest he would certainly have won against anybody.

Only Sir Mordred had the guts to do something about this ridiculous situation and let Arthur know that his best friend and his wife were hooking up behind his back. Mordred and his half-brother Agravaine put together a band of knights and decided to catch the two adulterous lovers in the act. They waited for Lance to enter the queen's chamber, gave them a couple minutes, and then rushed in and caught the lovers mid-bone. Lancelot, being the total meathead douche jock that he was, immediately decided to murder all the witnesses to the event, so he grabbed Sir Agravaine's sword out of his hand, impaled him with it, and then slashed his way through the voyeuristic party. Only Mordred escaped Lancelot's kill-boner with his jugular vein intact.

Mordred publicly exposed the affair and Arthur had no choice but to dutifully sentence his wife to be burned at the stake as a traitor. But then, just as she was about to be incinerated, her boyfriend Lancelot busted into the castle John Cleese–style, slaughtered a bunch of Arthur's knights (including Mordred's half-brother Sir Gareth, who was a stand-up guy that never really did anything wrong), rescued the queen, and took her back to his castle in France. Arthur immediately put together a huge army, sailed across the Channel, and besieged Lancelot in his stronghold. Lancelot sent Guinevere back to England and prepared to battle his one-time liege in an epic war for honor and glory.

Mordred decided he'd had enough of this crap. While Arthur was away in France playing grab-ass with Lance, Mordred usurped the throne, expelled the Archbishop of Canterbury from his post (and subsequently got excommunicated for it), and asked the recently returned Guinevere how she felt about hooking up with a real man for once. The sources differ on her response—Sir Thomas Malory has her barricading herself in the Tower of London while Mordred laid siege to it with catapults, but Geoffrey of Monmouth claims that she took the whole Arthur-wants-to-burn-you-at-the-stake thing pretty seriously, married Mordred out of spite, and then had a couple kids with him.

It is interesting to note, however, that Sir Mordred may not have been as diabolically malevolent as he's portrayed nowadays. According to Malory, "Those who so readily transferred their allegiance to Sir Mordred did so with the excuse that whereas King Arthur's reign had led them into strife, Sir Mordred promised them peace and prosperity." That doesn't sound so bad, actually. Maybe the average-Joe citizens were getting a little tired of Arthur's knights running around with their knees bent like silly people, because let's face it—questing, while heroic, doesn't really do a whole lot to improve the day-to-day life of your typical medieval peasant. They probably also weren't too keen on being conscripted into the army and shipped out to France to have their heads chopped off by some dickhole knight in a petty high school pissing contest between Lancelot and Arthur over who loved the king's girlfriend more. When Mordred rode by promising them that he would end these stupid wars, return peace and order to the world, not murder their children, and make it start raining bacon, they all lined up for a gauntlet of running high-fives like the pregame introductions at a basketball game. Of course, Geoffrey of Monmouth claims that Mordred's entire army was comprised of vagabonds, bandits, and, even worse, Germans and Irishmen, but Geoff was writing his history for a bunch of guys that claimed to be direct descendants of Arthur so it would stand to reason that he probably wouldn't want to go out of his way to make Mordred look like a sympathetic character.

Whatever the case may be, Arthur was, of course, honor-bound to return to England, reclaim his throne, and start laying waste to his one-time subordinate. He pulled the e-brake on his actions in France (Lancelot was kind of kicking his ass anyway), landed on the beaches, and fought his way toward London.

The slaughterfest that ensued was super-gruesome and bloody, with thousands of warriors savagely disemboweling each other with the fiery hatred of a million burning supernovas. After a flurry of donkey punches and spear thrusts, all that remained amid a heaping field of perforated bleeding carcasses were four men. The powerful King Arthur, his legendary blade Excalibur drenched in blood, and the last two surviving Knights of the Round Table stared across the carnage-filled warzone at the arch-traitor Sir Mordred. Mordred was resting up against his sword, which was stuck down into a huge heap of dead bodies he had just finished chopping up like diced tomatoes, his black armor dotted with dents, battle damage, and the blood of Arthur's knights.

Arthur stepped forward, drawing forth his lance and preparing to end this war and assert his dominance over Camelot once again. Sir Mordred, finally seeing a chance to gain the vengeance he had been seeking his entire life, silently stepped forward, gripping his blade with both hands. The two men broke into a run, charging one another with the full force of their anger, uttered their battle-cries, and simultaneously unleashed their most devastating attacks on one another.

Arthur's lance pierced Mordred's armor, went through some vital organs, and came out the traitor's back. The wound was incredibly fatal, and Mordred knew his time was short. He looked at Arthur, who was still just barely out of reach, triumphantly and unblinkingly staring into Mordred's eyes with the knowing look of a man who has just slain his mortal enemy. But Mordred wouldn't let his father have the satisfaction. Summoning the last reserves of his unquenchable rage, Mordred harnessed his inner badass powers and forced himself down on the spear, pushing the lance through his own body, jamming the weapon through himself just far enough that he could bring a savage sword-blow down onto Arthur. Both men crumpled to the ground. Mordred died a badass's death, grimly content with the satisfaction that his revenge was finally complete.

Arthur's body was conducted to the island of Avalon, where he was never heard from again. Lancelot died alone, miserable, and still French, and Queen Guinevere gave up the tabloid lifestyle to become a nun. Camelot as we know it ceased to exist. Sir Mordred, the Black Knight of Round Table, the abandoned son the king never wanted, had single-handedly brought about the destruction of the kingdom with the blade of his sword.

The corpus of knowledge on the legendary King Arthur was compiled in the fifteenth century by a guy named Sir Thomas Malory. As a soldier and a knight, Malory had fought battles across England, Scotland, and France, but in terms of chivalrous deeds, he was far more in line with Mordred than with Lancelot. While he was a sitting member of Parliament, Malory was arrested for attempting to ambush and murder the Duke of Buckingham, and during his career he was imprisoned eight different times, for crimes ranging from breaking into Coombe Abbey and punching the abbot to highway robbery and cattle thievery. Malory, being awesome, broke out of prison twice—once by swimming a moat and once by fighting his way out with cold steel. He assembled his tome of Arthurian knowledge while serving a life sentence in the infamous Newgate Prison.

While most people would think of the Round Table at Camelot as having somewhere between eight and twelve chairs, according to Malory this bizarrely gigantic table actually had seats for a hundred and fifty knights. Sure, at any given time there were empty seats for those dudes who were currently questing and/or deceased, but this was obviously one epic table. In case you're wondering what sorts of refreshments were served at meetings, I have it on good authority that these brave warriors ate ham and jam and Spam a lot.

Arthur's Excalibur is the most popular magical sword in literature, but the Welsh blade Dyrnwyn is also pretty rad. While it's probably most associated these days with the adventures of Taran, Assistant Pig-Keeper, the Dyrnwyn of ancient myth was a powerful weapon belonging to the legendary Welsh king Rhydderch Hael. The white-hilted sword was kept in a magical scabbard, and if a worthy man drew it out, the entire blade would be engulfed in raging white fire to better immolate your enemies.

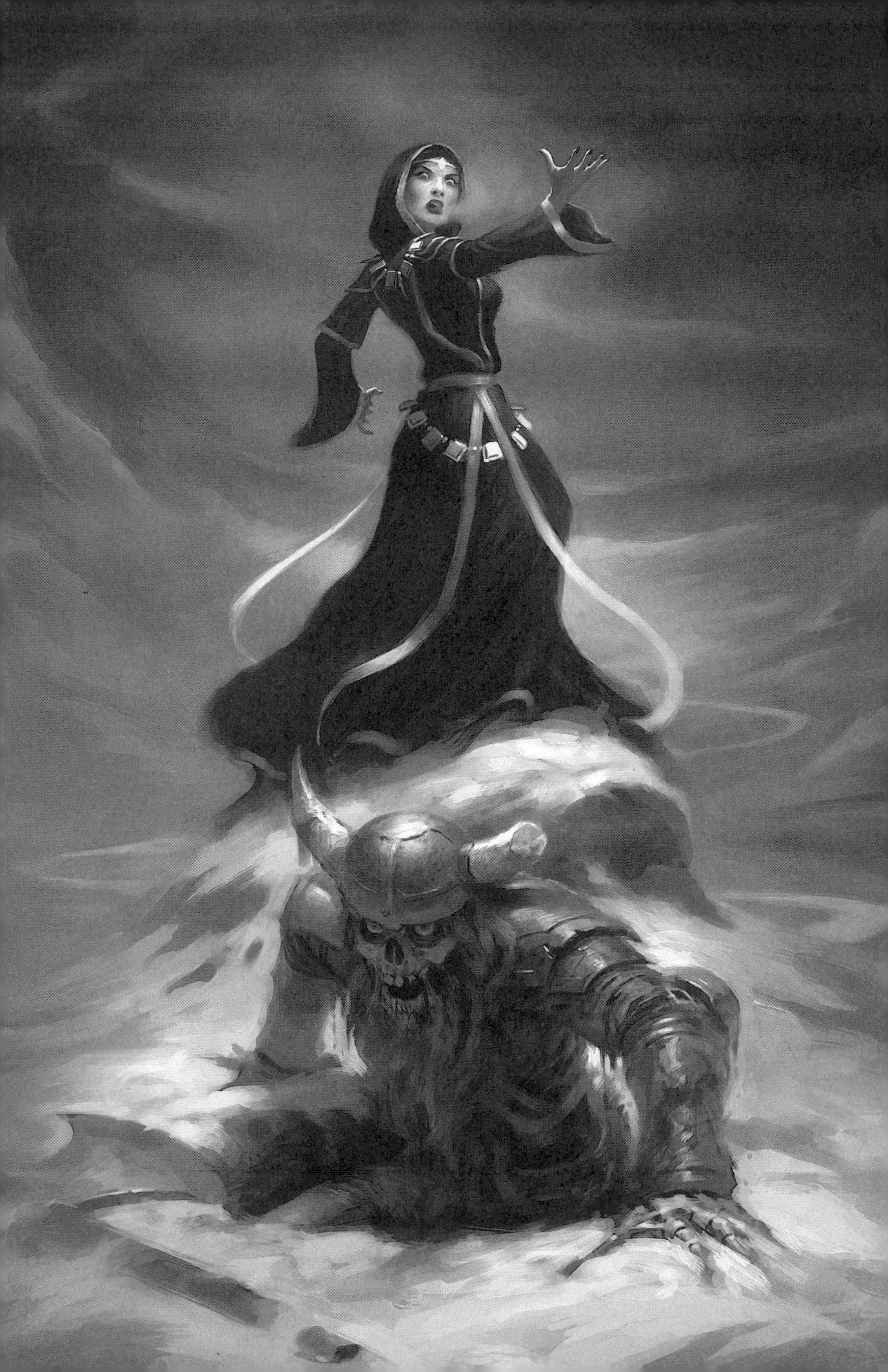

24

SKULD

*I fear now that the dead stir here, rise up again and fight against us, and
hard will it prove to fight with fetches; and for all so many limbs as here
are cloven, shields split, and helms and corslets hewn in pieces, and many a
chieftain cut asunder, these the dead are now the grimmest to contend with,
nor have we the strength to cope with them.*

—BOTHVAR BJARKI

VIKING SAGAS ARE EASILY SOME OF THE MOST BADASS PIECES OF
WRITING EVER. Produced by a bloodthirsty assortment of ludicrously
violent warrior-poets who spent just as much time slinging spears as
spinning tales, these merciless legends feature heroic quests, magical
spells, endless battle, withering trash-talking, and fearsome monsters,
with a lusty maiden or two busting out of her blouse thrown in just
for good measure. By the time the story is through, you can be pretty
damn sure that nearly every single character is heroically lying facedown on top of a pile of corpses with a gaping slash wound prominently displayed on some vital portion of their bodies and their blade
lodged in the head of their most hated nemesis. These sagas are the
blockbuster action movies and flaming six-minute guitar solos of

medieval literature—and while the endless parade of proper nouns can make it a little difficult to read at times, it's damn near impossible to argue with the badass cred of any short story in which a humorless asswhomper avenges his murdered brother by using a battle-axe the size of a Lexus to slaughter an entire city full of warriors.

The Saga of Hrolf Kraki is no exception to this time-honored tradition of literary blood-bathing. The epic story of a couple generations of semilegendary Danish kings who asserted their dominance by plowing people's skulls to bone dust with a bulldozer, Hrolf's saga is about as subtle and delicate as a game of beer pong played with live grenades. But while Hrolf himself is a hugely powerful ass-wrecker, no one in his tale can assert a better claim to badassitude than his vengeful sister, the pitiless necromancer sorceress known as Skuld.

Skuld's story begins with a Danish king named Helgi. One year, around Yule time, some rough-looking homeless chick knocked on King Helgi's door in the middle of the night, begging for shelter from the rain and maybe a little bit of jerky or something. When Helgi found it in his heart to let her in, he was rewarded for his kindness by quickly realizing that underneath her tattered rags this beggar was actually a super-hot elf babe. Being a typical Viking hero, Helgi celebrated his discovery by snatching this chick up and having his way with her. The next morning, after he was done ravishing this strange elf woman he just met, she informed him that she was carrying his kid, and that he should stop by this boathouse near his home in nine months to pick up his daughter. Helgi, being the sort of dude who probably fathered *a lot* of kids in his days pillaging and plundering every single European settlement that was accessible by Viking longship, of course completely forgot about his child and went back to the business of burning people alive and dousing out the smoldering ashes with a steady stream of urine. Luckily for people who enjoy things that kick ass, he wasn't going to get off the hook that easily this time—three years later, a group of elves showed up in the middle of the night, dropped a young girl off on Helgi's doorstep, and placed a totally gnarly curse on the king and his family forever.

That curse was Skuld.

The sagas say that Skuld was "by evil spirits ill-created," and as such she grew up learning all the forbidden dark arts you might expect from a woman whose primary goal in life was to hone her magic to the point where she could obliterate entire civilizations just by thinking really mean things about people until their heads caught on fire. She went on to marry a mighty Swedish king named Hjorvarth, who was known for being super-strong, well-endowed, and not averse to women who could conjure apparitions through their knowledge of the dark arts, and together they ruled a vast kingdom of Geats, which are like Swedish Goths. King Helgi, meanwhile, inaugurated his newfound curse by accidentally marrying his own daughter, producing a son named Hrolf Kraki, and then dying in a fire.

Skuld and Hrolf Kraki got along well enough, considering that they were brother/sister and aunt/nephew, but things started to take a turn for the worse one day when Hrolf tricked Skuld's husband, Hjorvarth, into accidentally becoming a vassal of Denmark. You see, Hrolf had given Hjorvarth a magical sword, and the Swedish ruler accepted the gift without realizing that taking a sword from the king was a symbolic Viking way of publicly declaring that you were officially his bitch. Bound by bro honor, Hjorvarth had no choice but to accept Hrolf as his master and pay him a yearly tribute, even though this was total crap.

Hrolf Kraki went on to become super-famous and powerful, kicking ass all over the world in his quest for plunder and glory and alcohol, and amassing all of the greatest heroes in the land to serve as retainers and lords in his empire. This guy was so popular that he's even mentioned briefly in *Beowulf*, a story that wasn't even written by Vikings.

Skuld and Hjorvarth, meanwhile, looked longingly on as Kraki and his champions living it up with games, mistresses, swimming pools, and diamond-encrusted toilet seats while they had to cough up tribute every year like chumps, and they quickly came to the conclusion that this sucked their asses on fire. Skuld told her husband to sack up and tell Hrolf to shove that tribute up his vas deferens, but Hjorvarth apparently didn't have the balls to stand up to the Danish hero. So Skuld did it herself. She asked her half-brother/nephew for a three-year break in tribute-paying, as long as she agreed to pay the full amount at the end of the three-year cycle. Hrolf didn't really give a crap, and basically just said, "Whatever."

Given a three-year break, Skuld took all the money she was supposed to give to Hrolf and instead put it to work building a huge-ass army of Vikings, criminals, summoned monsters, elves, evil spirits, and other ridiculous monstrosities from the bowels of the Underworld. She used her magic to conceal her actions from Hrolf, silently building up a mindless horde suitable for her purposes.

Now, while Hrolf Kraki was pretty cool in his prime, around this point in his lifespan he was kind of a total d-bag. He and his men had grown fat, arrogant, and pretentious, and instead of questing and warring, they spent their time throwing half-eaten chicken bones at innocent people, drinking themselves into oblivion, disrespecting the gods, and biting off the noses of prostitutes without warning. These guys were so confident in their badassitude that they didn't even notice Skuld marching a damn massive army right up to the gates of their castle in a situation that can best be described as being sneak-attacked by the Pacific Ocean.

Even when he noticed that he was completely surrounded by a force several times larger than his own, Hrolf was all out of give-a-crap. He just ordered a messenger to go to Skuld's camp and tell her that he and his champions were going to have one more drink of ale, then come out and beat her ass back into submission.

That was it. Skuld ordered her army to set their phasers to "decapitate" and the two armies met in a huge beat-down that quickly littered the entire battlefield in a thick layer of corpses. Guys were exploding all over the place; elves were fistfighting Vikings; everything larger than a cantaloupe was being sliced in half; and bodies were stacking up so high that warriors had to climb over mountains of dead people just to properly kill each other. One of Hrolf's berserkers, the mighty hero Bothvar Bjarki, awesomely responded to the carnage fest by transforming himself into a huge ghost bear, and the Viking grizzly monstrosity started swatting men apart with his gigantic paws and biting horses in half with one chomp of his ferocious, iron-like jaws. I picture it wearing a hilarious horned helmet while doing so, though the legend isn't specific about this.

Skuld, commanding her army from an ominous black-flagged witch's tent, responded to the Norse bear massacre of her army by summoning a fearsome demonic ox-sized wild boar into the fray to counter it. The wild boar is one of the most ill-tempered, meanest, and murderous crap-covered land animals to ever exist, and when they're summoned from a super-evil dimension beyond the mortal realm, you may as well just run up and hurl yourself into the thing's mouth to save yourself an excruciatingly slow, painful death. In addition to flinging people around with its tusks and shredding armor like tin foil in the microwave, this meat-tank had a super-tough hide that was impervious to sword blows from even the manliest Viking berserker, and could even shoot arrow-like quills out of its back, which hit so hard it could tear dudes in half.

The bloodbath raged on. Hrolf's berserkers and champions flailed wildly against the armies of Skuld. Those warriors fortunate enough to still be in one piece now found themselves covered from sword-hilt to shoulder in the blood of their enemies. It was just that kind of party. Hrolf's men fought a desperate stand, and against all odds started to push Skuld's forces back, but this is when things somehow get even more crazy. Skuld, seeing her army's resolve falter in the face of this army of human-size bandsaws, knew it was time to break out her secret weapon—her command over the forces of life and death itself. She furiously stormed out of her tent, entered the battlefield, and began rezzing dead warriors with her necromancy— reviving the slain and sending them right back out there to continue the fight. That's right, folks, we are talking about goddamn VIKING ZOMBIES here.

This has to be one of the most epic, insane showdowns of all time. Let's picture this for a second. It's the middle of winter. The towering spires of a huge Viking fortress are engulfed in flames, and the stench of smoke and corpses mix with the bitter cold and heavy winds of a snowy Scandinavian December to whip around the combatants. With no hope of survival, the half-drunk king of Denmark bravely defends his throne room in what he knows to be a triumphant last stand worthy of Valhalla. His personal champions, the twelve greatest and most accomplished warriors in the realm, fight for their lives Helm's Deep–style alongside a giant killer ghost-bear, while the ultrapowerful sorceress Skuld leads her mish-mashed army of Dark Elves, Viking Zombies, and a house-size angry pig that shoots arrows out of its ass.

For every man Hrolf's warriors cut down, another half-dead walking corpse was there to take his place. Bothvar the Ghost-Bear Viking Man even engaged the Swedish king Hjorvarth in single combat, cut off both of the guy's arms, sliced off a leg, and cleaved the dude in half through the torso, but Skuld just reanimated her husband's corpse and hurled his cobbled-together body back into the fray anew. I can only assume that squaring off against a barely stitched-together warrior you just took great pains to slaughter was pretty demoralizing to everybody involved.

With Hrolf's champions on the defensive, slowly being bashed into submission by the never-ending stream of undead, Skuld charged up to the fray, burst into the throne room, and personally oversaw the final destruction of her half-brother and his precious douche-champions. The woman who was once unwanted by her own father had now single-handedly destroyed thirteen of the most feared and deadliest warriors in the world, and triumphantly took her place on the bloody throne as the new queen of the Viking world.

Hrolf Kraki carried the magical sword Skofnung, a weapon so hardcore that it was simply referred to as "the best of all swords carried in the Northern lands." Sure, it had some minor design flaws—it couldn't be unsheathed in the presence of a woman, or when the sun was shining on the pommel—but wounds inflicted by the blade could not be healed except by the sword itself, and every time it cut into bone it ripped off a terrifying sound that struck fear into the hearts of all who heard it. The saga isn't clear on what it sounded like when the blade "sung," but in the context of the zombie mythos, I like to think of it as being something akin to the business end of a chainsaw.

Skuld ruled for a while, but was eventually overthrown when Bothvar's similarly badass brother Elgfrothi rolled into town looking for vengeance. Like his brother, Elgfrothi was the son of a Danish prince who was cursed to live as a cave bear during the day and a man at night. Elgfrothi's dad bit it when he was finally hunted down by a huge group of soldiers and got himself so worn out from pulling men in half all day that he passed out from exhaustion and was killed in his sleep.

Being the son of a werebear has some adverse physiological effects on a guy, though, and as a result, Elgfrothi was born with the upper body of a man and the lower body of an elk, making him half-Elk, half-Frothi. This guy was superstrong, which kicked ass, and was so tough that much of Bothvar's legendary strength had come from simply drinking a small taste of his brother's blood.

When Elgfrothi was twelve, he entered the county wrestling tournament and ended up crippling every single man in his village over the course of one afternoon. Exiled from his people for his inability to fistfight Viking warriors without breaking them in half, Elgfrothi moved into the wilderness and became a bandit leader. Wielding a short sword that had roughly the cutting power of a lightsaber, Elgfrothi became super-rich by killing travelers and robbing them of all their gold. He lived in an awesome pimped-out tent in the middle of the wilderness, and rationalized his line of work by saying that pretty much everyone he annihilated with his sword was a total wussbag and probably didn't deserve to live anyway. Hell, he was doing them a favor by putting them out of their misery.

After Skuld's conquest of Denmark, Elgfrothi got together with Hrolf's mother/sister, snuck into the castle, and captured Skuld before she could use her magic. Together they killed her with "divers torments" (which is just the old way of writing "diverse torments" rather than some sort of bizarre nautical-themed torture procedure) and incorporated the empire into Hrolf's sister/mother's dominion.

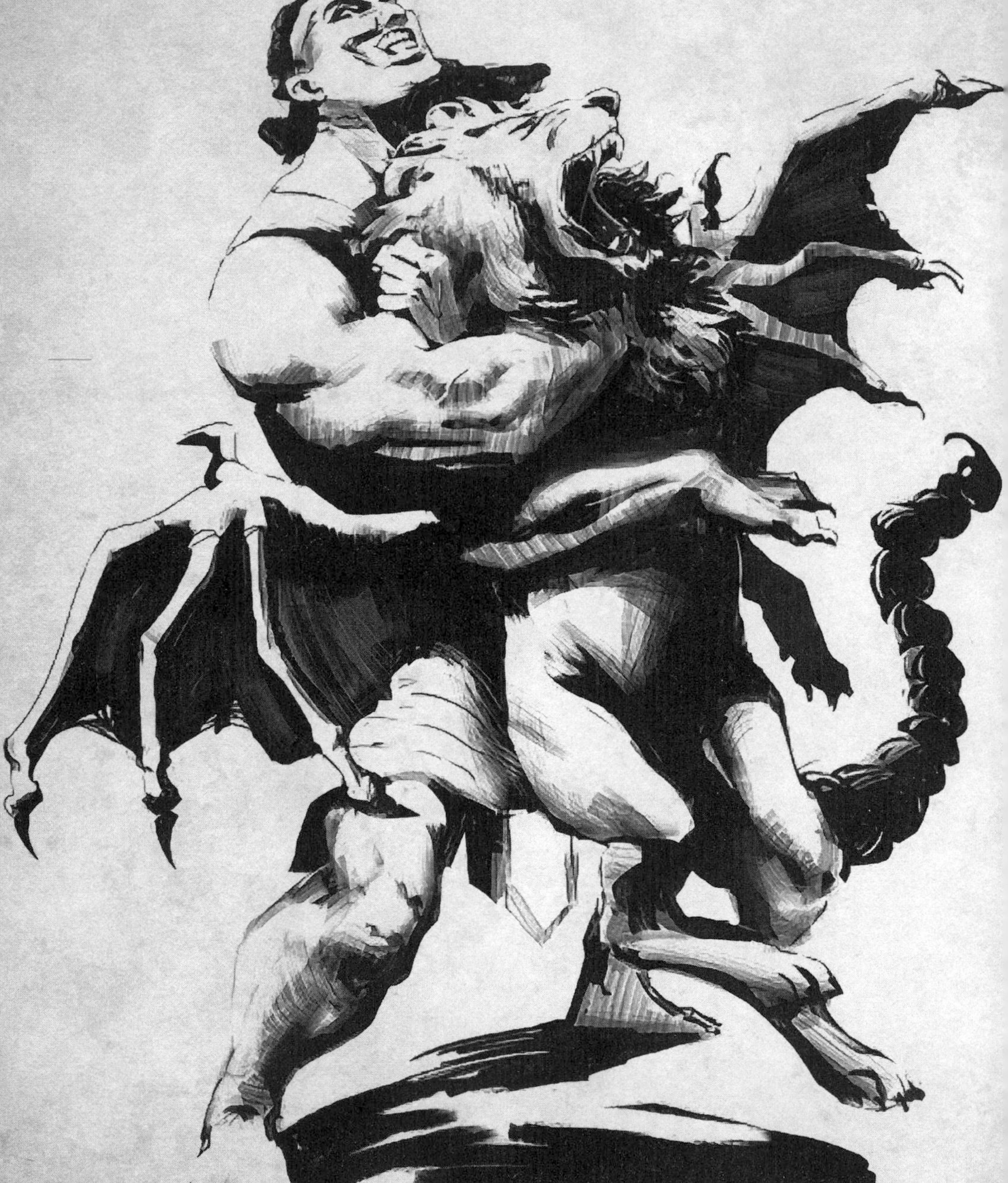

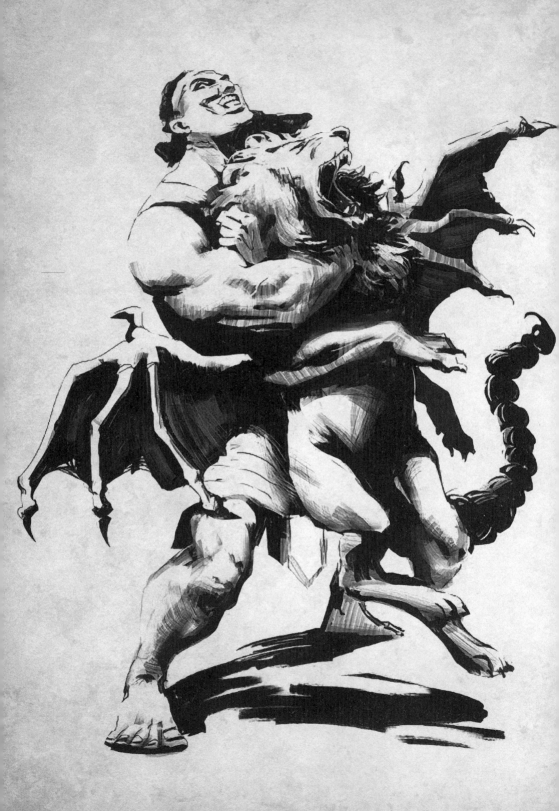

25

GILGAMESH

Surpassing all other kings, heroic in stature,
brave scion of Uruk, wild bull on the rampage!

—*THE EPIC OF GILGAMESH*

IT MAY SEEM A LITTLE WEIRD FOR ME TO INCLUDE HUMAN HISTO-
RY'S FIRST EPIC HERO AMONG A LIST OF BORDERLINE-PSYCHOTIC
VILLAINS, BUT AT THE BEGINNING OF *THE EPIC OF GILGAMESH*—
A STORY SO HARDCORE IT HAD TO BE CHISELED ONTO STONE
TABLETS BECAUSE NO MORTAL PAPER COULD CONTAIN IT—THE
MONSTER-SLAUGHTERING, POWER-MAD DESPOT GILGAMESH UN-
DOUBTEDLY FIT INTO THIS CATEGORY. Two-thirds god and one-
third man, Gil was the epic king of the super-ancient Babylonian city
of Uruk, where he spent his days tyrannizing the populace with a se-
ries of completely unreasonable edicts that served only to prove how
great he was and how much everybody else in his kingdom sucked.
He routinely challenged all men in the land under two hundred pounds
to no-holds-barred wrestling contests, beating their asses and snapping
their arms like toothpicks in back-alley, semilegal street fights. As if that

wasn't degrading enough, he then further emasculated the male population of Babylon by claiming the old-school rite of *jus primae noctis* on all newlywed brides in the land, meaning that he slept with every girl in Uruk on the night of her wedding. As much as this wedding-crashing and bride-humping situation was a good deal for Gilgamesh, it's not outside the realm of possibility to believe that it pissed off a lot of people unfortunate enough to be stuck under his rule. Eventually, his citizenry got sick of his bad attitude and desperately begged for the gods to send someone to free them from this cruel oppression and bring sanity back to the kingdom.

The gods took pity on the poor people of Uruk and called down a guy named Enkidu—an animalistic wild-man with bulging muscles, "tresses like a woman," and an impressive amount of *Magnum, P.I.–*style body hair. After being called down into the world like the Terminator, this superstrong, mostly naked beast-person ran around, killing animals with his bare hands, eating grass, and scaring the local hunters and farming villages. One day, a wise local farmer had the good sense to hire a prostitute to "tame" Enkidu with her singular talents. The prostitute babe went out into the woods, found Enkidu, got it on with him for six days and seven nights straight (!), and as a result of this epic boning, he gained what the Babylonian tablets refer to as "reason and understanding." After Enkidu was somehow made civilized through the medium of wild, freak-out monkey sex, the super-robo-prostitute informed her client of Gilgamesh's bastardly policy regarding newlywed brides. The hardcore wild-man instantly went off on a mission to beat the hell out of the tyrant king and stuff Gilgamesh's mangled corpse into a wood-chipper.

Enkidu went to Uruk and made the generally foolish decision to block the god-king from entering the honeymoon suite of some woman who was just married that day. Gil was obviously a little pissed that some heathen dirtbag was trying to prevent him from getting some action, and they immediately got into a hardcore fistfight that demolished a couple city blocks. After a severe superhero-style battle that smashed a quarter of the city into sweaty rubble, Gilgamesh and Enkidu developed a mutual respect for each other's powers, called the fight a draw, and decided to stop fighting and team up to accomplish super-manly awesome deeds by unifying their powers. In an effort to allay the concerns of his newfound ally, Gilgamesh agreed to stop wantonly sexing newlywed brides, and together they created the time-honored axiom of "brethren before wenches," which was later modernized to the more familiar "bros before hos." This was great for Gilgamesh, but the gods' plan to overthrow the tyrant with violence had now backfired spectacularly. Gilgamesh and Enkidu quickly became the Snoop and Dre of Ancient Sumeria, raising hell and crushing everything in their paths. I think that "Nuthin' but a G Thang" is based on their relationship, with the "G" being an obvious reference to "Gilgamesh"—a detail Dr. Dre was able to subtly work into his composition by virtue of the fact that his PhD is in Classical Mesopotamian Literature (or at least that's my assumption). Either way, Babylon had never been on a ride like this before—these guys put the rap down, put the mack down, and if bitches talked trash, they put the smack down.

Convinced that there was nothing left in Uruk to either beat up or sleep with, Gilgamesh decided to leave his harem-filled palace, climb the distant forbidden Mountain of Cedar, and do battle with a ferocious fire-breathing ogre named Humbaaba. Everyone, even Enkidu, thought Gil was nuts for even suggesting such a ridiculous quest, but Gilgamesh thoughtfully responded to their protests by calling everyone impotent cowards, buying some pimped-out gold-plated weapons, and heading over to fight the behemoth monster anyway. You and I might wonder who cares about a huge mountain covered with cedar trees anyway, but for Gil it was the principle of the thing. He hated the idea of some punk ogre thinking it was better than him just because it was huge and ate people.

Enkidu, not being a tremendous fan of having cowardice accusations thrown in his direction, finally started drinking the Kool-Aid and joined Gilgamesh's quest to beat the crap out of Humbaaba and steal all the cedar on his mountain. These two bone-breaking Nietzschean *übermenchen* mounted up, rolled out, traveled a ridiculous distance, and then battled the monster in a ferocious duel. After receiving what can perhaps only be described as a beatdown of stone-tablet epic proportions, the Guardian of the Forest fell to its knees, desperately pleading for its miserable life. Gilgamesh just killed it anyway, pulled out its lungs, and cut off its tusks for trophies. Then the G-child deforested the Mountain of Cedar, built a raft out of some of the freshly cut logs, floated back to Uruk on his wood, and built city walls out of it.

After single-handedly clear-cutting the most famous forest in Babylon down to a semi-pathetic stump-riddled field, Gilgamesh switched his mind back to freak mode and instantly became even hotter in the eyes of the Babylonian goddess Ishtar—the patron deity of sex, death, and hardcore fornication. Ishtar immediately came down to Uruk and offered to hop on Gilgamesh's bozack, but he inexplicably turned down some from the sex goddess, stating that she had a pretty bad track record of ruining the lives of her previous lovers. It's hard to understand why a world-class poon-hound like Gilgamesh would refuse to make the beast with two backs with the Goddess of Sex, so maybe this is another thing you just have to chalk up to principle. Ishtar didn't see the irony here, however, and Gilgamesh's none-too-delicate proclamation of "Get bent" really pissed her off something fierce. She stormed off to the land of the gods and demanded access to the Bull of Heaven, a huge Babe the Blue Ox bastard known for his horns and stomping/ crushing powers, so that she could use it to demolish Gilgamesh's precious city. The pantheon of gods told her to take a chill pill, but she threatened to "bring forth the dead to consume the flesh of the living" if the gods didn't comply with her demands. Not willing to have something as intense as the Zombie Apocalypse on their collective conscience, the gods relented and gave Ishtar the Bull of Heaven, and she immediately proceeded to send it to Uruk, where it killed a few hundred people by causing earthquakes and impaling people with horny death. Gilgamesh and Enkidu rose to the occasion, however, and after a seriously epic battle Gilgamesh overcame the monster by stabbing it in a place colloquially known by the ancients as "the slaughter spot." That's right, the ass. Then, to further vent his frustration, he cut off the monster's dick and threw it in Ishtar's face, which I guess is kind of funny if you think misogyny is humorous. After beating the bull's ass and de-*cojones*-ing it, he went back to his household of adoring servants and proclaimed, "Who is first among men? Who is the most glorious of fellows?" to which they unanimously and emphatically replied, "You are!" I picture this going down kind of like Sho'Nuff, the Shogun of Harlem, asking his cronies who was the baddest mofo low down around this town, which is something I think all of us can really appreciate.

The gods finally got tired of Enkidu and Gilgamesh's murderous rampages, and, realizing that there was no monster the Gs couldn't take down with their combined deity-smiting powers, went the more bio-terrorish route and afflicted Enkidu with some bizarre, incurable illness. He fell sick for twelve days, became feverish and delirious, hallucinated about a bunch of whacked-out crap, and promptly died.

This kind of threw Gilgamesh into something of a midlife crisis. Deciding that he didn't want to die the lame, wussy death of a mortal, he

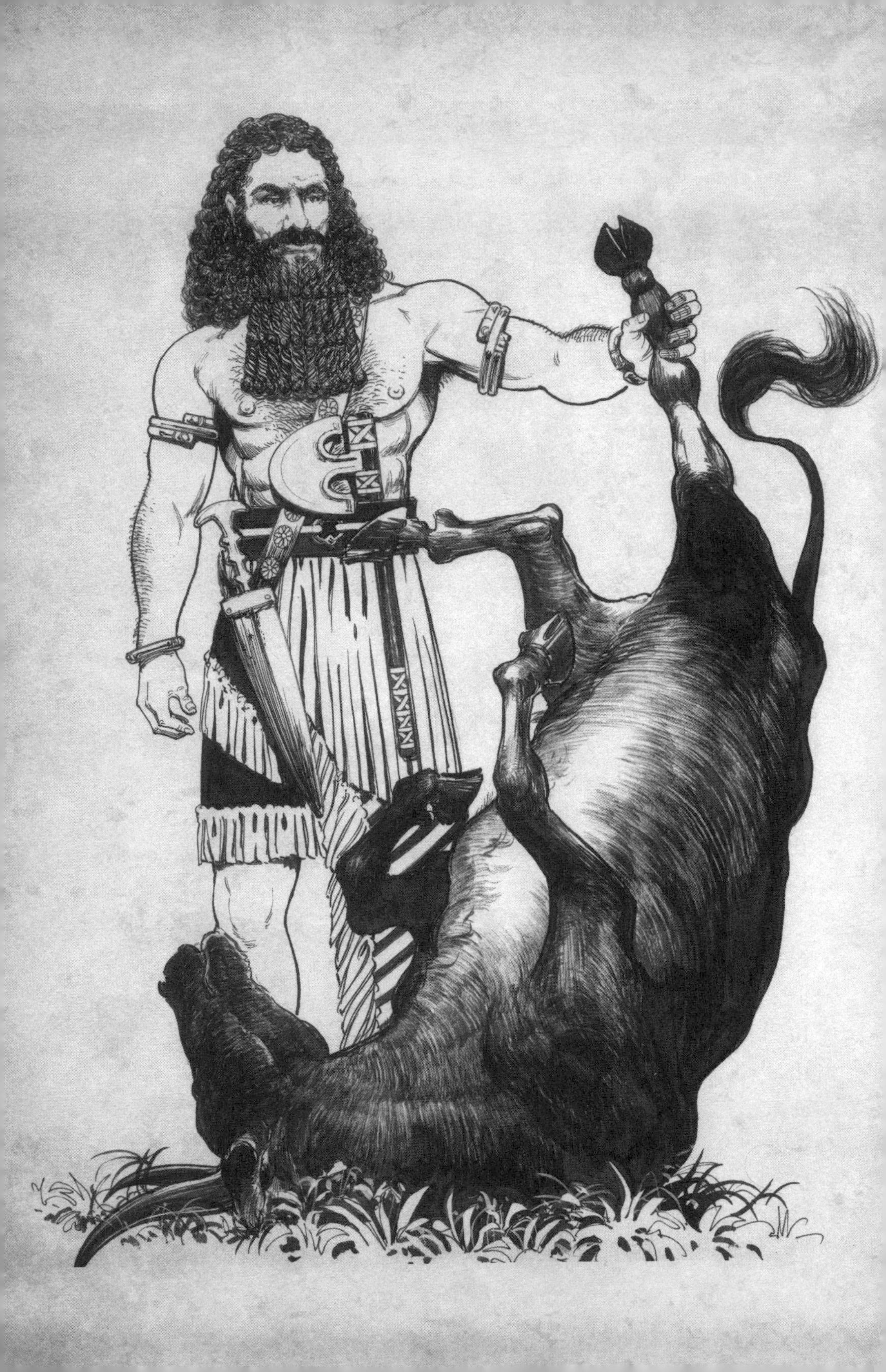

figured it made perfect sense to travel to the end of the world, find the one immortal dude on Earth, and figure out what the hell that guy's secret was. So Gil started his journey toward the mountains at the end of the world, sustaining himself by wrestling a bunch of lions and manticores to death with his bare hands and eating their flesh. When Gilgamesh finally got to the mountains, he blew past the two scorpion-men guarding the pass (even after they told him to chill the eff out), and headed down to the Waters of Death—a huge ocean at the end of the world, with water so crazy-polluted with neurotoxins it instantly killed any man who touched it. When Gilgamesh reached the shore, he found a ferry driver standing there smoking a cigarette with a bunch of huge stone men, which I imagine to look like fully articulated versions of those ancient Chinese terra cotta warriors. Without even asking any questions as to why there were a bunch of crazy animatronic stone soldiers walking around minding their own business like assholes, Gilgamesh just pulled out an axe in one hand and a dagger in the other and charged into battle. Using the element of surprise and the element of beating the holy living crap out of solid rock with his fists, Gilgamesh smashed all the stone knuckleheads into rubble and threw their blown-to-hell rock corpses into the Waters of Death. Then he forced the boatman to take him across the ocean, which he did.

At the end of the world, Gilgamesh met the Babylonian version of Noah—a guy named Utnapishtim, who got eternal life from the gods as a reward for surviving a great flood that wiped out most of the population of Earth. "Noah" told him that there was a weirdo magical plant that would give him eternal life, but that it was, unfortunately, buried at the bottom of the ocean. Gil, never being one to be held back by that which was deemed impossible, of course just swam out, dove to the bottom of the ocean, found the plant, and pulled it up to the surface. While he was taking a quick break to catch his breath, however, some stupid snake came up and ganked away the last immortality plant on Earth, proving once again that it doesn't matter what kind of religious or mythological belief system you're dealing with—snakes are always bastards. You just can't trust those guys with anything, especially if it's food-related.

Gilgamesh freaked out, got pissed, punched Noah in the head, said forget it, and went back home to lead the meaningless existence of being fabulously wealthy, ruling over the most powerful city on Earth, and having a harem of a few thousand wives running around his sprawling palace.

Gilgamesh eventually died of super-pissedness when he kept losing on the same stupid level of a frustrating video game and got so angry that a vein in his forehead exploded. According to the Sumerians, he currently spends the afterlife governing over the ghosts and souls of the Underworld, though Dante seems to have left this detail out of his description of Hell for some dumb reason.

Babe the Blue Ox was a giant crazy bull from American folklore who tore ass around the American countryside leaving nothing but shredded geological wreckage and destruction in his path. Standing thirty feet tall at the shoulder and with hide so blue you'd think he was a cartoon character, Babe was the best buddy of the heavily bearded lumberjack Paul Bunyan. While Paul clear-cut the forests of the North American continent Gilgamesh-style, Babe hauled goods around and carried all of the ridiculously gigantor equipment Paul needed to single-handedly wreak ecological havoc on the lumber of the universe. Babe was famous for his ravenous thirst for pancakes and blueberries, created the lakes of Minnesota by stamping the earth down with his feet, and accidentally created the Grand Canyon by dragging a huge pickaxe behind him for a few hundred miles.

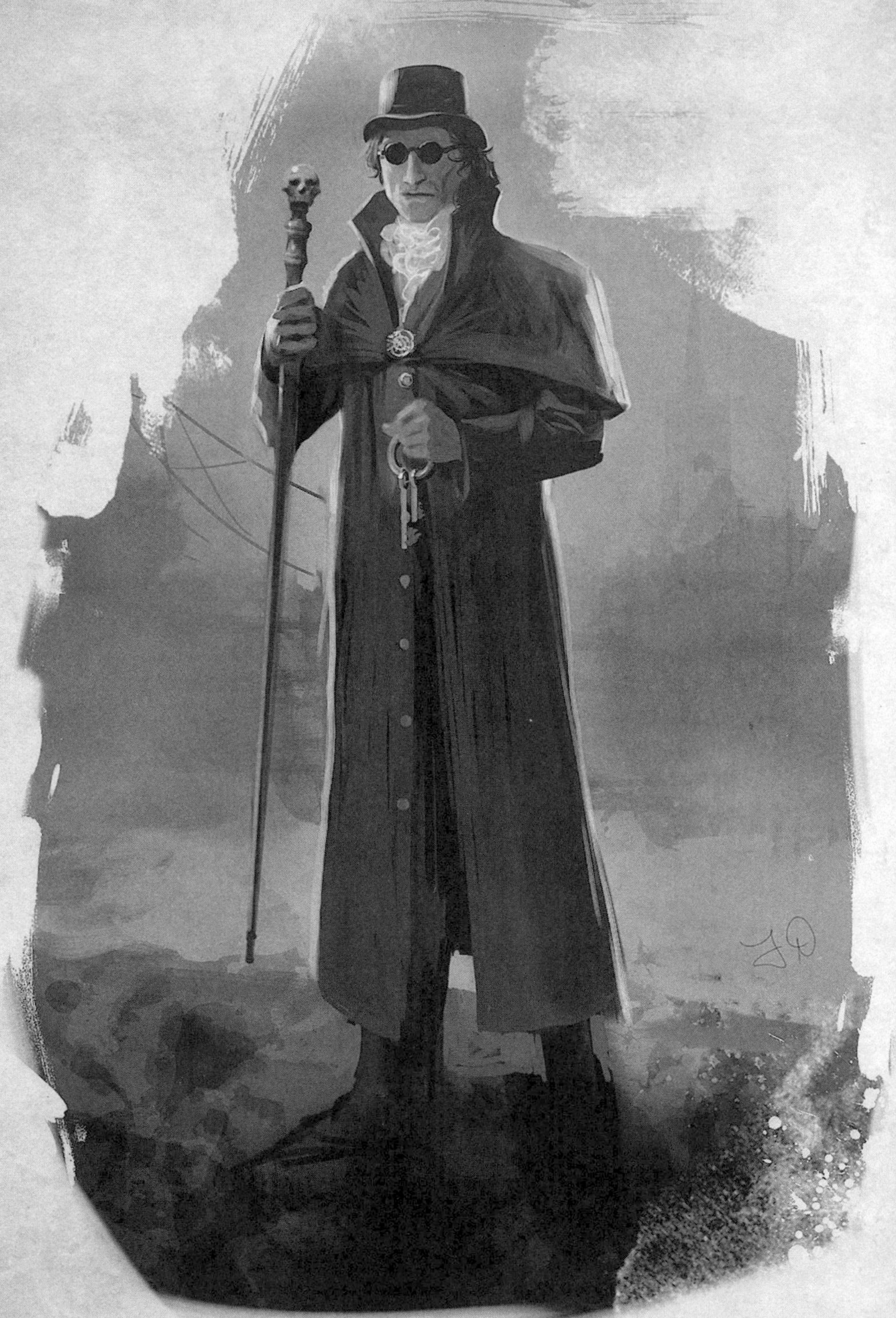

26

PROFESSOR JAMES
MORIARTY

This is not danger. It is inevitable destruction. You stand in the way not merely of an individual, but of a mighty organization, the full extent of which you, with all your cleverness, have been unable to realize. You must stand clear, Mr. Holmes, or be trodden under foot.

EVERY GREAT HERO NEEDS A WORTHY ARCH-NEMESIS. Whether it's a goatee-wearing evil twin from another dimension, an unstoppable cyborg killing machine sent back in time to destroy all of the world's cupcakes, or just a super-annoying upstairs neighbor, everybody needs a mortal enemy who seems to foil their efforts at every turn and constantly attempt to ruin their lives. These are the folks who are diametrically opposed to everything a brave hero stands for, and who are so incurably, delightfully evil that the only possible way to settle the dispute is through a ridiculously badass life-or-death showdown with the fate of the free world hanging in the balance. For Victorian England's greatest fictional detective, the peerless, pipe-smoking mega-sleuth

Sherlock Holmes, that foe was Professor James Moriarty—the supreme criminal mastermind, a diabolical evil genius of the highest order, and one of literature's first great arch-villains.

Sherlock Holmes is so famous for his exploits recovering stolen artifacts, thwarting international conspiracies, and solving heinous murders that his name is still synonymous with crime-fighting over a hundred years after his tales were written. When it comes to cloak-and-daggering douchebags in the kidneys with the shank of justice, Holmes was like Jack Ryan, Jack Bauer, and Lennie Briscoe all wrapped up into one ultra-arrogant, pretentious dick who solved crimes with his brain tied behind his back and then went off to mainline cocaine and think about how great it was to be so much smarter than everybody else. The unbelievably prolific author Sir Arthur Conan Doyle featured this cultural icon of Victorian England in a ridiculous fifty-six short stories, as well as a couple of novels, so you'd have to assume that anyone who could conceivably go up against this crime-solving machine and give him a run for his money would have to be pretty hardcore. Professor Moriarty fit that bill—even though he only directly appears in two stories, Holmes himself was so impressed that he once remarked, "If I could beat that man, if I could free society of him, I should feel that my own career had reached its summit." Considering that Holmes basically assumed that in an intellectual debate ninety-five percent of humanity was unfit to hold his codpiece, this is high praise indeed.

Moriarty's rise to become head of the world's largest underground criminal syndicate isn't what you might expect from your typical evil genius these days. Rather than being born from some mutagenic sludge or driven insane by a failed super-experimental military operation, he was just your average super-genius whose incredible intellect predisposed him to a life of ruthlessly taking advantage of stupid people. Born to an upper-class British family, by the age of twenty-one Jimmy

Mo had already written a treatise on binomial theorem that was so brain-crushingly genius that it got him a chair at a university near London. He would then later write a book titled *The Dynamics of an Asteroid*, which sounds so boring that reading it might have made you want to stick small, pointy objects into your eyes, but was apparently so scientifically airtight that no scientist in England even attempted to screw with it. Moriarty's title of full professor would also indicate that he presumably had tenure, which is an impressive and diabolical accomplishment in its own right. Plus it let him be as evil as he wanted to be, because it was too much of a bureaucratic pain in the butt for the administration to even attempt to fire him. The fact that he's a math professor only further illustrates how evil he is.

ProMo's claim to badassitude doesn't stem from being physically imposing or beating do-gooders' heads into sausage with an aluminum softball bat—it comes from being so subversive that he could manipulate a vast empire of meathead goons and loyal thugs to carry out his nefarious plots like a Victorian England cross between Keyser Söze and Stephen Hawking. Working behind the scenes like the final boss in a video game, this guy led an army of lemming-esque henchmen into battle against the semi-incompetent forces of justice, and constantly found new and exciting ways to make law-enforcement officials look like inept morons. He worked like an independent contractor of evil, taking criminal jobs from buyers and then finding the right minions to carry out the dirty work. His agents executed jobs ranging from robbery and extortion to kidnapping, murder, and stealing candy from orphans. If his people were picked up on charges, the police never linked the crimes back to Moriarty, and he would use his clout and hard-stolen wealth to get the perps acquitted or bailed out of the dock.

The best part was that Moriarty himself always stayed completely off the grid, no matter how many of his guys were running around bashing people's kneecaps with tire irons and stealing their priceless paintings and diamonds. He just walked the streets of London like a gangsta, with nobody even realizing that he was a super-villain on par with Doctor Doom, Magneto, or the Joker. It helped, of course, that he didn't go all crazy with the spandex tights or the makeup. Instead, Moriarty kept it simple—an appropriately dastardly black suit, usually with a black cloak, awesome black top hat, and a pimped-out custom-made cane that doubled as a silenced high-powered sniper rifle. Most people outside his sphere of influence just thought of him as "that asteroid dude," and even some of the henchmen carrying out his evil deeds were unaware that they were actually working for his syndicate. Moriarty is such an über-secretive character that a lot of Holmes's fans have come out and questioned whether he was even a real character or just an epic-level figment of Holmes's drug-induced hallucinations. It's impressive when you're such a mysterious fictional character that you've got avid enthusiasts debating your existence within the mythos.

Real or not, the character of Moriarty represents the personification of crime itself. Those members in the highest levels of his organization knew that even though Jimmy Mo looked like a tall, skinny math nerd, he wielded supreme power over the criminal underworld, and you didn't cross him unless you wanted to deep-throat the barrel of a twelve-gauge. He kept his records clean, using twenty different bank accounts to launder funds around, and this shadowy presence kept order in his organization by brutal retribution, the swift execution of traitors, and ruthless utilization of dunce caps and the "time out" corner. Those who crossed him were killed in such a way that it seemed like they simply disappeared, vanishing off the face of the Earth and ending up buried beneath the concrete at the old Giants Stadium with Jimmy Hoffa and the Loch Ness Monster. Holmes himself once said that when Moriarty needs to get crap done, it's like "crushing a nut with a trip hammer," which works perfectly for the purposes of this book, because it's an analogy that features badass overkill, extreme hyperbole, and a reference to nuts.

In the winter of 1890, Holmes was hired by the French government and a Scandinavian royal family to thwart the underhanded theft of some incredibly rare *Magic: The Gathering* cards, and Sherlock ended up chasing the criminal mastermind and his syndicate around the French countryside Carmen Sandiego–style, trying to figure out where the holy living balls he was hiding. After a crazy shakedown, the likes of which, Holmes remarked, "would take its place as the most brilliant bit of thrust-and-parry work in the history of detection," the cunning London detective somehow managed to catch the "Napoleon of Crime" in a fatal mistake, and in one fell swoop managed to gather enough evidence to convict the murderous crime boss of a borderline-ridiculous forty hangable offenses. Knowing what we know about Moriarty, we can only presume it was one of his goons who slipped up rather than the genius himself, but either way, this dude was all kinds of screwed.

But here's the cool thing about Moriarty: beneath all the murder, blackmail, and arson, he was a true gentleman, and had an unexpectedly honorable way of dealing with his enemies. Before sending his hired guns to take down the one man who could ruin his entire criminal enterprise, Moriarty opted to take the significantly more badass route: he hunted Sherlock down, confronted the detective in his own hotel room, threatened him in no uncertain terms, and gave him one chance to withdraw from the duel before being violently eliminated. Holmes, of course, refused, and the two men then spent the next couple of days desperately trying to eliminate each other. Moriarty torched Holmes's home and sent thugs to run him down in the street; Holmes escaped several attempts on his life and delivered the evidence to the police, who went out on a raid that rounded up every member of the gang . . . except one.

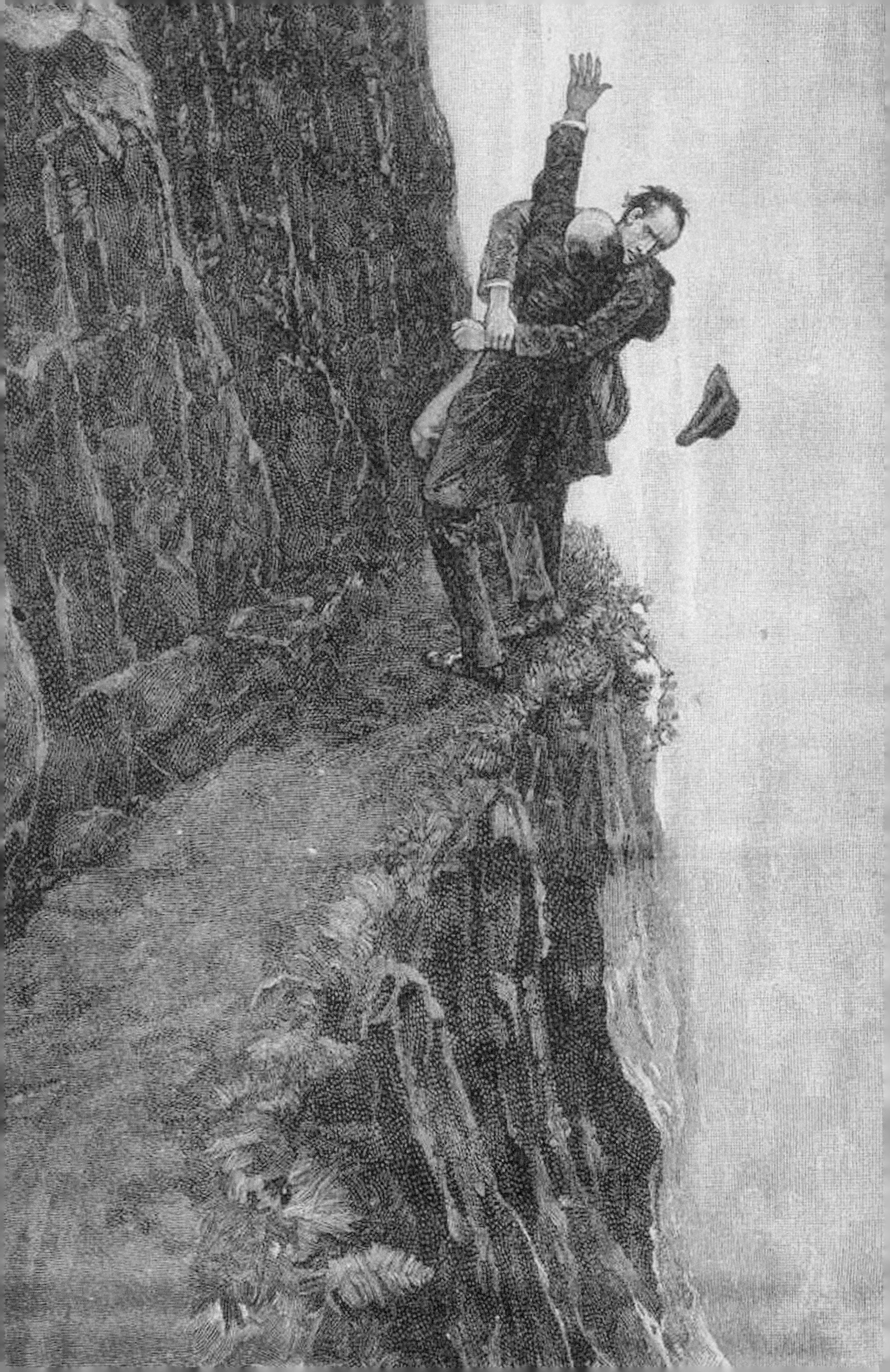

The battle between Holmes and Moriarty wasn't going to be settled in the courts. The two geniuses settled it in a manner in which all intellectual debate should culminate: with fisticuffs. They faced off old-school, fighting one of the greatest duels in literary history at the top of the Reichenbach Falls in Switzerland. After a tough beatdown between two experienced fighters, Holmes got a move on Moriarty and threw him over the ledge, but at the last second, the evil professor grabbed Holmes and pulled him down with him, dedicated in true badass fashion to making sure that if he died his enemy would go down in flames with him. Both men went careening into the abyss. The 1980s British TV series has them falling for thirty-one seconds (yes, I timed it), which is a damn long time to watch two dudes plummet to their deaths in slow motion.

Moriarty was such a hardcore literary character that his destruction of Holmes even ended up having an effect on real-life England. The day after Arthur Conan Doyle's story "The Final Problem" proclaimed the death of Holmes on the pages of the *Strand* magazine, twenty thousand people canceled their subscriptions. Men went around London in black armbands. Women wore black veils. Moriarty had put the British Empire into mourning.

Moriarty's kung-fu grip was supposed to be the official end of Sherlock Holmes, but even though it was kind of a perfect way to bring the series to a close, an obscene amount of public pressure and an even more obscene amount of money brought Doyle back into the habit of writing detective fiction. Eight years after "The Final Problem," Arthur Conan Doyle released "The Hound of the Baskervilles," a prequel, and a year after that, he officially went on a reunion tour that brought Sherlock Holmes back from the dead. Doyle retconned Holmes and had him surviving the falls, climbing up a rocky cliff face, and spending the next three years traveling the world high-fiving the Dalai Lama and playing Yahtzee with Arab sheiks (or some such nonsense), but it was pretty obvious that Sir Arthur was done writing these stories by this point. The later adventures were nowhere near as good, and even Holmes himself mentions in a later story that "from the point of view of the criminal expert, London has become a singularly uninteresting city since the death of the late lamented Professor Moriarty."

The character of Moriarty is based in part on a bizonkers real-life Prussian-American dude named Adam Worth. An artillery sergeant in the American Civil War, Worth spent his postwar years picking pockets in Boston, tunneling into bank vaults in New York City, running illicit gambling operations in Paris, stealing priceless paintings from art galleries in London, and ganking ping-pong-ball-size diamonds in South Africa. Engineering a criminal enterprise across three continents, Worth (who, like Moriarty, was also known as "The Napoleon of Crime") escaped from the federal penitentiary at Sing Sing, and routinely evaded the NYPD, Scotland Yard, and the Pinkertons every time they tried to ensnare him. He was finally caught in Belgium but, despite all of his evil deeds, Worth ended up spending just three and a half years in prison. After he got out, he somewhat ironically became good friends with Allan Pinkerton, and Worth's son would go on to become a lifelong Pinkerton detective.

Moriarty's chief lieutenant is the fearsome Colonel Sebastian Moran—a hardass ex-soldier with a bitchin' mustache and an irrational hatred of man-eating tigers. This guy was an avid hunter and marksman who spent his time in the Indian service hunting giant killer beasts and snapping people in half with his bare hands. Moran was the ultimate sniper, the best marksman in England, and a total rampaging mustachioed beast in hand-to-hand combat. After the events in "The Final Problem," Moran came to

London and attempted to avenge Moriarty's death by assassinating Holmes, but it didn't work out so hot—Holmes built a freakishly elaborate wax statue of himself and tricked Moran into shooting that instead, then he, Watson, and half of Scotland Yard ambushed the colonel while the latter tried to make his escape.

———

With all due respect to Drs. Blofeld, Faustus, Moreau, Jekyll, Mindbender, and Claw, I'd have to say that Hannibal Lecter is probably the most badass villain to ever tough it out and earn his MD from Evil Medical School. Not only does this guy eat brains with fava beans and help hot FBI babes hunt down sadistic killers, but he always seems to find a way to twist the situation to his advantage and come out victorious, regardless of how badly odds are stacked against him or how many different chains, straps, muzzles, and straitjackets are being used to render him immobile.

———

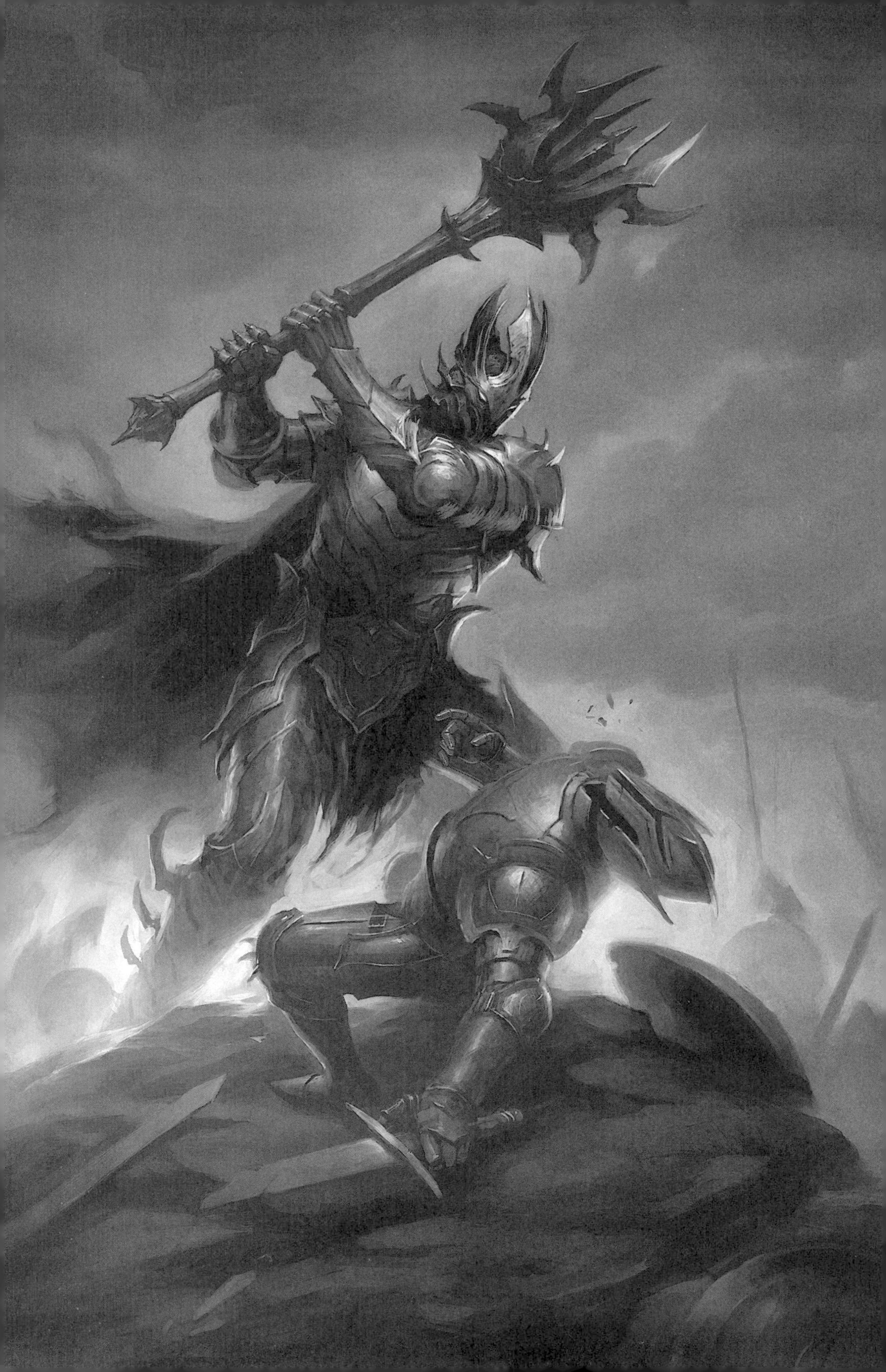

27

SAURON

Now Sauron's lust and pride increased, until he knew no bounds, and he determined to make himself master of all things in Middle-earth, and to destroy the Elves, and to compass, if he might, the downfall of Númenor. He brooked no freedom nor any rivalry, and he named himself Lord of the Earth. A mask he still could wear so that if he wished he might deceive the eyes of Men, seeming to them wise and fair. But he ruled rather by force and fear, if they might avail; and those who perceived his shadow spreading over the world called him the Dark Lord and named him the Enemy.

—THE SILMARILLION

ANY TIME YOU'RE TALKING ABOUT THE BIGGEST AND MOST BAS-TARDLY VILLAINOUS ENTITIES IN THE REALM OF FICTION, YOU'VE GOT TO TALK ABOUT SAURON—THE ULTIMATE PROTOTYPE FOR ALL THE SUPER-EVIL, ALL-POWERFUL FANTASY VILLAINS WHO CAME AFTER HIM. A moderately omniscient, mind-dominating magical being who almost conquered Middle-earth on three separate occasions (including once when he was imprisoned inside little more than a floating eyeball and a small gold ring), the mysterious Sauron not only donkey-slapped his enemies into submission with a titanium codpiece and terrified fantasy-novel aficionados for half a century, but he also once ruled over a place known as the Isle of Werewolves, which is probably one of the more awesome things that has ever been written.

Ultra-evil dark lords like Sauron aren't simply conjured out of thin air with their feet already wedged up justice's rectums. It takes a lot of time and effort to fall spectacularly from grace, and Sauron was no exception. This guy was originally just a lesser spirit in the service of the god of blacksmithing, armoring, and dwarf-forging (which is, of course, the timeless art of forging dwarves out of materials you find randomly lying around your house), yet he somehow managed to become so powerful and evil that every elf from here to the North Pole developed a drinking problem and an anxiety disorder because of him. Sauron isn't even the dude's real name—it's just a title that, depending on which dialect of Elvish you speak, translates to either "The Abhorred" or "The Abomination." I won't get too much into the psyche-crushing world of Middle-earthling etymology here, because, for whatever reason, J. R. R. Tolkien had some inescapable boner for giving a hundred different proper names to every person, place, geographical region, and inanimate object in his already name-intensive legendarium, and attempting to convey the intricacies of his border-line-obsessive naming conventions in detail is enough to make even the most devout linguistics professor start spewing blood out of their eyes and nostrils. I'll just say that Sauron, Annatar, Mairon, Gorthaur the Cruel, King Excellent, the Giver of Gifts, the Necromancer, the Nameless Enemy, and the Big Funky-Fresh S-Ron from Planet Funk-o-Tron are all the same guy, while Fingon, Finrod Felagund, Finarfin, Fingolfin, Finwë, Findis, Finduilas, and Fëanor are all names of different members of the Elven Royal Family. Awesome.

It didn't take long for a power-mad megalomaniac like Sauron to realize that he had better things to do with his time than stand in front of an anvil all day slapping together miscellaneous dwarf parts.

When the über-powerful evil god Morgoth—"The Dark Enemy of the World"—came by looking for peeps to come help him fist-bump a handful of tyranny up Middle-earth's rectum, Sauron was one of the first guys to toss aside his spare dwarf-beard collection and hop aboard a nonstop flight to eternal damnation. Sauron was placed in charge of the delved subterranean stronghold of Angband, where no mortal adventurer would ever dare venture without a torch, and he used his evil magic and above-average skills at elf-torture to twist the native peoples of the land and craft unruly bloodthirsty barbarian horde of mindless orc, dragon, troll, and balrog minions. During the insane war that followed, Sauron served as the chief lieutenant of Morgoth's forces, using a combination of extreme cruelty, sinister magic, and brute force to overcome the free peoples of Middle-earth. One of his most deliciously evil tactics was to line up in battle formation and then start publicly executing prisoners of war in full view of enemy battle lines in an effort to provoke the dumbass elves to charge foolishly into a trap. When that didn't work, he just bashed people into ground beef with a giant two-handed mace and dumped the remnants of their mangled corpses into an active volcano.

Sauron is so unabashedly evil that a lot of people think he was modeled after Adolf Hitler. Tolkien was pretty adamant that his writings were influenced by his own personal experiences as a soldier in World War I rather than anything related to the Nazis, so that would make Sauron the mace-swinging fantasy equivalent of Kaiser Wilhelm II, which is way cooler anyway. I'm pretty sure this is why Peter Jackson chose to represent him with a giant pointy helmet in the movies, though, for whatever reason, Jackson has refused to respond to my e-mails asking for clarification on this important matter.

Sauron and Morgoth succeeded in driving the gods out of the land, destroying the armies of the elves and dwarves and conquering almost the entirety of Middle-earth. Sauron personally captured the Isle of

Werewolves, and sent an army of wolfmen around to bite the throats of any imbecilic cretins who didn't think it would be super-incredibly awesome to have Sauron shove his boot into their face until their eyes popped out of their heads. Eventually, the gods regrouped and launched a balls-out assault on the dominion of our friends S&M. Dragons and giant eagles were locked in totally metal midair fighting, lightning bolts were crashing, and the fighting was so ferocious that it broke apart entire continents and irrevocably altered the geography of Middle-earth. Morgoth's forces were finally defeated; he was dragged back to Heaven in chains and thrown into the limitless void beyond the mortal realm.

Sauron, however, wasn't the sort of malicious spirit who would give up just because his boss was overthrown and he was bitten in the neck by the Hound of the Gods. A thousand years after Morgoth's defeat, Sauron showed back up in Middle-earth, moved in with the elves, and told everyone, "Hey, it's cool, guys, I totally repented and don't have such a raging hard-on for enslavement and uncontested omnipotence anymore. Oh, and speaking of which, here are some awesome rings I made for you!" Then he distributed sixteen rings of power among the rulers of men and the dwarves to show how chill he was (and taught the elves how to make three more). These rings not only looked fashionable and conferred some totally sweet magical powers like invisibility, but they were also covered by a lifetime warranty and guaranteed to bring all the ring-bearers power, wealth, babes, and immortality. Sauron then surreptitiously moved to the Black Land of Mordor, an ominous volcanic wasteland with mountains on three sides; built the giant, impenetrable Black Gate on the fourth side; and raised the skyscraper-esque phallic tower of Barad-Dûr to represent his giant, evil, raging hard-on for enslavement and uncontested omnipotence. Then he invented a language called Black Speech, which is primarily used to tell dirty jokes, secretly plot world domination, and find out whether or not you're about to sell black-tar heroin to an undercover narc. You'd think that inventing a language called Black Speech in the Black Realm of Mordor may have set off some red flags, but Sauron was still somehow secretly able to sneak into Mount Doom and forge the One Ring in infernal fires hotter than Lucifer's balls without anyone really noticing or giving a crap. Putting the majority of his extensive magical power into the ring, Sauron then acquired the ability to utterly dominate the minds of those kings wearing the other rings of power, corrupting them with greed, anger, jealousy, hooliganism, and miscellaneous other tomfoolery. He twisted the kings of men into totally freaky ringwraiths dedicated to carrying out his appropriately evil whims, and gave them all the ethereal thumbs-up while they rode around Middle-earth skeeving everyone out.

Now firmly entrenched in an incredibly fortified stronghold and in control of nine kingdoms of men, Sauron repaid his enemies for their encyclopedic ignorance by going on the offensive, banging his iron boot on the negotiating table, and telling the empires of Middle-earth, "We will bury you!" His rampaging armies de-meated their opposition, and Sauron tyrannically ruled his foes through an ever-so-subtle use of extreme terror and scrotalitarian oppression. He anointed himself with the title Lord of the Earth and King of Men, conquered most of the world, and ushered in a period known as the Dark Years of Dark Blackness. During this soul-sucking time period, if Middle-earth were a 1980s sitcom, he would have been Tony Danza, because he was the boss. If it were a 1990s sitcom, I guess he would have been Uncle Phil.

One group of hardworking humans, the battle-hardened warriors from the island kingdom of Númenor, started drinking the Hateo-rade about the whole "King of Men" thing, so they raised an army and attacked Sauron when he least expected it. Not wanting to deal with crushing these Doúchenorian fools in a protracted war, Sauron agreed to go to their homeland as a "hostage" instead. As soon as he arrived on the island, he immediately corrupted the king, took command of the royal court, and convinced the native population to build five-hundred-foot-tall statues to Morgoth and commit grotesque human sacrifices all over the place. The Númenorians began referring to Sauron as "King Excellent," which is totally, well, excellent, but the gods got pissed about it and sunk the entire island into the ocean Atlantis-style, killing the majority of the population in the process. Win-win.

The survivors of Númenor were unhappy about having their entire homeland turned into a barrier reef like it was part of a celestial dunk-tank carnival game, so they joined forces with the elves in the cleverly titled Last Alliance of Elves and Men. Together, the final remnants of goodness and purity launched a particularly balls-out invasion of Mordor. The torch-and-pitchfork mob breached the Black Gate and headed up Mount Doom, only to find Sauron waiting there to personally crush their brains with the black mace Grond, a weapon so hardcore it was also known as the Hammer of the Underworld. Sauron bashed in the heads of both the Last High King of the Elves and the King of Gondor, smearing their corpses along the slopes of Mount Doom and splattering their battalions. He was only finally defeated when the One Ring was cut from his finger in a freakishly lucky critical hit from the broken-in-half sword of the aggressively incompetent Prince Isildur. Isildur claimed the One Ring for himself, and then promptly lost it in a river like a moron.

But Sauron *still* wasn't done. Harnessing only the extreme power of his unbearable murder-rage, King Excellent somehow managed to overcome the hurdle of not having a physical body and manifested himself solely as a being of pure hatred. Barad-Dûr became topped by the giant glowing Lidless Eye of Sauron, which caught a lot of people off-guard, and the Dark Lord started scouring the land in search of the now lost One Ring.

Considering that he'd put the majority of his worldly strength into the ring, Sauron fighting a full-scale war without it was kind of like a guy kickboxing a robot with one leg tied behind his back. It also didn't help that he was severely hindered (as he was throughout his entire career) by the substandard quality of his mooks. Sure, the orcs tried hard and were super-enthusiastic about the whole crush/kill/destroy thing, but let's face it—a horde of green-skinned unintelligent mutants with crudely fashioned axes is only going to get you so far, especially when you're sending them up against sentient kung-fu trees and a fireball-flinging wizard who comes back from the dead every fifteen minutes. Even the mighty ringwraiths repeatedly failed

in their attempts to rough up a couple of three-foot-tall noncombatants, and their leader, the much-feared witch-king of Angmar, ended up being jobbed in the face by a hobbit and an amateur warrior-woman appearing in her first career battle. Sauron didn't even talk (he had a guy who did that for him, which is kind of kickass, by the way), and his primary mechanism for interacting with the physical realm was little more than an inanimate piece of jewelry hanging from the neck of an elusive and constantly whining hobbit, yet he still somehow defeated the armies of Gondor, penetrated the walls of Minas Tirith, and only failed to ransack the last bastion of hope for humanity when his army's flank was sneak-attacked by an army of undead spirits. Sauron finally had his power broken in the moment of his victory when a couple puny halflings snuck into Mordor and accidentally incinerated the One Ring in the fires of Mount Doom by fighting over it like idiots while Sauron was distracted wiping out the last remnants of humanity. I guess that's the price you pay for creating an ultrapowerful artifact out of your own magical life essence and then not locking the door to the only location in the universe where that item can be destroyed.

If it wasn't for the great eagles of the Misty Mountains, Middle-earth would have been totally boned. These giant, flapping monstrosities of beak-pecking viciousness were responsible for defeating the dragons and overthrowing Morgoth during the War of Wrath; they overcame the goblin hordes at the Battle of Five Armies; they defeated the ringwraiths at the Black Gate; and they saved the future of the universe by flapping around bailing out Frodo, Sam, Bilbo, Gandalf, and Thorin Oakenshield on a number of occasions. Sure, Aragorn gets all the publicity and gets to make out with elven Liv Tyler, but if it weren't for these giant, magnificent, winged bastards and their hundred-foot wingspans, everybody in Middle-earth would have been fluent in Black Speech for at least a couple millennia.

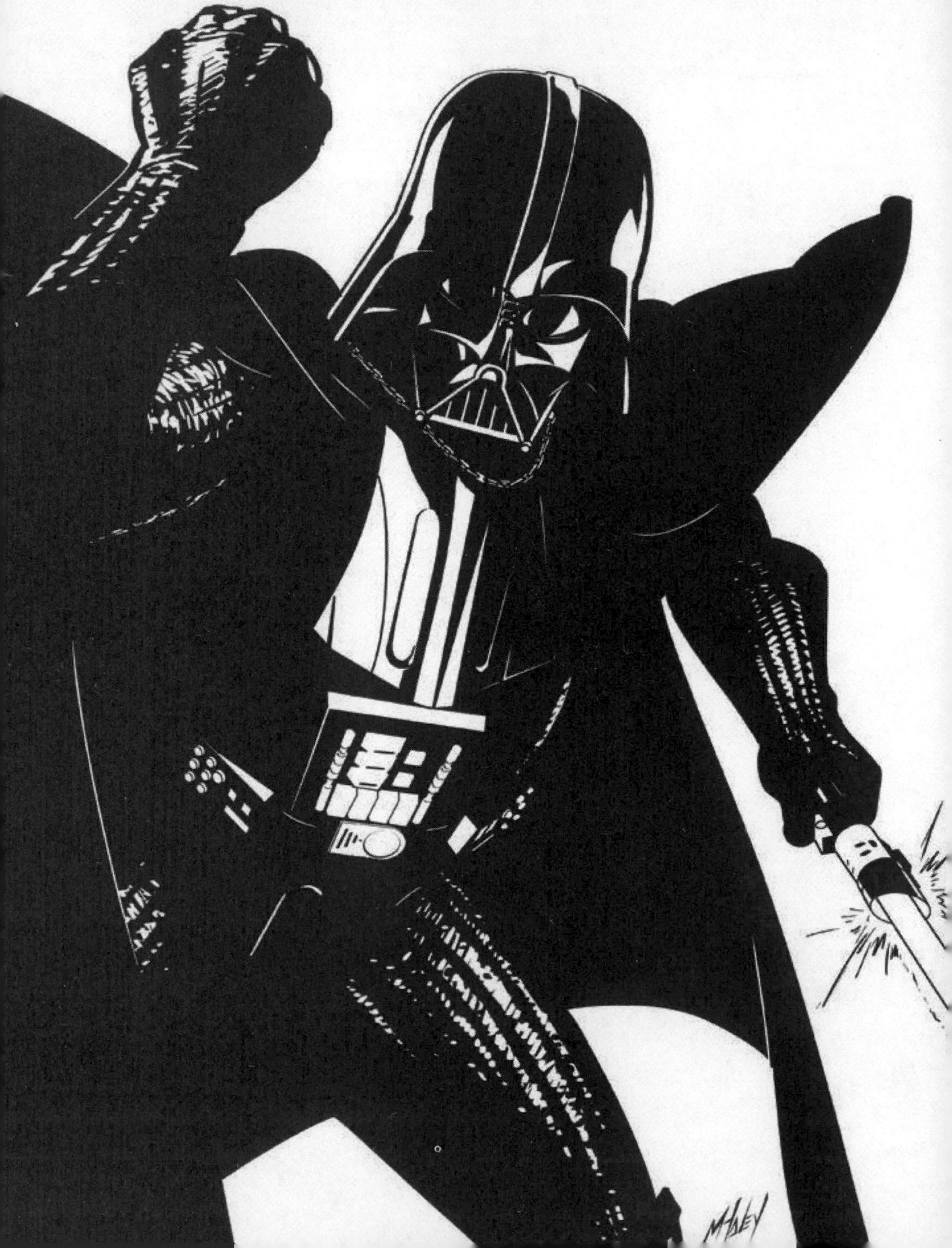

28

DARTH VADER

*A young Jedi named Darth Vader, who was a pupil of mine until he turned to
evil, helped the Empire hunt down and destroy the Jedi knights. He betrayed
and murdered your father. Now the Jedi are all but extinct.*

—OBI-WAN KENOBI

DARTH VADER IS THE SINGLE MOST ICONIC VILLAIN IN THE HIS-
TORY OF CINEMA. A seven-foot-tall intergalactic killing machine who
can murder you with his mind when he's not bifurcating your torso
or manually choking you out with a black glove. With his intimidating, commanding James Earl Jones voice, his impressive Welsh body-
builder body, and his cold, unfeeling attitude toward all life in the
galaxy (sentient or otherwise), Darth Vader commands fear, respect,
and awe from anyone who is a fan of science fiction, movies, or things
that don't suck. He's more dangerous than an underwater electric chair,
more intimidating than a freight train made out of rabid velociraptors,
and his jet-black armor, red lightsaber, and badass attitude are still totally cool even after pretty much everything else from the 1970s went
the way of Luke Skywalker's mullet.

Unlike many things from that largely unfortunate decade, being an unfeeling, emotionless hardass never goes out of style, and that's a hardcore talent Vader has perfected through a lifetime of not giving a crap about anything. His power comes largely from his furious anger and unquenchable blood-rage, but like any real badass, Vader harnesses his ferocity in a controlled way. He never loses his cool, shows emotion, or presents an outward demeanor that indicates anything other than the fact that he is goddamned scary. His fighting style isn't built around jumping or doing ridiculous crazy backflips or other show-off pointless bullcrap—it's all raw, overwhelming power designed to club his enemies into submission with sheer brute strength and his giant, robotic, steel-plated nutsack. You can have your somersaults, your double-bladed lightsabers, and your Jedi mind tricks—the Iron Fist of the Empire was single-mindedly dedicated to ruthlessly battering down your defenses with a vicious series of crushing attacks no man could withstand, leaving you a shriveled, weaponless, simpering, one-handed husk of your former self, and then using the power of the Force to choke out what remained of your miserable, pathetic life.

While we're on the subject, I just have to say that Force Choke has to be one of the most underrated powers to ever explode out of George Lucas's brain. Among most nerd circles, the Emperor's Force Lightning is by far the "sexier" method of utilizing the Dark Side to lovingly deliver a slow, excruciatingly painful death to your foolish enemies (insomuch as death by tasing can be considered "sexy"), but the Prime Minister of Pain's ability to asphyxiate someone through a cameraphone is some seriously next-level stuff. Strangulation in general is a brutal, terrifying way to go, and even though Vader could probably easily choke someone out from halfway across the galaxy, any time someone failed him or lacked adequate faith in the Force, he made absolutely sure he was able to look them dead in the eyes as he was snuffing out their lives.

Ultimately, let's face it—the Dark Side of the Force was good to Anakin Skywalker. I'm not exactly sure what his standing was like among the Jedi before he cliff-dived off the precipice of evilness, but Vader ended up being the second most powerful dude in the galaxy, and that ain't bad. Simply by somehow harnessing the unbridled power of his own limitless fury, we're led to believe he almost single-handedly annihilated every member of a militant order of warrior-monks that had dominated the galaxy for millennia, crushing all resistance except for a handful of old, under-the-radar, washed-up Jedi knights who had given up their lightsabers for lonely lives as crackpot hermits on crappy backwater planets barely capable of sustaining human life. He commanded the Imperial Fleet, personally oversaw the destruction of the Jedi Order and the creation of not one but two Death Star Battle Stations, and hunted down every trace of the Rebel Alliance across the galaxy. Vader not only directed massive space battles and planetary ground invasions from the bridges of planet-crushing Star Destroyers, but was also a mean pilot in his own right, screaming through the vacuum of space in a badass-looking bent-wing TIE Fighter. Sure, the TIE Advanced had great stats in the awesome old LucasArts *TIE Fighter* games, but it takes some serious chops to earn your keep as the most hardcore pilot in the Imperial Navy. Hell, the dude became an ace in a day just picking off fools in the Death Star trenches, smoking Porkins and all his douchey friends before finally getting knocked out by a cheap shot to this blindside right as he was preparing to send Luke cockpit-first into the Death Star trench floor.

In fact, when you really take the time to look at it, you'll notice that Darth Vader completely owns every major character in the trilogy at different times during the story. He taunts, overpowers, and kills Obi-Wan in a lightsaber duel on the Death Star. He doesn't just defeat Luke Skywalker on Bespin, he completely dismantles him—pummeling him incoherent by telekinesising giant pieces of heavy equipment into his head, chopping his hand off just to show him he's being a bitch, and then crushing his fragile psyche with one five-word sentence before kicking him down a super-deep hole. He viciously interrogates the princess aboard the Death Star with the help of a super-scary, syringe-dispensing robot, and then orders the utter destruction of her homeworld when she doesn't give up the info he wants. He captures Chewie and dismantles C-3PO on Cloud City. He knocks out Wedge's X-Wing and shoots R2-D2 in the head during the Battle of Yavin IV. He catches Admiral Ackbar's fleet in a trap (with hilarious results) at the Battle of Endor. He barks orders at Boba Fett and Lando whenever the hell he feels like it, and still goes out and double-crosses Calrissian just to be a bastard and demonstrate the minuscule amount of respect he has for the dude. Even Han Solo, probably the coolest guy from the entire series, failed miserably against this planet-smashing face-wrecker—when the two badasses squared off at that weird dinner table on Cloud City and Han busted out his puny broom-handled Mauser-looking blaster, Darth just gave him the old "talk to the hand" gesture, and the next thing you know, Solo is strapped to a table with a bunch of zaptastic electrodes shocking the crap out of his face. Then Han is dumped into the Carbonite fridge, handed over to the bounty hunter, and turned into a macabre window treatment in the dirty, breast-filled palace of Jabba the Hut.

Sure, in the imperial hierarchy, Vader was number two to the Emperor, but he obviously wasn't satisfied with that, either. Darth tried to overthrow his boss, but even when Luke wasn't interested in being awesome Darth still managed to get the kill shot on his former master, unceremoniously dumping the old man down a freaking service shaft into the central power core of the Death Star while lightning bolts shot all over the place. And yes, Luke overcame Vader in the Death Star throne room, but only after Darth talked a bunch of trash and pissed him off so hard that young Skywalker had to harness his inner Dark Side to accelerate his fighting spirit. So it's kind of like a moral victory for Vader anyway.

Darth Vader was eventually redeemed from the Dark Side when he hurled the Emperor into Mount Doom in order to save his son from death by painfully slow electrocution. Sure, turning traitor isn't exactly badass, but the end of *Jedi*, when the half-melted head of Anakin Skywalker tells Luke that there's still some good left in him, is one of the most touching scenes in cinematic history (perhaps second only to the heartwarming moment at the end of *Die Hard*, when Carl Winslow overcomes his fear of shooting kids and caps Karl the Terrorist in the face with a .38). Plus, I love the idea that despite all of this horrible evil crap he did during his life, Anakin Skywalker still gets to party in Space Heaven with Yoda and Obi-Wan. I bet Yoda is hilarious after he gets a couple margaritas in his system.

———

An astute reader will notice that I made every possible attempt to completely ignore the existence of the prequel trilogy in the writing of this chapter. I feel confident that this is something that will be appreciated rather than criticized.

———

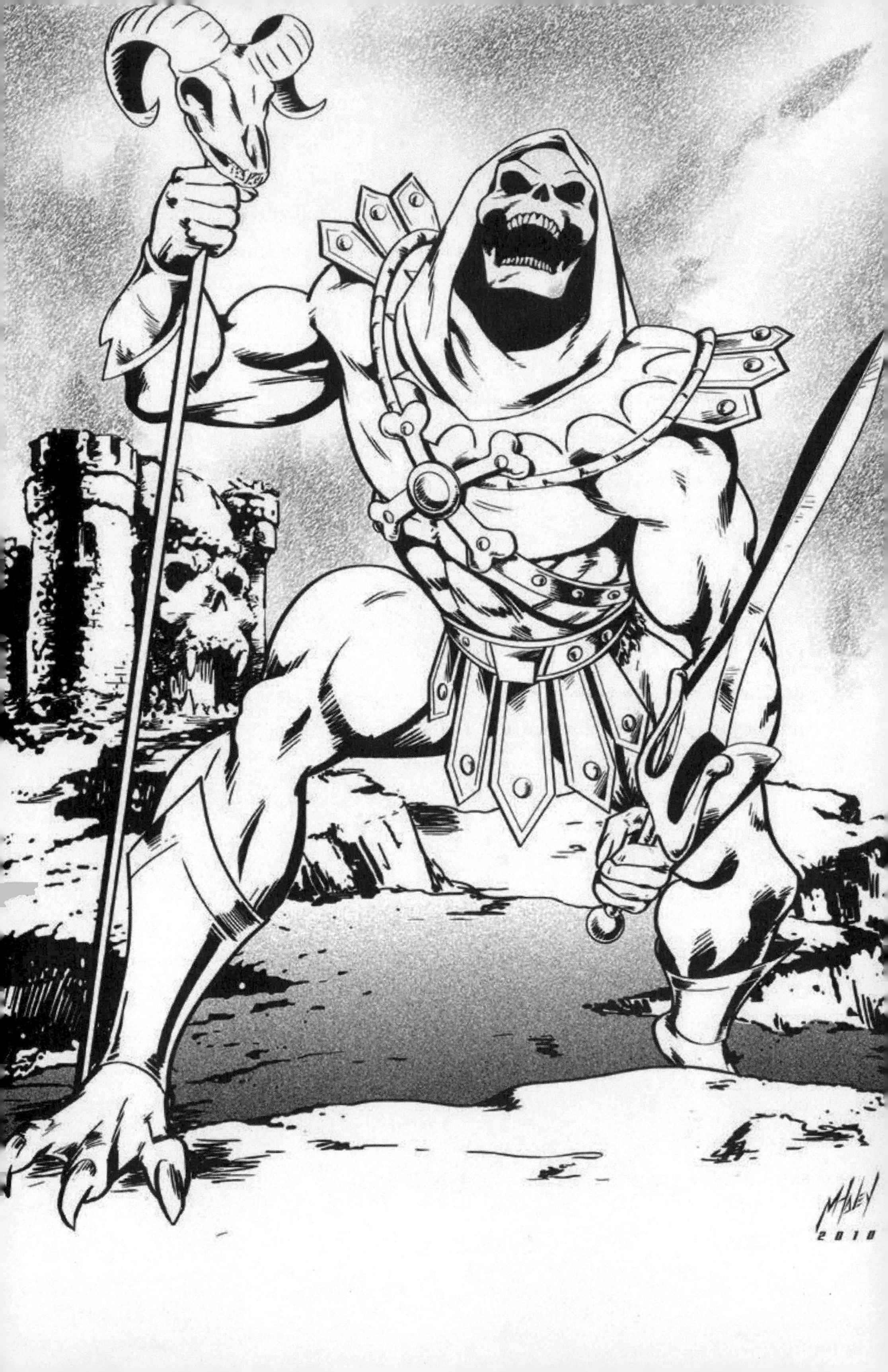
2010

29

SKELETOR

Very clever, you muscle-bound moron! Perhaps this will amuse you!

SKELETOR IS A SUPER-EVIL ARCH-VILLAIN WITH A TALKING SKULL FOR A HEAD AND THE MIGHTY TORSO OF A BEEFY-ARMED BODY-BUILDER. He's also an interdimensional time-traveler, a power-mad megalomaniac, and a badass-looking evil genius who made a career out of shaking his fist in disdain and hilariously berating everyone around him as incompetent morons.

Skeletor came to the land of Eternia when he overthrew his master and backflipped into an interdimensional gateway he created by blowing a shotgun-size hole in the fabric of the universe with his giant raging ego. Once in Eternia, a super-annoying touchy-feely planet of do-gooders and muscle-bound hippies, Skeletor took up residence in the awesome Snake Mountain, completely lost his sanity, built a bitchin' throne out of human bones, and now orders around his incompetent menagerie of underlings in an effort to crush the life out of the hopelessly lame Prince Adam of Eternia, conquer Castle Grayskull, and become the true master of the universe. This never works.

Skeletor's shrill cackling and unending hatred for guys with bowl cuts is only tempered by the soul-crushing ineptitude of his miserable henchmen, who range in general uselessness from a really hairy beast-man with atrocious posture to the notorious Skunkor—a dude whose only real superpower is that he constantly smells like he just crapped himself. You're not really going to be conquering any universes with these clowns bungling up even the most routine operations, and most of the time Skeletor was stuck just pointing in a general direction, sighing loudly, and watching all of his incompetent subordinates get their faces punched concave by He-Man. Skeletor summed it up succinctly, in the way that only he could, when he once exasperatedly told his arch-nemesis, "I have to be brilliant, just to make up for *them*!"

The only useful minion under Skeletor's power is his girlfriend, the powerful witch Evil-Lyn. The fact that this guy seems to exclusively date women who have the word "Evil" appearing prominently in their names should be some indication of how diabolical he is. Skeletor also has a badass giant purple panther that he can ride around on, though he doesn't really do this nearly as much as I feel he should. Hell, if I owned a saddled-up panther, I would be riding that thing to the damn grocery store, though I guess Skeletor is so confident in his masculinity that he doesn't need to go around flexing nuts. When you're built like a professional wrestler and have a bleached human skull for a head, your toughness kind of speaks for itself. Either that, or Panthor is a lazy piece of crap, which is understandable considering that he's really just an evolutionarily advanced version of a typically apathetic house cat.

The good news is that Skeletor has the sense to constantly verbally castigate his cronies for their crippling idiocy every time he gets the opportunity. As one of the only characters in the entire series with anything resembling a personality, Skeletor enjoys hurling wave after wave of useless supervillains head-first toward their own destruction, and then calling them boobs and fools when they inevitably end up being ruthlessly crotch-punched into crumpled heaps across the landscape of some barren, godforsaken, desert wasteland. An abusive boss with no respect for his troops, Skeletor leads through terror and fear, and by constantly threatening to taxidermy his friends and use their skins to reupholster his furniture and luggage. His threats aren't solely directed at his allies, however—as a power-hungry, super-arrogant megalomaniac, Skeletor also doesn't hesitate to utilize his ascerbic nonexistent tongue to mock and taunt He-Man and his douchey friends whenever possible. Generally, this manifests itself in Skeletor prematurely boasting about how awesome he is just before someone busts out a crazy maneuver that turns the tables on the forces of evil and generally results in Skeletor running away from an entire army of Eternian soldiers on flying motorcycles, but that's just how life works when you're a sinister cartoon villain. You're never going to win, so you may as well enjoy the moment and do as much damage to your opponent's self-esteem as you can while you have the chance.

In a lot of ways, Skeletor is the long-shot underdog in his eternal struggle with the forces of good. Despite being more jacked than a baseball player on HGH, he's still no match for He-Man in hand-to-hand combat, and his mishmashed handful of barely sentient associates don't stand much of a chance of overwhelming the armies of King Randor and the entire population of the planet Eternia. I mean, He-Man is best friends with a dude named Ram-Man, who can break doors down with his head, while Skeletor's got a dude named Mer-Man, who is basically a criminally idiotic frog-fish thing with legs. How could that possibly be useful? Skeletor has to improvise, goes to war with the army he's got available, and compensates for his organization's inability to pull its head out of its ass by devising a ton of harebrained Wile E. Coyote–quality schemes and honing his mastery of powerful badass Dark Magic.

No plan is too weird for Skeletor to attempt, and his mastery of evil magic seems to be as eclectically bizarre as the monster-creatures he tends to associate with. He avoids the boringly predictable crap like fireballs and lightning bolts from his fingers in lieu of crazy over-the-top insanity, like the ability to make trees come alive, turn himself invisible, create evil clones of his enemies, and summon a giant pink blob monster to fall on his enemies' heads when they aren't looking. Every time some rumor pops up about a long-lost staff, a helmet that gives the wearer a huge boner, or a planet-crushing comet with magical powers, the next thing you know Skeletor is sitting in the backseat of a speeding hovercraft cackling maniacally, elbowing Beast Man in the throat, and triumphantly shouting his weirdo diabolical plans at nobody in particular. Even if the execution of these harebrained machinations generally leaves something to be desired, you've really got to appreciate this guy's originality, and his ability to go balls-to-the-wall in the name of being completely out-of-his-mind crazy.

Speaking of balls, Skeletor is one of the few people in the world badass enough to pull off wearing purple armor, rocking a purple loincloth, and carrying a huge purple sword. The musician Prince is probably the only other guy who can get away with something like this, and then only because he gets more ass than a toilet seat and his powers of not-giving-a-crap border on the legendary—although I have a feeling Skeletor wouldn't be able to maintain composure while prancing around in assless chaps and wailing a solo on a guitar shaped like a penis. Skeletor does carry a totally righteous-looking staff with ram horns, which doesn't actually do anything useful other than look completely awesome and occasionally help him cast some bizarre spells, but it's not really the same thing.

One of the great mysteries of the universe is how exactly Skeletor's head connects to his body. He's always wearing his purple hood (which, incidentally, only sometimes connects to a cloak or a cape), which is cool and all, but we don't know if he has a normal-looking neck with a skull mounted on top, or whether his bare-skull-ness extends to a bony spine heading down toward his torso. Or if his body is straight across and the skull-head hovers above it magically. We'll never know. Also, his skin is blue. Like, bluer than a baboon's balls. Why is it blue? Who knows. It's probably the same reason why he has a super-nasal voice without actually having a nose.

Skeletor's evilness is celebrated in the moderately well-known holiday known as Saint Skeletor's Day, which is internationally recognized every year on February 15. The antithesis of Valentine's Day, Saint Skeletor's Day is a day dedicated to not giving a crap about anything. The appropriate way to celebrate is basically by just doing whatever and maybe drinking a beer while doing so.

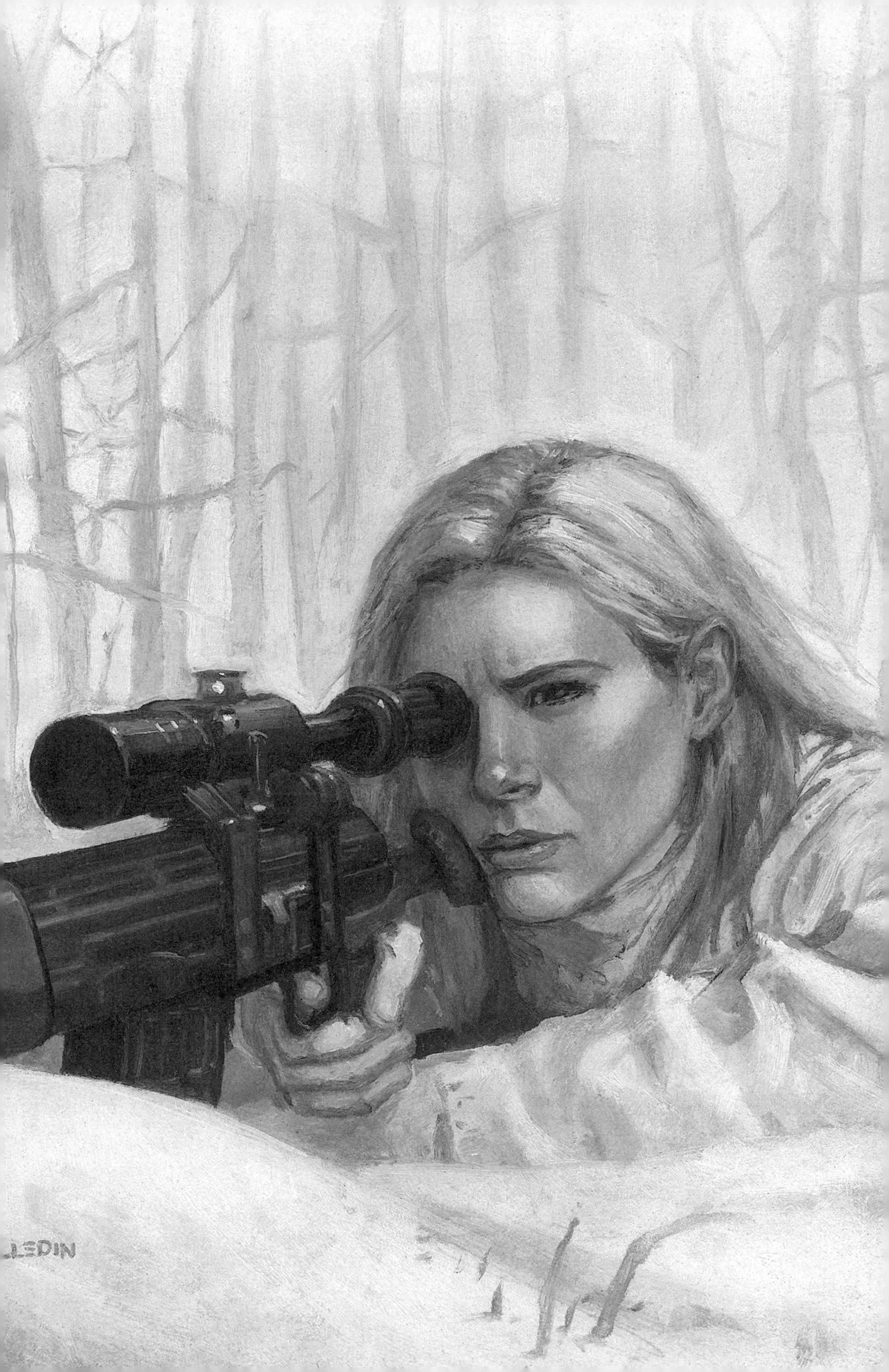
LEDIN

30

THE WHITE TIGHTS

I'll kill you slowly, because I love. First I will shoot you in the leg . . .
I promise I aim at the patella. Then the hand. Then the egg. Don't worry,
I am a world-class athlete. I do not miss.

—ALLEGED TRANSCRIPT OF A WHITE TIGHTS SNIPER SPEAKING TO
RUSSIAN CONSCRIPTS OVER A SECURE MILITARY RADIO FREQUENCY

ANYBODY WHO'S EVER WATCHED THE CRAZY CRAP THEY PUT ON
THE WINTER OLYMPICS NETWORKS AT LIKE TWO O'CLOCK IN THE
MORNING KNOWS THAT WOMEN'S BIATHLON IS ONE OF THE MOST
RIDICULOUSLY SWEETEST SPORTS EVER INVENTED. For those unhappy few of you who have never had the glorious, life-altering opportunity to watch this badass-athalon in action, it's basically just a
bunch of tall, superathletic Nordic and Eastern European superwomen
sprinting through the snow on cross-country skis with rifles slung on
their backs, then dropping down to a prone position every once in a
while, somehow instantaneously managing to completely control their
heavy breathing and exhaustion-induced hand-shaking, and blasting a
series of perfectly aimed rifle rounds through the bull's-eye of a target a
couple hundred meters away.

The much-feared *Beliye Kolgotky* (White Tights) are what you would get if you took a small detachment of these semi-mechanical sniper babes, dropped them right in the middle of a raging goddamn war zone, and told them to completely flip out and just go nuts on anything that moved. The fearsome product of an utterly unsubstantiated urban legend that has been circulating through the ranks of Russian enlisted men for nearly four decades, many front-line troops swear that the White Tights are a company of elite blond-haired nationalist biathletes from the Balkans or the Ukraine who abandoned their sport (presumably for it being "too pussy") and took on new careers as manslaughtering anti-Russian mercenaries. Gunning down Russian soldiers and officers without mercy. Rumors of these death-slinging sharpshooters are known to every man serving on the battlefront of Russia's post-Soviet wars.

The White Tights (also known as "White Stockings," or, alternatively, "Bitch-Cuckoos") are so named for their customary battlefield dress: tight-fitting white camouflage jumpsuits designed to help them remain unseen amid the snow-covered wilderness of the Caucasus Mountains. The story goes that these women were master athletes and marksmen who harbored intense nationalistic pride for their homelands (usually the Ukraine, Latvia, or Estonia), and decided to dedicate their lives to shoving their fists up the USSR's rectum at every opportunity. Trained by elite foreign sniper instructors, equipped with top-of-the-line overseas weaponry, and motivated by unbending hatred of the Cyrillic alphabet and a seething desire to kill everyone in the world, these women now go around offering their particular services to the enemies of Russia. War stories of these white-clad black widows smoking chumps from concealed sniping positions have persisted through every Russian conflict since the Soviet invasion of Afghanistan in the 1980s—they've even been cited as battling alongside the Georgians during the South Ossetia campaign as recently as 2008.

While I should mention that I typically wouldn't refer to any group of soldiers fighting for what they believe in as "villains," I include the

Tights among this category simply by virtue of the fact that they are always depicted as antagonists in the stories involving them. Every time you hear about these women, it's from someone who was on the receiving end of their handiwork, and in the legends, the White Tights aren't seen as noble freedom fighters or revolutionaries—they are vicious, cold-blooded ice queens. Sitting completely motionless in bombed-out husks of old buildings for days at a time, these calculated killers lie in wait for their unsuspecting prey, deal an insta-kill headshot with all the effort it takes most of us to brush our teeth, and vanish into thin air even before the dead man's comrades hear the gunshot.

The Tights are primarily believed to target Russian officers, dealing them a silent death from a couple hundred yards away with one in the brain and throwing their troops into disarray. When a high-ranking military commander isn't available, these black widows particularly enjoy torturing and tormenting their victims like a cat playing with its prey before finishing it off. They much prefer putting the first round into their victim's kneecap, sending him crumpling to the ground. The next round goes into his right hand, preventing him from working his rifle, and then one more directly through the balls to dish out the maximum amount of pain possible. From there, she lets her prey sit there and die a slow, painful death, bleeding out through three 7.62 mm–size holes in three very painful parts of his body. If any of the guy's friends come out to help, she drops them with one shot, sometimes trying to arrange it so that the corpses fall in a way where they spell out swear words. In addition to being motionless, deadly accurate, and utterly undetectable without some kind of long-range thermal imaging, the Tights are also credited with packing top-of-the-line rifles with effective ranges that more than double the range of standard-issue Russian-built sniper systems, making them damn near unkillable once they've got your range zeroed into their scopes.

In another badass display of fear-inspiring awesomeness, the Tights are occasionally mentioned as being capable of tapping into protected Russian radio frequencies and using the channel to taunt their prey, telling the enemy soldiers exactly what they plan on doing to them. *Metal Gear* fans will immediately recognize it as the modus operandi of Sniper Wolf, the terrorist rebel warrior chick who captured Solid Snake, shot his girlfriend a bunch with a high-powered .50-caliber sniper rifle, and then died one of the more epic deaths in video-game history. The common presumption is that the Slavic-accented, blond-haired, white tights–clad sniper chick from the game was based on this myth, but when you're talking about anything involving game designer Hideo Kojima you can never really be sure what the hell is going on.

Of course, the idea of hardcore, mysterious sniper chicks isn't completely unprecedented. Aside from the fact that there were actually women snipers fighting for the Soviet Union during World War II—women like Heroine of the Soviet Union Lyudmila Pavlichenko, who won the nation's top award for military bravery by notching 309 confirmed sniper kills during her career blasting Nazi skulls on the Eastern Front—these sorts of tales date all the way back to antiquity. The most famous was, of course, that of the Amazons. A fierce, mysterious society of asskicking warrior women who allegedly lived in uncharted lands and only ventured back to civilization once a year so that they could hook up with guys (and hopefully produce female children as a result of their one-night stands), these militaristic slaughter-mongers excelled at archery, javelin-hucking, and cleaving people with battle-axes. The Amazons were similarly masters of ranged combat, and, perhaps even more interesting, the Greek historian Herodotus mentions them as living "North of Scythia," which geographically places them roughly in present-day Ukraine—the same place the Russians suggest the White Tights originated. Also like the Tights, the Amazons were completely mysterious, only exist in hearsay accounts, and are widely believed to have been a figment of some guy's overactive imagination.

In terms of cultural anthropology, it also shouldn't be overlooked that these unseen killer women have blond hair and blue eyes. While this may seem like a pretty standard physical description for an Eastern European woman to you or me, it's also the stereotypical appearance of some of Russia's oldest and bitterest enemies. Sure, some Russians share these physical attributes, but between two world wars and the Cold War, these blond/blue-eyed women play directly on deep-seated fears instilled through a century and a half of conflict and tension against countries such as Germany and the United States. Taking these ultra-Aryan superwomen (*überwenchen?*) and dropping them into a war zone alongside Russia's other greatest cultural enemy—radical extremist Muslim militants—is kind of like grabbing a bullhorn and telling a battalion of U.S. troops that they're going to war against Nazi-Commie Taliban Zombies who drive Japanese-made automobiles and hate barbecue cookouts.

Despite the fact that no reliable documented evidence has ever been uncovered confirming the existence of these super-shady death babes (the closest thing is one Kremlin spokesman being quoted as saying, "They exist. Military intelligence says so, and they don't make mistakes"), and the fact that no Western journalist has ever seen them, this urban myth is so pervasive that most front-line Russian troops implicitly believe in the existence of these women without question. The very thought of some assassin woman lying in wait, expecting them to make one false step so they could take a gunshot to the balls, is enough to inspire belief. To this day, no one knows the truth behind the legends, a detail some folks chalk up to the rumor that these women are never captured alive. The theory is that they realize that survival and capture is not an option for them (there have been unconfirmed, presumably propaganda, reports of captured women being drawn and quartered by APCs for their suspected involvement in the terror-inspiring elite sniper cadre), and so they carry a sidearm to put one in the dome if they think there's a chance of being taken alive.

In the end, there are really only two explanations: the White Tights are either really good, or they're nonexistent.

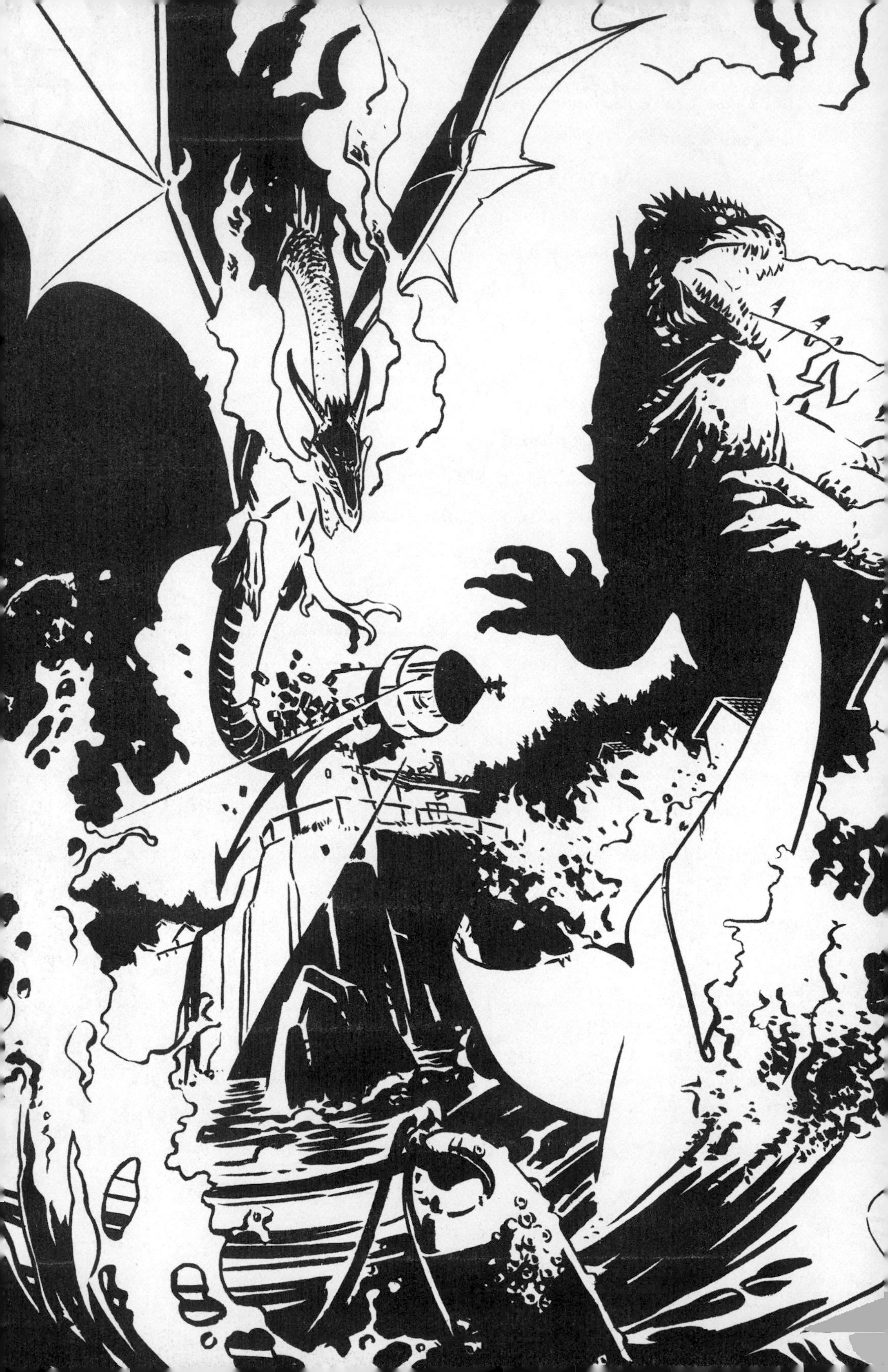

SECTION IV

Monsters, Fiends, Hellspawn, and Worse

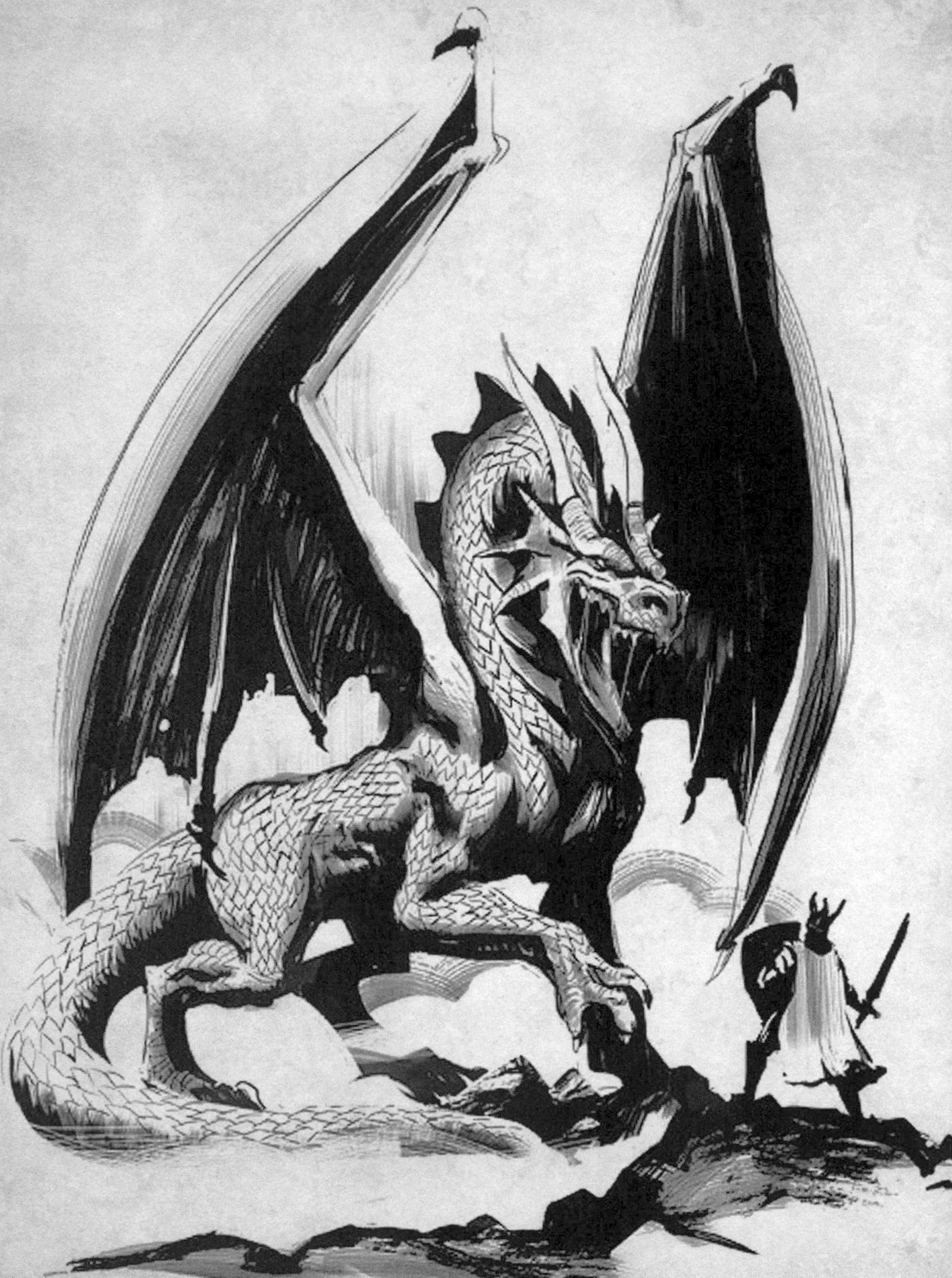

31

DRAGONS

My armour is like tenfold shields, my teeth are swords, my claws spears, the shock of my tail a thunderbolt, my wings a hurricane, and my breath death!

—SMAUG, *THE HOBBIT*

ONCE UPON A TIME, DRAGONS KICKED ASS.

Do you ever wonder why you don't see a whole lot of maidens or damsels running around anymore? It's because dragons ate them all. Those few maidens lucky enough to escape were usually married off to the valiant knights that saved them moments before they were chomped apart, thereby making them, by definition, no longer maidens, and the rest met an inglorious end inside a giant serpentine esophagus. Between marriage and consumption (and I don't mean tuberculosis), by the mid-sixteenth century the maiden was almost completely extinct, having been replaced almost exclusively by the wench and the pirate babe.

Most unlicensed amateur crypto-archaeologists believe that the typical European-style dragon, largely believed to be extinct today, ranged in size from a small pony to a medium-size aircraft carrier. While these monsters were still working their magic on the unsuspecting jerks of the world, the flame-belching beasts usually preferred to live in caves, rivers, dungeons, or anywhere that was really dark and scary and had enough space for a respectable treasure horde and a nearby supply of maidens, livestock, and/or children. According to various modern sourcebooks, these creatures could shoot anything from streams of acid to lightning bolts out of their mouths, though most primary-source material from the Middle Ages appears to limit them to breathing either fireballs or poisonous gas mouth-farts that killed on contact.

Every nerd worthy of his twenty-sided dice knows that dragons are some serious shiz. Facing a dragon in combat is like playing Russian roulette with a flamethrower, and should only be attempted by people who have completely lost their already-fragile grip on reality. Dragons have crazy magical powers, are covered in ultra-thick, steely scales, kitted out with claws, wings, and horns, and in the unexpected case when they get wounded, they shoot blood EVERYWHERE. I've already discussed the Eight-Headed Dragon of Koshii, and how that thing chucked out such an impressive river of crimson that it flooded an entire valley and almost submerged Brave-Swift-Impetuous-Male, but that's far from an isolated incident in the annals of blood-spewing draconic lore. A Russian hero, the peasant-knight Dobrynya, also had a near-death experience drowning in dragon's blood, and he was only saved from choking to death on the creature's interior parts when Mother Earth herself caused an earthquake that made the crimson sea drain into a giant fissure in the Eurasian tectonic plate. The infamous dragoness Tiamat's story was even more ridiculous. Far from the multiheaded Queen of Chromatic Dragons that we all know and love, the real mythological Tiamat was the Babylonian dragon-goddess of the sea and the mother of all of the other gods. One day, the über-god Marduk got pissed off, faced off against Tiamat in mortal combat, and after an intense duel managed to kill her by shooting an arrow down her throat as she was trying to masticate him (this was her one weakness, as her scales were too titanium-like to be dented by anything short of an armor-piercing depleted-uranium tank shell). When Tiamat died, Marduk mourned his slain dragon-mother by ripping her in half, turning her guts into the universe and her blood into the oceans. That's a lot of blood.

Another gore-intensive, badass reptilian monstrosity was the well-known dragon Fafnir. Originally either a dwarf or a giant (depending on who you ask), Fafnir compiled a Scrooge McDuck–size treasure horde, became a totally greedy bastard, and was such a total dick about the whole thing that he actually morphed into a giant man-eating dragon to better protect his wealth. After slaughtering a few thousand warriors who wandered into his cave like idiots, Fafnir was eventually slain by the great hero Siegfried, who snuck into the beast's lair, hid in a hole, and stabbed the beast in the belly with a magical sword when Fafnir wasn't even looking. Fafnir gushed out such a comically intense fountain of Troma film blood that it knocked Siegfried down and almost drowned him, but the brave knight somehow survived, swam to the surface, and ate the creature's heart—a meal that, for some reason, granted him the ability to communicate with birds. I know it's tough to beat Finn McCool and his Nuts of Wisdom, but this is pretty tremendous. Siegfried was later stabbed to death in his sleep by his jealous brother-in-law, because apparently being able to converse intelligently with parakeets is just one of those superpowers that have limited usefulness when you're being ambushed by a cabal of murderous, knife-wielding assassins.

Obviously, there's a pattern emerging here, and quite honestly we all know how nearly every dragon-related story ends: the mighty flame-retardant hero proves his worth to humanity by assaulting the vicious creature's lair and slaying the rampaging beast in mortal combat. But we also all know how these stories begin: the dragon is ravaging the countryside, popping princesses like Vicodin, and igniting every flammable object in his general vicinity. Every brave warrior sent to battle it perishes in flame, painfully and horrifically, leaving behind just a charred field of dead losers and a fat, happy dragon wantonly gorging himself on the defenseless populace.

Consider the winning percentage here. For instance, take the Wawel Dragon of Poland. This tremendous beast lived in a cave underneath an old castle, destroying cattle and sheep and maidens, and nobody could stop it. In some versions of the story, this fearsome beast slaughtered every single hero in Poland before a man named Krak finally took upon himself the task of saving the last princess in the land from the crushing chomp-jaws of this horrible monstrosity. Realizing that fistfighting a dragon is about as wise as urinating on a Tesla coil, Krak

instead stuffed a cattle carcass with sulfur, salt, and tar, and fed the taxidermied Trojan Cow to the monster. The dragon ate it, got super-thirsty out of its mind, and drank from the river until it exploded like an overfilled water balloon (which, as far as I'm concerned, is just further proof that these things are more extreme than ski-jumping rocket ninjas). Everybody got pumped, Krak married the princess, and to this day the city of Krakow is named after him. Sure, Krak was ultimately successful in using underhanded treachery to destroy the beast of Wawel, but where's the love for the beast that single-handedly cut a swath of ruination through the nobility? What was his record, like 100-1? It's a shame that we don't know more about that thing yet there's a whole song about Puff.

One notable dragon who breaks free from the cycle of getting worked over by dudes a hundred times smaller than them is the Norse serpent/dragon Nidhogg. Living in the Dark World far below the regular world, the "Hateful Striker" of Norse mythology dwells in the well of Hvergelmir—the place where all rivers from the Underworld begin—and is surrounded by enough snakes and serpents to give Indiana Jones an aneurysm. Nidhogg spends his days gnawing at the roots of the World Tree, tormenting the bodies of the dead, and ripping apart corpses with his flesh-tearing gross dragon-teeth. He also has a squirrel servant named Drill-Tooth who runs up and down the World Tree passing insults and curses between himself and the Noble Great Eagle, a heavenly creature that sits perched at the top of the tree in Valhalla. At Ragnarok, it's said that Nidhogg will fly through the sky with corpses in his mouth, and his appearance signals the end of existence as we know it.

Dragons really love gold, shiny objects, and virgins; they also love to frighten horses, kill knights, and call forth the Apocalypse; but if there's one thing they vehemently despise with the realness, it's

Roman Catholic Saints. They can't stand 'em. Generally speaking, the Christian tradition likes to use the imagery of dragons to symbolically represent the Devil, sin, paganism, and people from Mongolia (who probably don't deserve to be lumped in there, no matter what the medieval Russian monks have to say on the subject), yet still it seems like you can't open a catechism without some poor dude donning his holy armor and going toe-to-toe with a reptilian abomination unto God. The most famous of these tales is that of Saint George, who swooped in and saved a princess in distress from the dripping jaws of a maiden-eating dragon that up until that point had devoured two children a day everyday for an indeterminate period of time, but he is far from the only holy person to exert his dominance over a monster five steps above him on the food chain.

In the fourth century, Saint Margaret the Virgin was attacked by a dragon while she was being tortured in a dungeon, but even after the creature swallowed her whole, she stayed pure, got super-psyched-up, started glowing, and burst out through the dragon's stomach like she was popping out of a stripper cake (only, you know, holier). Saint Sylvester, the bishop of Rome, is credited with slaying a moat-dwelling dragon that killed three hundred people a day with his poisonous breath; Saint Anthony lived in a cave for twenty years, being constantly harassed and tormented by dragons and demons; and Saint Martha somehow overcame the Tarasque (an ox-size, half-fish, half-dragon monster that jumped out of rivers and ate travelers without warning or apologizing) using nothing more than the power of the Lord and the sign of the cross. These dragons almost always seem to get the worst of their duels with the followers of Catholicism, but a little bit of fail-dogging never stopped these true badasses from trying and never diminished their resolve to chomp down on holy people and churchgoers at all times.

Many dragons can also morph into people sometimes, though this generally doesn't make them any less prickish. My favorite example of this is the beefy-armed dragon-man Tugarin Zmeyevitch, who is easily one of the most badass jerkwads in Russian folklore.

Tenderly described by the Russian folklorists as "that infidel monster, the Dog Tugarin Zmeyevitch," Tugarin was a colossal jack-ass who was hilariously ill-mannered and inappropriate. The story goes that when the holy knight Alyosha Popovitch went to Kiev to visit the prince, he was sufficiently horrified when this ferocious barbarian busted into the dining hall in the middle of the appetizer course, completely disrespected everyone, and sat down right be-tween the prince and his beloved wife without even acknowledging the prince's presence. Tugarin then ate an entire swan, jamming his knife into the cooked bird, wolfing it down in one bite, and spitting the bones out onto the table when he was done. He chased that down by throwing an entire meat pie up into the air and catching it in his mouth. Being a courteous paladin who was unable to witness such a draconic affront to common courtesy and decency, Alyosha called Tugarin out for his blatant insolence. Tugarin, being awesome, com-pletely ignored the knight and then proceeded to shamelessly hit on the princess right in front of her husband. This dragon-man just didn't give a crap—it's obvious that even though he had taken human form, he retained his giant, dragon-size balls, and nothing was going to get in his way. The princess dug the attention, make no mistake, but everybody else in the dining hall was left wondering what the hell this guy's problem was. Alyosha again told Tugarin to mind his damn manners, but instead of apologizing or repenting or even pre-tending like he gave a porpoise's starboard nut, Tugarin just laughed and chucked a dagger at Alyosha's head, nearly de-facing the paladin with one flick of his wrist. In the duel that inevitably ensued, Tuga-rin spit fire, flew around on wings made of paper, and wore a suit of armor emblazoned with dragons, but Alyosha used the power of the Lord to destroy the wings by calling down a rainstorm. When Tugarin tried to trample the Russian knight with his horse, Alyosha jumped out of the way, brained Tugarin's head off with a holy monk's staff, and brought the barbarian dragon-man's head back to Kiev on a pike. Still, it was awesome while it lasted, and even to this day, many clubgoing and bar-hopping bros still pay tribute to Tugarin's legacy by acting like total douchebags while wearing silk shirts with dragons printed on them.

The Eastern traditions also feature dragons as central figures in their mythologies, though they generally don't try to bang too many princesses or eat a whole lot of monks. Eastern dragons are typically less badass in terms of arbitrarily maiming and dismembering members of the local populace, but do usually have totally sweet 'staches and beards. They're like the cool, stoned uncles of European dragons—they're always totally chill and awesome, and when they show up, everybody's pumped up about it because they kick ass and bring good fortune. These dragons are typically used to represent the symbol of imperial power, and according to ancient myth, it was a cosmic dragon that brought writing to people of China. Chinese writing is pretty intense, so you can tell that these guys were serious.

These days, you can also hike through the Dragon's Den in Krakow, which ends with a huge, six-legged bronze statue of the Wawel Dragon that breathes fire whenever you SMS-text the word "SMOK" (Polish for "DRAGON") to the number 7168. I assume this costs money. That's just how dragons are—if there's no cash involved, they're rarely interested. They're like giant leprechauns that tear people apart with fangs the size of broadswords.

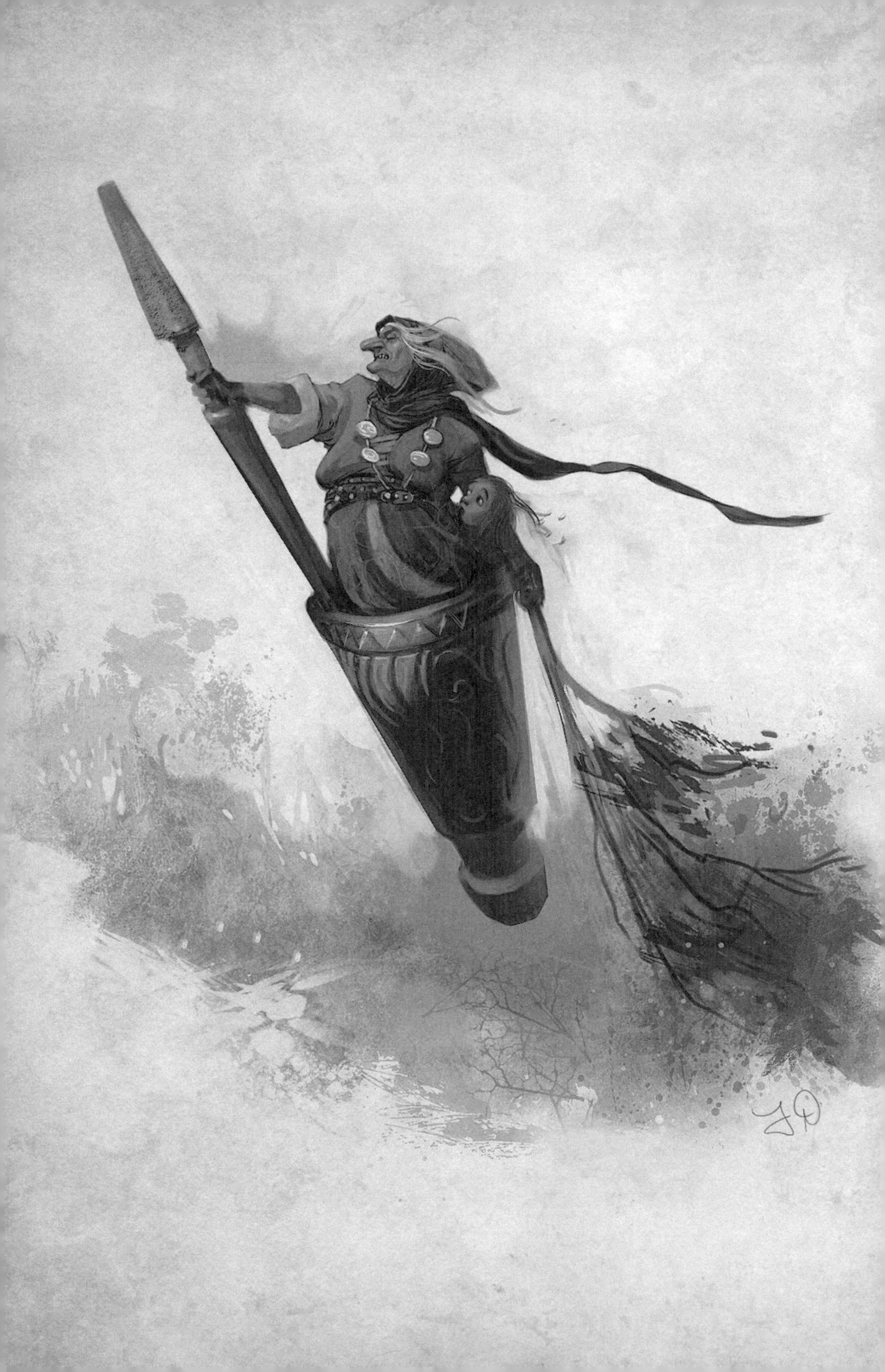

32

BABA YAGA

Dusk began to fall, the black horseman flashed by the gate, and night came;
only the skulls' eyes were shining. The trees crackled. The leaves rustled.
Baba Yaga was coming.

—*THE TALE OF VASSILISA THE BEAUTIFUL*

DEEP IN THE HEART OF THE MOST HAUNTED AND CREEPIEST FOR-
EST IN RUSSIA, BEHIND A SIX-FOOT FENCE CONSTRUCTED FROM
HUMAN BONES, STANDS ONE OF THE MOST RIDICULOUS BUILDINGS
EVER DESIGNED. A small, cramped, one-room hut mounted on gigantic, three-story-tall chicken legs that dance around all of the time
like they're on the set of *Breakin' 2: Electric Boogaloo.* Each post of
the bone fence, which is crafted from the unfortunate victims of the
foul beast that resides within the funkalicious chicken hut, is topped
with a human skull with eye sockets that glow with unnatural lights
at night. Between the dancing chicken hut and the heads that swivel
around with glow-sticks jammed into their eye-holes, this place is sort
of like a really jacked-up Halloween party all the time.

The creature that lives here is just as insane as her abode would indicate. Baba Yaga is a super-mean old fairy-tale witch who grinds the

flour for her bread from the bones of lost children, seasons her soup with fingers and eyeballs, flies around in a mortar, and plays a central role in seemingly every Russian folk tale ever written. All things considered, I could presumably end the story right there, but the tale of this powerful sorceress goes so much further than that. It's layers upon layers; like an onion or a mummified head.

Only the most hardcore adventurers have encountered this sinister crone and lived to tell the tale. She is described as a very old woman with razor-sharp iron teeth, iron breasts, and an iron nose. I'm not sure how "iron breasts" would work, but I try not to give too much thought to the cleavage of a several-hundred-year-old witch, so we'll leave it at that. She's inconsistently described as having snakes in her hair, though everyone agrees that she's so completely hideous and terrifying that one glimpse of her ugly mug causes

the weak of heart to instantly become paralyzed with fright. Baba Yaga digs this. Once you've been scared into a state not unlike rigor mortis, she tosses you under her arm, carries you back to her hut, and kicks you head-first into the oven so she can cook you up for dinner and begin desecrating your corpse for fun, food, and profit. When she gets bored with chilling inside a twenty-foot-tall dancing-chicken house (unthinkable, I know), she hauls ass through the night sky, flying on either a mortar, a broomstick, or a giant, raging boner. She also owns a fire-breathing horse, but that thing doesn't fly so it's practically worthless.

In terms of mythological significance, the primary responsibility of "The Devil's Handmaiden" is to manage the day-to-day order of the universe. No small task, true, but she goes after it with the sort of gusto you don't really see outside of a documentary on wolverines or an asylum for the criminally insane. From her humble break danc-ing chicken-legged hut, Baba Yaga spins the thread of life by jam-ming the bones and entrails of the dead into some bizarre tricked-out custom device that looks like a cross between a loom, a sewing ma-chine, and one of those things you put cows into when you want to de-meat them. I assume that this is mostly for the parts that aren't already being used in food products, home-defense fortifications, or diabolical witchy brews, but you never know. When you're sur-rounded by as many corpses as Baba Yaga is, I guess you really need to be resourceful with those materials that are most readily available to you. She's also supposedly present at all childbirths in Russia, but as you can probably imagine this isn't because she really loves babies or anything—it's because she's trying to decide whether she wants to kill the infant outright or give it a chance to do something useful with its life before she snuffs it out of existence. It's also explicitly noted that Baba Yaga is the entity in charge of regulating how much milk cows produce, and she's also the creature who controls earthly wealth, nature, animals, light, darkness, disease, nightmares, erections, fertility, and the weather. Yes, you read that correctly.

While all of this stuff makes Baba Yaga sound like kind of a totally miserable old, cantankerous wretch, she's pretty cool to those people she has some modicum of respect for. Basically, any time a Russian hero or heroine needed to get something awesome done or overcome a seemingly insurmountable obstacle, all paths to success ran right between the legs of the only house in the world capable of doing the Dirty Bird. But the big BY wasn't going to bail out some worthless chump just because he'd misplaced his favorite princess— she gave these would-be heroes some ridiculous task to do, and provided them with two options: succeed, and receive her help; or fail, and become witch food. It was like a medieval cannibal eugenics program designed to weed out unworthy d-bags who didn't deserve to be heroes.

One time, this guy came to her looking for help in rescuing his wife from the clutches of an evil ruler. Baba Yaga told the guy he was a dumbass for coming to visit her (he was), and that she was going to grind a broken beer bottle into his stupid chump face and kick him down a flight of stairs unless he went out and found a way to tame these forty psychotic horses that were tearing up her lawn. The guy turned out to be pretty seriously awesome at taming horses, got the forty mares under control, and she was so pumped up about not having racehorses doing doughnuts outside her porch all night that she gave him her magical fire-breathing steed. The guy took the horse, got the girl, and slaughtered his enemies, thereby living happily ever after. Another time, Baba Yaga hooked a knight up with a sword that flew off on its own and started slicing people's heads and arms off, which is cool.

On the other side of the coin, Baba Yaga turned Koshchei the

Deathless into an unkillable evil wizard man, and summoned a multiheaded fire-breathing dragon to guard the Waters of Life, so don't go thinking she's soft or anything.

My favorite story involving Baba Yaga is the tale of Vassilisa the Beautiful. Basically, this is the Russian version of Cinderella, only it's way more hardcore. The story starts off similarly enough—Vassilisa is beautiful and charming and sickeningly perfect, but her bitchy stepmother and stepsisters work her half to death for their own amusement. On one particularly brutal chore, Vassilisa was sent into the woods to ask Baba Yaga for a cup of sugar or a match or some other asinine thing. Baba Yaga of course immediately captured Vassilisa, and when the peasant girl tearfully told the witch her emo sob story, Babs was like, "Dude, this is awesome because I need some housework done too," and set Vassilisa to work busting her ass around the dirty chicken hut, taking full advantage of the chance to exploit the poor girl's extensive experience in backbreaking slave labor. Vassilisa then performed a series of seemingly impossible household tasks, and Baba Yaga was so jacked up about it that she pulled one of the skulls off the post of her fence and sent Vassilisa home with a macabre souvenir of all their fun times together. Well, no sooner did Vassilisa get home than the friggin' skull's eyes lit up like fire and freaked everyone out. The severed head slowly swiveled, fixed its eyes on the stepmother and stepsisters, and burned fiery holes right through their faces, leaving the wicked stepwomen completely charred to cinders. Then a strong gust of wind blew the cinders away, leaving behind a triple-homicide crime scene that not even *CSI: Miami* would be able to piece back together. So you can take your glass slipper and shove it, because brain-melting face-incineration is exactly how a badass fairy tale is supposed to end. I will hear no further discussion on the subject.

Baba Yaga is also kind of rad because nobody really screws with her. For instance, one time this knight named Dobrynya Nikitich rolled up all decked out in his armor and battle gear looking to joust some worthy adversary, but Baba Yaga appeared to him as a super-badass warrior carrying a lance so gigantic that it reached the skies, and the dude barely had a chance to choke on his pride before his head went on a point-first date with a hundred-foot-long spike.

If that's not enough for you, she can also morph into a bear and claw off faces whenever she wants, plus there's those Bond villain–like iron chompers and the whole thing about being so pants-soilingly terrifying that people seize up just looking at her. Baba can also launch out walls of fire on a whim, and one time she was trying to keep a guy out of a magical meadow so she summoned a teeming mass of woodland animals to block him from entering the field. Sure, conjuring deer and adorable bunnies isn't exactly badass in and of itself, but when you're an iron-toothed witch who can call forth an endless stream of pandas and gorillas and God knows whatever the hell else to come flying out of nowhere and wall off an entire section of the forest, that's a different story altogether.

Koshchei the Deathless was a villain from Russian folklore who was famous for hypnotizing maidens and tricking virgins and princesses into falling in love with him through some kind of weirdo diabolical mind-control roofie-colada. When self-righteous heroes inevitably showed up at Koshchei's evil castle looking to save their girlfriends, Koshchei would either fight them in a duel or turn them to stone with his magic. Koshchei the Deathless's name also can be translated as Koshchei the Invincible, Koshchei the Immortal, and Koshchei Who Never Dies, but none of these were very good nicknames, because every time you turn around some knight is impaling him with a lance or stabbing him in the balls with an arrow or something and leaving his dead ass rotting on a battlefield. Yet somehow Koshchei just kept on coming back, randomly reappearing in the next story without any explanation. He's like the Kenny McCormick of Russian folklore. It eventually came to light that his immortal soul was actually kept inside a needle inside an egg, which was inside a duck, which had been eaten by a hare, which, in turn, was buried inside a casket under an old oak tree that grew on a glass mountain. It was the Russian stacking-doll version of Achilles' Heel. Koshchei died his final death when the medieval hero Tsarevitch Ivan found the egg and threw it right into Koshchei's face, exploding it and him with ninety-mile-per-hour fastball to the dome and breaking the needle in the process. To bring this whole myth thing full-circle, Tsarevitch Ivan ended up marrying Vassilisa the Beautiful, and they lived, as they say, happily ever after.

33

SURT

That one is called Surt, who sits there at the end of the world as a guardian.
He has a burning sword, and at the end of the world he will travel and harry
and defeat all the gods and burn the entire world with fire.

—SNORRI STURLUSON, *GYLFAGINNING*

RAGNAROK IS PRETTY MUCH THE MOST INTENSE EVENT THAT
WORLD MYTHOLOGY HAS TO OFFER. This epic battle is like the Biblical Apocalypse cranked up to eleven and shoved into an industrial-
size blender along with a fifth of Jack, World War II, a battle-axe, the
complete works of Megadeth, and the still-beating heart of the Norse
God of Bloodshed. It's the ultimate showdown, where gods, monsters, demons, freakishly huge wolves, and reincarnated Vikings run
around with axes clubbing the brains out of each other until everyone is dead either from exhaustion or head-cleavery. And while Odin,
Thor, and the Norse pantheon get most of the name recognition and
the restricted-access rock-star parking spots in the mythology of
medieval Norway, it's the ultra-pissed fire giant Surt who is personally
responsible for torching the Earth into cinders with one of the most

hardcore flaming swords ever forged, defeating all of the gods in combat and causing the destruction of reality and the universe as we know it.

As with all good badass legends, the tale of the Surt and his insane incineration (insaneration?) of all life on the planet is a story of revenge. Back in the days before the Big Bang created Pangea and the dinosaurs through mitosis or whatever, the universe was just one huge boring-ass void of nothingness. Then one day, all of a sudden, this huge giant named Ymir popped up out of nowhere and arbitrarily started spawning a race of Frost Giants to keep him company. The gods got all pissed off at Ymir for some reason (Snorri Sturluson says that it's because Ymir was "wicked and evil," and possibly even "naughty," but he doesn't really elaborate), so they all jumped him one day and beat the crap out of him with their swords, spears, and axes until he was roughly the same consistency as applesauce. As Ymir was dying a gruesomely violent death, he started spewing so much blood out of his wounds that it drowned all of the Frost Giants that he had created. After the Frost Giants were genocided, the gods then thought it would be totally rad to tear open Ymir's body and mutilate it completely out of control. This is where the Earth comes from—it's Ymir's hacked-apart corpse twisted and bent into a fun, happy place where people live and farm and kill each other with axes, and the gods sit back and kick their legs up on their godly ottomans.

However, unbeknownst to the gods, two Frost Giants survived the attempted eradication of their species. One male and one female had hidden themselves away in a mountain cave, far above the oceans of gore. They got to work repopulating the Earth with their giantkin and plotting the day when they would finally get revenge on the gods for completely dicking them over.

Surt would be the instrument of that vengeance.

Seething in the land of Muspell, a land of fire and flames so ludicrously hot that no man or god could enter, Surt spends eternity sitting around sharpening his blade and thinking about how pissed off he is. This guy is a huge giant, towering over men and gods alike, and he carries a flaming sword so bright with fire it resembles the sun, and so impractically huge it would make Sephiroth pop a boner. His skin is black and charred from sitting around in the burning flames all day every day, but he doesn't seem to mind. His sole thought is the doom he is inevitably going to bring on his hated enemies in the heavens—a doom known as Ragnarok, the "Twilight of the Gods."

Ragnarok kicks off Al Gore–style with a little bit of extreme climate change. The world goes through Fimbulvetr, the "Great Winter," where three years of constant snow batter the land. The moon is eaten by a celestial monster known as the Moon Dog, who bites the thing so hard that it splatters the earth, sky, and heavens with blood. Another wolf swallows the sun, shrouding the land in perpetual darkness. The sea floods, possibly because of the whole lunar consumption thing throwing the tides all out of whack. Things generally just suck ass, though, interestingly, people really only seem to complain about the weather marginally more often than they do nowadays.

In the midst of this inconvenient weather, the Final Battle for Earth is set into motion. Loki, the Slanderer of the Gods and the Disgrace of All Gods and Men, breaks free from his nightmarish prison and advances at the head of an army comprised of all the damned souls of Hel. The Midgard Serpent rises from the waters of the Earth looking for someone to hock a venomous loogie onto. The monstrous wolf Fenris goes off his leash in a blood-rage, seeking to fulfill his destiny by tearing Odin a new one. Nagalfar the Death Ship—a gigantically huge vessel created from the fingernails of the dead—shakes free of its moorings, loads up with Frost Giant pirates, and sets sail for destruction. Surt, the personified fury of the giants, grabs his sufficiently sharpened blade and rides forth from the fires of Muspell at the head of a band of mounted warriors so freakishly tough and completely engulfed

in flames that they look like a cross between the Hell's Angels and a well-worked barbecue grill on Super Bowl Sunday. The death ride of the Sons of Muspell blitzes up the Rainbow Bridge that separates the earth from the heavens, and the sheer weight of their charge exceeds the maximum weight allowance for rainbows and shatters the bridge into Skittles.

Opposing this terrifying assortment of Harley-riding explosions and skyscraper-size carnivorous beasts is the combined might of all the gods of Asgard, supplemented by the souls of all the valiant warriors from Valhalla and Sessrúmnir. These two armies smash together in a battle so intense that it shakes the foundation of the World Tree, and the beatdown that ensues is more intense than a drunken four-player game of *Goldeneye* on License to Kill, Slappers Only. Odin, the leader of the Norse Gods, is chomped apart by Fenris, who then in turn gets his mouth ripped in half by the god Vidar. Garm, the evil hound, and the war god Tyr battle until both are dead. Loki and Heimdall double-kill each other with grenade launchers. The Midgard Serpent is killed by Thor in a valiant, protracted battle, but unfortunately for the Norse God of Skull-Crushing, the venom of the Midgard Serpent has an LD_{50} that makes Australian Death Adder fangs look like syringes filled with the polio vaccine, and Thor only gets nine steps away from the serpent's corpse before he collapses and dies of extreme poison damage.

During the bloody carnage that ensues, Surt kills Frey, the brother of Freyja and the Norse god of rain, sunshine, fertility, and peace (if you can't see the symbolism in this, then it's time to hand in your copy of *The Lion, the Witch, and the Wardrobe*), presumably in addition to a few hundred other nameless warriors of Valhalla. Finally, when everything is completely spiraling out of control and gods, monsters, and insane beasts are becoming corpsified all over the place, Surt casts his fire sword at the earth, setting the World Tree ablaze and annihilating everything—including himself—in a giant wall of superheated flame so over-the-top that even Oppenheimer would have been impressed.

When the fires finally subside, pretty much everything is annihilated. As far as we can tell, only four gods will survive the carnage—two of Odin's sons and two of Thor's—and a mortal man and a woman who hid from all the fireballs and destruction. The two humans get busy with the humping and will eventually repopulate the world, and everyone will live in a happy new fun-land where they don't have to worry about getting their heads eaten by Godzilla-size wolves or being stabbed in the eye by vengeful gods. Sure, there aren't a lot of people around to appreciate the hope for better days, but hey, at least Surt got revenge for the destruction of his family, right?

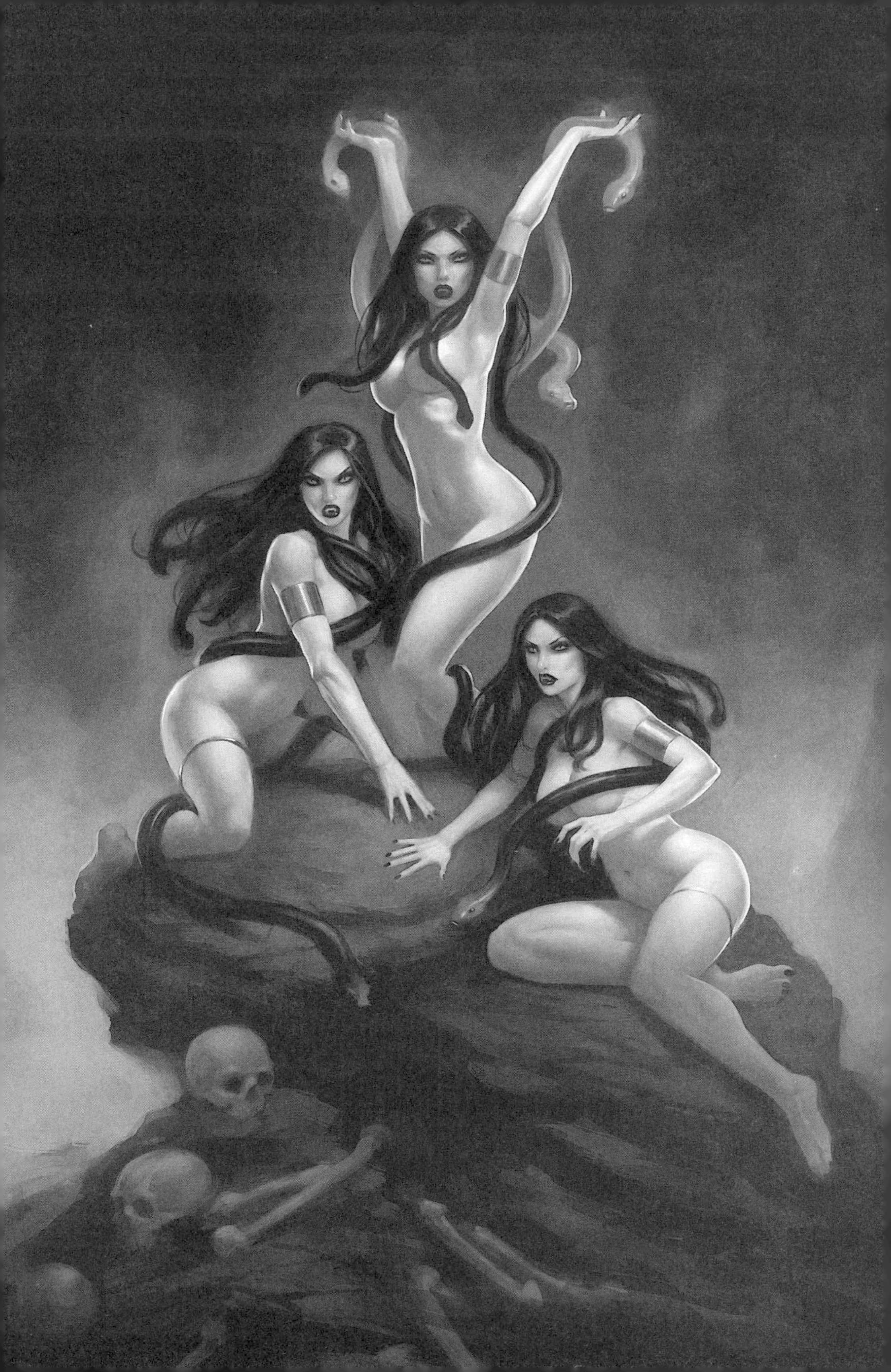

34

THE FURIES

We will drink the thick red liquid libation of your limbs
and quench our thirst with a sickening toast.
We will bleed you dry then banish you below.
We'll see you in hell, one more for the wicked,
with the men who sinned against gods, guests,
and their own dear parents.
You'll suffer the pain that Justice ordains.

IN TERMS OF KICKING ASS AND EMOTIONLESSLY AVENGING WRONG-
FUL MURDERS, THE FURIES WERE LIKE THREE NON-MUSTACHIOED
CHARLES BRONSONS FROM DIFFERENT ITERATIONS OF THE *DEATH
WISH* SERIES.

Known to the Greeks as the Erinyes (meaning "the angry ones"),
the three Furies—Alecto (the Unyielding), Tisiphone (the Avenging),
and Megeara (the Grudging)—were badass demonic spirit-chicks who
spent most of their time living in the Underworld, where they lashed
the hell out of doomed souls with awesome scourges made out of giant
scorpion tails. These merciless, world-ruining hatchet-women wore

wreaths of snakes in their hair, taking a page from *Medusa's Guide to Fashion*, and had bat-like wings, seriously bad attitudes, and the ability to shoot blood out of their eyes whenever they wanted. According to both Virgil and Dante, they resided in an impenetrable fortress behind a river of fire that could not be crossed by man or god, or even by a god wearing a fireproof suit made out of men. When people on the surface world committed a grievous sin such as murdering their parents or not putting the lid back on the sour cream, the Furies would haul ass out of Tartarus on matching Segways, trip the dude up with a lasso of snakes, beat him with scourges and burning torches, and eventually drive him completely insane.

The physical embodiment of vengeance, the Furies were originally created by the blood that gushed forth from Uranus' crotch after his cringe-worthy castration by a razor-sharp sickle. You see, Zeus wasn't the first disgruntled kid to take over as ruler of eternity by stiff-arming his dad through the turf and into the Underworld— the king of Olympus' own father, Cronus, had taken over from his dad, Uranus, by cutting off his johnson with the ultimate symbol of proletarian ascendancy. The Furies came from the blood resulting from this catastrophic crotchal trauma, and when Cronus threw the detached dick in the ocean, the love goddess Aphrodite sprung up from the waves in the spot where the flying dong splashed down. Greek myth was really bizarre like that. I do find it kind of hilarious, though, that a dude named Uranus was killed by being shanked in the taint.

The Furies' chief job was to ensure that vengeance was righteously inflicted on all those chumps who deserved it—murderers, mother-killers, oath-breakers, Internet spammers, drug dealers, and people who cheated death by foolishly not dying when they were supposed to. These hardcore monstrous goddesses were relentless—they never rested, never gave up, and never felt pity for any of the miserable wretches they persistently tormented. No matter what the killer's rationale was or how sorry he was for his crime, they just kept on beating his friggin' ass off with brass scourges and screeching their talon-like nails down the chalkboard of his mind until he completely blew a gasket and became a raving lunatic. Screwing with these hellions was like revving up your rocket-powered motorcycle and playing chicken with a parked car, only worse.

The Black Goddesses also maintained order in the universe, which means that they violently hated things that were creepy and weird, like talking horses. And Oedipus. Oedipus was a Theban king who accidentally murdered his father and married his mother, which is so horrible and wrong it makes most people want to pull out their eyes with the hook end of a claw hammer. When the truth of his actions was revealed, Oedipus was exiled from his kingdom and ultimately tormented by the Furies until he died a slow and painful death by their hands. As beings of pure retribution, the Furies didn't even give a crap that Oedipus' accidental incest-patricide double feature was brought about by a terrible, terrible case of mistaken identity—they don't listen to bullcrap excuses, don't make exceptions, and can't be deterred once they've achieved a missile-lock on their targets.

The best example of this is probably the groin-grabbingly tragic story of the Greek hero Orestes. When Orestes' father, Agamemnon, came home from the Trojan War and was immediately stabbed to death by his cheating wife and her murderous boy-toy lover, Orestes went to the Oracle of Delphi and requested permission to avenge the extreme douchebaggery of his dad's brutal, underhanded murder. The crime against Agamemnon was so bastard-licious that the god Apollo himself actually came down from Olympus, not only to personally give

Orestes moral absolution on the subject but to threaten that if Orestes *didn't* go get revenge, the gods of Olympus would inflict him with leprosy and break all of his favorite video games. Orestes mentioned offhandedly that he was somewhat worried about drawing the ire of the Furies, but Apollo said it was all good and gave Orestes a magical bow that was supposed to drive the Dark Goddesses away if they even actually appeared.

Orestes would have been better off with the leprosy and the Red Ring of Death. Immediately after he murdered his mother and her lover, the Furies appeared in all of their snake-wearing, black-clad glory, shaking their scourges at him and crying tears of blood. Orestes nocked an arrow on Apollo's godly power–infused bow and released a shot into their midst, only to watch in horror as it did absolutely ass-nothing.

Uh, crap.

Seeing that the bow was about as useful as a liberal arts degree, Orestes ditched it and ran off into the wilderness with the Furies chasing hard after him. In case you're thinking that it might not be so bad to have a trio of mostly naked women running after you, this wasn't like a Russ Meyer film—these chicks were hardcore, pissed, and terrifying like crazy as hell. Orestes fled across Greece for a year, traveling to every sacred place he could find, purifying himself in every body of water larger than a shot glass, and getting blessed by every holy man, woman, and animal he could get his hands on. Nothing worked. For months, the Furies haunted him, driving him completely insane and making him constantly flail his arms around like he was being swarmed by an imaginary cloud of killer bees. Finally, he went to Athens, and was put on trial by the gods to defend himself against the Furies and their accusations. The gods Apollo and Athena ruled that he was in the right, and that the Furies should cease and desist from their misery-inducing antics. They didn't. What's worse, they were so offended by this affront to their unassailable moral righteousness that they threatened to barren the earth, destroy all of the crops, and slaughter the firstborn children of Athens. Their rage was only pacified after Athena intervened, promised them a bunch of primo worship spots around the city, and required from that point on that all the citizens of Athens sacrifice the first crops of the season to them. Even Orestes went out and built a bunch of temples in their honor. After seeing it firsthand, he just couldn't deny their badassitude any longer. They did eventually chill out and leave the poor guy alone so that he could go off and get busy with Helen of Troy's daughter, which was magnanimous of them.

The coolest thing about the Furies is that the Greeks looked at them as the physical manifestation of your own guilty conscience. These creatures were only visible to those whom they were pursuing; they knew all of your crimes even when no one else did; they could not be silenced or escaped; and they could drive people to insanity, suicide, and intense depression. Their relentlessness and inescapability is what made them so terrifying, since no one can escape their own conscience. They were like the Tell-Tale Heart or Jiminy Cricket, if Jiminy Cricket bitch-slapped you with his umbrella and started spraying blood out of his eyes like a broken fire hydrant.

Nobody was too hardcore to stand up to the Furies and their withering wrath. Their vengeance drove the mother-murdering military commander Alcmaeon completely insane, and when the warrior-hero Meleager committed a similar offense against his brothers, the Furies used a flaming spear to turn him into a human voodoo doll. Even the mighty Amazon warrior-queen Penthesilia wasn't immune to their rage: when she accidentally killed her own sister with a javelin during a wacky hunting mishap, the Dark Sisters pursued her so hard that she enlisted in the Trojan Army and fought a duel with Achilles just to escape them. These chicks were so terrifying to the people of Greece that you weren't even supposed to mention the Furies by name—in regular conversation, the Greeks referred to them as the *Eumenides*, which means "The Kindly Ones," and when the real-life playwright Aeschylus featured them in a stage production, some of the pregnant women in the audience miscarried and other members of the audience either went into convulsions or instantly dropped dead from fright. Aeschylus himself had to flee town and promise never to put the play on again.

———

A close relative of the Furies is the similarly vengeful goddess Nemesis. The daughter of Night and Darkness, Nemesis was the personification of justice, capital punishment, order, and, for some reason, torture. Despite beating people with scourges, she is always seen as right and just, and is the vessel for bringing retribution to those who were guilty not only of felony-related crimes but also those who give in to excessive pride, hubris, and arrogance.

———

Another group of badass flying goddesses are the infamous Valkyries of Norse mythology. Soaring through the clouds on Pegasus-like steeds, these death-dealing helmeted Viking babes are responsible for bringing half of all the battle-dead back to Valhalla and determining who gets to spend the afterlife eating bacon burgers with Odin and partying like crazy until the great battle at the end of the world. The Valkyries determined who died in combat, which army would be victorious, and who came back to Asgard afterward. While they were terrifying on the battlefield, in the Halls of Valhalla the Valkyries were totally cool—they bring you mead like whenever you want, and they're reborn as virgins every morning no matter how wild the party got the night before.

———

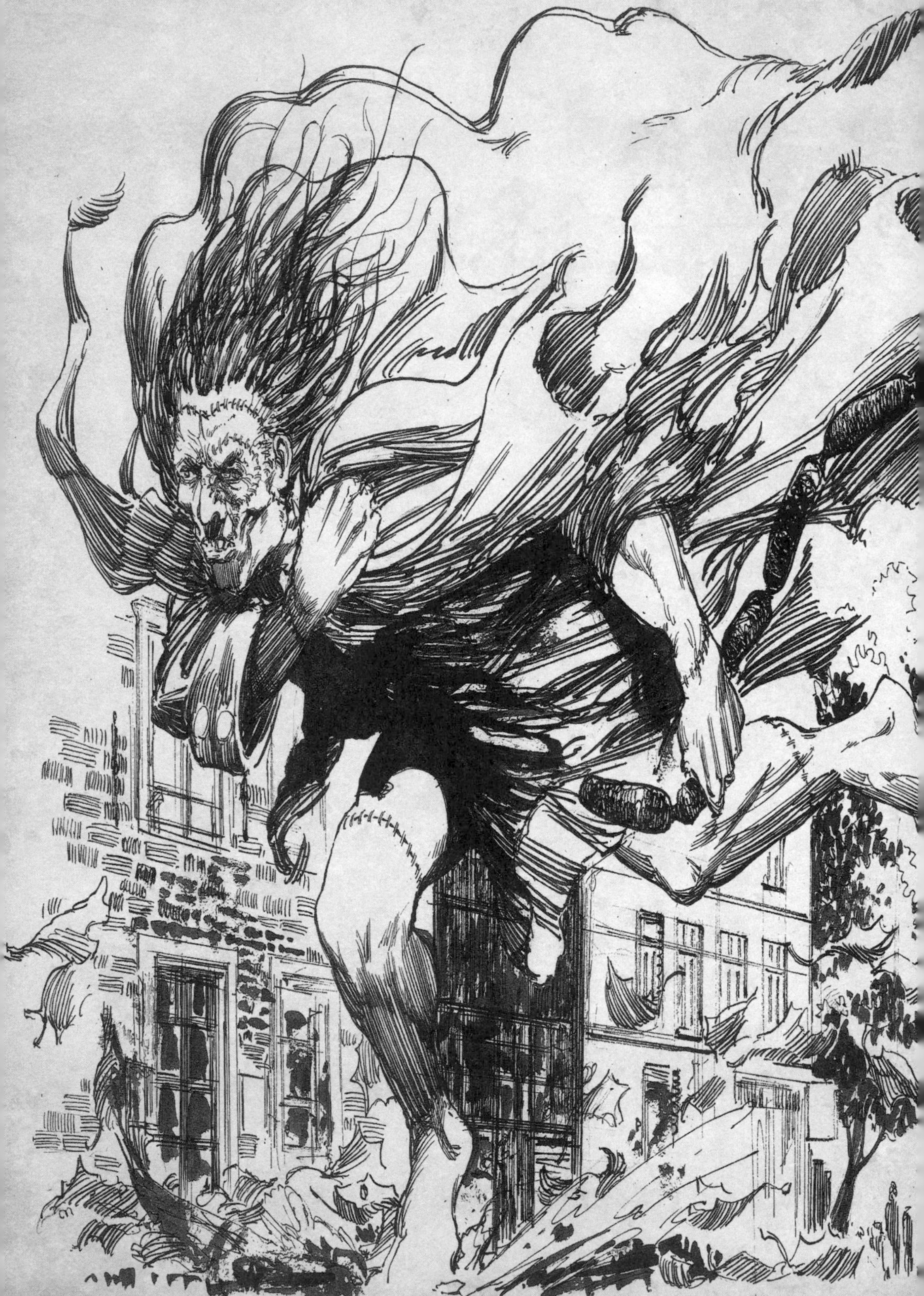

35

FRANKENSTEIN'S MONSTER

You purpose to kill me. How dare you sport thus with life? Do your duty and the rest of mankind. If you comply with my conditions, I will leave them and you at peace; but if you refuse, I will glut the maw of death until it be satiated with the blood of your remaining friends.

IN ORDER TO FULLY APPRECIATE THE AWESOMENESS OF FRANKEN-STEIN'S MONSTER, YOU SHOULD FIRST CLUB YOURSELF IN THE FORE-HEAD REPEATEDLY WITH A RUBBER MALLET UNTIL YOU COMPLETELY FORGET EVERYTHING YOU KNOW ABOUT THE FRANKENSTEIN STORY. Sure, there's a certain boyish charm to watching iconic monster-man Boris Karloff in extreme horror-movie makeup drunkenly lurching around sound stages like an uncoordinated zombie that accidentally chased his muscle relaxants with Jack Daniels, but if Mary Shelley had seen that particular bolt-necked portrayal of her hardcore literary creation stumbling down the stairs and howling like an incomprehensible dumbass, she probably would have crapped enough bricks to reconstruct a life-size replica of the Great Pyramid of Giza. The real Frankenstein's Monster—the one she wrote about back in 1818, at a time when the world's most renowned biologists couldn't have coherently explained DNA to you if you'd cracked them in the jaw with a double-helix-shaped lead pipe—was a tough, well-educated, and eloquent neck-snapping super-mutant motivated purely by the unwavering, vengeful desire to further ruin the life of the already-miserable man who created him.

Frankenstein's Monster isn't just a clever name. This creature was a totally psycho beast, and I don't mean that in a good way. As his moniker might also indicate, the creature was created by a completely unethical mad scientist named Victor Frankenstein. Victor was a nice young nutjob from Geneva who spent the formative years of his educational career studying natural philosophy, chemistry, and general mad science at Ingolstadt University, and who accidentally discovered the secret of life while messing around with dead bodies in a lab for reasons that are never quite fully explained. Putting this knowledge to use in only the way a delusional man of evil science might possibly consider, Vic then immediately began construction of an eight-foot-tall superhuman creature that he could potentially reanimate. Frankenstein didn't really think too much about the consequences of what it meant to give life to another creature, but for his part, he didn't really seem to give a crap, either. Mary Shelley isn't specific on how the monster was created, but I'm pretty confident that it has something to do with sewing together a bunch of dead bodies, cackling maniacally in a lab loaded down with bubbling beakers and zapping electrical arcs and then frying your human Mr. Potato Head with a lightning bolt. Shelley does mention that, rather than the Karloff representation of Frank that we love to think about, the actual monster was built completely in proportion, with yellowish skin barely covering the muscles and arteries, long black hair, pearly white teeth, lifeless-looking watery eyes, and super-creepy black lips. Frankenstein himself refers to the creature as "beautiful," but it's generally a good idea to take most mad scientists' proclamations with a grain of salt, particularly as they apply to their evil, unholy creations.

While he's never clear about his rationale behind this boneheaded decision to play God, Victor presumably built the creature for many of the same reasons why the similarly evil Doctor Wily built his Robot Masters (i.e., he's completely out-of-his-mind gonzo insane). However, instead of giving Frank Jr. a cool side-scrolling level with a bunch of flying robots, systematically disappearing blocks, and bottomless, spike-walled pits, as soon as the Beast opened its eyes, Victor just kind of flipped out, ran screaming from his laboratory, renounced the study of natural philosophy, barfed his face off a couple times, and then spent the next couple months laid up in bed with a terrible unexplained sickness. This is just irresponsible mad science, if you ask me. Animating corpses and then leaving them unattended while you puke your guts out is exactly how zombie apocalypses start, people. Get it together here.

But Frankenstein's creation, known variously as the Wretch, the Creature, and the Beast, wasn't just some animated hunk of semiconscious shambling flesh with terrible AI and a never-ending thirst for delicious human brains. He was competent, agile, strong, intelligent, and fully aware that his life totally sucked so much it needed kneepads. Being cobbled into existence from the stitched-together corpses of a bunch of dead dudes isn't as cool as you might think it would be, and this guy was obviously pretty upset that he'd been brought to life just in time to see some crazy Swiss med student turn around and flee for his life. The Beast wandered around, thoroughly confused as to why he was created, and continually ran into frightened and angry villagers who alternately feared, hated, or actively tried to kill him.

The Wretch decided to lie low for a while. He learned English by listening to people, and brushed up on his literary chops by reading *Paradise Lost*, *The Rime of the Ancient Mariner*, and Plutarch's *Lives*, thus making himself potentially more well-read than most high school students out there these days. The Beast eventually tried to befriend a local family, but they ran away screaming like everyone else. He wandered off and saved a young girl from drowning in a river, but instead of having a shiny medal pinned on his chest, some freaked-out villager took one look at this hideous monstrosity, loaded a lead bullet into his musket, and tried to blow it through the Wretch's torso. Eventually, the monster came to the sad realization that most humans don't want to be friends with eight-foot-tall reanimated corpses, so of course he flipped the hell out, declared war on humanity, and swore vengeance on Victor for giving him such a crappy, miserable existence.

The Monster spent the next couple years getting his revenge by killing every important person in Dr. Frank's life, eventually driving the creepy scientist even more completely insane than he already was. First he went to Geneva, strangled Victor's little brother to death, and then framed Victor's friend Justine for the crime. Victor saw his monstrous creation at the murder scene (the Beast escaped him by climbing up a sheer cliff face in the middle of a driving rainstorm, which is hardcore, by the way), but Victor couldn't divulge the identity of the true killer without people correctly believing he was absolutely out-of-his-mind crazy. In the ensuing trial, Justine was convicted of murder and hanged, because even in the nineteenth century the judicial system was totally whack.

Despondent and crushed, Victor went out for a walk around some old glaciers. Then, all of a sudden, the freaking Monster came leaping over the ice with superhuman speed, caught up with Frankenstein, and demanded that the scientist create a second beast—a Bride of Frankenstein, if you will. Someone to love him even though everyone else on the planet hates his damn guts with the burning fire of a thousand malfunctioning Bunsen burners. Victor, who was understandably looking for a good way to make the Monster stop choking out everyone even moderately associated with Clan Frankenstein, agreed to make a Mrs. Monster. However, as the creature was nearing completion, Victor came to the realization that he was getting ready to spawn a new race of superhuman asskickers with incredible strength and a distinct genetic advantage over humanity, and he kind of wondered if that was really such a good idea. Also, since his first Beast was such a dick, he could have only assumed that the next one would be equal in dickishness. Victor tore the half-made Bride of Frankenstein to pieces and dumped her in a river.

Needless to say, the Beast was a little unhappy about the re-dismemberment of the pile of body parts that was eventually going to become his wife. The creature swore on the spot to murder Frankenstein and everyone he loved in the appropriately badass fashion you would expect from a hulking behemoth of pain and throat-crushing suffering, saying, "I will revenge my injuries; if I cannot inspire love, I will cause fear, and chiefly towards you my arch-enemy, because my creator, do I swear inextinguishable hatred." Then he strangulated Victor's best friend and left the dude's rotting corpse on a beach for Victor to unexpectedly stumble into while going for his morning stroll. Heh.

Victor eventually married his stepsister Elizabeth, thus further proving that scientists have no morals, and once again the Monster was there to do the most evil thing he could think of. The Creature psyched Vic out, making him think that a huge, awesome showdown was coming, and then, when Victor came running outside like a moron, the Creature snuck into the honeymoon suite and choked the dude's brand-new wife to death. Then he ran outside, told Victor that evil will always win because good is dumb, and jumped in a lake just to prove how completely over-the-top balls-out he was. Victor's dad died of sadness from the homicides, and we'll just tack that on to the Wretch's kill count.

For the next couple year Frankenstein traveled around trying to find his Monster, but the Beast was always one step ahead. He pursued the Wretch across Germany, Eastern Europe, and Russia, but every time Vic got somewhere there was a letter saying something along the lines of,

Ha ha, welcome to Moscow, loser! I'm currently in London murdering your entire family. Love, F.M.
P.S. I rubbed my balls on this piece of parchment.

The Beast eventually lured Victor out to the middle of the arctic tundra, where the scientist died of hypothermia like a dumbass. His work finally complete, the Monster ran out to the North Pole, jumped on a homemade funeral pyre, and burned himself to death.

Mary Shelley was kind of a badass as well, and not just because she somehow managed to inexplicably put up with Percy Bysshe Shelley on a regular basis. This British feminist wrote the horror/mystery tale of *Frankenstein* on a double-dog dare from Lord Byron, and ended up busting out an epic work of face-melting awesomeness that is now believed by many to be the forerunner of modern science-fiction. Suck on THAT, romantic poetry! Nowadays Shelley's story lives on in the diabetes-inducing deliciousness that is Frankenberry cereal.

→ ABRAHAM VAN HELSING ←

It seems like you can't huck a crucifix into a crowded room these days without accidentally impaling some crappy vampire-centric romantic comedy/drama about a dark, brooding, impeccably dressed blood-chugging metro douchebag flitting about in the woods with his whiny high school girlfriend and talking about forbidden love ad nauseam until pretty much everyone watching it wants to barf up whatever is left of their rapidly shriveling brain cells. Well, back in the nineteenth century, everybody just thought vampires were complete bastards that were only good for one thing—getting pointy wooden stakes rammed through their chests at high velocity by Abraham Van Effing Van Helsing. This grizzled hardass old Dutch physician/cryptozoologist/crazy-occult-genius dedicated his long and single-purposed life to training his mind and his body in the fine art of murdering the undead with extreme prejudice all the way up their cadaverous asses, and he was so good at his job that nowadays his name is pretty much synonymous with stomping vampires' balls into a thick, marinara-like sauce smelling faintly of garlic and guano.

In Bram Stoker's *Dracula*, the novel that pretty much invented the horror genre as we know it, Van Helsing was called to London by a former student of his and asked to investigate a mysterious illness plaguing the guy's totally slutty harlot of a girlfriend. When Abe first arrived and noticed two giant fang-holes in the chickie's neck, he knew that this lady was boned. Realizing he couldn't save her, Van Helsing still tried to treat her symptoms, but of course she eventually died, and our boy AVH didn't seem to have a problem staking her in the heart and decapitating her with a machete once she came back as a vampire. Sorry about your girlfriend, dude, but that's just how it goes when you roll with Doc Van Helsing. It's as the good doctor says in the original text: "I say to you men tonight, and I mind you heed these grave words with all the weight in which I intend them to be understood, that from henceforth you shall always place bros before hos, particularly in such instances in which those aforementioned nefarious hos are bloodsucking undead servants of the villainous Prince of Darkness."

Abraham, now seeking to avenge the dead girl in the most violent way possible (and to rid the land of the living of the vile scourge of vampirism in the process), put together a group of average Joes, gave them all the necessary equipment to pummel the hair gel off of Dracula's unsettlingly pale dome, and led a full-scale assault on Nosferatu's evil lair. After traveling halfway across the world and gunning down a couple of fools who got in his way, Van Helsing and his crew did battle with Count Dracula himself. Even though Drac was the King of All the Vampires and one of the most asskicking undead monsters on the planet, the weirdly caped nobleman didn't stand a chance against this epic-level fighter/cleric and his posse of Simon Belmonts. The Transylvanian aristocrat met a grisly death on the pointy end of a wooden stake when he was stabbed repeatedly until he exploded into a giant geyser of fake plastic fangs and arterial blood spray. Van Helsing got so jacked about being awesome that he smashed the vampire's coffin into timbers with a karate chop before silently heading off into the night in search of other unholy fiends that needed a size-ten Puma sneaker crushed up their asses.

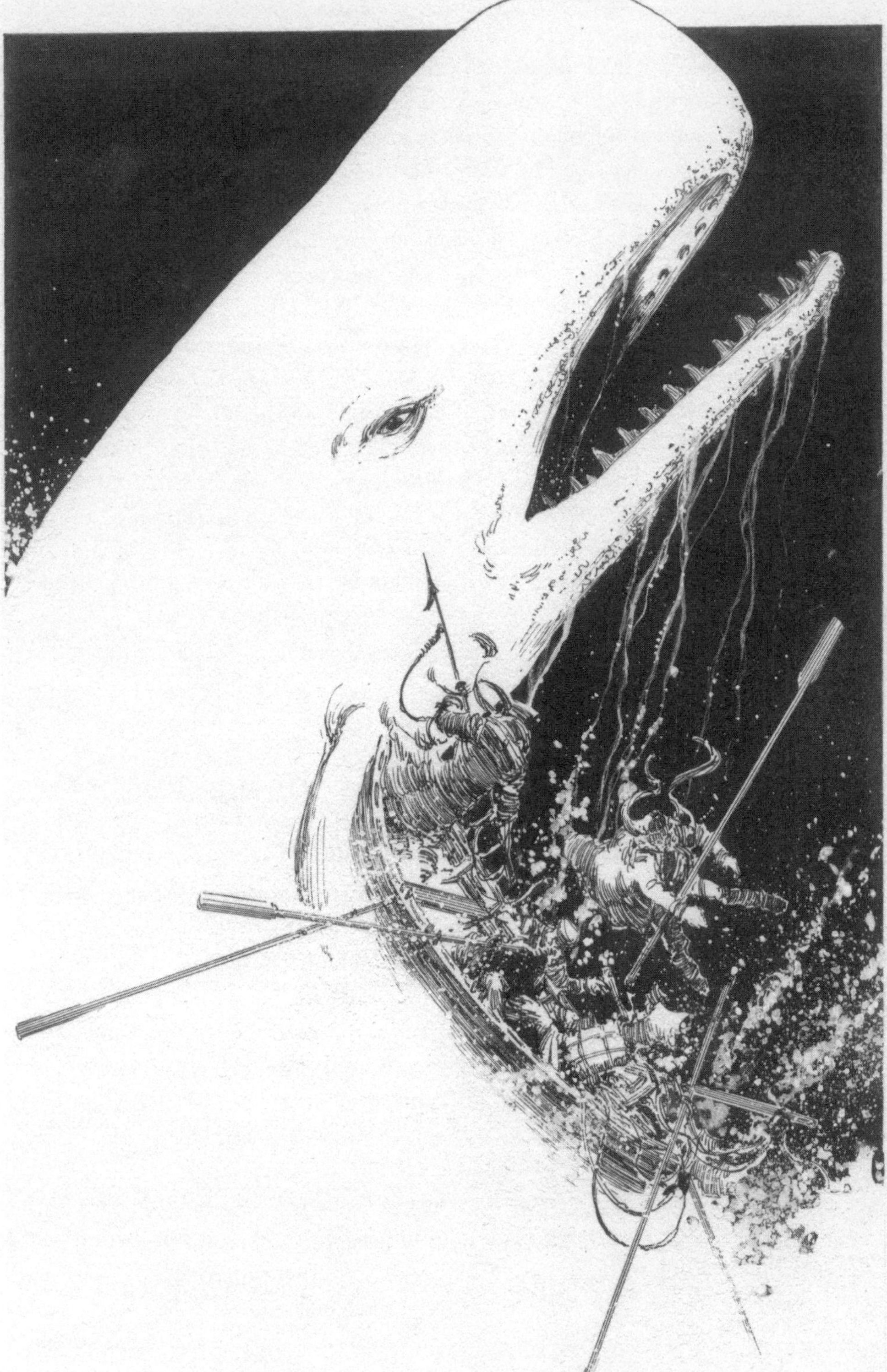

36

MOBY-DICK

Retribution, swift vengeance, eternal malice were in his whole aspect, and spite of all that mortal men could do, the solid white buttress of his forehead smote the ship's starboard bow, till men and timbers reeled.

—HERMAN MELVILLE, *MOBY-DICK*

MOBY-DICK WAS THE EIGHTY-TON, HATE-FILLED, MURDEROUS EM-BODIMENT OF GOD'S WRATH. An evil albino sperm whale of "great ferocity, cunning and malice," this vicious white-skinned leviathan from the darkest recesses of the ocean's ass-crack was five miles of solid muscle welded onto an iron chassis of seething, unbridled rage. Covered in twisted spears and shattered lances from shiploads of flaccid-armed harpooners, Moby-Dick's scarred, iron-like hide was only rivaled in its badassitude by his deformed, scythe-like toothy lower jaw (which, by the way, was the perfect shape for lopping off arms, legs, and other semi-useful appendages).

Sperm whales usually like to swim to the bottom of the ocean to eat giant squid, which are the second most-evil animals on Earth after the sperm whale (for reference, please see the following section on the Kraken). However, after encounters with whaling ships, sperm whales are often overcome by an unquenchable bloodlust that causes them to sustain themselves on a diet of broken oars and the bodily fluids of sailors.

All Moby-Dick wanted to do was attack whalers, sink ships, and eat all the seamen. This guy sank about a million boats, one of which carried a crotchety old hardass named Captain Ahab. After dumping the grizzled seafarer into the drink, Moby-Dick ferociously tore off Ahab's leg, but stopped short of killing him, because Moby-Dick preferred to leave his victims maimed, insane husks of their former selves. Many a time a sailor would meet another that had been torn limb from limb by Moby-Dick. "Such calamities did ensue in these assaults—not restricted to sprained wrists or ankles, broken limbs, or devouring amputations—but fatal to the last degree of fatality." In the homicidal murder-spree of this blood-consuming death-fiend, Moby dispatched the first mate of a ship called the *Jeroboam* by tail-slapping the dude off the deck, sending him flying fifty yards into the ocean, and then swimming over and disemboweling him. The Dickmeister also tore the arm off the captain of the *Sammy Enderby* (after a similarly well-placed tail-slap), devoured the full crews of a couple whaling vessels, and chomped down on a guy named Radney, who served as first mate on the *Town Ho*. Even though this short-yet-graphic list of whale maulings would have been sufficiently villainous without including the crushed-to-death corpse of poor Radney, I felt compelled to include him among the body count simply because I couldn't possibly ignore the fact that there was a ship in this book called the *Town Ho*.

While most knuckleheads couldn't so much as sustain blood circulation to their brains after being pimp-slapped halfway across the Pacific by Moby-Dick and his flailing flukes of bone-crunching human annihilation, Captain Ahab survived, went completely off-his-gourd crazy, and swore vengeance at all costs against the Great White Whale. This raving whalicidal lunatic somehow convinced a couple of wealthy idiots to lend him a boat, ostensibly so that he could go out and hunt some whales to bring back their valuable whale-parts, but instead of giving a crap about his assigned mission Ahab put together a gnarly crew of salt-encrusted sea dogs, took the helm of the *Pequod*, and turned this stupidly named vessel into a death-ship dedicated solely to the purpose of impaling Moby-Dick with dozens of javelin-size ice picks. Ahab, who by this point was a hardcore old mariner who hated everything that ever existed, decorated his intimidating whale-slaying conveyance with whale bones across the hull and two giant sliced-off whale heads attached to either side of it. Ahab also made a custom harpoon with his own hands, tempered it in his dead crewmates' blood, and sealed its power by getting it struck by a bolt of lightning. If that's not enough, he hired a six-foot cannibal harpooner from the Pacific Islands who was covered from head to toe in tattoos, sold human heads on the black market, shaved his face with a harpoon blade, and smoked tobacco out of a pipe he made from a hollowed-out (and still functional) tomahawk.

Decked out in all its most whale-murderingly badass gear, the *Pequod* set sail from Nantucket, tore ass around the Cape, and steamed toward the waters where Moby-Dick was having a wild time smasher-ating and masticating wayward vessels. What follows is a ridiculously long series of chapters that largely read like a how-to guide for people who always wanted to know every single boring mundane detail of a seafaring vessel. Thanks, Melville, for giving us this awesome setup about bloody vengeance between a grim crew of whale-hunters and a vicious, ultra-evil killing machine roughly the size and weight of a seven-story building, and then spending ten chapters explaining the difference between the forecastle and the poop deck until everyone reading this thing wants to take a chainsaw to their own faces. It's no exaggeration when I say that you can effectively summarize everything between chapters 43 and 123 of *Moby-Dick* by simply saying, "They were on a boat."

Eventually Ahab and the crew of the *Pequod* caught up to Moby-Dick, who at the time was taking a break in the South Pacific. He had just eaten the children of another sea captain when he was spotted. Ahab and the guys went after him, but no amount of harpoons or lances could stop Moby-Dick. He just kept smacking these guys with his tail and eating them. On the first day of battle, Moby-Dick bit Ahab's whaling boat in half, circled the smashed pieces of the obliterated rowboat a couple times like Bruce the Shark from *Jaws*, and then suddenly disappeared without warning just to screw with the old bastard's already fragile psyche.

The very next day, Moby-Dick rushed in, taking on three of the *Pequod*'s smaller rowboats at the same time like he didn't even give a crap. Two of the boats launched harpoons that nailed him in the sides, but Moby was all like, "Whatever, chumps"—he used the ropes attached to the harpoons to smash the two ships into each other like dumbasses. One of the whalers not only drowned in the splintery crash, but got caught up in the harpoon ropes, went overboard, and his mangled carcass continued to dangle from the whale's side for the next day and a half. The poor bastard's lifeless body was clearly visible when Moby-Dick breached and smashed Ahab's replacement rowboat into shrapnel with his head shortly thereafter.

Ahab still wasn't ready to call it quits yet, so he went back to his main ship and returned on the third day to fight Moby-Dick again. He didn't have to go far—Moby was already following the *Pequod*, just looking for an opportunity to crushinate it into flotsam with his gigantasaurus white muscle-bound torso. The boats were lowered into dangerous, shark-infested waters, and the whalers once again did battle with the beast. After sundering two more rowboats, Moby-Dick plowed the *Pequod* itself, annihilating the hull and bringing the entire ship down under the crushing weight of eighty tons of raging blubber. Ahab launched his special lightning-blood spear at the mighty unstoppable personification of brutal vengeance, but Moby-Dick was like, "Sorry, sucker." Ahab got clotheslined by the rope attached to the harpoon and dragged into the water, never to be seen again. After cruelly drowning Ahab, Moby ate the rest of the crew, sunk all the remaining boats, and left one guy alive, floating on a coffin. He wanted that guy to go back and pass on his story so that everyone would know what they were in for if they mess with Moby-Dick.

Towards thee I roll, thou all-destroying but unconquering whale; to the last I grapple with thee, from hell's heart I stab at thee, for hate's sake I spit my last breath at thee! Sink all coffins and all hearses to the common pool—and since neither can be mine let me then tow to pieces, while still chasing thee, though tied to thee, thou damned whale! Thus I give up the spear!

—CAPTAIN AHAB'S LAST WORDS

The scariest thing about Moby-Dick is that his story actually has a basis in historical fact. Melville drew his inspiration for the book from an 1820 incident when the 238-ton whaleship *Essex* was crushed and sunk by an aggressive sperm whale in the Pacific—between whale bites, exposure, and eventual cannibalism, only eight men survived to tell the tale. Then, in August 1851, just one month before the publication of *Moby-Dick*, a New England whaling ship called the *Ann Alexander* got its ass kicked by a giant sperm whale that chomped two of its rowboats in half and then rammed a hole in its bow, sinking the vessel.

➳ THE KRAKEN ⬳

The Kraken is a giant-ass emotionless cephalopod who lives solely to eat boats, destroy all life in the ocean, and violently implode warships with his ultrapowerful crush-o-matic appendages of doom. Say you're just some sailor chilling out minding your own business, cruising the high seas on a sweet boat and thinking about cool stuff like mermaid boobs when all of a sudden POW—you're getting a singing molest-o-gram from a half-dozen gigantor rubbery tentacles while a godless multi-limbed killing machine from the deepest uncharted reaches of the ocean's asshole smashes your brain apart and turns your ship into a useless hunk of flotsam.

For starters, giant squids are probably some of the grossest, creepiest things ever. They have two humongoid eyes that fall somewhere between The Lidless Eye of Sauron and a botched Botox face-lift on the freak-out scale, and their unblinking stares never seem to register any emotion other than cold, unfeeling rage. If that's not enough, there are so many suckers and noodly rubber appendages flailing about on this thing that it makes even the most cracked-out Japanese hentai tentacle-rape porn look like an unmarried Mennonite couple holding hands at a funeral. If you somehow survive being squeezed into Cheez Whiz by its eight legs or two barbed, suction-cupped tentacles, you can always look forward to being violently inserted into a beaked mouth and crushed out of hand by giant champing toothless jaws for a while. There aren't too many creatures this side of a Hitchcock movie that are capable of beaking a man to death, but hey, that's the Kraken for you. If the Kraken possesses most of the same feeding mechanisms as the giant squid, after the beak, your broken-down carcass will pass through something called the radula, a nightmarish mechanism that can best be described by saying that this thing has a cheese-grater for an esophagus. After that fun stuff, you head for the stomach, where you're slowly devoured Boba Fett–style. Good times.

Crushing and shredding aside, the main thing about the Kraken is that he's really damn huge. Believed to be something on the order of like fifty feet long, these foul beasts have supposedly been so massive that their arms were able to reach to the top mast of some old-school wooden sailing vessels. Honestly, what the hell are you supposed to do against a giant tree-trunk-size, fifty-foot-long hunk of suction-cup-equipped fleshiness capable of generating the same destructive force as a wrecking ball? Sure, you could try to go out there Captain Nemo–style and wave a harpoon at it like a spastic idiot, but unless you're a super-badass submarine commander who knows no fear and responds to every situation with extreme violence, you're probably just going to wind up getting a pointy tentacle jammed up your Krak.

The crazy thing about this Krake-sanity is that it's not even completely mythical—there are unsubstantiated accounts of multiarmed Krake-hem slapping around fishing boats and warships dating back to antiquity. The Greeks, Vikings, and others all have stories about vessels coming under attack from the tendrils of some terrible ferocious Cthulhu-esque sea monsters, which is pretty sweet.

The Kraken as we know it was originally written about in the sixteenth and seventeenth century by some Scandinavian survivors of his insane crush-tacular wrath, but most rational people from that time period figured that the authors had just been hitting the crack pipe a little too hard. It wasn't until 1870, when people started finding actual giant squid pieces washing up on shore, that science-types started putting it together that this might not be some weirdo shroom-induced hallucination. When a New Zealand crew discovered a sixty-five-foot-long squid in 1880, the entire scientific community pretty much barfed.

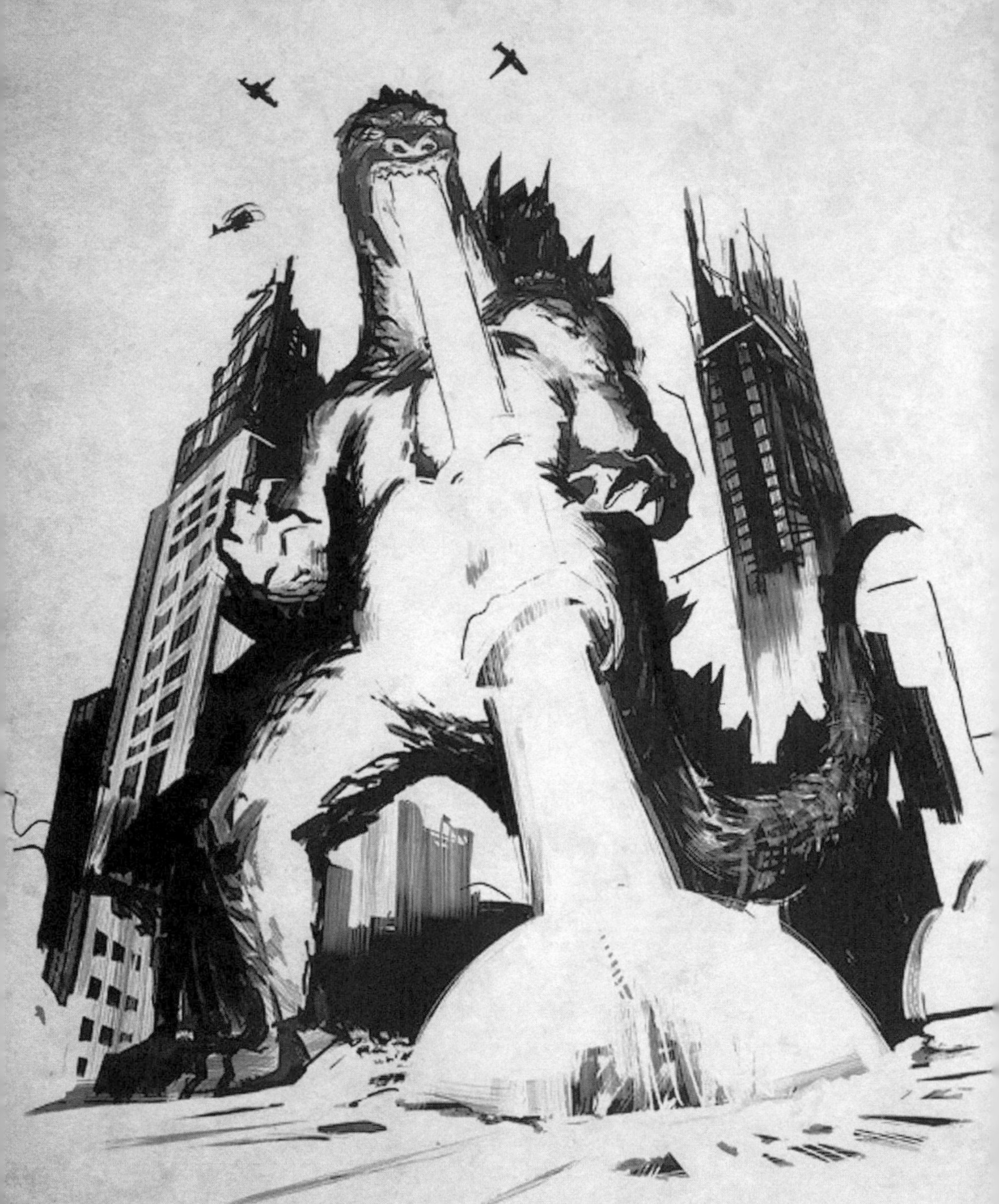

37

GODZILLA

The sky was blood red and filled with smoke. And through it a devil appeared. Its face was twisted with rage and hatred. When it was over my parents were gone. I will never forget the wretched cries of the dead . . .

—ADMIRAL TAIZO TACHIBANA IN *GODZILLA, MOTHRA AND KING GHIDORA: GIANT MONSTERS ALL-OUT ATTACK!*

GODZILLA IS THE PRIME EXAMPLE OF WHY YOU SHOULD NEVER SCREW WITH THE POWER OF SCIENTIFIC EVOLUTION. The legend goes that when the damn Americans dropped Fat Boy and Little Man on Japan back in 1945, the colossal nuclear fallout and intense radiation turned a regular everyday foul-tempered prehistoric flesh-eating lizard-dinosaur on a remote island somewhere in the Pacific into a gigantic, airplane-crushing monster capable of head-butting skyscrapers into the next time zone and obliterating an entire city block by ripping a really loud nuclear-powered EMP fart. Nowadays, he shows up and terrorizes the countryside every so often in a crazy drunken rage, bashing everything he sees and flexing his nuts before returning to the murky depths of the ocean to hibernate underwater somehow.

Godzilla is huge. And by huge, I mean really goddamn huge. He's so big he makes the T. rex from *Jurassic Park* look like something out of one of those calendars with pictures of newborn kittens on them, and unlike a lot of epically large things out there, he has the good sense to use his massive size as a means with which to destroy anything that crosses his path—smashing buildings with his tail, punching pagodas until they become flaming explosions, and using commuter trains as nunchucks with which to pummel the life out of other giant mutated monsters that get in the way of his mission to completely eradicate all human life on the planet.

Another sweet thing is that Godzilla is completely unpredictable, and, as such, represents the Ultimate Duality of Awesome: when he leaves the warm beaches of Monster Island and emerges from the dark waters near the Japanese coastline, you don't know if he's there to smash orphanages or save the universe from a rampaging giant space monster who shoots lasers out of its forehead and spits acid on hot Japanese babes. That's just how he rolls. One minute he's Earth's savior, the next minute he's grabbing handfuls of cheering humans and grinding them between his massive, pointy teeth.

The most daunting thing about Godzilla is that he's virtually indestructible, and his scaled hide is tougher to penetrate than a home-schooled Mormon chick. Tank shells, surface-to-air missiles, and armor-piercing ammunition only succeed in making him angry. You can crash jet fighters into his eyes and he won't blink—he'll just clench his fists and start breakdancing in the middle of downtown Tokyo. Shooting him in the face with a nuclear warhead only makes him EVEN MORE POWERFUL, because he sucks up radiation like a Geiger counter in Chernobyl and it has roughly the same effect on him as if he drank the contents of a gasoline tanker filled with Red Bull, Viagra, Four Loko, and pure Colombian cocaine. Hell, every once in a while he gets randomly struck by lightning for no reason, and the next thing you know he's shooting damned bolts of electricity out of his hands and lighting up downtown with a few billion volts of raw electrical power. Even on the off-chance that some monster gets a lucky shot and knocks Godzilla out of action, or the humans come up with some crazy ridiculous sleep ray that sends him into hibernation or some bull-crap, Godzilla has a mutant healing factor that makes Wolverine look like a hemophiliac and he comes back to life more regularly than Jason Voorhees. You can't finish him off—the guy has been around for almost sixty years with no signs of slowing down, and he's never going to get bored with stomping asses across the Tokyo skyline. The dude's completely leveled that city like a hundred times, yet those wacky Japanese just keep rebuilding it only to somehow still act like they're really inexplicably surprised when Godzilla shows up and trashes it again.

Of course, Godzilla is not out to just destroy the entire population of Japan—he also enjoys beating the pants off of the vast array of bizarre mutated monsters who dare to step on his turf. It doesn't matter how crazy the thing is, how many heads it has, or what bizarre melty substance it shoots out of some part of its body, Godzilla just emits his trademark ear-piercing, window-shattering scream, beats his chest like a giant green Tarzan, and starts Greco-Roman-wrestling the giant cockroach until its arms break off and it gets its limbless body used as a surfboard. He's got mad Bruce Lee kung-fu skills and a tail that delivers more force than the demonic love-child of an F5 tornado, a 10.5 earthquake, and a category 5 hurricane, and if that doesn't knock his enemy out of action, he shoots a giant beam of blue atomic energy out of his mouth and immolates anything he wants with his mouth-deployed blowtorch. Nobody can screw with him—he's taken out Ghidrah, Mecha Ghidra, Jet Jaguar, Megalon, Rodan, Mothra, Gigan, Anguirus, Biollante, Space Godzilla, and Mecha Godzilla (and a bunch of other strangely named beasts that may or may not feature the appropriate number of servos and metal plates to earn them the title "Mecha") and turned them all into giant bloody smears (and gears) across the Japanese countryside. He's the King of the Monsters, and he's willing to prove it to any giant, two-hundred-foot-tall, carnivorous, fire-breathing, flying, eating machine that thinks it can front on him. Sometimes, when he gets bored, he even joins up tag-team with other monsters in epic four-way giant monster fights, which is pretty rad.

As if it's not badass enough that Godzilla is a huge lizard that levels cities, eats Humvees, and judo-throws giant floating moths into the sides of Mount Fiji, he's also accomplished what few actors in history ever have—he's got his own star on the Hollywood Walk of Fame. Not too many walking apocalypses receive awards for their acting ability and on-screen presence, but there you go.

Making a turtle seem badass is no easy task, yet the video-game villain Bowser has somehow wedged himself into popular culture as one of the most iconic digital bad guys ever coded into a database-a-tron. Covered in a thick, Fireflower-proof carapace lined with spikes and inexplicably blessed with a truly impressive vertical leap, flame breath, and the ability to throw dozens of hammers simultaneously with unnerving accuracy, Bowser has made quite a career out of kidnapping oblivious princesses and confining them inside a vast number of towers surrounded by really angry-looking monsters and impractically deep pit traps. The bane of plumbing aficionados everywhere, Bowser seemingly has little use for princesses once they're under his control, yet still seeks to kidnap them simply to show the world that he's a huge bastard.

→ CTHULHU ←

Cthulhu is expressly defined as simply being the most terrifying monster you've ever seen in your life, a fact that makes this Lovecraftian behemoth somewhat difficult to overlook when one is making even the most rudimentary attempt at discussing some of the great monstrous badasses of literature. Basically, this disgusting, mountain-size, squid-headed, fleshy alien monstrosity lives several thousand nautical light-years beneath the sea in a fortress that resembles a cross between an M. C. Escher painting and the inside of a kaleidoscope, and he busts out every couple of millennia or so to party with humanity in a massive kegger of dead bodies, utter madness, desecrated corpses, writhing tentacles, and chattering mandibles. Descriptions of the beast are purposefully vague, leaving visualization of Cthulhu a task for your own out-of-control imagination, but he's generally described as some kind of winged octopus-dragon-humanoid thing that eats sanity and craps out nightmares. So at least he has that going for him.

Cthulhu is the high priest and leader of the Great Old Ones—a group of similarly minded grisly abominations from outer space that ooze a wide variety of revolting fluids that run the full spectrum of viscosity from every orifice on their hate-filled demonic bodies. These space bastards are worshipped by a bunch of weirdos here on Earth, which is actually a pretty sweet deal if you happen to be a Great Old One. Sure, Mothra had those two pint-size Japanese chicks who sang those ridiculous songs that seemed to go on for a mild eternity, but the hopelessly devoted zealot worshippers of Cthulhu really seem to understand what it takes to be a crazy-ass cultist—their method of showing support for their master is less about belting out annoying musical chants and more about strangling sailors to death with their bare hands, leaving creepy statues behind to taunt the police and doing a bunch of secret handshakes and/or badass behind-the-back high-fives. Their mission is to bring Cthulhu's chamber of horrors back above the waves like the ship at the end of *The Abyss*, so that he can effectively turn the surface of the Earth into a giant pile of phantasmagoric suck, although the one time they happened to be successful at resurrecting their awful lord, the mighty Cthulhu was only able to eat a couple dozen guys before some crazy drunk Norwegian sailor accidentally crashed a boat into his head. The massive, pulverizing head wound really only served to make Cthulhu even angrier, however, and I'm kind of under the impression that he's currently just biding his time until he's ready to return to the surface and simultaneously ruin the lives of 8 billion people in a pretty spectacular fashion.

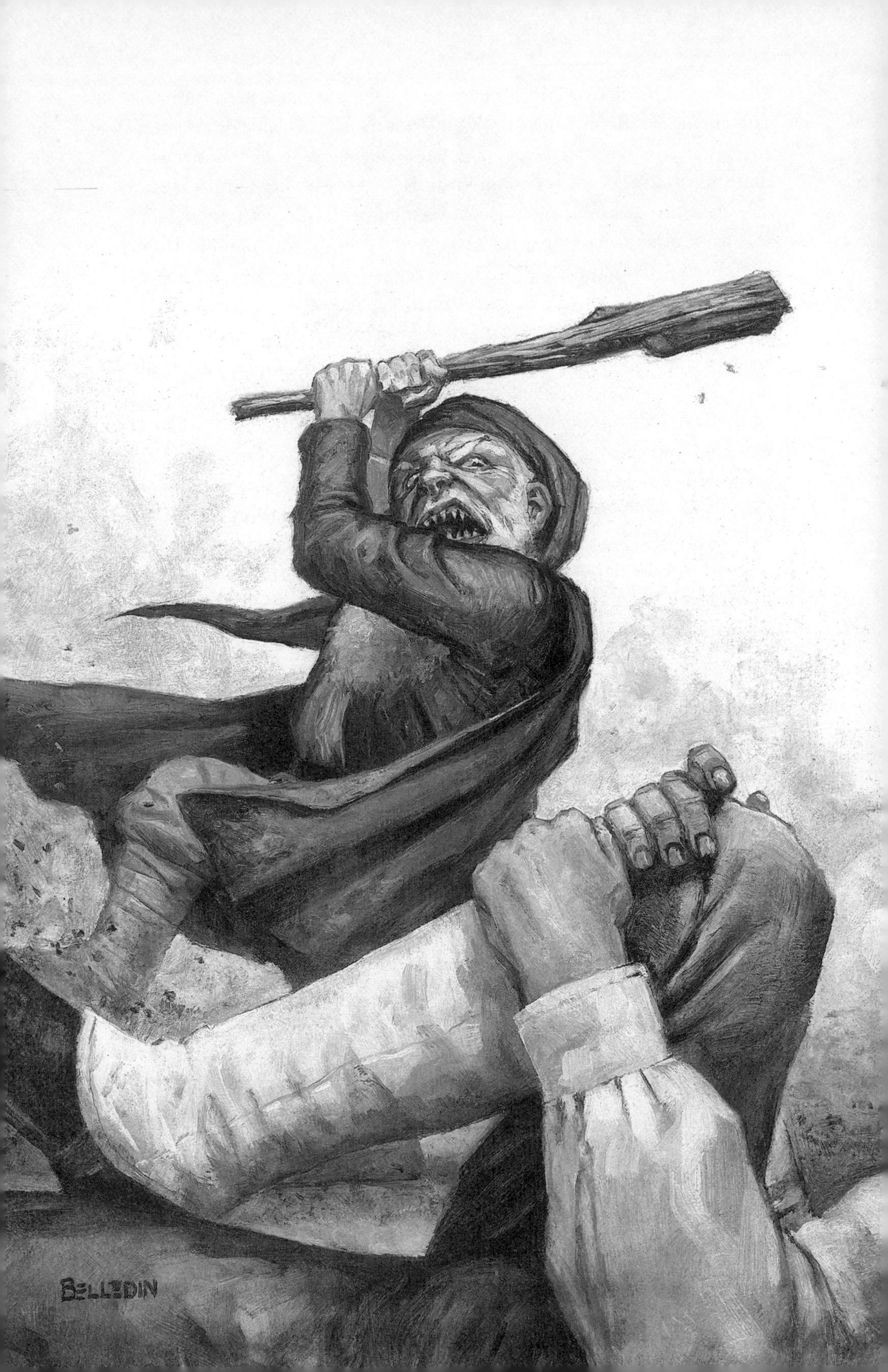
BELLEDIN

38

THE RED DWARF OF
DETROIT

The creature approached nearer. It was neither Indian nor white man,
though perchance the worst embodiment of both; a being, apparently, half-
human, half-gnome, short of stature, very red in the face, and with a blazing
eye whose horrible stare, instead of burning, turned the blood in one's veins to
ice. The apparition was enwrapped from head to foot in a blanket that I took
to be crimson, as well as I could see it in the moonlight, and his diabolical
grin displayed a wide mouth and sharp fang-like teeth.

—ALLEGED ACCOUNT OF THE DWARF GIVEN BY A MEMBER OF
CADILLAC'S TRAVELING PARTY

FALL **1701.** A small group of daring French explorers, led by the intrepid Antoine Laumet de la Mothe, sieur de Cadillac—the first white
settler brave enough to penetrate this previously uncharted territory—
quietly made their way through the dark woods outside the newly
founded settlement of Detroit. The only sounds wafting through the
night air were the eerie whipping of the frigid wind, the gentle rustling
of the leaves, and the quiet splashing of the Detroit River running just
beyond the small dirt path. The fog was thicker than a chunky New

England clam chowder—denser than usual, and so oppressively heavy that the men pushing through it felt like they were marching through a hyperactive fog machine while being constantly shot in the face from close range with a fire extinguisher.

The small group of hardy explorers were on edge even before the fog rolled in. No one vocalized their uneasiness—they had reputations to uphold, after all—but all of them had heard the creepy-ass tales passed down from the native Ottawa Indians. Freaky references to a super-pissed-off demon man who haunted the woods tirelessly looking for his next victim. These men had all swallowed their fear as the cryptic old fortune-teller in the foreboding Castle Saint Louis had croaked out the grim future that awaited Cadillac in this vast, uncharted wildland. How his fortunes would be great, only to be snatched away like the last bratwurst at a tailgate.

Just then, a small, almost imperceptible sound from the road ahead caused the edgy Frenchmen to halt in their tracks. Down the path, slowly, silently, an ominous three-foot-tall apparition made its way through the fog toward the men. As it drew nearer, the grim features of this demonic being slowly came into focus. Its skin was bright red, and the strange goblin, bundled in a red cloak, was sporting an overdeveloped set of canine teeth and an attitude that could best be described as surly as hell.

Before anyone could make a move, the creature sprang into action like a crazy jack-in-the-box with a two-by-four and an intense hatred of everything in the universe. The creature whipped out a small, heavy hickory stick, cackled like a creepy asshole, ran up, and started viciously clocking Cadillac in the knees really goddamn hard. Repeatedly. Cadillac jumped back, shocked and horrified at this overgrown Underpants Gnome smacking him ruthlessly in the patella and presumably calling him a "pussy" while doing so. The Frenchman instinctively drew his sword and swiped at the angry little monster, but it deftly avoided him and continued punishing his kneecaps with its instrument of blunt-force wooden viciousness. After a brief, painful battle that could only be described as "retarded," the creature suddenly hopped back, leered menacingly at the Frenchmen, cackled once more, and disappeared back into the fog.

Less than a week later, Antoine de la Mothe Cadillac was recalled to France by order of the king to stand trial for shady business practices he'd been perpetrating for the last couple of years. He would wind up stripped of his wealth, publicly disgraced, and rotting in the misery of the Bastille. A few years later, his town, Detroit, would fall into the hands of the British (who would, in turn, lose it to the Americans almost immediately), thereby cementing Cadillac's complete failure as a human being.

But Cadillac's tragically hilarious story is just the beginning of Detroit's problems. True, the Motor City is a tough, blue-collar metropolis full of squid-chucking survivors who have earned a reputation for being about as durable as they come—from the hardhat-wearing machinists putting in backbreaking nine-to-fives in auto plants to Ted Friggin' Nugent pioneering the art of hunting wildlife by chasing them through the woods on foot with an electric guitar that doubles as a chainsaw, there's a lot of crazy crap happening around Motown. The innate toughness of the 313 doesn't, however, nullify the common perception among Americans that the city of Detroit pretty much sucks balls. Sure, this may be varying degrees of untrue, but even the most devoted Red Wings fan has to admit that it's really not a good sign when the first white settler of your city ends up getting Tonya Harding–ed by a demon-man and spending the rest of his life sweating his nuts off and going completely straitjacket-insane in a French penitentiary.

There's an admittedly less-than-widely-held belief, however, that Detroit's various woes aren't the product of poor luck or a football program that hasn't been watchable since the days of Barry Sanders. They claim the city is cursed. Tormented by a demon spirit that was present at the inception of Fort Detroit, and which still roams the streets and neighborhoods of the city to this day—the infamous "*Nain Rouge.*" The Red Dwarf of Detroit.

I'm not going to lie to you—this thing kind of scares the piss out of me. The idea that there's some weird-as-hell little monster running around the forest like a cross between Warrick Davis from the *Leprechaun* series and "Hacksaw" Jim Duggan is unsettling at best. I have no idea why this eerily happy creature is out in the woods beating Frenchmen with sticks, but I don't like it.

But, as I said, Cadillac's epically bruised legs were the least of the trouble caused by this little bastard. The Red Dwarf once again haunted Southeastern Michigan during the 1763 rebellion of Chief Pontiac, a badass Native American warrior whose name I pretty much only mention because I think it's kind of awesome that the first two people to see Detroit's personal arch-nemesis now have automobile companies named after them. One night, during the campaign, two British infantrymen standing watch in their camp allegedly saw this cackling maniac running around doing cartwheels in the woods like a dumbass. The Brits chased it away by shooting at it, but the next day, the entire company—fifty-eight battle-hardened soldiers—were ambushed by Pontiac's warriors and massacred in a slaughter that was said to have turned a nearby river red with the blood of the slain.

Known as "The Harbinger of Doom," the infamous Red Dwarf continued being a total jackoff throughout the history of the cursed city. There's an account in 1884 of a woman being attacked by this thing—she mentioned being particularly unsettled by its "lascivious leer"—and some of the city's earliest settlers complained about a small man with bright red skin running around the woods offering to baptize people just to screw with their heads. In 1805, the Red Dwarf was seen again, this time running around through the streets of the city just hours before a devastating fire melted two hundred houses and torched every structure in Detroit except for one well-made stone building. With this info in mind, you can almost understand the wussbag actions of American general William Hull during the War of 1812—when Fort Detroit was surrounded and besieged by the British, Hull saw the Red Dwarf running through the woods outside the city walls, and immediately surrendered his garrison despite having strict orders to defend it at all costs. While this calculated maneuver may have averted some kind of thermonuclear disaster, the curse of the angry gnome still grasped General Hull in its tiny fist—the disgraced commander was subsequently court-martialed for his actions and sentenced to death by firing squad, and is now remembered as a coward and an incompetent numbnuts.

Even to this day, the *Nain Rouge* continually reappears just before times of groin-crushing hardship, arguably in a pretty badass effort to prematurely taunt Detroiters immediately before they get their asses kicked by some kind of soul-obliterating misery. In 1967, it was seen running down 12th Street, doing backflips just hours before a series of brutal race riots that left forty-three people dead and hundreds more injured and hospitalized. It gave the finger to a pair of Detroit power company workers just twenty-four hours before the worst ice storm in history blasted the city, leaving sixteen people dead and 400,000 homes without electricity for days. In 1996, two super-drunk Detroiters apparently saw it breaking into a car, and in 2008, the Lions completed their decade-long death-spiral of futility and became the first 0-16 team in NFL history. This is all the work of the dwarf and his leering angst of evil. Also, Matt Millen, who isn't particularly red or goblin-like, may have at some point had a never-mentioned meeting with the beast that cursed him throughout his days in Detroit.

Leprechauns are pretty well known for their pots o' gold and lucky charms and whatnot, but their drunken cousins the Chluricauns are a lot less about playing hopscotch with rainbows and a lot more about pounding whiskey, swearing, lasciviously dancing around mushroom circles, and swinging Jamison bottles around during out-of-control pub brawls. These Surlychauns wear red instead of green (so as not to be mistaken for their douchey bros), drink a ton of wine, and get DUIs for drunkenly riding around on the backs of dogs or sheep while well above the legal limit. If you're nice to them and leave them little plates of booze like alcoholic Santas, the Chluricauns are said to protect your wine cellar from intruders, keep your booze casks from leaking, and sing badass old Irish folk songs in your basement all night long. If you piss them off, however, they'll spoil all your wine, trash your basement, and upper-deck every toilet in your house before storming out and never returning.

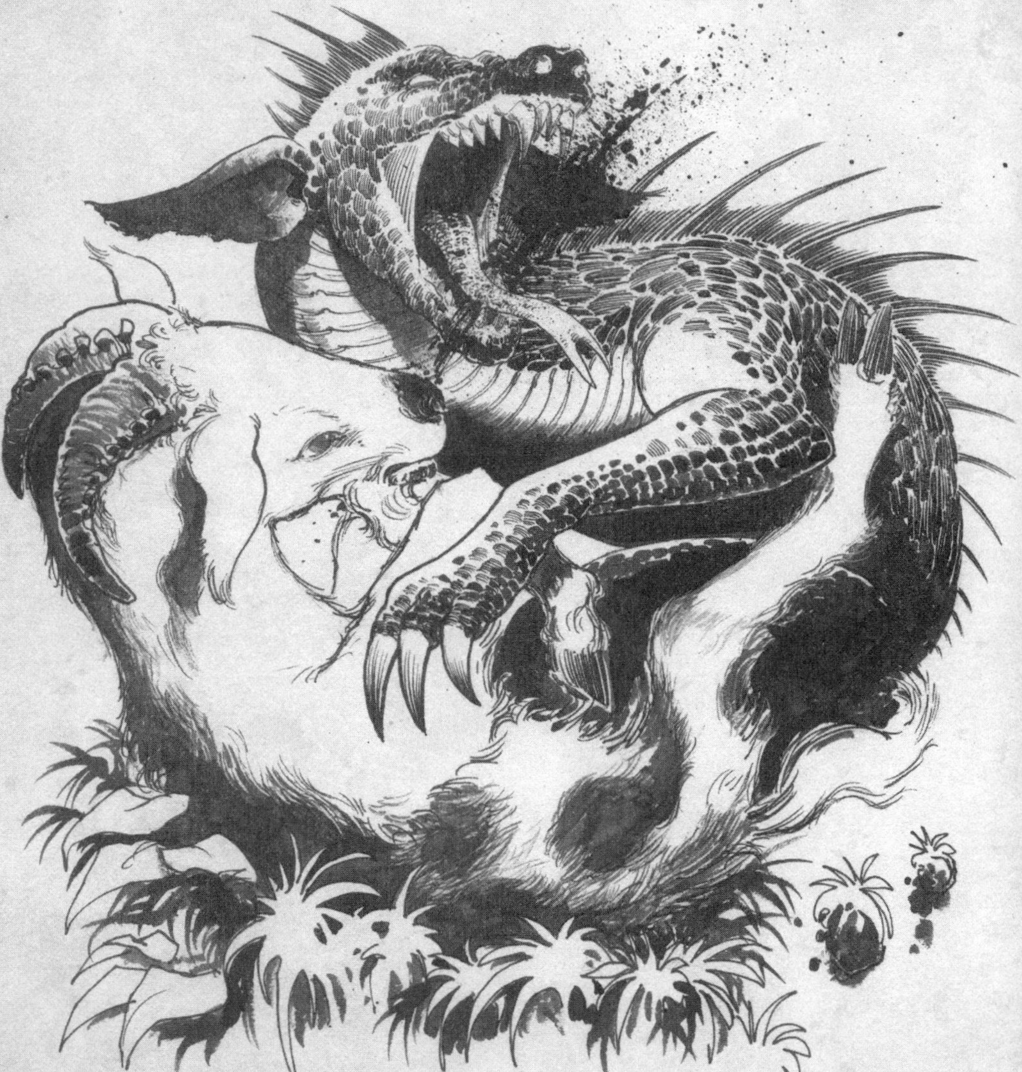

39

EL CHUPACABRA

The carcasses were like discarded rags, as though everything had
been sucked out of them through the eyes. Internal organs—heart,
liver, stomach—were all gone.

—ALLEGED POLICE REPORT DESCRIBING A SERIES OF
PUERTO RICAN ANIMAL MUTILATIONS IN 1991

DEEP IN THE HEART OF PUERTO RICO, A VICIOUS, UNSEEN PRED-
ATOR STALKS THE LAND IN SEARCH OF UNSUSPECTING VICTIMS.
Blood-curdling screams routinely echo throughout the picturesque rain-
forests and expansive farmlands of this terrorized island as a ferocious
beast ruthlessly tears its prey limb from limb, leaving nothing but a mangled husk of what at one point was presumably a living creature. Goats,
cattle, and even occasional human beings are considered prey for this
freakadelic ass-reaming spawn of Satan as it tears nuts around the land in
its dark rampage of blood-drinking disgustingness. The foul creature's
arsenal of carnage ranges from ungodly mutilation and disembowelment
to mass disappearances of entire herds of livestock, and no mammal is
safe from its voracious appetite for destruction. All of its victims share
one common, totally unsettling symptom: exsanguination. The complete draining of all blood in the body. The severity of their injuries may

vary, but these white, bloodless corpses all bear the mark of the beast—two small puncture marks in the neck from a pair of hollow, ultra-sharp fangs. These are the victims of the silent, invisible, super-weird hunter known only as El Chupacabra.

Despite all of this horror movie–style bloodsucking freakiness, the fearsome Chupacabra actually gets its menacing-sounding name from a Spanish phrase meaning "goat sucker," or, more literally, "it sucks goats." I guess this is a pretty straightforward description of the one unifying factoid that we know about this mysterious, modern-day cryptid—its unquenchable thirst for the blood of ruminants—but I have to admit that "it sucks goats" isn't really the sort of nomenclature that strikes crippling fear into the hearts of all who hear it. Considering that many of this thing's victims are torn to shreds and have all of their entrails forcibly removed through holes bored in their torsos, you would think they would have come up with some more fearsome terminology. A vicious demon that eviscerates cows deserves something better, like "Chupacabrasaurus Rex: The Livestock Mutilator."

For the last couple decades, there have been hundreds of eyewitness accounts of El Chupacabra in all of his goat-sucking glory, though perhaps somewhat interestingly, the accounts of the beast never really seem to synch up with each other in anything resembling a coherent unifying description of its appearance. To this day, amateur cryptozoographers still struggle to comprehend exactly what the balls this thing actually looks like, a detail that is usually a hindrance when you're trying to track something down and prove its existence. Generally speaking, there are two main variants: the first is a half-alien, half-dinosaur, kangaroo-like hopping creature with leathery gray reptilian skin, quills running down its back, a spiked tail, and a face that resembles the creepy anal-probing aliens from *The X-Files*. Other people swear that it's a quadripedal hairless dog-monster with a forked snake tongue and giant canine teeth, which, honestly, is kind of the exact opposite of a sociopathic, spike-laden, vampire space kangaroo. Both camps can agree that Chupacabras are three to five feet tall, or somewhere between the size of a huge dog and a small, angry bear. The 2004 Sci-Fi Channel masterpiece *Chupacabra Terror* depicts the beast more like the fleshly love-child of the Creature from the Black Lagoon, a burn victim, and a compost heap, which doesn't really fit either description, but it's okay because he fights Navy SEALs on board a cruise ship while shredding a bunch of rich jerks into ribbons so you kind of have to cut the dude a little slack.

Almost all eyewitness accounts of the Chupacabra mention that it has the ability to either hop, leap, and/or fly, and that it's super-aggressive, vicious, and completely unfazed by any humans not currently pointing automatic weapons at it. One dude said he saw one of these things snatch a full-size cow and friggin' leap twenty feet through the air hanging on to it like it was going to top-rope bodyslam it through a meat grinder, which rips ass. They also smell strongly of sulfur, which they presumably picked up from all the fire and brimstone that permeates whatever circle of Hell they typically reside in. Chupacabras have hardcore night vision, and sport glowing red eyes that have the power to induce nausea and make you spontaneously start barfing and crapping all over the place, presumably from all the awesomeness. When frightened, challenged, or pissed off, the Chupacabra emits a long, low, hissing sound followed by a ridiculously high-pitched screech that's more obnoxious than speaker feedback and better at making you deaf than jamming a matching set of ice picks into your eardrums.

The first documented reports of weird-as-hell Chupacabra-related phenomena actually date back to 1540, when the Spanish conquistador Francisco Vásquez de Coronado was moseying around present-day Arizona futilely searching for the nonexistent Seven Cities of Gold. According to a report from one of the members of Coronado's expedition, the Spanish were attacked in the middle of the night by a pack of creatures described as small, gray-skinned men with knives attached to their backs.

These weird attackers were driven off with torches, gunfire, and foul language, but not until they'd already killed or dragged off a bunch of Coronado's cattle and collectively given the entire expedition the finger. The Spanish asked the local Zuni Pueblo Indians what the deal was with these weird-as-hell gray dwarf monsters, and were informed that those jokers were actually a race of evil demons that had fought skirmishes against the Pueblo for years. Apparently, these angry little gray men had a bad habit of bear-hugging Indian warriors and tossing them off cliffs to their deaths, though their preferred method of ambush involved leaping down onto the heads of unsuspecting warriors, killing them, and drinking all of their blood. Coronado, of course, thought this was the most ridiculous bullcrap he'd ever heard, and wrote these guys off as unruly natives who probably didn't have anything worth pillaging anyway.

After Coronado, news on the Chupacabra front was pretty quiet for the next couple hundred years until 1975, when a bunch of turkeys, sheep, and other miscellaneous farm animals in Puerto Rico suddenly found themselves missing all their blood and internal organs. The mysterious animal murders were chalked up to the work of the "Mocha Vampire," a legendary goat-sucking savage believed by local farmers to be the soul of an evil man returned to Earth as a gray, blood-drinking dwarf. The Puerto Rican government attributed these killings to local birds and snakes, even though neither of those things have really been known to drink blood, and everybody pretty much forgot about it because what's the point in arguing anyway.

El Chupacabra surfaced yet again in 1991, when a bunch of Puerto Rican dogs had their insides sucked out by a monster that left two small puncture wounds on their necks and one giant hole where their bodies used to be. From that point on, it's been pretty much complete anarchy across the world as Chupacabras rampage throughout Earth like a plague of small, angry, blood-drinking space vampires. In 1995, over 150 sheep were drained entirely of blood in an attack that was witnessed by over thirty people in Canovanas, Puerto Rico, including the town's mayor, who utterly blew a gasket and went insane thereafter. A Puerto Rican journalist was so pumped about these grisly deaths that he released a mind-crushingly bizarre story claiming that this monster was actually a psychotic, genetically modified experiment developed by the Soviet Union during the Cold War when some Chinese scientist cross-bred an alien corpse with a Cuisinart and then sewed a bunch of chainsaws to it. The story of a maniac Communist space-predator tearing up non-proletariat-approved livestock created such a hullabaloo that the director of the Puerto Rican Department of Agriculture had to publicly come out and soothe the populace in person, and reassure them that the entire island wasn't totally screwed. The spokesman wrote the killings off as nothing weird, attributing them to panther maulings and cultists, two things that evidently aren't weird at all.

The Chupacabra epidemic went global in late 1995, when exsanguinated livestock started to turn up in Guatemala, Mexico, South America, and the United States. In 1996, half the town of Calderón, Mexico, saw one of these bastards wolf down a sheep, and for the next month they formed Old West posses to go out with AK-47s and torches to find and hunt the creature down. In 1997, two really drunk bros outside Perth, Australia, claimed they were attacked by a "vampire kangaroo," though the claims of two hammered Aussies weren't really enough to mobilize the populace to assemble riotous, assault rifle–slinging mobs in the middle of the night. Forty sheep were eviscerated in Argentina in 1999. Seventy goats were murdered in Nicaragua in 2000. A police officer was mauled by Chupie in Guadelupe in 2004; and in 2007, three hundred sheep vanished from a fenced-in farm in Colombia. Attacks have also turned up in Chile, Brazil, Texas, California, Arizona, and Costa Rica. Even if there's no such thing as a Chupacabra, this is a really jacked-up series of events. It's a bad time to be a goat.

In 2009, a San Antonio farmer caught some hairless dog thing that might have been the Chupacabra, but rather than a gray alien with spines, a barf-inducing gaze, and a vertical leap that makes LeBron James look like Homer Simpson, the creature this guy caught looks more like an unflattering mix between the Crypt Keeper and a scrotum. What a flattering mix between those two items would look like, I have no idea, but you get the point. Scientists have identified this wannabe-Chupacabra as a hairless coyote with extreme male-pattern dog-baldness, which was disappointing. Chupacabra sympathizers are quick to point out that this still doesn't explain how thirty sheep had their blood sucked out near Moscow in 2005, since Russia doesn't have coyotes. I would argue that it is still Russia, and who knows why the hell anything happens over there.

Other things that suck goats include artificial turf, spray-on tans, working as a receptionist, and the bubonic plague.

The closest thing that real life has to the Chupacabra is the African Honey Badger. This thing, like Chupie, isn't particularly massive (it stands about three and a half feet tall), but has been known to take out lions, cheetahs, poisonous snakes, and even wildebeests in combat. Using its size as a boon instead of a setback, this thing murders its adversaries in one of the most vicious ways possible—by tearing off it enemy's nutsack with its teeth and then mauling the poor de-balled bastard while it laments the passage of its most favorite piece of built-in equipment.

→ A CRYPTOZOOLOGICAL MENAGERIE OF WEIRDNESS ←

THE MONGOLIAN DEATH WORM

In addition to having one of the most awesome names of any pseudo-real creature ever, the Mongolian Death Worm is especially badass because it's one of the only land creatures reported to murder its prey with super-charged electrical voltage. Tearing ass *Dune*-style beneath the burning sands of the Gobi Desert, these reddish, five-foot-long worms alleg-edly pop up in front of wayward douchebags and money-shot them in the damn face with acid until their eyes melt out of their heads. If you somehow manage to avoid the fire hose of acid, the Gobi nomads swear that it is charged up with so much static electricity that just touching it is enough to overload your heart until it fibrillates out of your chest. Semi-legitimate scientific expeditions were launched into the desert to find this creature in 2003, 2005, and 2007, but as of yet nobody has been able to turn up any concrete evidence of the monsters' existence. This is prob-ably a good thing.

THE ABOMINABLE SNOWMAN

Himalayan Sherpas have long told the legend of the Yeti—a mysterious, shadowy gorilla-like man who wanders the ball-freezing environment of the world's tallest and most inhospitable mountain range. These mysteri-ous snow-Bigfoots have been known to leave behind Shaquille O'Neal–size footprints in the snow, some of which were spotted by New Zealand mountaineer Sir Edmund Hilary in 1953 when he became the first man to summit Mount Everest. Hilary returned to Nepal seven years later and spent ten months looking for Yetis, but was not super-successful in his efforts to discover Mr. Cold Miser. That wasn't even the creature's first brush with fame, however—in 1959, American Academy Award–winning actor Jimmy Stewart smuggled a suspected Yeti hand from India to Lon-don. People still can't figure out what the hell the deal is with that thing.

THE BONASUS

According to Pliny the Elder's *Historia Naturalis*, the Bonansus was a cow/bison kind of beast with giant, curved horns that bent back almost into a circle. The Bonasus didn't have any real natural weapons, but when it was attacked its primary defense was to run away and leave a *Spy Hunter*-style oil-slick of bison crap in its wake. This thing could al-legedly defecate two acres worth of feces in one explosive blast, and this mountain of crap was so deadly that it would set fire to any grass, trees, dogs, and people miserable and unfortunate enough to come into contact with it. It doesn't get a whole lot grosser than that.

40

THE DALEKS

Now Davros has created a machine creature—a monster—which will terrorize and destroy millions and millions of lives and lands throughout all eternity. He has given this machine a name: a Dalek. It is a word new to you, but for a thousand generations it is a name that will bring fear and terror. Now undoubtedly Davros has one of the finest scientific minds in existence, but he has a fanatical desire to perpetuate himself in his machine. He works without conscience, without soul, without pity, and his machines are equally devoid of these qualities.

—THE FOURTH DOCTOR, *GENESIS OF THE DALEKS*

THE DALEKS ARE AN ULTRA-EVIL RACE OF INTERGALACTIC, TIME-TRAVELING, ALIEN NAZI SPACE-TANKS THAT HATE EVERYTHING AND SCREAM MANIACALLY AT YOU IN SUPER-OBNOXIOUS ROBOTIC BRITISH VOICES SO SHRILL THAT IT SOUNDS LIKE YOU'RE TAKING A CHEESE GRATER TO THE INSIDE OF YOUR BRAIN. The most powerful and bad-ass villains on *Dr. Who,* the longest-running science-fiction television series of all time, these murderous automated salt-shakers are vile constructs of pure evil and hatred that seek nothing less than the complete extermination of all non-Dalek life in the universe and the utter destruction of all organic creatures and inorganic stairwells in the galaxy.

The Daleks were created by an evil, wheelchair-bound super-genius mutant named Davros, who used to live in a bombproof bunker on the war-torn planet Skaro. Correctly realizing that a few centuries of non-stop nuclear, chemical, and biological warfare was rapidly mutating the generally human-looking Kaled people of his homeworld into a horrible race of disgusting amorphous radioactive alien snot-balls, Davros (who amused his evil genius by working on bizarre, vaguely useful scientific experiments like engineering a species of man-eating oysters for some inexplicable reason) began work on the project that was destined to save his newly mutated civilization of freaks and slime-monsters from a life of sedentary misery—the soon-to-be-notorious self-contained military tank known as the Mark III Travel Machine.

Though this may seem like a noble (if not misguided) undertaking, don't be fooled into thinking that Davros was some selfless humanitarian hero who wasn't totally creepy-looking, psychotic, and evil, or that his motives were anything other than ulterior and perhaps even diabolical. This guy was a whacked-out delusional fascist megalomaniac who ate crushed-up orphans through an IV drip, and while ostensibly helping the Kaled race along in their evolutionary cycle for the good of civilization, he also decided to take the liberty of genetically engineering them to have no feelings, no pity, no compassion, and nothing that resembled a conscience or legs. These vicious alien blob-monsters were bred solely to survive, murder, and perpetuate their species through extreme violence, and were specifically designed to only be interested in mightily rolling over the groins of the worthless denizens of the universe any time they happened to be lying down on a piece of relatively flat pavement.

The Kaled booger monster itself operates the tank-like Travel Machine and is the ultimate source of its species' unrelenting universal hatred for everything in existence. Without the Dalek casing, however, these things would really just be a miserable little race of stationary angry globs that sat around all day waiting for someone to come within arm's reach so that they can strangle him with their noodly appendages, which, while cool, isn't exactly the most menacing thing ever. The full Dalek machine is really what makes them shine in their role as the badassholes of the universe. In addition to being impervious to all kinds of conventional weaponry, Daleks have propulsion and life-support systems that allow them to hover, fly, survive in space, travel underwater, and move through any number of incredibly inhospitable environments. They come equipped with a tremendously named eight-inch-long phallic device known as the gunstick, which shoots a vicious beam of electrical energy that can rearrange your ass faster than a sonic screwdriver enema, as well as a "manipulator arm" that makes it look like they have huge black toilet plungers sticking out of their torsos. The plunger can be used to interface with objects, manipulate heavy explosives, and rip information from a humanoid's brain, but sometimes they like to just wave it around menacingly at people as a means of making them uncomfortable. One time I saw a Dalek use the plunger to crush a dude's skull, murdering him in a hilariously humiliating manner. This manipulator arm, while strangely versatile considering that it operates solely by suction, can also be replaced with everything from flamethrowers to pestilence-filled syringes depending on how evil the Daleks feel they need to be on that particular occasion. The Kaled mutant driver looks out through an eyestalk attached to a swiveling head at the top of the Dalek, which, while capable of identifying and tracking human footprints, doesn't seem to help a whole lot whenever the Doctor and his companions have the good sense to tactfully duck behind some random nearby object. As utter megalomaniacs intent on asserting their superiority over the inferior douchebags of the universe, the Daleks love screeching about how awesome they are and talk incredible amounts of trash to their victims whenever possible.

In negotiations, they act like true badasses by speaking only in threats and responding to any arguments or disagreements by simply screaming louder and repeating themselves incessantly until their enemies either give up or get their neurons fragged apart by the death ray. Arguing with these guys is like getting in a shouting match with a broken MP3 player that can shoot lightning bolts out of its earphone jack.

The warriors of the Dalek Empire warp around the universe in flying saucers arbitrarily attacking every sentient civilization they encounter. They feel no pity or remorse, cannot be reasoned with, and demand universal genocide of all non-Dalek races (as well as any factions within the Dalek Empire that disagree with them). As cyborg monsters with no respect for organic or synthetic life, they rarely negotiate or accept surrender. They only waste their time forcibly subjugating a species if they feel like they need a little bit of help in the prehensile-thumbs department or if they decide they want to test out some experimental weaponry on captives, who they typically view more like expendable hostages than legit prisoners of war. For instance, one time the Doctor tried to actually negotiate with the Daleks, so they just grabbed a bunch of prisoners and started executing them in front of the Doc until he gave up all attempts at diplomacy. They're just bastards like that.

It's pretty beneficial to their existence that the Daleks uncovered the secrets of time travel at some point in their intergalactic crusade against sanity, because the thing about these ultimate alien jerkwads is that they're hardwired for survival at all costs and are never fully defeated. No matter how many times you think they've been destroyed, they just time-warp to a different era of history, and the next thing you know, there's a damn human-size salt-shaker wandering the streets of 1930s Manhattan wearing a fedora and a trenchcoat in a ridiculous attempt at rolling incognito.

Perhaps the most impressive thing about these creatures is that they were created back in 1963, and nearly fifty years later, they're still out there appearing in new episodes and exterminating humans just as fiercely as ever.

According to the story, the Daleks got their name because it's an anagram for the Kaleds. Other anagrams for Kaleds include "La Desk" and "Sad Elk."

Throughout their existence, the Daleks have invaded, defeated, and occupied the Earth on at least a couple different occasions, but they never really had the same humanity-obliterating success as another fictional race of robotic bastards—the Cylons. A similarly powerful race of angry, synthetic conquer-bots, the Cylons were vicious machine warriors that used treachery and deception to utterly wipe out twelve planets' worth of humans in the span of just a few hours, killing somewhere between 20 billion and infinity billion people in one day's worth of orbital nuclear airstrikes. Just to prove how dedicated these guys were to the cause of *Homo sapiens*' extermination, the Cylons then spent quite a bit of effort in tracking down and attempting to blow up the handful of people lucky enough to have survived a thermonuclear holocaust that would have made World War III look like Gorbachev farting in a bathtub.

ACKNOWLEDGMENTS

Writing a book is an adventure. To begin with, it is a toy and an amusement; then it becomes a mistress, and then it becomes a master, and then a tyrant. The last phase is just as you are about to reconcile yourself to your servitude, you kill the monster, and fling him out into public.

—WINSTON CHURCHILL

Once again, my most sincere gratitude goes out to the people who helped to get me through a grueling process that doesn't seem to get any easier with experience:

To Andrea—my publicist, PR guru, research assistant, events manager, editor, PowerPoint slide-advancer, audio/visual engineer, booth babe, marketing department, and copilot on all my wild misadventures in the world of writing. You are seriously the only thing that keeps me sane sometimes.

To my brother Clay, for helping me with a great deal of research, proofreading, brainstorming, and editing, and for dutifully sitting through countless hours of film that ended up running the full spectrum of awesomeness.

To J. Matt, for putting together the original "Moby-Dick" piece for the website, which I cannibalized in part for the updated version printed in these pages, and to J. Matt, Andrew, Clay, and Shane, for their excellent feedback and proofreading.

To all of my family and friends, for your continued support throughout everything.

To my editor, Matthew Benjamin at HarperCollins, for being crazy enough to want to read a second volume of my writing, for constantly championing the book, and for his much-needed ability to cleave an over-wordy manuscript in twain until the pages bleed red with tracked changes.

To graphic designer Lorie Pagnozzi, for her incredible work laying out the interiors both for this book and for *Badass*; to production editor Mary Beth Constant, for overseeing the seemingly grueling copyediting process; to copyeditor Olga Gardner Galvin, not only for painstakingly correcting my gratuitous capitalization and hyphenation errors but also for providing me with some excellent additional information regarding the more badass aspects of Russian folklore.

To my agents, Farley Chase of the Waxman Agency and Sean Daily of Hotchkiss, for having six to eight times more confidence in my abilities than I do, and for their tireless work in going around telling everybody how brilliant I am and why they should pay me lots of money in exchange for my writing.

To Scarecrow Video in Seattle, Washington, for having the ultimate collection of badass movies. Your two-for-one Wednesday rental deal provided me with more hours of research material than I could have ever wanted, and your stacks always seemed to contain every obscure movie I was looking for. Few things in my life have been more fulfilling than writing off a five-day rental of *The Ultimate Dirty Harry Collection* as a business expense on my taxes.

To Midtown Espresso, Top Pot Doughnuts, and Diva Espresso, for always providing quiet places to write and hot cups of coffee to fuel my caffeine-induced hysteria.

To Steve Lieber of Periscope Studio, for helping coordinate quite a few last-minute art commissions, and to all of the illustrators in this book—your incredible artwork sufficiently demonstrates these characters' badassitude before I even have to write a word.

And once again, to all the fans of the website, all the Facebook and Twitter followers, and all those who enjoyed the first book and came back for more. None of this writing stuff could have ever been possible without you, and your continued support never ceases to amaze me.

ILLUSTRATION CREDITS

Steven Belledin (www.stevenbelledin.com): Cover art, Atalanta, Sinbad, Beowulf, King Minos, The White Tights, Nidhogg the Dragon, The Red Dwarf

Miguel Coimbra (www.miguelcoimbra.com): Medea, Gilgamesh, Dragon vs. Knight, Godzilla, The Daleks

Thomas Denmark (www.studiodenmark.com): Rama, Monkey, Saint Michael, Finn McCool, Sir Mordred, Moriarty, Mount Doom, Baba Yaga, Baba Yaga's Hut, Surt

Matt Haley (www.matthaley.com): Zeus, Thor, Diomedes, Samson, Captain Kirk, Dirty Harry, Baracus, Darth Vader, Skeletor

Sidney Paget (1860–1908): Moriarty vs. Holmes

PERISCOPE STUDIO
(periscopestudio.com)

  ✳ **Ben Bates**: Section intro (Gods), Samson destroying the temple
  ✳ **Jonathan Case**: Section intro (Monsters), The Dragon of Koshii
  ✳ **Ben Dewey**: Section intro (Villains), Kali, Ragnarok
  ✳ **Rich Ellis**: Section intro (Heroes), Diomedes vs. Ares, Bradamant
  ✳ **Jesse Hamm**: Rama vs. Ravana, The Kraken
  ✳ **Aaron McConnell**: Mordred vs. Arthur

Raphael (1483–1520): Saint Michael vs. Satan

James Ryman (www.jamesryman.com): Sauron, Skuld, The Furies

Brian Snoddy (www.snellsoftware.com/briansnoddyart): Anubis, Brave-Swift-Impetuous-Male, Huitzilopochtli, The Templo Mayor, Gilgamesh vs. The Bull of Heaven, Frankenstein's Monster, Moby-Dick, El Chupacabra

Thom Zahler (www.thomz.com): Medea poisoning Theseus

BIBLIOGRAPHY

1000 Facts on Myth and Legend. Miles Kelly Publishing, 2004.

Abbot, Elizabeth. *A History of Celibacy*. Da Capo, 2001.

Abdulaeva, Maynat. "Where Do They Sew White Tights?" *Novaya Gazeta*. April 13, 2000.

The Adventures of Sherlock Holmes. Adapted for TV by John Hawkesworth. Granada Television, 1984–1985.

Aeschylus. *Eumenides*. Trans. Herbert Weir Smyth. Loeb Classical Library, 1960.

Alighieri, Dante. *The Divine Comedy*. Trans. C. H. Sisson. Oxford University Press, 2008.

Apollodorus. *The Library of Greek Mythology*. Trans. Robin Hard. Oxford University Press, 2008.

Apollonius of Rhodes. *Argonautica*. Trans. R. C. Seaton. Loeb Classical Library, 1990.

Appleton, E. R., and S. Parks Cadman. *An Outline of Religion*. Kessinger, 2005.

"Are Foreigners Fighting There?" *The Economist*. July 8, 2000.

Ariosto, Ludovico. *Orlando Furioso*. Trans. Guido Waldman. Oxford University Press, 2008.

Ashkenazi, Michael. *Handbook of Japanese Mythology*. ABC-CLIO, 2003.

Atapur, Alex Perry. "Killing for 'Mother' Kali." *Time*. July 22, 2002.

The A-Team. Created by Stephen J. Cannell and Frank Lupo. Stephen J. Cannell Productions, 1983–1987.

Axel, Olrik. *The Heroic Legends of Denmark*. Bibliobazaar, 2009.

Bailey, James and Tatyana Ivanova. *An Anthology of Russian Folk Epics*. M. E. Sharpe, 1999.

Baker, Mark, and Kit Fui Burczkowski. *Poland*. Frommer's, 2009.

Barnard, Alan. *Hunters and Herders of Southern Africa*. Cambridge University Press, 1992.

Bartlett, Sarah. *The Mythology Bible*. Sterling, 2009.

Bastian, Dawn Elaine, and Judy K. Mitchell. *Handbook of Native American Mythology*. ABC-CLIO, 2004.

Bates, Brian. *The Real Middle-Earth*. Palgrave, 2003.

Battlestar Galactica. Created by Glen A. Larson. Universal, 1978, 2004–2009

Berens, E. M. *The Myths and Legends of Ancient Greece and Rome*. BiblioBazaar, 2008.

The Bible. Authorized King James Version. Oxford University Press, 1998.

The Bible. Revised Standard Version. Cokesbury, 1963.

Bidwell, Margaret and Robin Bidwell. *Morocco*. Tauris Parke, 2005.

Bildhauer, Bettina and Robert Mills. *The Monstrous Middle Ages*. University of Toronto Press, 2003.

Boiardo, Matteo Maria. *Orlando Innamorato*. Trans. William Stewart Rose. W. Blackwood, 1823.

Bonfante, Lisa and Judith Swaddling. *Etruscan Myths*. University of Texas Press, 2006.

Brier, Bob, and A. Hoyt Hobbs. *Daily Life of the Ancient Egyptians*. Greenwood, 1999.

Brooks de Vita, Alexis. "Oya." *Encyclopedia of the African Diaspora*. Ed. Carole Boyce Davies. ABC-CLIO, 2008.

Brown, Robert. *The Unicorn*. Forgotten Books, 2009.

Budd, Deena West. *The Weiser Field Guide to Cryptozoology*. Weiser, 2010.

Budge, E. A. W. *The Gods of the Egyptians*. Courier Dover, 1969.

Burton, Richard F. *The Arabian Nights: Tales from a Thousand and One Nights*. Random House, 2001.

Burton, Richard F. *Vikram and the Vampire*. Echo, 2006.

Campbell, Joseph. *The Hero with a Thousand Faces*. New World Library, 2008.

Carroll, Robert T. "Chupacabra." *The Skeptic's Dictionary*. Skepticsdictionary.com, April 5, 2010.

The Catholic Encyclopedia. Robert Appleton, 1909.

Christ, Henry I. *Myths and Folklore*. Amsco, 1989.

Chupacabra Terror. Directed by John Shepphird. Sci Fi Pictures, 2005.

Clark, Mary Ann. *Santeria*. Greenwood, 2007.

Coleman, Loren and Jerome Clark. *Cryptozoology A to Z*. Simon and Schuster, 1999.

Colum, Padraic and Willy Pogany. *Nordic Gods and Heroes*. Courier Dover, 1996.

Conway, D. J. *Maiden, Mother, Crone*. Llewellyn, 1995.

Cross, Tom P. and Clark Harris Slover. *Ancient Irish Tales*. Trans. Tom P. Cross. Barnes & Noble, 1969.

Crowley, Mary Catherine. *A Daughter of New France*. Little Brown, 1901.

Curran, Bob. *Lost Lands, Forgotten Realms*. New Page Books, 2007.

Curran, Bob. *Vampires: A Field Guide to Creatures that Stalk the Night*. Career Press, 2005.

D'Aulaire, Ingri and Edgar Parin D'Aulaire. *D'Aulaire's Book of Greek Myths*. Delacorte, 1992.

Dalley, Stephanie. *Myths from Mesopotamia*. Oxford University Press, 1988

Daniels, Cora Linn, and C. M. Stevans. *Encyclopedia of Superstitions, Folklore, and Occult Sciences of the World*. Minerva, 2003.

Darlington, William. *A Catechism of Mythology*. W. R. Lucas, 1832.

David, Ann Rosalie. *Egyptian Mummies and Modern Science*. Cambridge University Press, 2008.

Davies, Carole Boyce. *Encyclopedia of the African Diaspora*. ABC-CLIO, 2008.

Davis, Kenneth C. *Don't Know Much About Mythology*. HarperCollins, 2005.

Day, John. *Molech: A God of Human Sacrifice in the Old Testament*. Cambridge University Press, 1989.

The Dead Pool. Directed by Buddy Van Horn. Warner Bros., 1988.

De Grummond, Nancy Thomson. *Etruscan Myth, Sacred History, and Legend*. UPenn Museum of Archaeology, 2006.

De Rouen, Karl R. *Civil Wars of the World*. ABC-CLIO, 2007.

De Sahaguin, Bernardino. *Primeros Memoriales*. Trans. Thelma D. Sullivan. University of Oklahoma, 1997.

Destroy All Monsters. Directed by Ishiro Honda. Toho Company, 1968.

Dirty Harry. Directed by Don Siegel. Warner Bros., 1971.

Dixon-Kennedy, Mike. *Encyclopedia of Russian and Slavic Myth and Legend*. ABC-CLIO, 1998.

Doctor Who. Created by Sydney Newman. British Broadcasting Corporation, 1963–1989, 2005–2010.

Dorsey, George A. and Alfred L. Kroeber. *Traditions of the Arapaho*. Kessinger, 2006.

Dorsey, Lilith. *Voodoo and Afro-Caribbean Paganism*. Citadel, 2005.

Douglas, Jim. "A Chupacabra Sighting?" *KENS 5 News*. January 18, 2010.

Dowson, John. *A Classical Dictionary of Hindu Mythology and Religion*. Trübner, 1870

Doyle, Sir Arthur Conan. *Sherlock Holmes*. Bantam Classics, 1986.

Doyle, Sir Arthur Conan. *The Sherlock Holmes Mysteries*. Signet Classics, 2005.

Du Chaillu, Paul Belloni. *The Viking Age*. C. Scribner's Sons, 1889.

Dunn, Brad. *When They Were 22*. Andrews McNeel, 2006.

Dutt, Romesh C. *The Ramayana and Mahabharata*. Courier Dover, 2003.

Dybis, Karen. "Banishing the Nain Rouge." *Time*. March 22, 2010.

The Egyptian Book of the Dead. Trans. E. A. W. Budge. Forgotten Books. Peter Smith Pub., 1967.

El-Saddik, Wafaa and Sabah Abdel Razek. *Anubis, Upwawet, and Other Deities*. American University of Cairo Press, 2007.

The Empire Strikes Back. Directed by George Lucas. 20th Century Fox, 1980.

The Enforcer. Directed by James Fargo. Warner Bros., 1976.

Ennis, Garth and Steve Dillon. *Preacher*. Vertigo, 1995–2000.

The Epic of Gilgamesh. Trans. Andrew George. Penguin, 2003.

Euripides. *Medea*. Oxford University Press, 1907.

Euripides. *Orestes*. Trans. Arthur S. Way. Loeb Classical Library, 1978.

Fairbanks, Arthur. *The Mythology of Greece and Rome*. D. Appleton, 1907.

Faurby, Ib. "The Battle(s) of Grozny." *Baltic Defense Review*. February 1999.

Fee, Christopher R. and David A. Leeming. *Gods, Heroes, and the Battle for Mythic Britain*. Oxford University Press, 2004

Geoffrey of Monmouth. *History of the Kings of Britain*. Trans. Lewis G. M. Thorpe. Penguin, 1966.

Ghidrah, the Three-Headed Monster. Directed by Ishiro Honda. Toho Company, 1964.

Ghose, Sanujit. *Legend of Ram*. Bibliophile South Asia, 2004.

Gierasch, Peter J. and Philip D. Nicholson. "Jupiter." World Book Online Reference Center. World Book, Inc., 2004.

Gill, Sam D. and Irene F. Sullivan. *Dictionary of Native American Mythology*. Oxford University Press, 1994.

Gleason, Judith. "Oya: Black Goddess of Africa." *The Goddess Re-awakening*. Ed. Shirley J. Nicholson. Quest, 1989.

Godfrey, Linda S., Mark Moran, and Marc Sceurman. *Weird Michigan*. Sterling, 2006.

God of War. Created by David Jaffe. Sony Computer Entertainment, 2005.

God of War II. Created by David Jaffe. Sony Computer Entertainment, 2007.

God of War III. Created by David Jaffe. Sony Computer Entertainment, 2010.

Godzilla. Directed by Ishiro Honda. Toho Company, 1954.

Godzilla 1985. Directed by Koji Hashimoto. Toho Company, 1985.

Godzilla 2000. Directed by Takao Okawara. Toho Company, 1999.

Godzilla: Final Wars. Directed by Ryuhei Kitamura. Toho Company, 2004.

Godzilla, Mothra, and King Ghidorah: Giant Monsters All-Out Attack! Directed by Shusuke Kaneko. Toho Company, 2001.

Godzilla vs. King Ghidorah. Directed by Kazuki Omori. Toho Company, 1991.

Godzilla vs. Mechagodzilla. Directed by Takao Okawara. Toho Company, 1993.

Godzilla vs. Mothra. Directed by Takao Okawara. Toho Company, 1992.

The Golden Voyage of Sinbad. Directed by Gordon Hessler. Columbia Pictures, 1974.

Goodrich, Norma Lorre. *Myths of the Hero*. Kessinger, 2006.

Gott, Kendall D. *Breaking the Mold*. U.S. Department of Defense, 2006.

Grant, Richard. *American Nomads*. Grove, 2005.

Graves, Robert. *The Greek Myths*. Penguin, 1993.

Gray, Louis Herbert. *The Mythology of All Races*. Marshall Jones, 1920.

Gregory, Lady Augusta. *Cuchulain of Muirthemne*. Dover, 2001.

Gresh, Lois H., and Robert Weinberg. *Why Did It Have to Be Snakes*. John Wiley and Sons, 2008.

Guerber, H. A. *The Book of the Epic*. Biblio & Tannen, 1983.

Guerber, H. A. *The Myths of Greece and Rome*. Courier Dover, 1993.

Hahn, Theophilus. *Tsuni-i i Goam: The Supreme Being of the Khoi-Khoi*. Trübner, 1881.

Hamilton, Edith. *Mythology*. Penguin, 1969.

Hamilton, Sue L. *Monsters of Mystery*. ABDO Group, 2007.

Hard Boiled. Directed by John Woo. Rim, 1993.

Harding, Elizabeth U. *Kali: The Black Goddess of Dakshineswar*. Motilal Banarsidass, 1998.

Harris, Mark. *The Dr. Who Technical Manual*. Severn House, 1983.

Hart, George. *The Routledge Dictionary of Egyptian Gods and Goddesses*. Routledge, 2005.

Hartland, Edwin Sidney. *English Fairy and Folk Tales*. Kessinger, 2006.

Heaney, Marie. *Over Nine Waves: A Book of Irish Legends*. Faber & Faber, 1995.

Heller, Julek and Dierdre Headon. *Knights*. Schocken Books, 1982.

He-Man and the Masters of the Universe. Filmation Associates, 1983–1985.

Herodotus. *The Histories*. Trans. Macaulay, G. C. Spark, 2004.

Hesiod. *Theogany and Works and Days*. Trans. Martin L. West. Oxford University Press, 1999.

Hilton, James. *Lost Horizon*. HarperCollins, 2004

Homer. *The Iliad*. Trans. Richmond Lattimore. University of Chicago Press, 1951.

Homer. *The Odyssey*. Trans. Richmond Lattimore. Harper, 1965.

Ihelzon, Eugene. "Chechen General's Rose Litaeva." *Segodnya*. July 5, 2005.

Inbe no Hironari. *Kogoshui*. Forgotten Books, 2008.

Indiana Jones and the Temple of Doom. Directed by Stephen Spielberg. Paramount, 1984.

Jansen, Eva Rudy. *The Book of Hindu Imagery*. Binkey Kok, 1993.

Jason and the Argonauts. Directed by Don Chaffey. Columbia, 1963.

Jeans, Peter D. *Seafaring Lore and Legend*. McGraw-Hill, 2004.

Joseph, Frank. *The Atlantis Encyclopedia*. Career Press, 2005.

Journey to the West. Trans. Anthony C. Yu. University of Chicago Press, 1980.

"Kahless the Unforgettable." *Memory Alpha*. Memory-alpha.org/en/wiki/Kahless_the_Unforgettable, 2010.

Karade, Ifa. *The Handbook of Yoruba Religious Concepts*. Weiser, 1994.

The Kojiki. Trans. Basil Hall Chamberlain. Tuttle, 2005.

The Koran. Trans. N. J. Dawood. Penguin, 1990.

Hkerdian, David. *Monkey*. Shambhala, 2005.

Kinane, Karolyn and Michael A. Ryan. *End of Days*. McFarland, 2009.

Kinsley, David R. *Hindu Goddesses*. Motlial Banarsidass, 1998.

Krueger, Roberta L. *The Cambridge Companion to Medieval Romance*. Cambridge University Press, 2000.

Lang, Andrew. *Myth, Ritual and Religion*. Longmans, Green, and Co., 1913.

Leaman, Oliver. *The Qur'an: An Encyclopedia*. Taylor & Francis, 2006.

Lee, Matt. "St. Skeletor's Day 2010." Matt.lee.name/skeletor/2010/. 2010.

Leeming, David. *Oxford Companion to World Mythology*. Oxford University Press, 2009.

Levin, Anatol. *Chechnya*. Yale University Press, 1999.

Lindow, John. *Norse Mythology*. Oxford University Press, 2001.

Littleton, C. Scott. *Gods, Goddesses, and Mythology.* Marshall Cavendish, 2005.

Lovecraft, H. P. *The Call of Cthulhu and Other Weird Tales.* Penguin Classics, 1999.

Maberry, Jonathan and David F. Kramer. *The Cryptopedia.* Citadel, 2007.

The Mabinogion. Ed. Jeffrey Gantz. Penguin, 1976.

Mac Carthy, Ita. *Women and the Making of Poetry in Ariosto's Orlando Furioso.* Troubador, 2007.

Macintyre, Ben. *The Napoleon of Crime.* Delta, 1997.

Mackenzie, Donald A. *Egyptian Myth and Legend.* Kessinger, 2006.

Mackenzie, Donald A. *Myths of Pre-Columbian America.* Kessinger, 2003

MacKillop, James. *Fionn Mac Cumhaill.* Syracuse University Press, 1986.

Magnum Force. Directed by Ted Post. Warner Brothers, 1973.

The Mahabharata. Trans. John D. Smith. Penguin, 2009.

Mahler, Richard. *The Jaguar's Shadow.* Yale University Press, 2009.

Malory, Sir Thomas. *Le Morte d'Arthur.* Trans. Keith Baines. Signet, 2001.

Manguel, Alberto and Gianni Guadelupi. *The Dictionary of Imaginary Places.* Houghton Mifflin, 2000.

Martin, Richard P. *Myths of the Ancient Greeks.* NAL, 2003.

Massey, Robert. *The Natural Genesis.* Cosimo, 2007.

Mastny, Elizabeth. "Wolf in White Pantyhose." *Moskovskiy Komsomolets.* April 6, 2001.

McAnally, D. R. *Irish Wonders.* Gramercy, 1996.

McIntosh, Jane. *Ancient Mesopotamia.* ABC-CLIO, 2005.

Metal Gear Solid. Created by Hideo Kojima. Konami, 1988.

Milton, John. *Paradise Lost and Other Poems.* Signet, 2003.

Murdico, Suzanne J. *Russia: A Primary Source Cultural Guide.* Rosen, 2005.

Narayan, R. K. *The Ramayana: A Shortened Modern Prose Translation.* Penguin, 2006.

Nash, Jay Robert. *The Great Pictorial History of Crime.* Rowman & Littlefield, 2004.

Newton, Michael. *Hidden Animals.* ABC-CLIO, 2009.

Nivedita, Sister. *Kali the Mother.* S. Sonnenschein, 1900.

Oakeshott, R. Ewart. *The Archaeology of Weapons.* Courier Dover, 1996.

Orr, James. *The International Standard Bible Encyclopedia.* Howard-Severence, 1915.

Oswald, H. P. *Vodoo.* Books on Demand, 2009.

Ovid. *Metamorphoses.* Trans. Frank Justus Miller. Loeb Classical Library, 1984.

Pape, Frank C. *The Russian Story Book.* Macmillan, 1916.

Parker, Janet, Alice Mills and Julie Stanton. *Mythology: Myths, Legends and Fantasies.* Struik, 2007.

Pausanias. *Description of Greece.* Trans. W. H. S. Jones. Loeb Classical Library, 1933.

Philbrick, Nathaniel. *In the Heart of the Sea.* Penguin, 2001.

Pierce, Tony. "Is That a Chupacabra Being Stuffed in Texas?" *Los Angeles Times.* September 2, 2009.

Pinch, Geraldine. *Handbook of Egyptian Mythology*. ABC-CLIO, 2002.

Plato. *Dialogues*. Trans. Benjamin Jowett. Clarendon, 1953.

Pliny. *Natural History*. Trans. Harris Rackham. Loeb Classical Library, 1971.

Poe, Edgar Allan. *The Collected Tales and Poems of Edgar Allan Poe*. Random House, 1992.

Preston, Douglas J. *Cities of Gold*. UNM Press, 1999.

Price, Simon and Emily Kearns. *The Oxford Dictionary of Classical Myth & Religion*. Oxford University Press, 2003.

Rabb, Kate Milner. *National Epics*. Echo, 2007.

Redford, Doug. *The History of Israel*. Standard, 2008.

Return of the Jedi. Directed by George Lucas. 20th Century Fox, 1983.

Revai, Cheri. *Haunted New York*. Stackpole, 2005.

Rislaaki, Jukka. *The Case for Latvia*. Rodopi, 2008.

Robinson, Edwin Arlington. *Collected Poems*. Macmillan, 1921.

Robocop. Directed by Paul Verhoeven. Orion, 1987.

Robocop 2. Directed by Ivan Kershner. Orion, 1990.

Robocop 3. Directed by Fred Dekker. Orion, 1993.

Rosa, Greg. *Incan Mythology and Other Myths of the Andes*. Rosen, 2007.

Rose, Carol. *Giants, Monsters, and Dragons*. W. W. Norton, 2001.

Rosen, Brenda. *The Mythical Creatures Bible*. Sterling, 2009.

The Saga of King Hrolf Kraki. Trans. Jesse L. Brock. Penguin, 1998.

Sakaida, Henry. *Heroines of the Soviet Union, 1941–45*. Osprey, 2003.

Scharfstein, Sol and Dorcas Gelabert. *Chronicle of Jewish History*. KATV Publishing, 1997.

Schlosser, S. E. *Spooky Tales*. Globe Pequot, 2007.

Segal, Robert Alan. *Hero Myths*. Wiley-Blackwell, 2000.

The Seventh Voyage of Sinbad. Directed by Nathan H. Juran. Columbia Pictures, 1958.

Seymour, John D. *True Irish Ghost Stories*. Echo, 2006.

Shelly, Mary Wollstonecraft. *Frankenstein*. Barnes & Noble, 2005.

Shuster, Simon, Denis Dyomkin and Margaria Antidze. "Russia Says U.S. Mercenaries, Others Fought for Georgia." *Reuters*. November 24, 2008.

Sinbad and the Eye of the Tiger. Directed by Sam Wanamaker. Columbia Pictures, 1977.

Skinner, Charles Montgomery. *Myths and Legends of Our Own Land, Volume 1*. J. P. Lippincott, 1896.

Skinner, Charles Montgomery. *Myths and Legends of Our Own Land, Volume 2*. J. P. Lippincott, 1896.

Smith, Evan Lansing and Nathan Robert Brown. *The Complete Idiot's Guide to World Mythology*. Penguin, 2008.

Spence, Lewis. *Myths of Mexico and Peru*. Kessinger, 2003.

Square Enix, Inc. "Corporate Strategy Meeting (Eidos Integration)." Square-enix.com/eng/pdf/news/20090422_02en.pdf. 2009.

Star Trek. Created by Gene Roddenberry. Desilu/Paramount, 1966–1969

Star Trek: The Motion Picture. Directed by Robert Wise. Paramount, 1979.

Star Trek II: The Wrath of Khan. Directed by Nicholas Meyer. Paramount, 1982.

Star Trek III: The Search for Spock. Directed by Leonard Nimoy. Paramount, 1984.

Star Wars. Directed by George Lucas. 20th Century Fox, 1977.

Steinberger, Peter J. *Readings in Classical Political Thought*. Hackett, 2000.

Stoker, Bram. *Dracula*. Barnes & Noble Classics, 2004.

Stone, Michael E. *Jewish Writings of the Second Temple Period*. Fortress, 1984.

Stookey, Lorena Laura. *Thematic Guides to Literature*. Greenwood, 2004.

The Story of the Volsungs. Trans. William Morris and Eirikr Magnusson. Echo, 2006.

Strong Bad. "dragon." Strong Bad Email. Homestarrunner.com/sbemail.html. 2003.

Sturluson, Snorri. *King Harald's Saga*. Trans. Magnus Magnusson. Penguin, 1976.

Sturluson, Snorri. *Prose Edda*. Trans. Jesse L. Byock. Penguin, 2006.

Sudden Impact. Directed by Clint Eastwood. Warner Bros., 1983.

T., Mr. *Mr. T: The Man with the Gold*. St. Martin's Press, 1985.

Tales from the Thousand and One Nights. Trans. N. J. Dawood. Penguin, 1973.

"Taliban Trains 'Monkey Terrorists' to Attack U.S. Troops." *People's Daily Online*. June 28, 2010.

Taube, Karl A. *Aztec and Maya Myths*. University of Texas, 1993.

Tolkien, J. R. R. *The Hobbit*. Ballantine, 1997.

Tolkien, J. R. R. *The Lord of the Rings*. Del Rey, 1986.

Tolkien, J. R. R. *The Return of the King*. Del Rey, 1986

Tolkien, J. R. R. *The Two Towers*. Del Rey, 1986.

Tolkien, J. R. R., and Christopher Tolkien. *The Silmarillion*. Mariner, 2001.

Tolkien, J. R. R., and Christopher Tolkien. *Unfinished Tales of Númenor and Middle-earth*. Houghton Mifflin, 2001.

Twitchell, James B. *Preposterous Violence*. Oxford University Press, 1989.

Urban, Hugh B. *Tantra*. University of California Press, 2003.

Virgil. *The Aeneid*. Trans. David West. Penguin, 1991.

Wagner, Stephen. "On the Trail of the Chupacabras." About.com. Paranormal.about.com. Retrieved 2010.

Walker, Barbara G. *The Woman's Encyclopedia of Myth and Secrets*. HarperCollins, 1983.

Walker, Texas Ranger. Created by Canaan, Grief, Haggis, and Ruddy. Amadea Film Productions, 1993–2001.

Ward, Phillip. *Polish Cities*. Pelican, 1989.

Waters, Clara Erksine Clement. *A Handbook of Legendary and Mythological Art*. Hurd and Houghton, 1874.

White, Terrence Hanbury. *The Book of Beasts*. UW-Madison Libraries Parallel Press, 2002.

White, T. H. *The Once and Future King*. Ace, 1987.

Wheeler, Post. *Dragon in the Dust*. Read, 2007.

Whitmore, Brian. "Myth of Women Snipers Returns." *Moscow Times*. October 9, 1999.

Wilkinson, J. G. and Samuel Birch. *The Manners and Customs of Ancient Egyptians*. J. Murray, 1878.

Williams, George Mason. *Handbook of Hindu Mythology*. ABC-CLIO, 2003.

Williams, Joanna Gottfried. *The Two-Headed Deer: Illustrations of the Ramayana*. University of California Press, 1996.

Willis, Roy G. *World Mythology*. Macmillan, 1993.

Yearsley, MacLeod. *The Folklore of Fairytale*. Kessinger, 2005.

Zacharias, Pat and Baulch, Vivian. "Some Haunting Tales from Detroit's Past." DetroitNews.com. October 31, 1997.

Zelinga de Boer, Jelle, and Donald Theodore Sanders. *Volcanoes in Human History*. Princeton University Press, 2002.

Zenkovsky, Serge A. *Medieval Russia's Epics, Chronicles and Tales*. Meridian, 1963.

BADASS BOOKS BY BEN THOMPSON

BADASS

A Relentless Onslaught of the Toughest Warlords, Vikings, Samurai, Pirates, Gunfighters, and Military Commanders to Ever Live

ISBN 978-0-06-174944-5 (paperback)

An unstoppable collection of history's most ball-crushingly awesome figures to ever strap on a pair of chainmail gauntlets and run screaming into battle, from Julius Caesar to Bruce Lee.

BADASS: THE BIRTH OF A LEGEND

Spine-Crushing Tales of the Most Merciless Gods, Monsters, Heroes, Villains, and Mythical Creatures Ever Envisioned

ISBN 978-0-06-200135-1 (paperback)

A celebration of the most hardcore gods, monsters, wide-smiled heroes, and merciless arch-nemeses—including Zeus, Dirty Harry, and El Chupacabra.